LISZT

Liszt, 'en costume de ville,' from the painting by Lauchert, 1856

SACHEVERELL SITWELL

LISZT

Dover Publications, Inc.

New York

Published in Canada by General Publishing Com-
pany, Ltd., 30 Lesmill Road, Don Mills, Toronto,
Ontario.
Published in the United Kingdom by Constable
and Company, Ltd., 10 Orange Street, London
W.C. 2.

This Dover edition, first published in 1967, is an
unabridged republication, with minor corrections,
of the revised edition published in 1955 by Cassell
& Co. Ltd., London. It contains a new Preface by
the author.

Standard Book Number: 486-21702-7
Library of Congress Catalog Card Number: 66-26822

Manufactured in the United States of America
Dover Publications, Inc.
180 Varick Street
New York, N.Y. 10014

TO

MOIRA SHEARER

'The attraction of the virtuoso for the public is very like that of the circus for the crowd. There is always a hope that something dangerous may happen. M . . . x (Ysaye) may play the violin with M . . . y (Colonne) on his shoulders; or M . . . b (Pugno) may conclude his piece by lifting the piano with his teeth.'—CLAUDE DEBUSSY. *Monsieur Croche, the Dilettante-hater.*

PREFACE TO THE DOVER EDITION

There is so general a conception of Liszt by now as a mixture of charlatan and virtuoso that, as time goes by, it becomes not easier but more difficult to arrive at the truth about him as a composer. This is in part because of the recently awakened interest in the compositions of his old age, and it is true that in certain of these Liszt hints at and foresees the musical experiments of a later generation. But, whatever their appeal to specialists, they are not enough in themselves to hold an audience if only because by very reason of their experimental form, being indeed more of a searching than an achievement, they are lacking in the bravura and eloquence expected of him. We are therefore thrown back again upon the accustomed repertoire, and it becomes monotonous to see the same works by him advertised again and again in concert programmes.

This is the more disappointing because of the enormous number of his works there is to choose from. Why for instance is it always 'the *Mephisto-Waltz*', as though there were but one of them, when in fact there are no fewer than four, the third of these in particular being among his very finest and most powerful works in that vein of music in which Liszt is alone and quite unique? Or, to descend to more trivial things, why is it ever and again the familiar *Liebesträume* No. 3 when there are two others, the second of them being charming and beautiful indeed? Can the menu never be varied; or is it the virtuosi themselves, and not the audience, who are to blame? As long as forty years ago it needed a pianist of the stature and renown of Busoni to put across so great a rarity as his own arrangement of Liszt's fantasy and fugue on the chorale *Ad Nos ad Salutarem Undam* from Meyerbeer's *Le Prophète*, a major work lasting over half an hour in performance; or at the other end of the scale a little piano piece such as Liszt's *Die Zelle in Nonnenwerth* for which the inspiration was a small island in the Rhine, only big enough for a few fishermen's huts, a chapel and a half-ruined convent. In an appendix at the end of Edward Dent's life of Busoni, his piano repertory is given, including a dazzling number of pieces by Liszt which even now are seldom if ever performed.

It can be assumed that among the vastly enlarged number of listeners to music, due to broadcasting and to the gramophone, there is by now something approaching a working knowledge of most of Chopin, much of Beethoven, and even most of Mozart's Concertos. But in fact the situation has not changed or improved nearly as much in the case of Liszt. How few persons would recognize his *Ballade* No. 2 in B minor, or the magnificent and most moving *Bénédiction de Dieu dans la Solitude*, both of them among the splendours of all works written for the piano, and dating not from his early pyrotechnics or late experiments but from the full maturity of his great talents! Or, as said already, there are the other *Mephisto-Waltzes*; or such almost unknown and unheard delights as his *Waltz* on themes from Donizetti's *Lucia* and *Parisina*, or his transcription of Donizetti's *Nuits d'Été à Pausilippe*, works which in the general revival of interest in Donizetti as an opera composer should, and surely will, find favour. They are of a romantic elegance that has a place of its own in the whole Romantic movement, but to which it is difficult to find an equivalent or a parallel in either its poetry or its painting.

That Liszt lived too long and wrote too much is not a reproach that can really be laid against him when we consider the adulation and the amount of attention devoted in our time to another inventor and supreme virtuoso, but in the art of painting. He, too, has lived to old age, and the sum of the activities of the one, in respect of his supreme and unapproached genius as executant; his vast output in all fields of music; his support of Wagner and of the Russian school of composers, the innovators of their day; his role as an orchestral conductor which, also, was something new to the time; together with his fascination as a person, as a legend and no less so as a lover, all add up to a total that equates him to the Proteus of our day. Some of it may seem dusty and old fashioned now, but so will much of that other only too soon when the dross comes to be sifted from the bright metal of his genius.

The day is long past when only one or two living pianists could break in and ride the war-horses of the *Rhapsodies*. And by the same token what excited fifty or a hundred years ago no longer either interests or stimulates. But behind the fustian the real character of this enigmatic character emerges, and like a living being perceives he no longer dazzles and puts away his tricks. There is no more need for them. It is no longer so gullible and untrained a public, and as though in the knowledge of that he can begin to show his powers. This greatest of virtuosi in the history of music has more than that at back of him. He must be forgiven for exulting in his strength. How could he resist it? Why, then, did he give up his career as virtuoso and retire so early from the concert platform? We have to accept the genuineness of this move on his part, as also of his entrance into minor orders, neither of which things were affectation, but sprang from motives that were as genuine as they were obvious. That he was one of those born to be the centre of attention is not to be denied. Whatever he did, he was sure to attract it, but it is to be remarked that his best music was written after he had assumed the soutane. He was an unselfish and lovable character, generous to a fault, and who can never be forgotten. The more he is studied, the more unfathomable his talents, many facets of which are lasting when others are forgotten.

January 1967

CONTENTS

LIST OF ILLUSTRATIONS

Frontispiece: Liszt, from the painting by Lauchert, 1856
*(Nationale Forschungs- und Gedenkstätten der klassischen
deutschen Literatur, Goethe-Nationalmuseum, Weimar)*

facing page

NEW INTRODUCTION TO THE REVISED EDITION

During the twenty years since 1934, when this book on Liszt was first published, it is only natural that certain changes and modifications should have occurred in his reputation. For no artist in any of the arts is a fixed star; not even Rubens, not even Richard Wagner, both of whom have known the most constant of all fames. Neither one, nor the other, has yet been obscured or in eclipse. Their lot, posthumously, has been to be applauded all the time. But the position of Liszt has changed a little, following the eternal laws; and if the alteration can be expressed in a phrase, it is not that Liszt has grown more popular, but that, as time passes, he becomes still more interesting.

His character, both personally and as a musician, deepens: though depth means other things beside profundity. We know now, for instance, of which there was not evidence until recently, that he was the lover of *La Dame aux Camélias*; and does this, or does it not, affect the hearing of some of his music for us? That beautiful piano piece *Ricordanza* (one of the *Douze Études*), which Ferruccio Busoni describes as 'like turning over the pages of a yellowing love letter' (though, and this is quite typical of the contradictions in his history, it is true that the first version of the *Études* was published when Liszt was only sixteen years old)? Or the *Faust Symphony* which, surely, is one of the masterpieces of the whole Romantic Movement in all the arts? Or the 'air noble', for it is difficult to describe it in other than theatrical terms, of his *Sonata in B Minor*? In the light of this discovery, and increasingly, in the glare of all the lights that can be thrown upon him, Liszt emerges as a distinctly *rusé* character. At least, even in the Paris of the 1830's, that legendary epoch of the starving artist in the attic, Liszt was never a bohemian. He made use of the fantastic physical and sensual powers given to him for his own comfort and advantage. Or is it only that Liszt was first of all musicians to try and follow in the footsteps of Lord Byron?

All in all, we may ask ourselves, has there ever been a more extraordinary wearer of the soutane? For this, after all, is part of his mystery. I would like to add in a personal note that the Rev. A. K. Chignell, of the Charterhouse, Hull, a clergyman of the Church of England who kindly corrected the proofs and prepared the index for the first edition of this book, always crossed out in green ink every mention in my pages of Liszt as an Abbé and put, instead, 'curate', an interpolation on his part which I only perceived in time to get it altered, and which may be an accurate statement of fact, but it certainly detracts from the romance. We have to think of this 'curate' playing *L'Invitation à la Valse* at his farewell concert in the Palazzo Barberini and retiring next morning to a monastery in order to be prepared for his priesthood; or even being promoted in his old age to be a Canon of Albano, and paying the necessary fees by an advance from his publishers on his *Second Mephisto-Waltz*.

Yet, one cannot for a moment doubt the sincerity of his religious convictions. It is only that, like a 'street Arab' brought up in a good home, even in the most conventional surroundings he could not help dancing to the music of the street band. There are certain traits in his music which from over-repetition become insupportable, his two piano concertos in particular; but in all probability it was the shackles of his own virtuoso powers, and the sense that all eyes were fixed upon him, that made him put mere tinsel and glitter where, in what was only another phase of the same mood of vulgar display, he was capable of so much deeper feeling. It is not possible, for another example, to deny that Liszt seems to 'haunt' or 'possess' in the psychic sense his own setting of the *'Flower' Waltz* from Gounod's *Faust*. This is, indeed, among the most pointed and extreme of all his works, but it would be more true in this sense to say 'performances', and it is something other than only the setting of a highlight from a phenomenally successful opera. His treatment of the waltz theme is like a cat playing with a mouse. We have to consider that Goethe and Dante were the favourite reading of this Romantic of Romantics, and that all the energies of which he was capable had already been put into his own *Faust Symphony*, which, at this date (1868), had in all probability not been performed as many as half-a-dozen times. The softer, more appealing, more sentimental strains of the counter-waltz are conveyed with devilish insidiousness as though played by a Tzigane band of exceptional fire and eloquence to a half-mesmerized audience. No one hearing this setting of the '*Flower*' *Waltz* could doubt that Liszt understood the art and the wiles of the Gypsies, if, indeed, he was not part Tzigane himself, of which there is argument alike in his personality and in his music.

The prime interest in the history of Liszt lies in his extraordinary powers as a performer, which can never have been excelled; in his exultant enjoyment of those and his simultaneous desire to be rid of them in order, not to perform, but to compose; and in the last anomaly that no one would listen to his music. Yet, no body of piano music is more incomparably written for the instrument. Chopin and Liszt, beyond dispute, are the supreme composers for the grand piano. The argument is not that Liszt wrote too much music, which is true, but that even when he was young his own music dazed and astonished, and did not altogether please. It was too terrific as a performance. Perhaps a majority of the public prefer to be lulled by music, and not to have their skin tingle and their hair stand on end. But we must always remember, when Liszt, or Paganini, or Anton Rubinstein are under discussion, that they were first of their race, and that their public were in a state of innocence. Think of Paganini's provincial tours in England in the early 1830's, when he played in towns like Leeds and Shrewsbury! What 'easy game' it must have been! The most sophisticated persons in his audience will have been amateur players who knew a sonata or two by Mozart and Beethoven.

The advent of Liszt was coincident with the invention and perfecting of the modern pianoforte, to all intents a new instrument compared to the ancient spinets and half-pianos of the previous age, though we have to consider again that the Erard played by Chopin was tuned differently to our own contemporary pianos, permitting of effects and nuances and of a style of playing never heard in our generation. But, at least, the piano was a new instrument and Beethoven, Chopin, Schumann wrote new music for it. The impact of the full piano repertory must have been overwhelming in effect. Merely to have the whole world of Chopin thrown open to you at some time in the last century must have been a sensation we do not appreciate in our sated age. Liszt played so little in public after 1847 (when Chopin was still

living) that the public more in question are the audiences of
Anton Rubinstein. When Liszt came to London on his farewell
visit in 1886 he had not played in England since 1841, but
Rubinstein had been here on several occasions, had made a huge
American tour in 1872, and his great series of historical recitals
brought him to London for his farewell tour in this same year,
1886. He played music by Byrd, Bull, Couperin, Rameau, and
every composer of note, ending with the *Islamey* of Balakirev.
Then, indeed, the audience heard the whole piano repertory (if
we except the music of Ravel and Debussy). But a whole chapter
could be written on the insensitivity of the English intellectuals,
let alone the æsthetes! Tennyson, Ruskin, Swinburne were
entirely oblivious of music. It never dawned upon them that this
was the opening of a new world of art. Liszt, in the meantime,
had accrued to himself the advantages, as well as the disadvantages,
of playing so seldom in public. He had become a legend, and he
was the not unwilling actor in the centre of his own smoke-screen.
But his ceaseless industry had accumulated a body of music which
it was impossible for the public to digest. Even if he had toured
Europe and America like Anton Rubinstein, giving immense
recitals to packed audiences, the situation would have been little
different. A body of music so pianistically conceived, and performed with such phenomenal powers, may have daunted the
public. And in his simpler, popular pieces such as *Liebesträume*,
Liszt stands before you playing like a Tzigane in a restaurant.
It is as though he had wheeled up his piano and was playing it
into your ear. He is showing how easy it is for him to mes-
merize and fascinate; and while some submit, more are annoyed
by this.

Other music lovers are aggravated, or even maddened, by
Liszt's fireworks. Even 'plain persons', self-vaunted, will complain
that there are too many notes. There is, of course, sense in these
arguments; and in the end it becomes nothing other than a question of taste. You either like, or you do not like, Liszt's music;
since it seems never to occur to anyone to pick and choose among
it, admiring some and rejecting the rest. The advocate for Liszt
must, therefore, try to make the dissentients change their point of
view, for it is a taste that, once experienced, leads one through
all the gamut of his works. When you accept him, you accept
everything; not only with a grain of salt, but with a pinch of

curatical snuff, and even with the handful of pepper that he sometimes throws deliberately into your eyes. Probably the first step towards appreciation is to hear his music played by a pianist who is not frightened of his ornaments; which is likely to mean by a player who is in temperament with him. Then, the 'difficulties' fall into their place and are unnoticed. In his finest works there is the sensation that no one else has ever written, as Liszt did, for his instrument; that he is the transcendental composer for the piano; that Chopin for all his exquisite refinement of sensibility and febrile fire was ill and *maladif*, and that this shows in his music.

It is to be noted how writers on Chopin often hold up to ridicule what Liszt wrote about Chopin, and then proceed to quote from him. His remark that a pianist of the first rank should be 'harnessed' to each one of Chopin's mazurkas becomes hardly an exaggeration the more we know the mazurkas in their subtle and miraculous differences of mood. The lauding of Liszt is in no sense a disparagement of Chopin, perhaps the most complete and fulfilled of geniuses in the whole history of music, but Chopin never moved beyond certain boundaries which were his limitations. Within them he was master; but he had neither ambition nor curiosity for the world outside. There was nothing of the charlatan, mountebank, or Tzigane in Chopin, who was reserved and inward-growing, talked and behaved as though he would like to be looked upon as a man of fashion, and hid his deeper feelings. Ease and elegance were the models of this man of genius who in his life aspired no higher than the Parisian salons and the princesses and countesses to whom he wrote his dedications. But he was confined, of course, within his dreadful illness and knew his days were numbered. He set himself, therefore, to the perfecting of his talent and worked that till it could go no further. Chopin is complete, with nothing left unfinished. What else is there in the arts to compare with this saturation of his personality? At twenty years old Chopin was adult and 'in full plumage'. Nothing he composed later shows any fundamental change of temperament, although it is true that as in the case of all artists who are victims of consumption his works show the customary three periods of development, 'telescoped', as it were, into one short span of life.

Liszt, in contradiction, lived to old age and was composing all the time. Leaving his orchestral works out of the argument for the moment, his piano music falls easily and obviously into various grades and categories. His piano versions of Beethoven's nine symphonies, and of three of Beethoven's piano concertos for two pianos, prodigies of skill and labour after their fashion, he seems to have regarded, himself, as in the nature of engravings after famous paintings. They were prints by a skilled hand after well-known pictures. Amateurs who know his piano edition of Berlioz's *Symphonie Fantastique*, that astonishing translation from terms of one art into another, may think that Liszt is for once too humble in his pretensions. He, also, wrote versions for two or four hands, and some, as well, for two pianos, of his own *Faust Symphony* and *Divina Commedia*, and all thirteen of his own Symphonic Poems; works, we say, in which he regarded himself as master engraver or skilled translator, and for which there was neither time nor disposition in the few years of Chopin. But these, also, with the mass of other piano music of the same class, were the pedestrian works by which he earned an income. After 1847, we must remember, Liszt made no money by playing, teaching, or conducting.

His transcriptions of between fifty and sixty of Schubert's songs are among the most beautiful of his slighter works; but in all probability the same persons who find pleasure in those will be in antipathy to Liszt's *Fantaisies Dramatiques*, which are in fact his operatic transcriptions. Even the Schubert settings may be very little known to the younger generation. But in the decline of amateur music—how many persons are there, now, who sing Schubert songs in their flats or converted houses?—and the steadily increasing public for opera, it is not impossible that his *Réminiscences* and his *Fantaisies* on operas by Bellini and Verdi may be heard again. It perhaps needs no more than a single L.P. gramophone record by some eminent pianist for this to happen. Yet, it is doubtful. Times have changed so much during the hundred years since they were written. Probably Liszt's operatic fantasies could only be revived as curiosities, which would not do justice to their merits. Enough has been written about them in the body of this book, but it will be found that the *Grande Fantaisie sur Norma* is beautiful and fascinating to listen to. Those persons whose musical taste is not entirely Teutonic, but tends to the Italian, may discover that it whets their appetite, and that they become curious to hear Liszt's *Réminiscences* of Donizetti's forgotten *Lucrezia Borgia*, or *Lucia di Lammermoor*. London audiences, already familiar with Verdi's *Simone Boccanegra* performed at Sadler's Wells, have had little chance as yet of hearing Liszt's fantasy on this opera, one of his last works composed in 1882-3, and an interesting example of his later style. *The Skating Waltz*, from Meyerbeer's *Le Prophète*, a sensational 'firework' piece with its *glissando* imitations of skaters 'cutting figures' on the ice, is already in the repertory of more than one good pianist. The fantasy on Meyerbeer's *Robert le Diable* is not less effective as an encore piece at the end of a concert, and was often thus performed by Anton Rubinstein. It is a *Valse Infernale*, based on the ballet of nuns from that dead and ignored work of Meyerbeer, who was in his day the most famous name in opera.

The most charming and delightful of his operatic 'treatments' is, doubtless, the *Valse à Capriccio*, the third of Liszt's *Trois Valses-Caprices*, published in 1852, and based on motives taken from Donizetti's *Lucia* and on a waltz from *Parisina*, a forgotten opera by Donizetti to the poem of that name by Byron. It is already stated in the text, but perhaps will not harm from further mention, that this waltz theme from *Parisina* is identical with the *adagietto* in Poulenc's ballet of *Les Biches*. Were this *Valse à Capriccio* but better known, it would be among the most popular of Liszt's lesser works, in the style and manner, it could be so described, of Gavarni's fashion plates to *La Mode*, and of Gautier's *Mlle de Maupin*.

It is seldom appreciated that Liszt wrote, in all, fifty-eight piano studies or études, if we group together the three books of the *Années de Pèlerinage* and the twelve *Études d'Exécution Transcendante*. We will combine with these the *Deux Études de Concert* which are the well-known pieces *Waldesrauschen* and *Gnomenreigen*, and three further études, including the beautiful piece known as *La Leggierezza*. Further études, the *Paganini Études* and *Ab-Irato*, make up the fifty-eight, and form the hard core or main body of all his compositions for the piano. Busoni said of them that 'they should be put at the head of his piano compositions, because they were the earliest of his works, the fruit of his virtuoso aspirations, and because they reflect as do no others Liszt's personality'. I think, indeed, that we hear this very clearly in *Ricordanza* (one of the twelve *Études*) and in *La Leggierezza*.

These two pieces are remarkable as examples of effects, and subjects, that had never been achieved before in music. If we listen to them, we get a strong impression, as Busoni says, of his personality. It has been said of Beethoven's *Bagatelles* (op. 133) that in them it is possible to get the impression of what it must have been like to hear Beethoven improvise, for which he was famous, and therefore you can form some idea of Beethoven's style of piano playing. The loose, 'improvised' style of the *Bagatelles* suggests that they are improvisations written down, more or less, and Beethoven in a particular mood may not have been averse to this. In the same way, *La Leggierezza* and *Ricordanza* seem to contain in them the elements of Liszt's playing. They reproduce, we may like to think, his peculiar quality of touch, his runs and ornaments and lyrical feeling.

Feux Follets and *Chasse-Neige*, which are two of the *Études d'Exécution Transcendante*, raise interesting problems of derivation. There can be little doubt that their origin is in Paganini's violin caprices. Liszt and Schumann, at about the same time, and both strongly influenced by hearing Paganini play, had begun to give titles of this description to their piano pieces. It would not be difficult to describe Liszt's *Waldesrauschen* as typical of Liszt in its lyricism and its ornament, but influenced by Schumann, and owing much to Paganini. Yet *Waldesrauschen* is Liszt, pure Liszt; but what work of art in the whole world is entirely original, and without ancestor or predecessor? The violin caprices of Paganini, it is true, have no individual titles, but if you listen to them—and they can become monotonous!—names like *Feux Follets* or *Chasse-Neige* attach easily to them. *Harmonies du Soir*, or *Wilde Jagd*, two others of the *Études d'Exécution Transcendante* could, indeed, come out of the *Paganini Études*; yet *Wilde Jagd* is German Romantic in spirit. To my own taste this is among the most effective and most personal of all Liszt's études, and I can never listen to it without thinking to hear in it some ghostly echo of the most wonderful of pianists there has ever been; in his youth, certainly, for *Wilde Jagd* has the faults and exuberance and fire of youth.

In the first volume of the *Années de Pèlerinage* there are two marvellous études, *Au Lac de Wallenstadt* and *Vallée d'Obermann*, music which could have been written by no one else, and instinct with the moods and personality of this strange being. Pianistically, they are masterpieces in their way. *Vallée d'Obermann* is as much of a 'picture' as any of Turner's Swiss paintings. There is an æsthetic pleasure in listening to the mere technical skill with which it is laid out for the instrument. *Au Bord d'une Source, Pastorale,* and *Eglogue* are beautiful pieces from the same album, more in the mood of Schumann's *Arabesque,* free of the glitter and fustian which, often unfairly, have attached to Liszt's name. *Au Bord d'une Source,* it may be said, is indubitable parent to Ravel's *Jeux d'Eau.* The second or Italian album of the *Années de Pèlerinage* opens with *Sposalizio,* a piece inspired by Raphael's painting of the *Betrothal of the Virgin,* in the Vatican, and this beautiful étude opens another phase of Liszt's music and anticipates some of the greatest of his later works. The Italian album also contains the *Fantaisie, quasi Sonate: d'après une lecture de Dante,* one of Liszt's 'tremendous' pieces, a little too portentous, in fact, for many tastes; *Venezia e Napoli,* ending with the famous and too reiterative *tarantella*; and the much more interesting and beautiful *Tre Sonetti di Petrarca,* which were in the first place songs, and then were made by Liszt into piano pieces. It would be no exaggeration to say that the *Petrarch Sonnets* are among the most beautiful of all his works. A third volume of the *Années de Pèlerinage,* published in 1883, contains little of interest except *Les Jeux d'Eau de la Villa d'Este,* much admired by Debussy, and probably the strongest single influence in his piano music. But *Les Jeux d'Eau de la Villa d'Este* shows again in Debussy's *L'Après-midi d'un Faune,* and even in his *Fêtes.* Its discovery was, obviously, a landmark in Debussy's life. The *Années de Pèlerinage* apart, the most interesting of the études is *Ab-Irato,* a formidable piece made yet more intimidating by its sub-title, *Étude de Perfectionnement.*

The *Sonata in B Minor* is now universally admired, and socially accepted, as it were, in houses where its own brothers and sisters are not received. It is, of course, one of the master works of the whole Romantic Movement, and on a par with the *Faust Symphony.* The *Sonata in B Minor* was composed in 1853, and in it you can hear clearly this great musician and magician. But there are other works of Liszt not less deserving of general admiration and acceptance, but still unknown except to a small and specialized audience. Among these is his *Ballade No. 2 in B Minor,* dating from the same year as the *Sonata in B Minor* (except that Liszt was so constantly rewriting and altering his own works that it is nearly impossible to be certain of an exact date). This is among the most important compositions of Liszt's middle period, and it is unprofitable and pointless to compare it with Chopin's *Ballades*. The 'lay-out' of a master hand is apparent in it, and there is magnificent writing for the piano; indeed, this is one of the pieces in which Liszt seems to transcend the capabilities of the intrument. It is, at moments, as though two pianos were playing. The *Ballade in B Minor* may represent the ultimate phase of development for the 'concert grand', carrying its resources to a point at which they can be developed no further. The sections are beautifully contrasted, though the storm effects may be a little jejune to some tastes, but the 'grand air' is companion to the *Sonata in B Minor*. This is Liszt at his best, not only in technical bravura, but in nobility of expression and beauty of phrasing. The *Ballade* is neither German Romantic in style, nor does it bear traces of the years Liszt lived in Paris. His other *Ballade in A Minor* is disappointing.

La Bénédiction de Dieu dans la Solitude, one of the *Harmonies Poétiques et Religieuses*, is of the same quality as the *Ballade in B Minor*. Its virile, beautiful opening should endear it to any audience, and this again is one of the pieces in which Liszt's hand is apparent in every phrase. I would call the *Bénédiction*, and the *Ballade*, and the *Sonata* Italian in feeling. Their soaring melodies are Italian, and their broadness of melody. They appear to have been written under Italian light and clarity. The *Bénédiction* was inspired by the poem of Lamartine; and it is to be remarked that Liszt needed, it seems, to see his subject in a frame. The *Dante Sonata* is *d'après une lecture de Dante*, upon Victor Hugo's poem of that name; the *Hunnenschlacht* (or *Battle of the Huns*) one of the most impressive of his Symphonic Poems, was inspired by a huge and hideous painting by Kaulbach; the *Totentanz* had its inspiration in the marvellous medieval fresco of *The Triumph of Death* in the Campo Santo at Pisa. Two other piano pieces of Liszt's mature years which are imbued with this Italian feeling, and which must be the fruits of the many years he spent in Italy, are the *Deux Légendes*, *St. François d'Assise prédicant aux Oiseaux*, and *St. François de Paule marchant sur les Flots*. The second of these, in particular, is a splendid and beautiful example of music composed in the Italian feeling.

In addition to the two works of his middle period classed here with the *Sonata* (the *Ballade* and the *Bénédiction de Dieu*), there are two magnificent works written in the first place for organ. They are the *Fantasia and Fugue for Organ on B. A. C. H.* (B flat, A. C. B.), of which Liszt himself prepared the piano version; and the yet more tremendous *Fantasia and Fugue 'Ad Nos ad Salutarem Undam'*, based upon a chorale sung by three Anabaptists in the first act of Meyerbeer's *Le Prophète*. There is an edition for two pianos arranged by Liszt himself, seldom, if ever, performed; and a piano edition arranged by Busoni, taking three-quarters of an hour in performance. There may still be a destiny for this latter work. Perhaps the *'Ad Nos' Fantasia and Fugue* may be allowed to rank, eventually, with the *Sonata in B Minor*.

All the works mentioned were written by Liszt in the fifties of last century, when his Paris period was over and done with and he lived chiefly at Rome and Weimar, with occasional visits to his native Hungary. This was the period of his Symphonic Poems, which are more interesting in implication than in performance. *Festklänge*, with its echoes of processions and its *Polonaise*; *Héroïde Funèbre*, with its Hungarian national colour; and *Hunnenschlacht* (which I can no longer admire as I did when first writing this book), are probably the most interesting of the Symphonic Poems. What is more eventful is their progeny. The symphonic poems of Richard Strauss, from his *Macbeth* in 1884 to his *Alpine Symphony* and *Nursery Symphony* written thirty years later, are due to Liszt's example. Persons who do not admire Richard Strauss may not be grateful for this, or feel any more disposed to like the music of his progenitor. But, also, *Thamar*, *Schéhérazade*, and many other works by Balakirev and Rimsky-Korsakov, as acknowledged by their authors, were inspired by Liszt's music. The overwhelming genius of Beethoven, in whose hands the classical patterns of sonata and symphony were brought to their highest perfection, had a stultifying effect on the succeeding generation. A loosening of the forms of music was essential, and this was the service that Liszt rendered. It was his theories, and his work as conductor at Weimar, together with the effect of the concerts conducted by Berlioz in Russia, that fertilized the Russian School of composers. *Mazeppa* and *Les Préludes* were two of Liszt's Symphonic Poems which seemed new and revolutionary in their day. The *Faust Symphony*, Liszt's orchestral masterpiece, and the overlong and boring *Dante Symphony* were seldom given, if at all, except at Weimar, when that city for a decade or more was the capital of music.

Liszt had now embarked on his career. In his earlier years there were the perpetual comparisons with Chopin, and now the more complicated character of Richard Wagner is inseparably, and always, mentioned with him. If we return for a last moment to Liszt's years in Paris it is to remark that the rival biographers of Liszt and Chopin are ever in argumentative attitudes about their heroes in a manner reminiscent of the long past days of nurses and nurserymaids, the discussion being as to which of their 'charges' is the 'greatest little gentleman'. 'There were traits in Liszt's character that repelled Chopin from the beginning. His letters . . . make it clear that he could not bear Liszt's showmanship and his way of playing the *grand seigneur*. . . . At ho time was Liszt ever on the same footing as Chopin in the highest Parisian society. Something in his manner, some ineradicable trace of the parvenu, prevented his being accepted. . . . It is no slight to Chopin to admit that social and snobbish considerations played a large part in his enormous success as a teacher. It was something of a novelty for the aristocracy to find a piano teacher who besides being a superb virtuoso and composer was also a gentleman who lent distinction to a *salon*. . . .' And Chopin, we are assured, 'had a man-servant (unheard-of for musicians in those days) and a carriage, and his clothes, hats and gloves came from the most exclusive shops'.

All this, and more, is just criticism of Liszt at that stage in his career. But it is, also, true that the same Grand-Duke Karl Alexander of Saxe-Weimar who had invited Liszt to Weimar and made it the centre of music in Europe, when inviting Busoni many years later, in 1900, to hold the *Meisterklasse* and try to revive some of its past glories, made the historic observation to Busoni about Liszt—'Liszt *was* what a prince *ought* to be.'* On

---

*Sentences quoted, with permission, from *Chopin*, by Arthur Hedley, 'The Master Musicians Series', J. M. Dent & Sons, Ltd., 1946, pp. 49, 51, 52, 53. The above is the most informative book on Chopin in the English language, its author having gone to the trouble of learning Polish and visiting Poland in order to deepen his knowledge of his subject. Chopin only 'opened himself' to his Polish friends, and a vast amount of material concerning him is only available in the Polish language. The remark on Liszt by the Grand-Duke of Saxe-Weimar is quoted from *Ferruccio Busoni*, by Edward J. Dent, Oxford University Press, 1933, p. 128.

the other hand, it is pleasant to think of Chopin and Liszt as young geniuses in Paris—a marvellous echo of that time, in the opinion of the present writer, being the first of Chopin's *Préludes*, the opening or introduction to the whole series, and containing within the space of twenty or thirty seconds all the poetry of the Romantic Movement. Thinking of those few wonderful months or years it is impossible not to recall with envy and amusement that well-known occasion when Liszt visited Chopin in his apartment in the Chaussée d'Antin, seated himself at the Pleyel piano and played Chopin's *Études* in inimitable fashion, only interrupting his playing in order to join in writing a few sentences in a letter to Ferdinand Hiller. Chopin continues the letter, 'I write to you without knowing what my pen is scribbling, because at this moment Liszt is playing my études and transporting me out of my respectable thoughts. I should like to steal from him the way to play my own études.' The *envoi* of this letter in Chopin's hand, which reads, 'Heine sends his heartiest greetings . . . Love from Berlioz', may remind some readers of the recent film in which Cézanne, Degas, and other painters are always 'dropping into cafés' and into the conversation, and one of the female characters goes out of the room with the words 'So long, Toulouse!' (Toulouse-Lautrec). One expects the young women friends of this group of musicians, as reported in the letter, to leave with such phrases as 'Bye-bye, Liszt!' or 'Come up and see me some time, Paganini!' on their lips.

The reciprocal influences of Wagner and Liszt upon each other, and the extent to which each helped himself to a common amalgam of ideas, is a subject so complicated that even the life-long study of so great an expert as Mr. Ernest Newman can scarcely unravel it. There are surely instances in which one plagiarized the other, and perhaps it is only the continued and unbroken honour and glory of Wagner that inclines one in fairness to the side of Liszt, who worked so hard and long for the cause and has had more than his share of notoriety, but not enough of fame. How is it possible for there to be combined in one human being so many faults of the parvenu, so many tricks of the showman, such a degree of exhibitionism and so much reticence, the cloak of Lovelace and the black silk cassock of the priest, such a master of fireworks and so genuine a contrition and a religious feeling? This is the fascination of Liszt, and that this

most wonderful of musical virtuosos there has ever been was not only the vehicle for other men's music, was not only the lyre of Orpheus, but wrote incomparably for his own instrument, composing music good and bad. It is the contrasts and contradictions in his character and in his music that will always make him interesting.

Liszt has been much attacked on the subject of his Hungarian music. Had he only called the *Rhapsodies, Gypsy Rhapsodies,* and made it clear that they were Hungarian music *à la Tzigane,* no harm would have been done. But, unfortunately, he followed up his *Hungarian Rhapsodies* by the book *Die Zigeuner und ihre Musik in Ungarn,* published in 1861.* In this peculiar and sketchily fascinating work he misunderstood the situation he himself had created and given rise to. It was a fundamental error to confuse the Magyars and the Gypsies. The Gypsies never create musical forms, in Hungary any more than they do in Andalusia. Their talent is to ornament and improvise. It is the manner of their playing which makes Gypsy music. A Tzigane band, for instance, will play Viennese waltzes in the Gypsy style. The meretricious faults and defects of the *Rhapsodies,* which, yet, were works of dazzling originality in their day, has attached them more than any other body of his music to Liszt's name, and it was inevitable that a new generation would strip them of their ornament and enquire critically into their authenticity.

Béla Bartók, the head of this school of restorers of Hungarian tunes, let them appear again in their primitive simplicity, where they have a natural beauty, as of the mushrooms in the woods, or the wild cherries on the bough. How lovely after their fashion are the dozens or even scores of little pieces which form his *Peasant Songs,* his *For Children,* and his *Mikrokosmos*! But their wooden awkwardness, their rusticity, can become annoying. They are so brief in length; and when they turn it is like the turning of a weathercock, which only moves on a fixed base in the wind, upon a wooden steeple. One or two of the tunes are enough, and there is a monotony in numbers. When Bartók put aside his peasant tunes for his own music his mannerisms became not less awkward than his models. Having taken his tunes out of the soil he digs them back again deep into the earth, so deep that their roots cannot breathe. Would it not be true to say that the

*The Gipsy in Music. Translated by Edwin Evans, Senior. W. Reeves, 1926.

Violin Concerto or the *Concerto for Orchestra* of this lover of nature in music are more full of mannerisms and eccentricities than any work by Liszt? Will they be alive after a hundred years have passed, for the *Hungarian Rhapsodies* are now a century old? It is, after all, musical quality that makes a work live, and it is no use applying to music the standards of the old picture-restorer or the curiosity shop. Béla Bartók studied the folk music of the Magyars and followed it to its primitive origins, but the more it is studied the more remote it becomes. In the end, the ideal is a fledgeling of music played upon a badly made instrument that is out of tune. Liszt is, at least, 'the only great Romany Rye in music', and the composer who more than all others understood and paraphrased the Gypsies. In how many other ways, as well, will he be remembered when other and lesser musicians are forgotten!

There must certainly be material that has not yet come to light on Liszt's yearly visits to Hungary. So little is known of those, compared with his stays in Weimar and in Rome. Much study and concentration went into the composing of his *Rhapsodies*, which are now accepted, heedlessly, as though he wrote them down out of his head. How often he must have listened to Gypsy bands, and with what uncanny skill he 'translates' them for the piano! But there are too many of them, as with nearly everything else that Liszt wrote! *La Bénédiction de Dieu dans la Solitude*, let us recall, is one of a set of ten pieces. There are fifteen *Rhapsodies*, where there should have been three or four. Five more *Rhapsodies*, bringing the number up to twenty, are much later works written in his last years (1879–1886) in the wisdom of old age. But what is of interest is that, as in the case of all artists and writers who have made a study of the Gypsies, from Callot to George Borrow, something has passed between them more potent than the traditional 'crossing the palm with silver'. It is only different in kind from the truism that most musicians, writers, painters, are 'altered' once they have been to Italy or Spain. In the case of Liszt we may think that a childhood spent in a country district of Hungary in those distant years round 1820 where the popular music was that of itinerant Tzigane bands must have affected him to at least the extent to which Falla, Albéniz, Granados were influenced by their childhood environment in Spain. Further, the Gypsy influence is one of tricks and mannerisms. It has been conjectured, probably without foundation, that there may have

been some Gypsy heredity in Liszt, and that this would account for the instability in his personal character and in his history as a musician. Certainly he added the tricks of the Tziganes to the other wiles and graces in his repertory.

The final turn to the career of this ageing actor and magician comes in the last and experimental workings of his mind. There are pieces of some length, such as the *Second, Third,* and *Fourth Mephisto-Waltzes, La Lugubre Gondola,* the curious and late *Réminiscences de Simone Boccanegra,* the last five *Rhapsodies,* the *Czárdás macabre,* and *Czárdás obstiné,* some late arrangements of *Hungarian Folk Songs,* other late Hungarian pieces, *Mosonyi's Grabgeleit,* and *Dem Andenken Petöfi,* together with little and extra-ordinary musical fragments, though left complete, such as *Nuages Gris, Schlaflos, Frage und Antwort, Unstern. Sinistre. Disastro.* Some of these compositions are so curious in themselves and so full of anticipations, some not yet fulfilled, of music of the future that the renown of Liszt seems likely to descend upon these to the exclusion of his earlier works.

But there are, as well, unpublished manuscripts dating from other periods of his life, some of them proving a youthful originality which his detractors would deny to him. With Liszt's published works it is always to be noticed that the earlier editions are the bolder and more uncompromising, reflecting his own phenomenal powers as a performer. His first printed work, the earlier form of the *Études d'Exécution Transcendante,* published when he was only nineteen years old, is more difficult, more transcendant, and more interesting than the later edition of 1854. There are, also, many pieces by Liszt so long out of print that they have become collector's items. In this sense he is, perhaps, the most interesting of all composers to collect, owing to the rarity of some items and the many, differing, and revised editions of other works. His genius for the instrument and uncanny sleight of hand put him apart, and the collecting of his works could be the recreation of a lifetime. Yet what pianist, now, ever plays, as did Busoni, the twelve pieces of the *Weihnachtsbaum (Christmas Tree),* or *Die Zelle in Nonnenwerth,* or the twelve pieces comprising his setting of the *Soirées Musicales* of Rossini? Why does no player venture on the *Soirées Italiennes,* settings of songs by Donizetti and Mercadante; or the *Fantasia* on Verdi's *Ernani,* dating from 1860, and a work, therefore, of the middle period of his life?

Asserting, for the moment, a personal taste, one wonders if there will ever be a performance of the unpublished *Lélio Fantaisie* for piano and orchestra (1834), of which the manuscript is in the Liszt Museum at Weimar. For *Lélio* is the never played sequel to the *Symphonie Fantastique*. This was intended by Berlioz to be performed immediately following the *Symphonie Fantastique*, and was so given at one of the concerts he conducted at Weimar, in 1855. There it was performed in its proper stage setting, for it is a monodrama intended to be played in front of a curtain with an actor declaiming the part of *Lélio*. Mr. J. H. Elliot, in his life of Berlioz, says of this *Monodrame lyrique, Lélio, ou le Retour à la Vie*, that it 'must be the craziest work ever sketched out by a composer not actually insane'. It contains long passages of declamation, a *Song of Happiness*, the *Brigands' Song*, and the *Fisherman*, as well as a *Fantasia upon the Tempest*, but was much revised and altered for the performance at Weimar, and could obviously be played in its expurgated form. This supreme curiosity of the Romantic Movement has, so far as I know, only been given one performance since 1855, and this was at Cologne just before the Second World War. The transcription by Liszt for piano and orchestra should make this sequel to the *Symphonie Fantastique*, now one of the most popular of all orchestral works, easy of access to the public, and in this form it may be no more 'difficult' than Berlioz's *Harold in Italy*, which in recent times is often played. Of all works by Liszt, unpublished or published, the *Lélio Fantaisie* is the one which the present writer would most like to hear.

There have been signs of increasing interest in Liszt in this country, particularly in his late works, but this is a revival of which there are no symptoms yet in the United States. Their gramophone catalogues, a sure test, still have surprisingly few records of Liszt, and those the most obvious. The pieces mentioned here as being likely to attract the public are unrecorded. Will the revival of interest in Liszt be confined to an audience of specialists? The story of his life, when that becomes better known, is the best way to stimulate curiosity about his music. There is enough in that to suit all tastes and satisfy all moods. Liszt is in many ways, no less than Byron, one of the key figures or leading actors of the Romantic Movement. Both were men of action, and not recluses of the writing desk. That the spirit of Don Juan was in both, points only to the actor and his audience. This is the bravura in his character, a rôle in which he is without rival and unexcelled. Any piece by Liszt performed with phenomenal brilliance only infers that it would have been played even more brilliantly by Liszt himself. After a while there is ever more fascination in listening in simpler pieces for his sleight of hand. Then, the music that he wrote for his own ear alone in the certainty, almost, that it would never be performed becomes the mystery of his long life. Mozart, who is in no way comparable to Liszt, has this one shade of resemblance, that having been the infant prodigy, and having appeared in this rôle in many of the capitals of Europe, he could not earn a living while his genius was fulfilling itself, and was buried, to the shame of humanity, in a pauper's grave. Liszt, in a sense just because he was so wonderful a performer, was distrusted by the public and by many of his fellow musicians.

It is true, though, that Liszt always had admirers, and that he wrote too much. His production was on the scale of that of Victor Hugo, of Ruskin, of so many other writers and intellectuals of the nineteenth century. Liszt was of that generation who rose from their beds at four or five o'clock in the morning and sat down to their desks. His technique and his 'hand', or call it his personality, are apparent in even the smallest fragment of his work, a factor which still further annoys and irritates those tastes that are antagonistic to him. His works are inseparable from his life, and this to a greater extent than in the case of most other artists. Of Liszt, as of Wagner, more intimate knowledge makes the mystery deeper. It is a taste that grows stronger by indulgence until his extravagancies, his musical excesses, are self-explanatory, and these are no longer obscured by works of his that are accepted. His little known compositions that have waited so long for an audience fall into place, and we become eager to hear anything and everything that is by his hand. His measure of immortality is not yet filled. His immense output, if taken in entirety, would exclude all other music from the programme. But time, as it passes, makes more room for Liszt. In the two decades since this book was first published there has been a difference of attitude towards him. By all the laws of logic this will continue; the actor and magician will be merged in the hero, and the fustian be sifted from the sparks of gold. Then, one of the noblest, most unselfish, and most exciting figures in music will have his due.

November 1954.

BOOK I

1811-1839

Childhood and Youth

CHAPTER I

*The year of the Comet—Music and the Esterházy—Birth and
origin of Liszt—His first concert—He plays at Pressburg, and
his musical education is guaranteed for six years*

Liszt was born in 1811, the year of the Comet, a sensational,
extraordinary year when talk was of nothing but War.
Napoleon was waning, the disastrous Moscow campaign
threw its shadows before it, and the King of Rome, the Cæsarion
of the Empire, appeared in the world. There was change in everything, and no permanence.

The birthplace of Liszt, though it was so near to Vienna, was
on the confines of the civilized world and not far removed from
the dominions of the Turk. Indeed, the Turks had receded from
there. The minaret and the standard of the crescent moon had
been known in those lands, but the Hungarians lived, now, in an
antique, feudal peace on the very edges of the modern earth. The
wars and disturbances of Napoleon can hardly have reached them,
for their only connexion with the world was through the in-
sensate luxury and extravagance of their landlords. These were
the Esterházy. Their very name bespeaks that.

The Esterházy had been made Princes in 1687, and were the
chief of those Hungarian families who, on the expulsion of the
Turks, were allotted gigantic estates and allowed a semi-inde-
pendent condition. Their domain was some fifty miles to the
south of Vienna in a characteristically Hungarian district, that, by
the curious provisions of the Peace Treaty of 1920, is now divided
with Austria.* They had two great houses, not far apart, at
Esterháza and Eisenstadt, and lived at both in more than princely
splendour. We shall see that music was not the least part of this,
and that it is no matter for surprise that a great musician should
have been born upon their estates, since this family had been
associated with music to a quite extraordinary degree.

Eisenstadt was the first great palace of the Esterházy, but Prince

*Eisenstadt is in Austria, Esterháza is in Hungary.

3

Nicholas Joseph, 1714–1790, who had travelled to Italy and France, was not satisfied and began to build Esterháza, a few miles away from it. The circumstances of his life are hardly credible, but its glitter and brilliance were decidedly a part of the Orient. The palace and gardens of Esterháza were on an immense scale, and he kept open house there, to the extent that it became equivalent to what a modern hotel would be, were its owner a philanthropist. Every foreign visitor to Vienna made a point of staying there for three or four days. We may doubt whether Esterháza contained much in the way of works of art, but the gardens must have been delightful, and the horses, the carriages, the liveries were splendid.

However, the chief recreation of the Prince was in music, and this was, also, the amusement of his guests. There were daily concerts, and German or Italian opera on alternate nights, with an occasional musical piece played by the marionettes, or fantoccini. For all this, the great Haydn was responsible, and he was employed at Esterháza for thirty years, until the death of the Prince. During this time he wrote an infinity of music, the fame of which spread, by degrees, to the extreme limits of Europe. The atmosphere was of music, and of music in many different forms.

For it may be said that during these years Haydn invented the symphony and the string-quartet as we know them. And his theatrical music, which has been unduly neglected, cannot have been the least delightful part of his activity. Indeed, if we wish to regret music of his that is never heard, we may think of his comic operas and vaudevilles, of a Chinese pantomime for marionettes, of the marches for the Esterházy Grenadiers; and, when all these are added to his known and popular compositions, it must be conceded that the rumours and echoes of fine music may have lingered, twenty years after he left the place, until Liszt was born.

After the death of Prince Nicholas Joseph, in 1790, his successor, Prince Nicholas, 1765–1833, dispensed with the services of Haydn and allowed him to leave Esterháza and proceed abroad, into the world. The great period of his fame was at hand. He paid two visits to England, wrote the Twelve Salomon Symphonies, and became the musical idol of Europe.

But the Esterházy, though to a diminished extent, still continued their patronage of the art. Prince Nicholas had, by now, transferred his residence to Eisenstadt, which was old-fashioned and which he entirely remodelled in the classical taste of that day.

4

It is an enormous square building, flanked by seven towers, and encircled with a moat. It was this same Prince Nicholas whom Napoleon invited the Magyars to elect as King of Hungary in 1809, instead of the Habsburgs. But the Prince, true to his family character of loyalty to that dynasty, refused the honour. He was equally true to the Esterházy tradition of ostentation and extravagance, for it is reported that his immense expenditure on building and on the arts impoverished his family for two generations. His connexion with music is that Johann Nepomuk Hummel, the greatest piano-virtuoso of his day, was Kapellmeister at Eisenstadt from 1804 till 1811. Hummel, it will be remembered, was a pupil of Mozart at the age of seven years, and was, by the time he lived at Eisenstadt, the finest player of his day. There are, also, records of Cherubini having visited Eisenstadt for some performances of his works during his stay in Vienna in 1805 and 1806. So it will be seen that music was still the interest of the family.

To complete the picture of the Esterházy, we may add that it was the son of this Prince, Paul Anthony, 1786–1866, who was Ambassador in London and wore the famous suit of diamonds at the Coronation of George IV. He married the daughter of Lord Jersey, and it is said that she pined away in her adopted country because she had too few quarterings and so the nobles of Hungary could not speak to her. But the extravagances of Prince Paul Anthony brought about the final ruin of his family, and they have never recovered from him.

His history lies beyond our subject, but his father, the patron of Hummel and Cherubini, was in the full blaze of his splendour in the year 1811. Among his numerous retainers there was a land-steward, called Adam Liszt, whose father had filled a similar post and had, therefore, some hereditary claim to his Prince's consideration. This Adam Liszt was promoted, in 1810, to the post of steward of the Esterházy properties at the little town of Raiding, and, before going to live there, he married Anna Lager, or Laager, a native of Lower Austria, with German blood in her veins. His own family, like all Magyars not of the peasant class, was originally of noble origin, and persons of the name, notably a Bishop, occur as far back as the early sixteenth century. The connexion between them and Adam Liszt cannot be traced, but there is no reason to doubt its truth.

Soon after he was married, Adam Liszt moved to Raiding, and

there, on 22 October 1811, his son, Franz, or Ferencz, was born. Life must have been exceptionally quiet and provincial, for, even now, the house they dwelt in is the only respectable building in an overgrown village of wooden huts. It is certain that the father did not appreciate his exile, however much financial advantage it may have brought him, for he was a musical enthusiast of pronounced character, and all his interests were, therefore, at Eisenstadt. He played the violin and guitar, and only gave up the piano in despair at hearing Hummel's perfection and rapidity upon the keyboard.* He remembered Haydn at Eisenstadt, and knew Hummel and Cherubini well enough to presume upon it in later years. In fact, he cared for nothing but music. But he was one of those pathetic persons who have the rare good luck to see all their dreams for themselves realized in their children.

In spite of its dullness, his immediate surroundings at Raiding were much more picturesque than the ordinary squalors of a slumtown, or the usual dormant countryside of nearly every other landscape. And occasional visits to Eisenstadt were not the only musical relaxation, for the shepherds played their pipes and violins, and there were the Tziganes. This must have been the beginning of music with the young Liszt, and, at an extremely early age, under his father's tuition, he had started to make sensational progress with the piano.

In 1820, when he was nine years old, he gave his first concert at Oedenburg, a town near by, upon the Esterházy properties. A certain Baron von Braun, a blind pianist, who died before his twentieth year and must have been, therefore, in himself, something of a portent, had lost his interest with the public, and, in order to enlist their more active support, decided to give a concert with some other child prodigy likely to cause a little stir. The concert was such a success that the young Liszt followed it up with one of his own. We are told that he roused the audience to immense enthusiasm by his playing of a concerto by Ries, and by some improvisations upon well-known themes, and that his execution of these difficult pieces was wholly to be praised, 'malgré un accès de fièvre paludéenne'.

Soon after this he was taken by his proud father to Eisenstadt so that the Prince could hear him. There, too, he caused a

* Or, according to another version of the story, gave up violin and guitar and took to the piano, on hearing Hummel.

sensation, for the Princess gave the child the great Haydn's 'name-book', an album in which Haydn had collected the signatures of all the eminent musicians he had met, either at home or during the course of his travels abroad. It was a valuable present to give so young a child, and Franz quickly lost it.

The next event was a concert at Prince Esterházy's palace at Pressburg. This was organized by Adam Liszt with the express intention of attracting interest to young Franz so that steps could be taken to place his education in the right hands. The result was even better than could have been hoped for. Pressburg, as an important provincial capital, contained the palaces of the chief Hungarian magnates, and this concert, given during the season when they were in residence, was attended by many of them. Such was the enthusiasm, after it was over, that a committee was set up, and a subscription, headed by Counts Apponyi, Szapary, and Erdödy, guaranteed to young Liszt the sum of six hundred Austrian gulden a year for six years. Adam Liszt, thereupon, resigned his appointment to Prince Esterházy, who was reluctant to lose his services, and the Liszt family moved from Raiding to Vienna.

It was 1821, the year that Napoleon died; and Liszt was entering his second decade. It was also the beginning of the second phase of his life, for, if the first part of it was his infancy, the career of a prodigy upon which he was now entering cannot be called childhood. That would be a misleading term to use for its ardours and adventures.

But, though he left Hungary in his tenth year, and did not return to it till he was thirty, his early environment had profound effects upon him. He was no Viennese. He had the fire and brillance, the impetuosity and extravagance, of his surroundings and of the persons whom he heard of, or knew, in his infancy. He had the manners and fine bearing of a Court. If there was something a little unreal about him we must lay it to the credit of his environment. Those parts of him that suggested chicanery, and the wiles of the charlatan, were no more than the true proof of the peculiar circumstances in which he was born. In everything, he was rare and phenomenal and showed the strange surroundings, the charged atmosphere, in which he was bred.

But we must not emphasize, to the exclusion of everything

7

else, the glitter and the gilt of Eisenstadt. There was, also, its ragged side, and in saying this, we are thinking, not only of the Gypsies, but of the whole landscape, for, outside the gardens and the avenues of Eisenstadt or Esterháza, the landscape was of romantic monotony. It was an endless plain, low-lying, and broken with lakes and marshes. It had nothing, and left everything to the imagination. Its only colour was in the clothes of the people, in the Gypsies and their music, and in the ceremonies of the church. Liszt never forgot any of these things, and their effects lasted with him all through his life.

CHAPTER II

From Eisenstadt to Vienna—The age of Biedermeier—Lessons from Salieri and Czerny—The kiss of Beethoven—Introduced to Schubert

Though so little removed in miles, it was a big transition from Eisenstadt to Vienna; they were in the German world, and out of Hungary. German had been the spoken language of Eisenstadt, and even of the Liszt household at Raiding, but, in every other respect, there could not be more difference than between life on that feudal estate and the bourgeois, Biedermeier world in which they were now installed. It was the Schubertian Vienna, a sort of aftermath, or rest, of the old world, its last few years before the coming of the factory and the engine. It was the latest, the final, style in building and in the domestic arts. After this, the universal anarchy arrived, so far as the arts were concerned.

Vienna, and not Naples or Venice, was now the centre of the musical world. Haydn and Mozart had been the beginning of its fame, and Beethoven and Schubert were its present masters. The fame of Beethoven, and his deafness, made it nearly impossible to approach him; Schubert, on the other hand, could be heard or met anywhere, but his genius was only recognized by a few of

8

his friends. The careers of both men were nearly over: six years later they were dead.

The first step that Adam Liszt took was to ask Hummel to give lessons to his son, but Hummel would not accept less than a guinea a time, in spite of their old acquaintance at Eisenstadt, and so the project came to nothing. Instead, little Franz had lessons from Salieri and from Czerny.

Salieri was a very old man, deep in the traditions of eighteenth-century Viennese music; though it may be doubted if he ever discussed Mozart with his new pupil, for Mozart was still so much on his conscience that, as he lay dying, the year after this, he dictated a special denial of the story that he had poisoned him from jealousy. In any case, Salieri was so near to the brink of his own grave that his efficacy as a teacher may be doubted, and it is certain that Liszt derived much more benefit from the lessons given him by the redoubtable Czerny. It was a dry, pedantic system, but it instilled the right principles of hard work.

After the first twelve lessons were over Czerny' asked for no payment, but took him as a free pupil. This continued for the greater part of two years, during which time he must have played occasionally in private houses, for his fame had become the sensation of Vienna. It is true, though, that since the prodigy of Mozart developed into genius there must ever have been prophets in Vienna on the look-out for a new Messiah.

It was natural, this being so, that sooner or later the news of him should reach Beethoven, but the rumours of it were not calculated to please the master, for he detested child prodigies. They did, nevertheless, have personal contact, and the story of the kiss of Beethoven dates from this time.

The conversation books, in which questions were written by the persons who visited the deaf Beethoven, contain some mention of the young Liszt. He and his father had been presented to Beethoven by Schindler, and the following note sounds as though written by Franz, but may be in his father's handwriting. 'I have often expressed the wish to Herr von Schindler to make your high acquaintance, and am rejoiced, now, to be able to do so. As I shall give a concert on Sunday the 13th I most humbly beg you to give me your high presence.'

Later on, in Schindler's handwriting, it is written: 'Little Liszt has urgently requested me humbly to beg you for a theme on

9

which he wishes to improvise at his concert to-morrow. He will
not break the seal till the time comes. The little fellow's improvisations do not seriously signify. The lad is a fine pianist, but, so far
as his fancy is concerned, it is far from the truth to say that he
really improvises. Karl Czerny is his teacher. Just eleven years.
Do come: it will certainly please Karl to hear how the little
fellow plays. It is unfortunate that the lad is in Czerny's hands.
You will make good the rather unfriendly reception of recent
date by coming to little Liszt's concert. It will encourage the boy.
Promise me to come.'

It is amusing to read between the lines of this one-sided
correspondence, for Beethoven's answers were of course spoken,
and so we have only the evidence of the remarks addressed to
him. A great deal, obviously, depended upon the way in which
Beethoven was approached. Where Schindler regretted that
young Liszt was in Czerny's hands, he was trying to curry favour
for him with Beethoven; while Karl, whose probable delight in
the concert he used as a bait to persuade Beethoven to go to it, was
the nephew whom Beethoven loved and by whom he was so
much troubled.

What happened, as the result of these tactful advances, is
difficult to discover. It seems unlikely that Beethoven attended
the concert. He was too deaf to derive any pleasure from another
person's playing. He certainly did not give Liszt the theme he had
asked for upon which to improvise. But, on the authority of
Liszt himself, the story is true that Beethoven climbed upon the
stage at the end of the concert, lifted him in his arms, and kissed
him. This personal testimony cannot be lightly contradicted,
although it has been argued by his detractors that the story was
merely invented as an advertisement for the young virtuoso.

It is sufficient that Liszt knew Beethoven and that on some
occasion, in public or more probably in private, perhaps in the
master's own house, Beethoven should have been so impressed by
his playing that he embraced him. This possibility, that the
episode took place in Beethoven's own house, is certainly in
accord with the version of it that used to be told by Ferdinand
Hiller, a musician who was one of Liszt's early pupils. In any case,
if this is the general truth of the incident, its details are not
important, and are beyond the possibility of being confirmed at
this date. It is only mentioned here because it was the consecration,

so to speak, of Liszt's career, and because his extraordinary life, that extended over nearly the whole of the nineteenth century, would not be complete if he had not known Beethoven.

There would be this same sense of omission had he not met Schubert, but he was definitely introduced to him by Randhartinger. Whether he saw any of his music, or heard him play, may be considered more doubtful.

The two years that he passed in Vienna must have been a time of extreme importance to him, but more because of his discipline at the hands of Czerny than through any inspiration that he received through the example of Beethoven or of Schubert. He had not yet begun to write music—if we except the twenty-third of the set of Diabelli variations, which is by him—but he was already, at the age of thirteen, a pianist of most sensational quality. He arrived in Vienna as a foreigner, a Hungarian who spoke German; he was now to leave Vienna and become, to all intents and purposes, a Frenchman. We shall find that his early compositions, when he came to write them, had nothing of Vienna about them but were the productions of a most polyglot fancy.

CHAPTER III

Liszt arrives in Paris—Cherubini is inexorable—'Le petit Liszt'—Liszt is christened the ninth wonder of the world—Embraced by Talma—London—Plays to George IV at Carlton House—Plays at Windsor Castle—Don Sanche produced in Paris—Visits London again—Death of his father

Adam Liszt must have had the tours of Mozart in mind when he decided to take his son through the German cities, to Paris, and even to London. Franz played in Munich, Stuttgart, and Strasbourg, and was greeted with the same curiosity and the same applause that had been accorded to Mozart, sixty years before. But there was this difference. Liszt was twelve, twice the age of Mozart; he had not the strain of writing as well as performing; and it may be supposed that travelling was a little quicker and a little less tiring than it had been two generations before, even though the railway was not yet in use.

The morning after their arrival in Paris, the father and son hurried off to see Cherubini, the musical autocrat of the capital. They bore with them, as passport, a personal missive from Prince Metternich. The awe and terror of the little boy are well described in a letter written by Liszt, half a century later. They got to the composer's house at ten o'clock, to find that he had already left for the Conservatoire. Liszt tells how his heart failed him as they passed through the gloomy portal; how they were ushered into the pedagogue's presence; and how he fell on his knees to kiss the hand of Cherubini, and tears came into his eyes as he realized that this might not be the custom in an alien land. It was of no avail; Cherubini was inexorable. The regulations would not allow him to admit a foreigner, and even a letter from Prince Metternich could not alter this. They begged and entreated; and as they left the building, in despair, they felt as if their visit to Paris was a failure.

In the end, Reicha and Paer were the masters who took young Franz as pupil. Reicha had been taught by Michael Haydn and was a famous musical theorist, while Paer, who came from Parma, was the composer of a number of melodious operas, all completely forgotten, but extremely popular in their day. In fact, the arrangements for his musical education were as satisfactory as could be expected, apart from the refusal of Cherubini; and, as well as this, they delivered a number of letters of introduction to the French nobility from the nobles of Hungary and Austria. Little Franz played, thanks to these, in the salons of several private houses, and public concerts were arranged for him as well. The print-shops were full of his portraits, and within a few months the French public had christened him the ninth wonder of the world. Articles in the newspapers compared him openly with the young Mozart, and he was spoilt and lionized by all the fine ladies of the capital. Serious musical opinion, at the same time, agreed that he played, even then, as well as Moscheles or Hummel, the two acknowledged virtuosi of the day.

At one of his concerts, Gall, the founder of phrenology, insisted on taking a plaster cast of his head, that he might study it, while Talma, the tragedian, clasped him to his bosom with tender affection and foretold a great future for him. This was a scene in the great classical tradition; but his success was unanimous and universal. Soon, his proud father was able to send back one thousand gulden, the equivalent of a hundred pounds, to Prince Esterházy, who invested it on Franz's behalf.

The following year they went to London, where he played at the Argyll Rooms, on 21 June 1824. A week later, he gave a concert at Drury Lane, having, in the words of the original playbill, 'consented to display his inimitable powers on the New Grand Piano Forte, invented by Sebastian Erard'. He played a concerto by Hummel, Sir George Smart conducting, and at the end, when he asked for a theme upon which to improvise, a lady in the stalls suggested 'Zitti, zitti', from *Cenerentola*, and he treated this in the manner of a fugue, to the delight of the audience. His playing was the subject of immense interest, and he was received by George IV at Carlton House.

A tour in the French provinces followed his success in England, but he was back again in London the next year. He played to George IV at Windsor, gave a concert at the Duke of Devonshire's on 13 May, and played in Manchester, twice, during June. We have a delightful account of him in some reminiscences by Charles Salaman.* 'I visited Liszt and his father at their lodgings in Frith Street, Soho, and young Liszt came to early family dinner at my home. He was a very charmingly natural and unaffected boy, and I have never forgotten his joyful exclamation "Oh! gooseberry-pie!" when his favourite dish was put upon the table.'

On his return to Paris, *Don Sanche*, his operetta in one act, was given at the Académie Royale, on 17 October 1825. There had been immense excitement about this, and poets had vied with one another to furnish him with a libretto, but it was no more of a success than those early operas of Mozart with which it was meant to compare. After three performances it was withdrawn. The score was never published and has only lately been rediscovered. It was completely unremarkable in every way, and we may add that Liszt never again made a serious attempt upon opera.

His third visit to England took place in 1827, after yet another French provincial tour, and this time he played for the Royal Philharmonic Society. So much activity had begun to wear down

Blackwood's Magazine, September 1901.

his health, and on his return to France the doctors sent him to
Boulogne for sea baths. There, on 27 August, his father, Adam
Liszt, died of what was probably typhoid fever. His last words to
Franz were: 'Je crains pour toi les femmes', a warning of many
impending troubles. He was only forty-seven years old; and
Franz, who behaved with as much composure as did Mozart
when his mother died in Paris, agreed to pay all his father's debts,
and sent for his mother to come and join him. From now onwards
he supported himself and earned his own living. He was sixteen.

CHAPTER IV

First love affair with Caroline de Saint-Cricq—He is reported
dead—His first compositions

Franz was now entering that difficult stage between childhood
and manhood. Perhaps, in his case, it was accompanied by
more than the usual amount of introspection. He was passing
through a religious phase, in which he had serious thoughts of
becoming a priest; he was practising the piano, according to his
own admission in later life, not less than ten hours a day, and when
too exhausted to do this was reading all the romantic literature
on which he could lay hands. In addition to all these other
excitements he fell in love for the first time.

He had been giving music lessons, and among his pupils was
Caroline de Saint-Cricq, a girl of sixteen, whose father was the
Minister of Commerce and Industry to Charles X. A romantic
feeling quickly sprang up between them, which was known to
her parents, for as her mother lay dying, some months after it
had begun, her last words to her husband were: 'If they love
each other, let them be happy.' Probably the mother's death
made it easier for them to see each other, as the daughter could
pretend that she must have music to distract her, but one of the
servants, whom Franz had forgotten to bribe, gave away the
secret of their late meetings to the father, and Franz and the girl
were found prolonging a music lesson till long after midnight.

They had reached the stage, like Paolo and Francesca, of reading romances and poetry together, and the situation had reached such a point that Franz was turned out of the house and forbidden ever to come back.

He fell ill, as the result of this, and was in a state of breakdown for some two years. The seriousness of his feelings is proved from the fact that, in 1844, after his break with Madame d'Agoult, he paid a special visit to Pau, in order to see Madame d'Artigaux, as Caroline was then called, wrote an impassioned melody for her upon a poem by Georg Herwegh, and transcribed, and dedicated to her, two folk tunes of Béarn, her native province, *Faribolo Pastour* and *Chanson du Béarn*. Finally, years after this, at Weimar in 1860, when he wrote his will just before he took Holy Orders, he left her a jewel mounted as a ring. He was determined never to forget her.

For many months after the close of this thwarted love affair Franz was ill and did not appear in public. It was even reported that he had died; an obituary notice was printed in the *Étoile*, and a print of him was on sale with the title, 'Franz List, born Raiding, 1811; died, Paris, 1828.' It is probable that at some time during this period he had a cataleptic seizure, of the sort he had experienced before, during his childhood in Hungary. He may have lain unconscious and apparently dead for two or three days, and this would certainly be sufficient ground for the spreading of the rumour. And there can be no doubt that this false report helped his fame, for it was exactly in accord with every tenet of romanticism.

He led a life of monkish asceticism, read religious books, and played with Saint-Simonism. It might be said that Franz had read more, and had a wider culture, than any musician who had lived before him; but this statement, which is probably true, stresses his weakness as well as his strength. For he was outside life at this moment, and not sordidly struggling in it, which had been the fate of Mozart and Beethoven at his age. He lived by giving lessons, not in a garret, but in gilded drawing-rooms, to such pupils as the two daughters of Lord Granville, the British Ambassador. The Duchesse de Berri and Louis-Philippe, then Duc d'Orleans, were other patrons of his. The mention of such names would seem to contradict his solitary and contemplative life, but poverty drove him out of this, now and then, to earn his living, while his fine manners and aristocratic bearing lightened the fatigues of those high, if empty, circles. In his own early life, at Eisenstadt, he had seen the last and one of the finest blossomings of the feudal system, and now, in Paris, as a part of his romantic aspirations, and through reading Lord Byron, he was at the same time full of vague revolutionary fire, the prelude of the year 1830, and only happy with the famous names of France, in the Faubourg St. Germain. We shall see, later on, that in the reign of Louis-Philippe he would have nothing to do with the King or the circle of Orleanists, but would only play in the houses of the old Legitimist families. The very mention of this shows how his career had altered the whole status of a musician.

During all the six years of his residence in Paris the excitement had continued about him, unabated, and his infrequent public appearances made a rarity of his playing and caused it to be the more appreciated. His fame had spread, as we have seen, to the French provinces and to England. He was nearly nineteen at the time of the July Revolution, where this chapter leaves him, but the Progress of his Muse had been slow and he had not written much. A grand overture, played at his concert at Manchester, has been lost, and a concerto and a sonata have also disappeared. There remain an allegro di bravura, and an impromptu on themes by Rossini and Spontini, from the *Donna del Lago* and *Armida* of the former, and *Olympia* and *Fernan Cortez* of the latter. Also, and this is far more important, there are his *Études en douze exercices*, for these are the first works really typical of him, and, although printed as early as 1826, they form the basis of his famous *Transcendental Études* of 1838 and 1854. The fourth of them was to appear, much later on, as the symphonic poem *Mazeppa*. The *Études* were published at Marseilles, bore on their title page an engraving of an infant lying in its cradle, and were dedicated to a young woman who makes no further appearance in history, Mlle Lydia Garella, who may have been a pupil of his at Marseilles. It is only recorded of her that she played duets with him, gave him sweets, and had a hunch back.

What is remarkable in the *Études* is their embodiment of a new and terrific technique in a variety of fresh forms most admirably suited to their display. But this is not the right moment to discuss them, for they belonged to his future, to his period of transcendental execution, when he toured all over Europe with them.

At least, in these early versions of the *Études*, all the characteristics of his style are present, for, apart from the *Études*, Franz was suffering at this time from a lack of direction.

He may have been practising too much, and reading too many books, to be very prolific in composition. All that he published in 1829 was a Fantasia upon the Tyrolienne in *La Fiancée*, an opera by Auber. This, also, foreshadows a new and enormous volume of his work, and it must be dealt with in its proper place along with all his other Operatic Transcriptions and Fantasias; but certainly these two things, the *Études* and the Fantasia, show the leanings of his mind.

And, at this stage, his future as a composer did not show very much promise. It is easy to believe that he was already unrivalled as a pianist, but his own compositions cannot be described as at all remarkable, except in their dwelling upon difficulties which only his own consummate technique was capable of solving. In fact, he was waiting for a new direction. A strong wind was blowing, in the period just before 1830, and he could not know whence it came, or where it was going. We shall see, in the next chapter, that the most violent influences came to bear upon him at just the right moment for his own development, and that he was not slow to seize the opportunity they offered him.

CHAPTER V

The July Revolution—He meets Berlioz, Chopin and Paganini —Strange character of Paganini—His gaunt appearance—His 'terribilità'—Berlioz—The Symphonie Fantastique—*The* Queen Mab *Scherzo—Chopin arrives in Paris from Poland— Chopin and Bellini*

The Revolution of 1830 is a most eminent example of the false purposes and crooked results of revolution. It upset the dynasty which really came out of that antique past which the romantics wished to restore, and put in its place a bourgeois king, so safe and dull, that the glitter and martial clangour of the restored empire, false though they were, came as a relief after him. But, as ever, the people who made the Revolution knew not what they wanted. If it was excitement, and a life of more promise and greater beauty, they were disappointed, for the reign of Louis-Philippe was only more respectable, and not less dull, than the Third Republic. However, in 1839 this was not foreseen, and every young artist and person of ideas joined the students. The reason is not difficult to discover, for after the frantic excitement of Napoleon's campaigns the comparative peace and tranquillity of the Bourbons were hard to bear and spelt reaction. All the conditions of life were to alter; the modern world came into being, and the railway, the factory, the bourse were born. In fact, the Revolution of 1830 was to prevent things standing still.

It was a change in the life of everyone, and we may imagine how a young man of the age and sensibility of Liszt must have been waiting to see what would happen. But his personality, which was centred in music and not in politics, found a more certain direction than was discovered by the demagogues.

In his twentieth year, and before the July Revolution was a year old, Franz was to meet Berlioz, Chopin, and Paganini. It is no wonder that their impact upon him was more violent than the weight of impressions he had taken with him from Vienna. These three figures were of dazzling, intoxicating importance in his life, and indeed in writing of them it is difficult to know where to begin.

Ten years later, when Liszt's own first concert tour in Russia is described, we may be able to imagine back from that to the excitement and the mad frenzy caused by Paganini. But Liszt had his youth and his good looks to help him, while everything about Paganini was sardonic and diabolical, and he may be said to have frightened as much as he pleased. As Liszt grew older, he, also, turned Mephistopheles, but the credit for the invention, or for that state of nature, must lie with Paganini.

He had been famous in Italy since the early years of the century, when he had been appointed court musician, at Lucca, to Napoleon's sister, Elisa Bacciochi. Since then he had disappeared on more than one occasion for a period of years, only to emerge from retirement still more perfect in his technique and more gaunt and mysterious in his person. For years together he would neglect the violin and play the guitar, and when he resumed the violin he was as willing to resign it for the viola. At length, when nearly fifty years of age, at the height of his power and with a sufficient accumulation of curious pieces for the display of his technique, he determined to extend his fame all over Europe and set out on a tour of Germany. From there he came to Paris, and gave his first concert in the opera house, on 9 March 1831. This was followed by performances in London and a tour of the English provinces, and Paganini, henceforward, was to spend much of the remainder of his life in Paris.

The effect of his playing upon Liszt was of decisive and far-reaching character. New technical horizons were displayed to him, and perhaps Paganini taught Liszt as much in showmanship as he did in matters of execution. It must be remembered that even serious-minded persons believed Paganini to have been taught by the devil, or more arduous still, to have developed his uncanny powers during an imprisonment of twenty years where his only plaything was a broken violin with one string. His new and curious forms of composition caused even more astonishment than his performances of the classical repertory, and these were no mere technical exercises but the invention and creation of new moods. They may be compared to the enlargement in the scope of poetry wrought by the romantic writers in the dying classical body. All the romantic properties, mutterings of thunder, beating of rain, howling of wind, were there; and the human passions, anger, jealousy, dæmonic laughter, could be imputed. In his violin capricci there may be found, according to these precepts, the sighings, the flutterings, the tremolos, of the emotions; and, as well, fantasies based on the sound of distant church bells, on military bands, and on the music of the chase. If, also, he wrote fantasies on operatic airs, on the prayer from the *Mosè in Egitto* of Rossini, and would, as willingly, perform his *Fandango Spagnuolo* into which imitations of the farmyard were introduced, these were the playthings of his genius and were scarcely worse than the indulgences of some present-day conductors of famous orchestras.

The wildest reports of his appearance were exceeded when the eyes beheld him. He was so thin that he seemed tall, and so dark that even his haggard features left him ageless. His body was completely fleshless and his limbs were mere bones, everything being sacrificed, so it seemed, for his long hands and talon-like fingers. In his portraits, and in the wonderful statuette by Dantan, made in 1837, we have but the ghost of this strange being, for his music was an inseparable part of him and, without it, his is the soundless body of a cricket or a cicada, dead, and with no shrill and vibrant tones, but only the implements of its song.

Even the image of his clothes has a little of horror left in it, more especially about his black, bone-shaped trousers. They are the trousers of someone who has slept in them when too ill or too drugged to bother about it, and who has passed the entire night gambling with curious partners against sinister adversaries. Paganini was, in very truth, an inveterate gambler, and had, before now, been forced to pawn his violin in order to pay his debts. Later on, he was to nearly ruin himself with the Casino Paganini, a gambling hell for which he was refused a licence.

The long tails of his coat were preternaturally thin and flapping; his collar and cravat were formless and hardly visible, for his jaws, by long custom, leaned down to hold his violin, and were thus for ever sunk upon his chest. His features were wasted to nothing but an aquiline nose, sharp eyes, and a huge forehead lank with hair. This was in locks of a raven black, like his black eyebrows, with the metallic darkness of hair that never whitens as it grows old. In so far as his whole appearance conformed to any fashion whatever, save his own, it may be said that he belonged to the early years of the Empire, when men ceased to powder their hair and the knee-breeches of the eighteenth century had become elongated into trousers for the first time since the warriors of Gaul fought the Roman legions.

Already, at the time of his opening concert in Paris, Paganini was ailing in health and felt the first ravages of the disease that killed him. This was a tubercular affection of the larynx, and its results were noticeable in his voice and in the spareness of his diet. He was taciturn, partly from this necessity, and spoke no more than was needed; while, on his concert tours, he would hardly eat at all, and was content with a cup of soup, or camomile tea. He no longer practised his instrument, but would lie for hours stretched out upon a sofa on the days of his concerts; and perhaps there might be a mandoline on the table beside him. If he re-hearsed a concerto with the orchestra, when it came to the cadenza and the musicians waited in astonishment to hear him, he would bow with a sardonic smile and continue the music after the omission of his solo part. This made it nearly impossible to study his effects, for he could be heard once, and once only. He guarded his secrets with such jealousy that he would only publish his compositions at rare intervals, and many of them have been irretrievably lost because of this, or are only preserved in skeleton form without his embellishments. At last, but only as a proving of his powers, he was induced to print the twenty-four *Capricci* and their publication in no way diminished the astonishment caused by his execution of them.

It was the ambition of Liszt to transfer these effects of virtuosity to the piano, but the transition took some years to accomplish. His six *Grandes Études de Paganini* were not ready till 1837, and were not revised and published in their final form till 1851, three years before the whole body of his *Transcendental Études* was finished and perfected.

If we postpone our discussion of them till we come to deal with the whole of that part of his work, it is possible, even at this stage, to give a name to the atmosphere in which Liszt was involved by his study of Paganini, and this is best described by the Italian word 'terribilità', which is easy enough to understand in its application to the architecture of the early Seicento, when the influence of Michelangelo, or the misreading of his ends, let melodrama and terror into the art of building. This 'terribilità' is responsible for a whole division of Liszt's works: for the *Faust Symphony*, for the *Sonate : d'après une lecture de Dante*, for the *Mephisto-Waltzes*, for the *Totentanz*; indeed, for all the Mephistophelean side of him. So we see that the influence of Paganini was not directed wholly towards the gymnastics of music, but that his personality, more even than his compositions, put a new ideal before Liszt and gave a fresh development to his musical character. Where he did not follow Paganini was in his personal meanness and pettiness; but he seems to have formed in his mind a sort of sublimation of Paganini's appearance and its suggestions, and to have carried this out in a series of works where he played the diabolist rôle himself.

At the same time that he was caught up in this hurricane, and that his mind was full of projects of virtuosity, Liszt met Hector Berlioz. This extraordinary being was thirty years old, and in the high fermentation of his strange schemings. There has never been anything more individual than these; indeed, they are without a parallel in his own art, or in any of the other arts. The blaze and violence of his genius allowed him to achieve things to which no really sane person would have dared set his hand. He had already written the overtures to *King Lear*, *Les Francs-Juges*, and *Waverley*; and these were the years of the *Symphonie Fantastique*. This work, which keeps its originality after the lapse of a century, was a violent, explosive force in its own day. It was wild, violent, incoherent: an explosion of egoism. His vanity and ambition, and his belief in his own powers, had no limit; and they were justified, for the greater the scale the more sure was his accomplishment.

Any judgement of Berlioz by the usual, ordinary standards is fruitless and impossible, for at every turn he contradicts his own failures and successes. The *Queen Mab* Scherzo shows him in a world of small and subtle fancies, of fairy horns and sylvan enchantment. This is the spirit of that last scene in Verdi's *Falstaff*. The sounds are fluttering, hovering; and they move, not in the flashings of a bird's wings, but in zigzag, wavering flight, as a moth or butterfly. Foxglove and Canterbury bell, red campion and dark nettle, are the flowers of the wood, and, if you listen, there are little voices, muttered spells, and the loves and wars of the leaves. This miracle supports itself in the green-lit air, and never sags or drops to ground. The same mind can hardly be recognized in the *Carnaval Romain*, in the rolling and tumbling of its Saltarello, that comes nearer and nearer, like a procession, and gathers new actors at every street corner.

Berlioz must have been preparing for the *Requiem* during these years, and in this, and in the *Symphonie Funèbre et Triomphale*, he reached to the furthest possible limits of orchestral production. The addition, to full orchestra, of four brass bands in the one case, and of a military brass band in the other, makes the performance of either work a rare and expensive undertaking. From the scale of these pieces of music it is possible to guess the force and vehemence of his personality, and if these are his actual and finished achievements, he had schemes, still wilder and more grandiose, that never matured further than in his imagination and his talk. He dreamt of what his own phrase describes as Babylonian or Ninevean grandeur. In mastery of orchestral effect he has never been matched. But it is music of the nerves, not of the sensibilities, and its pleasures are a tingling of the skin, a firing of the blood. There is the very taste of blood in the *Requiem*, and in the *Rákóczy March*. His violent and frightful nervous energy carries these pieces right off the ground and projects them to their ends.

It took Liszt more time to assimilate Berlioz than to digest Paganini, but, as early as 1833, he had completed his piano version of the *Symphonie Fantastique*. The value and importance of this has diminished with the invention of the gramophone, and with the increased chances of hearing any work due to broadcasting; but, in spite of this, his piano score remains one of the most extraordinary productions of his skill. Last century, when the *Symphonie Fantastique* was given, perhaps once in five years, there was no other method by which to gain an aural knowledge of this revolution in music. Liszt was twenty-two years old when he finished his version of it, and it shows him already in possession of his phenomenal technical powers. Such an achievement could have been attempted by no one but him.

We hope to follow the careers of Paganini and Berlioz, step by step, as they reacted upon Liszt, until the one died and the other lost some of his blaze and refulgence. By the period at which this chapter closes, the *Paganini Études* of Liszt were not yet published, and his transcriptions of the overtures to *King Lear* and *Les Francs-Juges* of Berlioz were in his portfolio, but had not yet been engraved, though he had certainly played them at his concerts. His studies of both these composers were, indeed, a long time in maturing. Berlioz was to affect him very much later in his career, a score of years ahead of this time, when he lived at Weimar and wrote the Symphonic Poems.

Meanwhile, there was yet another shock in store for his susceptibilities. This was the arrival of Chopin from Poland, in 1831. He was but a year older than Liszt, and his personality was accented, even as early as this, by his unique and peculiar inflections, for Chopin, at that age, was the full-grown Chopin, and, if he improved, he never changed. This great artist had come from the same landscape as Liszt, for the difference between Poland and Hungary is only that Hungary lies more to the south. The inhabitants are Magyars and not Slavs, but both races belong to the Church of Rome, and the conditions of life are the same. Both countries are alike, also, in that they have no middle class, so that it was impossible for Poland to produce burgher-musicians of the type of Bach or Brahms. Instead, they would be drawn naturally into the salons of the rich aristocrats. We have seen that this happened to Liszt, and, as soon as he left his native land and went to Paris, his days were spent as if in the refinement of Eisenstadt or Pressburg. Chopin, as a parallel to this, may be said to have gone straight from the drawing-rooms of Warsaw to those of the Faubourg St. Germain. Here a small and select audience, largely female, was ready for him; and, indeed, Chopin never went outside this, or had any desire to increase it.

The music of Chopin is so instinct with his own personality, and his personality is so familiar through constant repetition, that he remains much less of a mystery to us than Paganini or Berlioz. It is easy to credit the invariable remark of all who heard Chopin play, that his music was as nothing at the hands of any other pianist than himself. He was entirely centred in it, to the exclusion of everything else in the world; the only other music he loved being that of Mozart. In this respect he was entirely the opposite to Liszt, whose overwhelming curiosity and interest in the music of other composers was strong enough to be a danger to him and to interfere with his own activities.

The appearance of Chopin was exactly in accord with the expectation of his music. He had a profusion of light-brown, curly hair, clear-cut features, and the most aristocratic manner and princely carriage. His skin is described as being of a diaphanous colour, he was thin and slight, and had a high forehead. Although delicate, the marks of consumption had not yet spoilt and ravaged his health; and he had eighteen more years of life ahead of him.

It was already evident that Chopin would be content with the piano, and was not ambitious to write for the orchestra or the opera house. He came, thus, as a reinforcement to assure Liszt's conscience, which was probably troubled by the wish to embark upon a larger career. And, if the influence of Paganini was towards greater technical perfection, and the forms of his *Capricci* brought Liszt many new motives for his piano pieces, the effect of Chopin upon him was to open new sources of poetry. The results were indirect, for there is but a small body of Liszt's work to which it is possible to point as being the direct outcome of his study of Chopin. On the other hand, both composers, just because of their origin, had certain things in common; such as a love of Italian opera. Liszt is always reproached for this, while Chopin is never blamed for his admiration of Bellini. Also, Chopin's adaptation of the forms of Polish dances, the mazurka, the cracoviak, the polonaise, opened another branch of composition to Liszt, though he did not avail himself of this till nearly twenty years later, when he spent more time in his native Hungary.

We see, then, that these three extraordinary figures, all appearing in the life of Liszt within the same year, wrought deep and far-reaching changes in him, and may be said to have altered, and indeed pointed, his whole subsequent career. Paganini was, for the present, the strongest influence of all. The whole technique of the piano was being altered, and Liszt was effecting unheard-of innovations and setting forth difficulties which, for a generation, only his own skill could put into performance. In the case of Berlioz, the labours of Liszt were directed towards reducing the most audacious orchestral scores conceived, till then, into a form in which all their subtleties could be made to appear on the keys of the piano. Nothing more than these transcriptions showed his study of Berlioz for many years to come. But perhaps the most valuable of all three influences was that of Chopin, for his example must have curbed some of Liszt's essays in extravagance.

His maturity of technical skill, which was just beginning, was the greatest danger and menace to his future. But, so far as his own music was concerned, he was still without direction; it is, therefore, all the more extraordinary that the next large body of his compositions, far from showing the influence of either Paganini, Berlioz, or Chopin, should be works of the utmost originality. But the reason for this lies in the restraint with which Liszt exercised his virtuosity. His public appearances were rare in the extreme, and all his efforts, at this time, were towards the perfection of his technique. From now onwards, for several years, he lived almost in retirement. He was only twenty years old; and the fatigue of practising, the weight of these various influences, and the amount of his miscellaneous reading, had reduced him almost to silence.

CHAPTER VI

A mood of Werther—*Another love affair—Liszt discovers*
Weber, Beethoven, and Schumann

Fifty years before this, the novel, *Werther*, had altered the
whole outlook of the world. Now it was *René*. Liszt was
carried so far on the wings of this romantic enthusiasm that
in a letter to Pierre Wolff he even apostrophized his friend as
René. 'Voici quinze jours que mon esprit et mes doigts travaillent
comme deux damnées; Homère, la Bible, Locke, Platon, Byron,
Hugo, Lamartine, Chateaubriand, Beethoven, Bach, Hummel,
Mozart, Weber, sont tous à l'entour de moi. Je les étudie, les
médite, les dévore, avec fureur; de plus, je travaille de quatre à
cinq heures d'exercices, tierces, sextes, octaves, tremolos, notes
répétées, cadences, etc. Ah! pourvu que je ne devienne pas fou,
tu retrouveras un artiste en moi. René, quel homme, quel violon,
quel artiste!' These sentiments show his obsession by Paganini.

A few months later, a letter from Chopin says, 'I write to you
without knowing what my pen is scribbling, because at this
moment Liszt is playing my études, and transporting me out of
my respectable thoughts. I should like to steal from him the way
to play my own études.'

These two documents give an accurate picture of the excitements and distractions by which Liszt was surrounded. There was
a new frenzy for every day, and in his exaltation he trod the air
and not the common earth. For nearly two years he led this
interior life, extending his emotions and putting the finishing
touches to his pianistic technique. He was living with his mother in
a small and modest apartment, and, not much in need of money,
could make all he required by giving a few music lessons.

His mood of religion was still strong in him, and friendship
with the Abbé Lamennais did nothing to lessen it. He stayed with
the Abbé at La Chênaie, in Brittany, and his host, who was a
devoted amateur of music, engaged him in long theosophical
discussions, and wasted, it may be presumed, a good deal of his
time. But Liszt was young, and time has to be wasted, somehow.
There were other distractions, and he had his first adult

love affair. The whole of the winter of 1832 was spent in this intrigue. It was in the depths of the country, at the château of Marlioz, between the Alps and Geneva, and the lady was the Countess Adèle Laprunarède, *née* du Chelerd, who afterwards became the Duchesse de Fleury. So secret was their attachment that nothing more is known of it than this. It will be remembered that Adam Liszt, on his deathbed, had said to Franz, 'Je crains pour toi les femmes'; and the first of these troubles had begun. But it did not last long, and Franz seems to have extricated himself without any damage to his feelings. At least, he was not ill after this, as he had been when his music lessons with Caroline de Saint-Cricq were interrupted by the father.

Perhaps his emotions were not seriously involved in this affair with the Countess: the air was too full of enthusiasms of a serious sort. It must not be supposed that he had only time for the music of Paganini, Berlioz, and Chopin. He had lately made another discovery—of Weber. This composer had been dead for some five or six years, but his romantic operas were the first signs of the new musical generation in Germany to reach Liszt. And he was as strong a partisan of Weber's piano compositions, and made his own arrangements of the *Invitation à la Valse* and the *Polacca Brillante*, which he adapted as a concerto, with orchestra.

Meanwhile, his cult for Beethoven had never ceased, and he was slowly preparing his piano scores of the nine symphonies, a work which did not reach completion till many years later. But that was the fault of his publisher, who kept the manuscript of half of the symphonies for twenty years. All the piano sonatas were in Liszt's repertory by now and we are told that he used to play them to Berlioz in the dark. The sonatas must have sounded different then; and the inclusion of Beethoven's name on the programme of a recital was a dangerous act, for the public wished to be pleased or astonished, and the sonatas of Beethoven were altogether too serious for them.

In the midst of this tumult of sound, and among all this babel of voices, Liszt saw the music of Schumann for the first time. Schumann was the same age as Liszt, and the same age as Chopin; and in his early years he was writing the most beautiful and characteristic of his compositions. *Papillons* and *Carnaval* had just been published, and Schumann was working on his own Paganini variations, for he, also, had fallen under the spell of the Italian. In those early years he was a person of as many enthusiasms as Liszt, and he had an admiration for Chopin which that composer never repaid to him, for he took little or no interest in Schumann. But Liszt immediately recognized Schumann; and we must admit that Liszt had now reached a pitch of receptivity that made it dangerous to him. His mind must have been choked with the music of other men; and, at the same time, his phenomenal skill, and the intoxication into which he could throw an audience, were calculated to make a virtuoso of him, and nothing more.

CHAPTER VII

Paris as art-centre—Rossini, Bellini, Meyerbeer—Account of a Liszt recital by Henry Reeves—An hysterical occasion—Appearance of Liszt—The Parisian salons—Madame d'Agoult—Her origin and history—Her character—Their liaison

In those years there was no musical life anywhere but in Paris; and, indeed, Paris was the centre of the World of Art. It had seemed, after the wars of Napoleon, as if England might be the scene of a great art movement, but the prospect of this was spoilt by a series of untimely accidents. The early and tragic deaths of Keats, Shelley, and Byron, of Girtin, and of Bonington, removed the excuses for our Victorian prosperity. So Paris had the writers, the painters, the musicians. Ingres, Delacroix, and Balzac lived there, while foreigners like Chopin and Heine left their homes and came to Paris. Liszt, at this period of his life, had forgotten his native Hungary, and was, in all things but fact, a French citizen.

It was not only that Chopin and Berlioz lived in Paris, but that city had every authentic, settled attribute of a centre of music. It had a great pedagogue, Cherubini, to preside over its musical academy; and opera seemed to have deserted Italy and come to France. *William Tell* was the climax of a career that no person of intelligence was afraid to compare with that of Raphael or Titian, and, even if Rossini had retired after this, no one could foresee that his silence was to last, and new operas were expected from him at each new season.

This was not all. Bellini had been invited to compose a grand opera for the French stage. He came to Paris for this purpose, and *Puritani* was the outcome of the contract. No one could have foreseen that he would die at only thirty-four years of age, with every opportunity at his feet, and with singers, such as Pasta or Tamburini, who were the old Italian art of song at its best, and, for want of whom, the operas of Bellini can hardly be given even a tolerable performance in our day.

There was, also, Meyerbeer, whom it is hard to appraise at his true value. It is, perhaps, sufficient to say that the quasi-military disposition and organization of his mediocre talent were dangerous enough to force Rossini from the field. No composer has ever worked more hard, or revised his scores as much, as did Meyerbeer, who was content if his new operas were produced at intervals of eight or ten years. Rossini, who was by then in a state of nervous collapse, from the speed with which he had been forced to spend his prodigious gifts of melody, was unable to face competition with this steadier, more plodding mind, and he retired for ever.

If Rossini, Bellini, Meyerbeer, were the lions of the operatic world, Franz Liszt, at even twenty years of age, was no less celebrated. His talent as a performer had never been equalled. It must be remembered, also, that he was the first pianist ever to give complete piano-recitals, without the aid of any other musician: as he was the first pianist ever to perform his programme by heart. These two considerations were sensational enough in their day; but, also, a whole world of music was thrown open to him, and the scope of the pianist was extended indefinitely by the works of Beethoven and Weber, to mention but the dead composers who figured in his repertory. He had, now, the youthful works of Chopin and Schumann to add to these, and his own intricate and dazzling adaptations, for Liszt cannot yet be described as an original composer. Thus, as a virtuoso alone, he had opportunities there had never been before; and, if the repertory of a pianist had altered and increased, it must be admitted also that the public were in a condition of high romantic tension, brought about by the novels and poems they had read. The years immediately after the July Revolution knew the heights of Byronic fancy. Red ties, untidy beards, and corduroy suits, were not yet the symbols of culture. It is typical of the time that Chopin and Liszt, two of the chief protagonists of the Romantic Age, should have had all the airs of the grand seigneur and the graces of the aristocrat.

A recital by Liszt, even in these early years, produced such an atmosphere of excitement as can hardly be credited. Henry Reeves, the friend of Greville, gives a good account, in his own *Life*, of a concert he attended in Paris, in 1835. 'Liszt', he writes, 'had already played a great fantasia of his own, and Beethoven's 27th Sonata. After this latter piece he gasped with emotion as I took his hand and thanked him for the divine energy he had shed forth. At last I managed to pierce the crowd, and I sat in the orchestra before the Duchesse de Ranzan's box, talking to Her Grace and to Madame de Circourt who was there. My chair was on the same board as the piano when the final piece began. It was a duet for two intruments, beginning with Mendelssohn's *Chants sans Paroles* and proceeding to a work of his own.

'We had already passed that delicious chime of the Song written in a Gondola, and the gay tendrils of sound in another lighter piece, which always reminded me of an Italian vine. As the closing strains began I saw Liszt's countenance assume that agony of expression, mingled with radiant smiles of joy, which I never saw in any other human face except in the paintings of Our Saviour by some of the early masters; his hands rushed over the keys, the floor on which I sat shook like a wire, and the whole audience were wrapped with sound, when the hand and frame of the artist gave way. He fainted in the arms of the friend who was turning over the pages for him, and we bore him out in a strong fit of hysterics. The effect of this scene was really dreadful. The whole room sat breathless with fear, till Hiller came forward and announced that Liszt was already restored to consciousness and was comparatively well again. As I handed Madame de Circourt to her carriage we both trembled like poplar leaves, and I tremble scarcely less as I write this.'

This description, that seems touched with comedy, is the account of an ordinary, average Englishman. The secret of the power and spell of Liszt lay in the new system that he had invented. His attack and brilliance, his speed and his exquisite arpeggios and runs, together with the extraordinary quality of his touch, these things gave him an unfair advantage over pianists of the old classical school. But, at the same time, there was the spirit of the *haute école* about his playing, and, though he had perfected a new method, he threw away none of the advantages of the old. It would, indeed, be possible to apply terms, like those of classical dancing, to the different figures of his ornament and embellishment.

There were, also, the extraneous enhancements of his effects, and among these a place cannot be denied to his good looks. The drawings of Ingres and Dévéria show him in his adolescence when his appearance was the embodiment of young genius. His figure was tall and slender, and his hair, in an exaggeration of the fashion, fell below his ears but not to his shoulders, as he wore it in later years. His features had already the Dantesque profile which was so much remarked, while it would be superfluous to mention the beauty of his hands, for no less than that could be expected of Liszt. His nationality would be difficult to determine, were it unknown to us; but, in the impossibility of his belonging to any one of the ordinary races of Europe, Liszt might be a Russian or a Pole. If he was this, he was a poet or a musician; and, from this, it is no great transition to be told that the subject of these two drawings was a Hungarian, that he was the greatest virtuoso the world has ever known, and, in fact, that he was Liszt.

When that has been said, the dangers that must lie ahead of him are as obvious as his gifts from nature. Beauty, male or female, is most happy with someone else of neutral looks. Liszt, according to this rule, was marked out to be the prey of any strong-minded woman who could think she loved him, and be, really, intent on her own aims in pseudo-literature, or pseudo-philosophy. He would not be happy, because he would be the victim and the instrument of her false ideals. We shall see this come true in a very short space of time, but meanwhile there were his other perils.

If he was living, at Paris, in an atmosphere far removed from squalor and poverty, it was also an environment not at all congenial to hard work, or at any rate to the labours of composition. His innate breeding and fine manners made him welcome in circles where it may be supposed that a gentle dilettantism passed for the highest intellectual attainment. He used frequently to play in the house of the Austrian Ambassador, Count Apponyi, and in the salons of the Countess Platen and of the Duchesse de Duras. This lady was the mother of two other hostesses who were his patrons, the Vicomtesse de La Rochefoucauld and the Duchesse de Ranzan, the latter of whom was among the agonized spectators when Liszt fainted at the concert we have just described. These ladies may have made pleasant company, but they cannot have helped Liszt to become a serious artist.

Chopin was in exactly the same circumstances, and that Liszt was aware of such weakening influences, to himself and to Chopin, is proved by the letter he wrote to Wilhelm Lenz, in 1872, some forty years later. 'You exaggerate, I think, the influence which the Parisian salons exercised on Chopin', he writes. 'His soul was not in the least affected by them, and his work as an artist remains transparent, marvellous, ethereal, and of an incomparable genius —quite outside the errors of a school and the silly trifling of a salon. He is akin to the angel and the fairy; more than this, he sets in motion the heroic string, which has nowhere else vibrated with so much grandeur, passion, and fresh energy as in his Polonaises.'

So Liszt was alive to the danger and was waiting, we may imagine, for an opportunity to remove himself from its orbit. His spirit was steeped in the most burning ideals of romanticism, his mind was more than a little muddled by the amount of miscellaneous reading he had done, and he was ripe and ready to fall in love.

To this fate he was doomed, and the person he had to thank for its immediate possibilities was his friend, Berlioz. The first meeting between the future lovers took place at a musical party, one evening; and, since it is probable, and cannot at least be contradicted, we may place Chopin, Rossini, Meyerbeer, the poets Heine and Mickiewicz, and the painter Eugène Delacroix among their fellow-guests. This affair was to last for ten years, and its results affected history. It calls, therefore, for some recession of facts.

Marie Catherine Sophie de Flavigny had been born at Frankfurt-on-Main in 1805, the year of Austerlitz. Her father, the Vicomte de Flavigny, was a French aristocrat, both of whose parents had suffered under the guillotine, who had become an officer in the army of the emigrant Bourbon princes. As a child, her father had been page of honour to Marie Antoinette. Her mother was the widowed daughter of a member of the Bethmann family, who were old-established Jewish bankers at Frankfurt. The Vicomte de Flavigny took the earliest chance of returning to France, and bought the Château of Mortier, in Touraine. He died in 1818, and his daughter's childhood had, till then, been passed between Mortier and Frankfurt. After his death, she was sent to a convent in Paris, and, in 1827, was married to Comte Charles d'Agoult, who held a Court appointment at the Tuileries, and was in attendance upon the Dauphine. Charles X, the Duc and Duchesse de Berri, and the Duc and Duchesse d'Orléans were witnesses to their marriage. Her husband was twenty years older than she. They lived in Paris, and at the Château of Croissy-en-Brie. Soon, they had three children;* and, as quickly, she grew tired of him. She was young, and he was middle-aged; he did not interest her, and their indifference soon grew into estrangement.

For her inclinations belonged to the romantic age, to the aftermath of Byron, while her German blood gave her a thoroughness and a dogged energy that forced her to initiative and changed her attitude from passive to offensive. She was not content to let her life with the Comte d'Agoult grow into a tepid permanence; she would take action, herself, as soon as the opportunity presented itself.

She was twenty-eight years old when she met Liszt, and he was twenty-two. She was blonde, handsome, and serious-looking, but had no humour. Above all, there was no sense of the ridiculous in her; she could never laugh at herself, and, from lack of this, we may argue that as she grew older and her looks faded, there would not be much of her charm left.

A century ago, a married woman of nearly thirty with children was an onerous responsibility for a lover to incur. But Madame d'Agoult so quickly enthralled Liszt that there could be no question of anything less than elopement. A curious point is that she did not especially like music, but she plunged blindly into this love affair, quite regardless of its consequences to her three children, and of the shame and calumny that would attach to her harmless but unintelligent husband. She was the captive of Liszt's good looks, of his miscellaneous reading, and of her own vague aspirations which she saw fulfilled in him, though in an art of which she knew nothing.

For his part, he must have been flattered by her affection; he was ardent and young, and he may have felt the pull of her

---

*The death of one of these children made a profound effect upon her, and much influenced her state of mind at the time when she made the acquaintance of Liszt.

personality upon him, which sort of force was new in his experience, for every other woman would look to him for energy
and driving power. She was his elder by much more than the six
years that really separated them, and it took him many years to
throw off her shackles. But, having once begun their relationship,
Liszt made no attempt to evade the responsibilities he had taken
upon himself, and this is in exact accord with everything that we
know about his character. Their liaison caused an immense scandal,
the consequences of which were not so immediately serious to
Liszt, himself, because he had no family to harm. There was only
his mother, who lived in Paris, of whom he was very fond, but
whose character was so negligible that she hardly appears at all in
his life. On the other hand, he was to be branded, from now
onwards, as a person of loose morals; and, in England at least,
these rumours spoilt his fame, till, after two unsuccessful concert
tours, he left these shores and did not return to them for forty-five
years, until a month or two before his death.

If these adverse effects of her influence upon him are not to be
denied, it is also the truth that she gave him the background of
peace and quiet that was urgently necessary to him. She took him
away from Paris, and his first serious compositions were the fruits
of this removal from popularity. All credit for this is due to her,
even if its occasion was no more than the necessary seclusion that
had to follow her escapade. Madame d'Agoult had been waiting
for a lover to change the course of her life and break the monotony
into which she was falling, while Liszt was waiting for a chance to
give up his virtuosity and embark upon the career of composer.
Thus, both Liszt and Madame d'Agoult found their ambitions
fulfilled, at least in the first few months of their friendship. Their
minds were full of romantic ideals, and their love was not yet
disillusioned.

CHAPTER VIII

They elope together to Geneva—The carnet de Genève—Birth of Blandine—George Sand arrives to visit them—The trip to Chamonix

It became necessary, for good and cogent reasons, that they should remove themselves from Paris, and their first stopping place was Lyon. This town seems to have left a powerful effect upon Liszt's imagination. It was a centre of industry, and revolutionary feeling had been endemic in it for forty years, since the 'glories' of the Terror; in fact, martial law was nearly a permanence in Lyon. There was widespread distress among the workers at the time of his visit, and with his customary generosity he gave concerts for their benefit, and kept little, or nothing, for himself.

But Lyon was only on their way, and after a few weeks they continued their journey, arriving at Geneva in August 1835. The next few months were probably the happiest time that Liszt had yet experienced. Geneva was well chosen as their place of refuge. It had all the amenities of life, and was so very nearly in France that it held little sense of estrangement for them.

His happiness was of a double sort, for this was also his first experience of the beauties of landscape, of the external world that lay before his eyes. He had come straight from the grand effects of literature to the grand effects of nature. Switzerland was, moreover, the land of romance, and the young generation, who were tired of classical sentiment, admired the mountaineers for their love of liberty and their sturdy sentiment. The opera of *William Tell* is the embodiment of these feelings, and was seen by contemporaries as a serious masterpiece only to be anticipated from the composer of the *Barbiere* and *Semiramide*. But Rossini had studied local colour with a persistence that his lazy lyric genius, with its flow of curving ornament and comic characterization, could never have been expected to show. No one could have foreseen this sort of labour from Rossini; we are even told that there are no less than twenty instances in his score of the employment of the '*Ranz des Vaches*', and other traditional tunes of the country.

Switzerland was the land of romance and sentiment, and under its inspiration, and from his new-found personal happiness, Franz was able to set to work on a scale of energy that had never come to him before. He worked at composition on alternate days, and spent the other half of his time reading, or following a course of philosophy at the University. The Conservatoire of Music had just been opened, and, on his own initiative, he agreed to give lessons, free of all charge, to the most promising of the pupils. These notes in his class book show a keen appreciation of their different qualities:

'*Julie Raffard:* sentiment musical très remarquable; très petites mains. Exécution brillante.

Amélie Calame: jolis doigts, le travail est assidu et très soigné, presque trop. Capable d'enseigner.

Marie Demallayer: méthode vicieuse (si méthode il y a), zèle extrême, dispositions médiocres. Grimaces et contorsions.

Ida Milliquet: artiste genevoise; flasque et médiocre. Assez bonne tenue au piano.

Jenny Gambini: beaux yeux.'

The citizens of Geneva, who had been somewhat scandalized by the arrival in their midst of Franz and Madame d'Agoult, were brought to reason by his generous participation in their interest. In this way, he entered into the life of the town, though, from the beginning of his stay there, he was far from friendless. Adolphe Pictet, the author; J. L. Fazy, the politician; and the historian, Sismondo de Sismondi, were natives of Geneva, who took the earliest opportunity to invite Liszt and Madame d'Agoult to their houses. In their turn, they came to hear Liszt play, and would spend the evening at their home in the rue Tabazan with the pianist and the Countess.

Geneva was on the way to Italy and, in the spring, people they had known in Paris came for a stay. They were Prince and Princess Belgiojoso and Countess Potocka, all of whom were friends of Chopin. Madame d'Agoult, for all her views on revolution, was delighted to see persons of her own class again, and, if they loved Chopin, they would understand her intrigue with Liszt.

Meanwhile, the prime purpose for which they had left Paris had accomplished itself, and a daughter was born on 18 December 1835. She was given the names of Blandine Rachel, and in the register her father appeared, under his true name, as Franz Liszt, 'musicien', while the mother was given as 'Catherine Adélaide Meran, rentière, agée 24 ans, tous deux non mariés et domiciliés à Genève'. It will be noticed that Madame d'Agoult had become, for the time being, the same age as her lover.

The birth of a child must have made difficult any return to Paris on the part of the Countess. She and her lover were to live together, for good or ill, and now she was finally committed to him. The news must have travelled quickly to Paris, and the effect of this notoriety was to deepen the solitude in which they lived. They could not be for ever exiled from France, but, if they did return, it must be as visitors. It was better for them to live abroad, and they began to lay their plans for a long stay in Geneva, and a move to Italy after that.

Not that life in Geneva was dull, for Franz was writing his own music, for the first time in his life; there were his lessons at the Conservatoire; and, in the evenings, Adolphe Pictet, Sismondo de Sismondi, or Countess Potocka and the Belgiojosos, would come round to the rue Tabazan, and he would be persuaded to play. Sometimes, even his pupils and their relations were admitted, and we have some delightful and naïve descriptions of this perfunctory courtesy. Sad to relate, Madame d'Agoult is mentioned as being considerably older than was the truth, and very materially more so than in her own statement at the birth of Blandine. Franz looked hardly more than adolescent; the length of his hair was ever a subject of comment, and we are told that he wore, on his index finger, a ring with a death's head in silver on a gold ground.

He also played, on one or two occasions, in public, notably at a concert for the eternal Italian refugees, organized by Prince Belgiojoso. Jérôme Bonaparte, the brother of Napoleon, the ex-King of Westphalia, was among the audience, and he brought with him his children, Prince Napoléon and Princess Mathilde.

Presently, George Sand, who had promised to come and visit them, but had been delayed by her divorce, wrote to announce that she was leaving Paris to join them. She had never met Madame d'Agoult, but she apostrophized her as an old friend, dilated on her blonde hair, and said she as good as knew her already. It was feminine curiosity that drew her to Geneva, for the mistress of Chopin had to see this ideal union between music and aristocracy. It was the sort of thing she had dreamed of, if she had not yet written about it. As the descendant of Augustus the Strong, and Maréchal de Saxe, George Sand held liberal views, and was no enemy to plurality. Liszt she had long admired, not without some suspicion of undue interest in his personality, and as soon as it could be arranged she started off for Switzerland with her two children. Madame d'Agoult had with her the two children of her first marriage, and Blandine as well. That would make five children, two women, and one man, for George Sand had promised to meet them in the first few days of September. But when she arrived at Geneva, a few days late for their appointment, she found them gone. They were on a holiday trip into the mountains, and had left a letter for her directing her to get into touch with Adolphe Pictet, who had also been delayed, and was on the point of starting to join them. The Poste Restante was hermetically shut, but she wrote to Pictet introducing herself; and with her children, and with Pictet for escort, dressed in his officer's uniform, she took the first diligence and followed them to Chamonix. She consulted the hotel registers, and tracked them, by this means, to the Hôtel de l'Union, where Liszt had inscribed himself as 'né au Parnasse, venant du Doute, allant à la Verité'. Her reply to this, on behalf of herself and her children, was:

'Nom de Voyageurs: Famille Piffoëls.
Domicile: la nature.
D'où ils viennent: de Dieu.
Où ils vont: au ciel.
Lieu de Naissance: Europe.
Qualités: Flâneurs.
Dates de leurs titres: toujours.
Délivré par qui: par l'opinion publique.'

She seems to have entered into the spirit of the party, at the door of the hotel.

The meeting between the two women must have been a curious spectacle. But Liszt and Madame d'Agoult were not alone; they had with them a child, about thirteen years old, whom they called 'Puzzi'. He was Liszt's favourite pupil, and his real name was Hermann Cohen. If he was a boy, he was more like Madame d'Agoult than like Liszt; and if he was a girl, he bore an astonishing resemblance to Liszt. At first sight, George Sand thought he was a page in travesty, a beautiful girl who found an operatic cliché the only safe approach to the master.

This trip to Chamonix lasted for eight or ten days, and we may find in it the personification of a new era of thought and expression. Liszt must have communicated some kind of electric excitement to those round him; and, so memorable did they think the occasion to be, that both George Sand and Adolphe Pictet afterwards wrote books about it. They were all very young, and they had an implicit belief in themselves, and in each other. It is so long ago, now—over a century has passed since then —that the thought of their enthusiasm is pathetic and beautiful. The wonderful person of Liszt, and his exquisite and terrific talent as pianist, had just blossomed into what he most longed for, himself, a flowering of his own creation. It is easy to believe that his personality had become transcendentalized in this process, and that these days spent in his company may well have been magnetical, miraculous hours, that could never be forgotten.

All day long they rambled in the mountain valleys, and ate their midday meal on the banks of a stream, or in the shade of a rock under the trees. Their discussions and arguments were endless, and the talk was abstract, and of course useless, except as fuel for its own fires. The five of them—for the children would run ahead and play by themselves—went, not by pairs, but in a haphazard gesticulating group. They were like a company of strolling actors on the march, and there should have been a cart, a little way behind them, loaded with their luggage.

Their appearance was most certainly calculated to cause surprise, and even distrust. 'Puzzi', who had the precocious talent of his race, and who talked not less long or loud than his elders, wore his hair long, 'à la Liszt'. So did the two children of George Sand. The authoress herself was in her famous blouse costume, equivalent to the modern workman's overalls. The hair of Liszt was longer, and more striking in colour, than the hair of anyone else. Pictet wore his uniform of an officer in the Federal army. All the party were hatless and sunburnt; and perhaps only the Countess looked ordinary, though from that very fact she was even more odd than the others, for her respectability, and her aloof, aristocratic air, were out of company with their freedom in dress and manners.

When they got back to their hotel in the evening the

commotion was extraordinary, and the inevitable Englishwomen, who were among the guests, barred their doors, and even veiled their faces from the profane gaze. The pandemonium was prolonged far into the night. They had a private sitting-room, upstairs, with a cracked piano in it, and they sang, and shouted, and played music till the early hours of the morning. Champagne was cheap and plentiful, and not the least part of the scandal was the cigar that George Sand always smoked.

So delightful was the excursion that they decided to prolong it. The view of Mont Blanc had been their objective, but now they went on to Bulle and to Fribourg. The church of St. Nicholas, in the latter place, had an organ built by the famous Mooser, on which Liszt played in astonishing fashion and with savage force working up to a free, extemporary fantasia on the *Dies Iræ*. He seems to have frightened even his friends. And that was the end of the trip; but no one of them ever forgot it.

CHAPTER IX

Return to Paris—Rivalry with Thalberg—A Liszt recital
described by Sir Charles Hallé—Thalberg vanquished—Liszt
and George Sand at Nohant—Madame d'Agoult joins them—
Her flirtation with Ronchaud—Liszt and Madame d'Agoult
leave France for Italy

When George Sand went back to Paris, shortly after this, Liszt and Madame d'Agoult accompanied her. It was a good opportunity, and there were sufficient reasons. Madame d'Agoult had been living long enough in discomfort, while what was hardship for her, after her luxurious upbringing, was unwonted luxury to the pianist. But, even more than this, they had their self-esteem to think of, and they must not hide their faces for ever. It was time that they showed themselves and were not ashamed. Besides, Madame d'Agoult, who was married in all but name to Franz, wished to take her daughter, Blandine, to see Liszt's mother.

But, above all else, there was this. Franz had been away from Paris for eighteen months, and he had left it as the supreme virtuoso of the day. During this interval he had taken to composing and had accomplished much, but his supremacy as performer was threatened, and it was urgently necessary that he should appear, once more, to assert his authority. Prodigies are too soon forgotten; if he wanted to uphold his fame he must appear in open competition with his rival.

This serious threat to the career of Liszt came from the pianist, Sigismond Thalberg, who was a year his junior. He was the illegitimate son of Prince Moritz Dietrichstein and a certain Baroness von Wetzlar. His fame had swept Europe before him, and already critics were saying that he played better than Liszt and that his compositions were superior to those of Chopin. It was essential that he should be destroyed.

Franz reached Paris, for this purpose, in December 1836, only to find that Thalberg had left in triumph just before his arrival. He must wait for the return of Thalberg in the spring; but, meanwhile, he made his own reappearance in the most sensational circumstances at a concert given by Berlioz. The quality of his playing had greatly improved during his absence, and, though he was given a chilly reception at the beginning of the concert, the audience was raised to frantic enthusiasm by his transcriptions of pieces by Berlioz. Sir Charles Hallé was among the public on this occasion and gives the following account of his playing. 'Such marvels of executive skill and power I could never have imagined. One of the transcendent merits of his playing was the crystal-like clearness which never failed for a moment, even in the most complicated and to anybody else impossible passages; it was as if he had photographed them in their minutest detail upon the ear of the listener.

'At an orchestral concert conducted by Berlioz, the *Marche au Supplice*, that most gorgeously instrumented piece, was performed, at the conclusion of which Liszt sat down and played his own arrangement, for the piano alone, of the same movement, with an effect even surpassing that of the full orchestra, and creating an indescribable furore. The feat had been duly announced in the programme beforehand, a proof of his indomitable courage!'

His next move, after the concert, was to examine the music of Thalberg and to write a slashing and destructive criticism in the papers. Chopin, in self-defence, joined in the attack and supported Liszt. 'Thalberg joue excellemment, mais ce n'est pas mon homme. Il joue les forte et les piano avec la pédale, mais pas avec la main, fait les dixièmes aussi aisément que je fais les octaves, et porte des boutons de chemise en diamants.'

When Thalberg came back to Paris, in March, the excitement was immense, and the whole world took sides. Thalberg gave his concert in the hall of the Conservatoire, which only held an audience of four hundred. He played his Fantasia on *God Save the King*, and his Fantasia on the *Mosè* of Rossini. Liszt hired the opera house, and, to an audience nearly ten times as big, played Weber's *Concertstück*, and his own Fantasia on the *Niobe* of Pacini. It would seem that he played, also, the *Hammerklavier Sonata* of Beethoven. Finally on 31 March, in the salon of Princess Belgiojoso's house, and for the benefit of the eternal Italian refugees, Liszt and Thalberg made their joint appearance. Liszt came first and played his *Niobe* Fantasia, and Thalberg, his Fantasia on *Mosè*. This ended the competition, and it was universally acknowledged that Liszt was immensely superior to his rival.

So complete was the verdict that Thalberg hardly appears again in musical history, but it would be a mistake to dismiss him altogether because of his defeat by Liszt. There can be no doubt that he was a most beautiful player. His touch and his phrasing were exquisite, but there were no improvements, there was no invention in his technique. What was supreme in his playing was his 'jeu perlé', his liquid runs, and his scales, which were like little cascades of water, seen separately, drop by drop. As well as this, he had a beautiful singing tone, and never showed the least sign of exertion at the piano, but maintained the aristocratic calm and indifference which gave distinction to his person, and must have been his birthright. He continued to delight his audiences for many years after this, often played in England, toured in South America, married the daughter of the great basso, Lablache, retired to a villa at Posilipo, near Naples, and died there in 1871.

It is probable that some among his numerous compositions have been unduly neglected; but the best of these will have been written by him much later in his career. It must be admitted that

Fantasias on *God Save the King* and on *Mosè* cannot have shown his talent at its best; but neither was the *Niobe* Fantasia representative of Liszt in the phase of composition to which he had now attained. The defeat of Thalberg by Liszt marks the end of that form of music, and in another year or two Liszt's own compositions were at last ready to be played, and his public could be induced to listen to Chopin and to Schumann. That came to pass as soon as he had disposed of Thalberg.

Liszt was content after his victory to retire again from the public, and he spent several months in the country with George Sand, at her house at Nohant, in Berry. For some time he was alone with her, for Madame d'Agoult was ill and did not want to leave Paris. It would be a libel on George Sand to infer that she did not make the best uses of this opportunity. Her custom was to write all through the night, from ten o'clock till five in the morning; and they worked in the same room and smoked the same box of cigars. Liszt was finishing his transcriptions of the Beethoven Symphonies, and he had begun a new enthusiasm—for Schubert. These were the years when Schubert was, in effect, first published, and his influence upon Liszt, which we must discuss at a later page, was important in moving away his interests from France, where he had lived for so long. It had seemed as if he was to speak French, and remain French, for the rest of his life; he had become, in fact, like Chopin, a native of Paris, but this phase of his life was coming to an end. It had been interrupted by his flight to Geneva, and he could never pick up the lost threads of it again.

When Madame d'Agoult joined them at Nohant, after a few weeks, she must have been conscious of the changed atmosphere. For some time, though, it seemed as if this triple friendship could run its course unchecked. There was no open quarrel between the two women, and life, except for its hours of work, was not far different from the trip to Chamonix. They had the same discussions, the same walks in the country, and, in the evening they masqueraded as at the Hôtel de l'Union. But this life could not continue, it was time to put a stop to it, and Madame d'Agoult asserted her authority over him and reminded him of Italy. They had promised each other they would go there together to read Dante and to see the picture galleries. The German side of Madame d'Agoult, the blood of the Bethmanns, made her want these experiences even more from an educational, than an emotional, point of view. She was resolute to have them, and was equally determined that Franz should share them with her.

So they left Nohant, in July 1837, and passed through Lyon again. The same distress and unemployment were still raging there, and, as ever, Liszt gave a concert and was able to place several hundred pounds at the disposal of the Committee. And there was a diversion of another sort. A young poet, Louis de Ronchaud, started an ardent friendship for the pianist, and an admiration, tinged with something more serious, for the Countess. It is probable that she welcomed this as a means of restoring her lover's affection, which had become jaded after his stay at Nohant, and she therefore gave some encouragement to the poet. Liszt was not jealous, and invited him to accompany them to Italy. But at Chambéry they parted company, and Ronchaud went back to his native Lyon.

After a detour to Saint-Point, in order to visit Lamartine, Franz and the Countess went on their way, and reached the Italian Lakes some weeks later. He had not been jealous of Ronchaud, but he could not resist writing to him in terms which settled any problem in the poet's mind and closed the question; for, as he said, 'Lorsque vous écrirez l'histoire de deux amants heureux, placez-les sur les bords du lac de Côme'. Perhaps, after Liszt left her, no one else ever loved Madame d'Agoult, for many years later, in 1876, she dedicated *Mes Souvenirs*, her book of Memoirs, to Ronchaud.

CHAPTER X

Lake Como—Birth of Cosima—Milan and Rossini—Some difficult themes—'Une soirée très animée'—The Danube floods —Liszt returns to Vienna, in order to raise money for the victims—Milan again—He drives in an open carriage round the town—Rome—Monsieur Ingres—Birth of Daniel—San Rossore —A parting on the road—Liszt goes to Vienna, Madame d'Agoult to Paris

This was Liszt's first experience of Italy, and the lovely autumn days must have followed on one another too quickly to count. They had lingered on the shores of Lake Maggiore, at Baveno, but were drawn onwards by the idea of Como until they reached Bellagio, and were satisfied to stay there, on the narrow arm of the lake, where the opposite bank is so near that the blue gulf between might be the placid waters of some deep river. The oleanders were in flower and the air was heavy with the scent of the magnolia. These perfumes were near to them, because they took the Villa Melzi which has a beautiful garden. Pasta, the great singer, owned the villa next door to them. They may have bathed in the lake, and they certainly rowed by moonlight on its waters.

The atmosphere was propitious for work. During his stay at Geneva, Liszt had finished the Swiss numbers of the *Années de Pèlerinage*, soon to be described in detail, and he now began a second volume of impressions and wrote, at Bellagio, perhaps the finest of the whole series, the *Fantaisie, quasi Sonate: d'après une lecture de Dante.* Also, at long last, he was completing the *Douze Études d'Exécution Transcendante* and the six *Paganini Études.* These were the fruits of his labours ever since he had first left Paris for Geneva, two years before. Now, at last, he had some original works worthy of him.

In the midst of all these labours another daughter was born, on 25 December 1837. This was Cosima, whose name will remain for ever linked with that of Wagner. She was called thus because she first saw the light upon the shores of Como.

Her birth was the reason for their repose at Bellagio, but Milan, the capital of the Lombardo-Venetian kingdom of Austria, was only a few miles away, and the fame of its opera drew Liszt out of his retirement. Milan was a capital of music and he must conquer it.

His introduction to the city was highly characteristic of him. Passing by the shop of the famous music publisher, Ricordi, he went in, seated himself at a piano and played in so astounding a fashion that Ricordi rushed in from his office, saying, 'Quest' è Liszt o il Diavolo' ('This must be Liszt or the Devil'). Having assured himself that the musician was a human being, Ricordi then opened his villa in the Brianza for Liszt, lent him his box at the Scala and his horses and carriages, and placed at the pianist's disposal his famous library of fifteen hundred musical scores.

Rossini, an old friend of Liszt, was then living at Milan, still more determined in his retirement from the operatic stage, but giving elaborate dinner parties to a society composed of musical amateurs and operatic singers. Rossini, the most celebrated artist in Italy, was the arbiter of Milan, and his friendship with Liszt was sufficient to establish the pianist's notoriety and to make the public curious to hear him. But Milan, one of the great cities of Italian opera, was quite outside the path of any other form of contemporary music.

The taste of the public was deplorably bad; all they would listen to were fantasias upon operas that they knew, and then they would whistle and sing the airs. A portentous arrangement that Liszt had made of the overture to *William Tell* was their favourite piece; but Rossini had lately broken his long silence to the extent of writing, or at least allowing to be published, a dozen songs called *Les Soirées Musicales*. Liszt adapted these for the piano, and he was certain of applause.

His concerts in Milan took place in a curiously humorous atmosphere, very typical of the native wit to those who know the Italians. At one of them, a silver urn, presented to the pianist by a group of admirers, and described by Liszt himself as being 'from the hand of one of the best pupils of Benvenuto Cellini', was placed at the entrance of the hall, and the audience were invited to place in it their themes, or suggestions for themes, on which he would improvise. At the end of the concert, when he took the notes out of the silver urn and opened them, he found he had been requested to improvise upon Milan Cathedral, upon the railway (a newfangled invention which had not yet lost its terror, or the variety of childish and Futurist delight with which it appealed to the Italians), and upon the question as to whether it was better to remain a bachelor. Liszt's reply to this last-suggested theme may be quoted from a letter: 'As I could only have answered this query by a long pause, I preferred to recall to the audience the words of a sage—whichever conclusion you may come to, whether to marry or remain single, you will always repent it.' From this anecdote it may be guessed that Liszt had to vanquish his public as much by a display of ready wit as by his prowess on the piano.

Liszt gave at least three public concerts in Milan. On 10 December 1837, he played at the Scala opera house, and on 18 February and 15 March 1838, at the Assembly Rooms. His programme consisted of his Rossini arrangements, some of his own études, and an adaptation he had made of the overture to the *Magic Flute*, for six hands playing on three pianos. Two hands were those of Liszt; the other four were those of hired assistants!

Milan cannot have been much to his taste, and, as soon as Madame d'Agoult was sufficiently recovered from the birth of Cosima, they set forth on their travels again, in February 1838, and made for Venice. The relationship between them was becoming more difficult; Liszt was entering upon rather a wild stage of his career, when his peculiar, almost mesmeric powers over an audience made him extravagant and vain and intractable. It must be remembered that there had never been anything like this before in history, and that his genius as a virtuoso was just entering into its most glorious phase. It made him impatient of stupidity. He knew he was like no other man and had no equal, and he longed for his opportunity. Up to this moment he seems to have been uncertain where it would occur. This feeling made him ready to embark, at a moment's notice, upon any course, however unlikely, that would lead him to fame.

Meanwhile, he was in Venice, and there is but little information about his stay in that town. His visits to its monuments of painting and architecture may be presumed, and during more idle moments he was still an assiduous reader. We are told that he and Madame d'Agoult read together, on alternate days, Dante, Shakespeare,

Goethe, and Tasso. For the rest, an entry in the Countess's diary gives an interesting little picture of their life. 'Soirée chez la Baronne W. très animée. Franz joue son étude, son galop, et la fantaisie des *Huguenots*.' This shows an odd mingling of subjects. The étude will have been one of the transcendental set; the galop was the famous *Galop Chromatique*, and the Fantasia on the *Huguenots* was the only work ever dedicated by Liszt to the Countess. Its full title was 'Réminiscences des *Huguenots* de Meyerbeer. Grande Fantaisie Dramatique. Op. 12.' After their separation, it was the only piece of Liszt's music that retained its favour in her eyes. When she, in later years, spoke disparagingly of his works she always excepted the *Huguenots* Fantasia, and called it his best work.

But the soirée musicale in the house of Baronne W. took place over a century ago. Liszt was not yet twenty-seven years old, himself, and the new kind of virtuosity was still in its infancy. We are rapidly approaching the point, though, at which his programmes were complete, when the works of Chopin and Schumann, and the finest of his own compositions, were played by him as they were never played before and as they never have been played since. The occasion was near at hand, and the opportunity came to him during this very stay in Venice.

He read in the newspapers of a fearful inundation of the Danube which had carried destruction far and wide into Hungary. The crops of the très peasants were ruined and they were menaced with starvation. This misery in his native land made an instant appeal to the chivalry of Liszt, and he set off, at once, for Vienna, leaving Madame d'Agoult, who was in ill health, behind.

It was fifteen years since he had been in Vienna, and, after the bad taste of Italy, the cultured audiences of the Austrian capital must have been a delight and an inspiration to him. In one month he gave no less than ten concerts, and each of these yielded a sum of some hundred and fifty pounds, all of which he forwarded for the benefit of the sufferers.

In fact, the concerts were an unparalleled success, and he introduced the public to entirely new spheres of music. When performing in private houses his programmes were still more varied and extended; he played anything and everything. Not only did he give all Chopin's works, but the pianist Clara Wieck, who was to marry Schumann, showed him *Carnaval* and the

Phantasiestücke, which were the latest compositions of her lover, and we are told that he played through them at sight, in inimitable fashion, and at once added them to his repertoire. His programmes, indeed, included all the good piano music then published, and his concerts were a revelation to all who heard him.

The Viennese, who had just realized in those years their extraordinary connexion with the history of music, but were aware of it too late to help any of its heroes, were quick to recognize the prodigy who was in their midst. But it cannot be too much stressed, that between the Liszt of 1838 playing in Vienna, and the Liszt of 1835 who astonished Paris, there were deep and far-reaching differences. For the whole of modern music, all the stock-in-trade which has lasted concert pianists from 1838 down to our own times, was at his disposal.

His fame penetrated even to the frigid circles of Viennese society. He played to the Emperor Ferdinand and the Empress Anna-Carolina of Savoy, in spite of a police report which mentioned his liaison with Madame d'Agoult and his affair with the dangerous Socialist, George Sand.

Some reflection of those evenings is to be found in the lately published *Diary of Baron Philip von Neumann*, Austrian Ambassador to the Court of St. James, and the reputed brother of Metternich. '16 April, 1838. The pianist Liszt paid a visit to Princess Metternich. He astonished us by the self-sufficiency of his manners. He is a product of "la jeune France" beyond anything one can imagine. 17 April. Heard Liszt, whose execution is the most massive and incoherent that can be conceived. He astounded more than he pleased, an audience composed of the first professors and connoisseurs of the capital. 23 April. Dined with Prince Metternich. Went, afterwards, to a concert given by Liszt, who played in an electrifying manner. He is a meteor. Under his touch the piano becomes an altogether different instrument.' Evidently, at a third hearing, Baron von Neumann was the captive of Liszt's playing, and his transition from cordial dislike to violent admiration is to be read in his somewhat laconic remarks.

When he left Vienna, Liszt had to promise to come back again at the earliest possible moment. He was given a banquet, an immense send-off, and a procession of his admirers escorted him some miles along the road.

It had been his original intention to go on from Vienna to

Budapest, but this project, which was dear to his heart, was frustrated by Madame d'Agoult, who wrote that she was ill and needed him. His ambition to visit his native land had to be postponed, and probably he had already decided in his mind that he would go there without the Countess.

Perhaps there was a touch of bathos about his return to Madame d'Agoult after all the excitement of Vienna. They did not, at least, stay more than a very few days in Venice, but left for the Italian Lakes once more, and spent the summer at Lugano. Here, again, he was near Milan, but the harmony of his late triumphs in that city was spoilt because of some articles he had written for the *Gazette Musicale* of Paris. He had attacked Italian musical taste, and had criticized the management of the Scala opera house; as a result of which the chief newspapers were loud in their vituperations of him, a shower of anonymous letters arrived, and it must have seemed as if he would not be safe in the streets of the city. He had to write back that he would accept any challenge to defend his honour, giving emphasis to this defiance by driving round the town in an open carriage. Nothing happened. The wordy warfare died away, and he was able to return to Lugano.

When the summer heats were over he started for the south, stopping on the way at Cattaio, the villeggiatura of the Dukes of Modena. His host was Francis IV, of whose petty tyrannies and restrictions Charles Dickens gives an amusing description in his Italian travels. He reintroduced the use of torture in the judicial system, and re-established the Inquisition in his tiny dominions. But he lived the patrician life of a sixteenth-century Venetian noble in this lovely palace, frescoed by the pupils of Veronese. No great musician had ever before been received on such terms of friendship; Liszt had altered the whole social status of the art.

From Cattaio, their way led by easy stages through Genoa, where he gave a concert, to Florence, in which town he made a stay of some weeks and played on several occasions, in public and in private. It was early in 1839 that he reached Rome, and here he remained for four months.

Rome was to occupy a large place in his life. It appealed to him in many different ways. It satisfied the religious cravings that had never left him since childhood, and that must have come back, now, with redoubled force. Some day he was determined to satisfy his longing for peace and for contemplation. This was

Portrait drawing of Paganini by Ingres, drawn in Rome in 1819

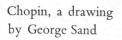

Chopin, a drawing
by George Sand

Comtesse
d'Agoult,
from a drawing
by Ingres in 1849

always contradicted by the worldly side of his nature, which, again, could find its consolation in Rome, for this dead and derelict town was thronged by all the nations of Europe, so that no one who lived a life of retirement in Rome had really left the world. The gorgeous church ceremonies attracted him; and, as well, a new source of enthusiasm revealed itself in the church music. The choir of the Sixtine chapel sang Palestrina, Allegri, Vittoria, and his mind filled itself with projects for great choral compositions in glorification of his faith.

This was not all. He felt himself, at Rome, in the very presence of the great masters, and, to Liszt, who read Dante, Shakespeare, Goethe, and Tasso on alternate days, it was no little thing to be near the masterpieces of Michelangelo and Raphael. His friendship with Monsieur Ingres, the director of the French school in the Villa Medici, amounted almost to a bargain, for Ingres was a devotee of music, and if he showed Liszt the pictures in the churches and galleries, Liszt would play to him, and would listen in patience to his violin. Ingres preferred his violin to the pictures, and it is not impossible that Liszt preferred the pictures to his piano. A delightful testimony to their friendship has been bequeathed to the world by the drawing that Ingres made of the pianist during his stay in Rome. It was seven years since Dévéria had drawn him, but he was still youthful in appearance. At the same time, there are the signs of change in this later portrait; the young genius has grown into a fine and polished courtier. There is a loss of innocence, but no diminishment in sensibility.

The effect of his travels may be seen in the letters that he wrote; and we are reminded, in them, of the tables drawn up by Stendhal in his comparisons between music and painting, for exactly the same thing is to be found in Stendhal's lives of Mozart and Rossini,* while even if these were to some extent plagiarized by the Frenchman, they must, nevertheless, represent his views. 'Raphael and Michelangelo', Liszt writes to Berlioz, 'make Mozart and Beethoven more easy for me to understand. Giovanni Pisano, Fra Angelico, Francia, explain Allegri, Marcello, Palestrina; Titian and Rossini seem to me like stars of the same magnitude. The Colosseum and the Campo Santo (of Pisa) are no longer strange if one thinks of your Heroic Symphony and your Requiem. Dante found his picturesque expression in Orcagna and Michelangelo;

* Stendhal's life of Rossini is an acknowledged pastiche.

perhaps, one day, he will find his musical expression in the Beethoven of the future!'

These letters are typical of an enthusiastic traveller of that day, and it may be that his mind was becoming a little muddled by an excess of sightseeing. A few years before, it had been important that he should leave Chopin and Berlioz and Paganini in order to think for himself. Now the time was clearly approaching when he must put on one side these extraneous emotions, derived from pictures and from works of art, must clarify his inspiration, and must think of music in terms of music. We shall see that this moment was unfortunately delayed, and that he was now to embark upon the life of a wandering virtuoso. For, in a sense, the months that he spent in Rome were the last rest that he was to enjoy for a long time to come.

During this time, his third child, a son, Daniel Liszt, was born; and he came into the world at a sad moment. Liszt and the Countess had been together for four years. They were disillusioned in each other. She had come to her senses and had realized that it was not music that interested her; and, as for Liszt, he found her temper trying. Also, Madame d'Agoult and her three children, making five children in all, were a serious impediment to his plans. Being in complete possession of that immense new repertory of music for his instrument he must travel in order to display his genius; and either he had to leave her, or, if she accompanied him with the children, his mobility would be impaired. As this was impossible, they had to decide on a partial separation. His next scheme was to visit Vienna again and go on to his native Hungary, where the presence of a mistress and several children, three of them illegitimate, would spoil his triumph.

When it became too hot in Rome, they left, in June 1839, and went by way of Lucca and Pisa to the little seaside village of San Rossore. Here they spent a quiet time, reading and writing and bathing in the sea. There were, also, the antiquities of the neighbourhood to be visited. The Campo Santo of Pisa, which they had seen before on their way to Rome, left a powerful effect upon Liszt's imagination, and the fresco of the Last Judgement by Orcagna gave him inspiration for one of his best works, the *Totentanz*, only completed many years later.

In the middle of October they left San Rossore. Liszt and the Countess parted at Florence, for he was going to Vienna and she

was bound, with her children, for Paris, where at first they shared
a house with Madame Liszt, the pianist's mother. It was a decisive
moment in their existences. Nothing was the same again with
them after this. They were to continue their lives together, at rare
intervals, but it was obvious that a permanent farewell was near.
The situation dragged on for another five years. It was only half
over, indeed; though, in effect, all of it was finished. Nothing
more ever happened to Madame d'Agoult; Liszt, on the other
hand, was on the very threshold of his fame. For, from this
moment, he embarked on his years of transcendental execution.
The moment has come, therefore, to examine what was his own
contribution to that extraordinary period. Its actualities lay ahead
of him, but the bulk of his virtuoso music, from which he created
that renown, was already written.

CHAPTER XI

The Grandes Études de Paganini—*A fantasy on* La Campanella, *and* La Chasse—*The* Douze Études d'Exécution
Transcendante

I f Liszt, as a virtuoso, was incomparable in the music of other
men, he was no less remarkable when playing his own compositions. There was, indeed, no other pianist of the time who
was capable of executing them. This was because they combined
fresh principles and systems of construction with new scales of
ornament; they required new gradations of tone; they called for
a flashing, scintillating rapidity and a power of endurance that
none of the old order of executants possessed. In fact, his own
piano pieces were the most sensational part of his programmes.

By the year 1840, at which we have now arrived, he had already
completed some eighteen transcendental études with which to
astonish and delight his public. These comprise the six *Grandes
Études d'après les Caprices de Paganini*, and the *Douze Études
d'Exécution Transcendante*. In writing of any of Liszt's compositions,
there is always this difficulty, that he was never satisfied. He was

continually withdrawing his published music in order to revise it. At the same time, it was often many years after he had finished a work before he would allow of its publication. In this way, these two separate bodies of his work were not finally issued, and allowed to remain without further correction from his pen until another ten or fifteen years had elapsed. But it is better to indicate these facts as the works are separately studied, according to the order in which they issued from his fancy.

It will be remembered that Liszt first heard Paganini play in the year 1831. He immediately set about the transference of his technical experiments and effects from the violin to the pianoforte. This was an arduous labour, but it was a work that fascinated the greatest musical minds of the day, for both Schumann and Brahms dedicated their talents to the task. Liszt was, however, the first of them to set to work, and it was a subject more within his province.

The twenty-four *Capricci* for the violin had been published by Paganini about 1830, and Liszt began his labour of translation with his Opus 2: *Grande Fantaisie sur la Clochette de Paganini*, which was finished in 1834. This proved of such excessive difficulty that it was withdrawn and published again three years later. The final version of his *Paganini Études* did not see the light until 1851.

Schumann's version, which was his Opus 3, consisting of *Six Studies after the Capricci of Paganini*, was published in 1833. A second set of six studies, his Opus 10, was printed in 1835. They belong, therefore, to the very best period of Schumann's genius, coming close after *Papillons* and just before *Carnaval*, but it would be useless to search in them for the same qualities that distinguish the transcriptions of such a master hand as that of Liszt. They are romanticized, as compared to the realistic, ruthless methods of Liszt. On the other hand, the contribution made by Brahms to the elucidation of the mysteries practised by Paganini cannot be said to compete directly with the similar work of Liszt, because they are not transcriptions of the *Études* at all, but a set of twenty-eight variations written on a theme taken from one of the *Capricci*. They are as terrific in technique as the Liszt set, but their underlying idea is entirely different, and they were not published until 1866. They form his Opus 35. Therefore, of all these works with which the name of Paganini is coupled, the Liszt transcriptions are both the earliest and the most remarkable.

Liszt may have originally intended to transfer all twenty-four of the *Capricci* to the piano, but he was deterred from doing so by the manifest impossibility of the task, and also, more probably, by the monotony of such labour. Twelve études were originally announced, but eventually only six made their appearance, and *La Clochette*, which he had first published separately, was now included among these. It is better known under its Italian title of *La Campanella*, and its first origin is to be found, not in the actual *Capricci* of Paganini, but in the second movement of his second violin concerto. Of the other studies, perhaps the best are those known as the *Tremolo* and *La Chasse*, a fantasy inspired in Paganini by the hunting horn.

The writer must confess to a special inclination towards *La Campanella* and *La Chasse*, if only because they recall the enthusiasms of his own childhood. He heard *La Campanella* played by Paderewski at a moment of his life when any such impression has an unbearable strength and potency. He was reading Strindberg at the time, and, finding a mention in it of *La Campanella*, was so strangely moved that he wrote down an impression of the piece which can, perhaps, be quoted here as an analysis of its effects. 'There is in a novel of Strindberg's, *The Inferno*, the description of how his impending nervous collapse became all but precipitated upon him by the insistence with which someone invisible in a near room played over and over again, so as to practise it perfectly, the most difficult passages from the Paganini-Liszt *Campanella*. The strings of notes, separated from each other and then sewed together again, came floating to him over the low garden wall, one hot summer afternoon. The tinkling and feeble imitation of the church bell, as it occurs all through the first part of the piece, seemed irritating and silly beside the huge, brazen clangour of the sun as it came beating down in a brazen shower through the leaves. The piano was like the church bell in one of those absurdly needle-shaped spires of Switzerland, rung early in the brittle morning, and hardly strong enough to scratch with its feeble point the ice that was lying on the little round mountain lakes. This passage was tried over and over again till the fingering was perfect, and each peal of bells rang out clearly by itself, without interfering with any of the spiked fir trees, or becoming muffled by the snow. Later on, in the middle, when there comes the long tremolo for the right hand, up in the high notes of the piano, a good performer will make them rattle out till the two notes, together, combine and sound forth like the whistle of a steam engine. This is the signal for the feeble church peal to sound out once more, now for the last time, and after this is over the real game of acrobatics begins. Up till this moment, Liszt has been hiding his strength and playing with the church bells like a cat with a mouse, but now the piece is to end with the display of all the technique of which Liszt was the master. What had been feeble before, now takes on a militant and extremely menacing tone, and the meekness of the first half of the piece has been obviously exaggerated, so as to give contrast to the magnificence of the display with which it ends. The whole range of the piano, and not only the treble register, becomes engaged in the conflict, and the sonority is such that it would seem he had the bells in every tower of Northern Europe to run among and thunder upon. The last notes end off suddenly in full force, and their echo grows even stronger before it has passed by and drifted on towards windows farther away.'*

The writer heard *La Chasse* played in just as favourable an environment. It was midwinter, and the flat fields of Northamptonshire had a matt level whiteness of snow upon them. This was blue with shadows where there was any bank, or a rise in the ground, and elsewhere the winter sun, out of a cloudless sky, powdered the snows with a fluid and opaque rose. The tall, leafless elms, and the chestnut trees with their guttering candles burnt down to the very wicks, were glittering and shining in the silver frost and were immensely exaggerated in height owing to the clear air; they were like a line of frigates, crowded with sail, waiting, motionless, for the breeze to blow. The far-off fields had a little mist upon them, as from a bonfire of dry leaves, with no wind to lift the smoke away. Suddenly, just as *La Chasse* was in the full torment of its sound, noiselessly the hunt came past, over the horizon of the next field. First the hounds, at full cry, and after them the huntsmen in their red coats. This was the Grafton Hunt, and they were gone and out of sight with the dying of a horn, the only sound they made. Then, and then only, did *La Chasse* come to an end, and its images had been transferred directly from imagination into reality. So magical was this transition that it will be impossible to forget that winter day. It will live in the memory, linked with the rattlings and tappings of this play

*See Appendix II.

56

of virtuosity, as though Paganini and Liszt were two ghosts in the wainscoting, while I looked from the old window of square frames into the white fields, and listened to *La Chasse*.

If *La Campanella* and *La Chasse* are the best of the *Paganini Études*, the others are not so noticeably inferior to them. But it must be stated that they are preferable in their earliest and most difficult form. Liszt clipped their wings when he came to revise them; though, many years afterwards, another great virtuoso, Ferruccio Busoni, edited them again, adding his own particular difficulties to those already there, and giving them, as it were, too copious and ruffled a plumage. Thus it came about that these *Études de Bravura* carry the names of the three greatest virtuosos of music, and are signed Paganini-Liszt-Busoni.

After the completion of these bravura studies Liszt devoted his time to the *Douze Études d'Exécution Transcendante*, the most important of all his compositions of this time, and the final and tremendous affirmation of his technical improvements and inventions. It will be remembered that their first appearance was in the *Études en forme de douze exercices pour piano*, published at Marseilles, as his Opus 1, in 1827, when he was sixteen years old. These were withdrawn in 1830, and six of them, rewritten and enlarged, were again issued as Opus 1, dedicated to his teacher, Karl Czerny, the following year. Their next appearance, still further revised, and with the number of pieces increased to the original twelve, was from the publisher, Haslinger, at Vienna, in 1839. Their publication was the result of his Viennese concerts during that year. The germ of his ideas for them had been in him, therefore, since his childhood, and this 1839 edition shows the *Études* in their fullest and most complicated form. The final and culminating edition, of 1854, amounted to a simplification of their difficulties, so that, if the *Études* are to be studied at the moment when they were most characteristic of Liszt, this edition of 1839, from Vienna, shows them in the form in which they were closest to his ideals and aspirations.

They are twelve in number, and their titles are:

1. *Preludio.*   5. *Feux Follets.*
2. *Paysage.*   6. *Vision.*
3. *Paysage.*   7. *Eroica.*
4. *Mazeppa.*   8. *Wilde Jagd.*

9. *Ricordanza.*   11. *Harmonies du Soir.*
10. *Harmonies du Soir.*   12. *Chasse Neige.*

If any of these can be specially chosen for discussion, it should be *Mazeppa, Feux Follets, Eroica, Wilde Jagd,* and *Chasse Neige,* though the other seven pieces in the collection are but little inferior to these. *Mazeppa* must have been an idea that haunted him continually, for he only found the title for it or betrayed the inspiration of the piece, after it had already undergone several revisions and rewritings. He eventually developed it still further and an orchestral version of it appears as one of his twelve Symphonic Poems. It was not suited for this, and is much more successful as a piano étude. It is laboured and banal on the orchestra.

The subject of *Mazeppa* was part of the stock-in-trade of every Romantic poet and painter; it was in their repertory, and was associated in their minds with the tragedy of Poland. The responsibility was Byron's, for this was a typically Byronic theme. A century earlier, the History of Alexander, or subjects from Ariosto and Tasso, had filled the place now occupied by *Mazeppa, Manfred,* or *Childe Harold.* But *Mazeppa,* like the waltzes that were fashionable, once, in the ballroom and that we hear many years later on the sanded floor of a circus, or at a country fair, was doomed to a descent from high dramatics. It lingered for many years at Astley's Equestrian Drama on the Surrey side of the river, where the rôle of Mazeppa, tied to the barebacked horse, was played by the circus rider, Ada Mencken, whom Swinburne loved. She inspired his poem, *Dolores,* and her love letters are among the surprises of literature. Her character would have made an immense appeal to Liszt. The lover of Lola Montez could not have been indifferent to Ada Mencken, but they never met. Nevertheless, the bedraggled, tawdry fate of *Mazeppa* is foreshadowed, perhaps, even in this music. The orchestral version, it has been suggested, is laboured and banal; and as for the piano étude, it may be described as a significant and typical work of Liszt. But this piece is one of the primitive beginnings of programme music. The stage directions are too apparent and the voice of the prompter too loud.

The other four études mentioned fall, of themselves, into two classes. *Eroica* and *Wilde Jagd* have their character sufficiently

58

indicated in their titles, and each is the progenitor of numerous other works. To the first of these, Liszt returned again and again, himself, more particularly in the Third and Tenth of the *Hungarian Rhapsodies*. This peculiar rhapsodical mood, this 'vibrating of the heroic string', to quote a phrase used by Liszt in discussing the polonaises of Chopin, was more essentially of his own invention, and it is, really, in Liszt that it appears for the first time in history. As for the *Wilde Jagd* its inspiration was more fruitful in other composers, and its theme does not appear again with Liszt. For some reason, it chiefly affected his French disciples; César Franck, in *Le Chasseur Maudit*, was indebted to the *Wilde Jagd*. Yet the subject was essentially German in origin, owing some of its possibilities to Weber and *der Freischütz*.

Feux Follets and *Chasse-Neige* are very different in intention. They are studies in deftness, lightness, and rapidity, more in character with the well-known étude, *Gnomenreigen*, that he wrote many years later. In their case, the programme was not so clearly defined as in *Mazeppa*, or *Wilde Jagd*, and this was much to their advantage. Obviously, in any studies of virtuosity, there had to be examples of this mood, and, having made two or three experiments in that direction, Liszt was lucky enough to find titles sufficiently suggestive of their meaning, but which did not too closely dictate their form. As a result of this, these are perhaps the finest of all the *Études Transcendantes*.

But, to be properly appreciated, it is necessary to hear the whole twelve of the *Études* played consecutively by some pianist of the calibre of Busoni. They emerge from such an ordeal as the perfect vehicle of virtuosity. After them, there is little, or nothing, for the piano to say. Even now, when their final edition is some eighty years old, they have never been surpassed, and the *Études Transcendantes* remain unapproachable as the machinery of display. For many years, Liszt was the only person who could dare to play them, and, even in our own plethora of pianists, there are but a half-dozen executants who can do justice to their beautiful hardships.

Armed with the *Douze Études* and the Paganini studies, it will be admitted that Liszt was in a formidable position to assert his technique. They were enough, in themselves, to frighten away any competition; for we have arrived, now, at his years of transcendental execution, a decade during which he toured all over Europe, with his unique personality at the full blaze of its effulgence. The histrionic and the anecdotal side of those years must soon be considered, but at present our concern is only with his actual compositions, and the list of these transcendental pieces is incomplete without a mention of the *Grand Galop Chromatique* (Opus 12). This is quickly dismissed as an absurdity, and, to-day, it would be almost impossible to include it in a programme, but it was a favourite war-horse of Liszt, and in his years of virtuosity it nearly always ended his concerts. It is dedicated to Count Adolphe Apponyi, the Austrian Ambassador in Paris, and Lina Ramann, the official biographer of Liszt, tells us, naïvely, that it owed its origin to the *Études Transcendantes*; for, in working them out at Como, a striking chromatic run originated under his fingers, the character of which seeming to challenge him, as it were, to compose this galop, he retained it as his motive.

This completes the list of his virtuoso pieces up to 1840, the year in which he really embarked upon his public career. If it was Paganini who had first inspired him, he had, by now, far surpassed his master. The *Études Transcendantes* had much more appeal to the memory than the *Capricci* of Paganini, partly, of course, owing to their definite adoption of a programme meaning.

It must have seemed as if they would remain alone in their kind but, unfortunately, nothing in the world is unique, and the études of the Parisian music-teacher, Alkan, who died in 1880, are no less difficult, not less strange and, were we given sufficient opportunity to hear them, perhaps no less effective and fine.*

But it may already be said, even at this stage, that Liszt was beginning to tread upon dangerous ground. In the *Études Transcendantes* he had proceeded to the extreme limits. No further advance was possible; and they were works of a kind that could not be indefinitely repeated. Luckily for Liszt, the pressure and strain of his concerts were so intense that, for the next few years, and, indeed, until his retirement from the concert platform, he had neither time nor energy to embark upon large works of a controversial nature. Instead, he devoted himself, almost entirely, to the transcription of songs; admittedly a minor art, but one in which Liszt has never been rivalled. In this way, the next period saw his arrangements of Schubert's songs, and of other German *lieder*, and the pyrotechnical side of his talent had a rest. Never-

* See Appendix I on the works of Alkan.

theless, it is difficult not to prefer him in a mood of display, rejoicing in his own strength.

CHAPTER XII
The Années de Pèlerinage. *First and Second books: Switzerland and Italy*

Apart from the Bravura studies, the tremendous transcendental *Études*, Liszt's chief work—always excepting certain miscellaneous pieces, and the operatic fantasies to which a subsequent chapter of this book is devoted—are the *Années de Pèlerinage*. They form his first body of really important original compositions if we remember that the *Douze Études* were already, to some extent, mature in his mind; and he was only able to attempt them owing to the seclusion to which he was forced because of his intrigue with Madame d'Agoult. With the enumeration of these, as of every other branch of his activity as composer, there are the same difficulties of date. The *Années de Pèlerinage* were published in three books, of which only the first two are our present concern. The earlier of these, to which the title was eventually given of *Années de Pèlerinage: Première Année: Suisse*, consists of nine numbers:

1. *Chapelle de Guillaume Tell.*　　5. *Orage.*
2. *Au lac de Wallenstadt.*　　　　6. *Vallée d'Obermann.*
3. *Pastorale.*　　　　　　　　　　7. *Eglogue.*
4. *Au bord d'une Source.*　　　　8. *Le Mal du Pays.*
　　　　　　9. *Les Cloches de Genève.*

These had their origin in three books of pieces called *Album d'un Voyageur:*

(i) *Impressions et Poésies* (7 numbers).
(ii) *Fleurs Mélodiques des Alpes* (3 numbers).
(iii) *Paraphrases: Trois Airs Suisses.*

They were published in 1835, withdrawn and rewritten, and only cast into their final form in 1852, with the omission of some of the smaller pieces, and the publication, under separate cover, of the Swiss Airs.

It must be admitted that the titles of these pieces sound jejune and old-fashioned to our ears, but it must be remembered that Switzerland was then the land of romance. Those were the years in which Turner made his finest watercolours of mountain scenery, and we may look in these pieces of Liszt for the same poetry that inspired one of the greatest of landscape painters. The scheme of the *Années de Pèlerinage* was of utmost originality for its time; while, if to call a piano piece by a place name seems to us a fruitless and pedestrian device, we must think of the *Ibéria* of Albéniz, where the names of Jerez or Almería are but a faint indication of what their title implies for picturesque evocation, a sunny languor and deliberate fire.

Liszt first found himself in the *Années de Pèlerinage*. Certain of these pieces, more particularly *Au lac de Wallenstadt*, *Au bord d'une Source*, *Eglogue*, and *Pastorale*, are among the most successful things that he ever accomplished. These collections of sounds do really call up a mood in the mind, which takes shape as the piece proceeds, until it exactly represents the sensation and the poetry of a mountain lake, or the chill cool of an Alpine stream. How this has been done it is not possible to describe, but no one could deny the charm and the effectiveness of these abstractions.* They are a century old, and while they are the definite and unmistakable works of a master, there is no use in exaggerating their scale. They have a place in the history of Romantic Art beside many small and delightful trifles—acquatinted views, vignettes in books, romantic poems and so forth. If their value, as works of art, is considerably greater than the worth of these confessedly minor things, it is because they are from the hand of Liszt.

The second volume, *Années de Pèlerinage: Seconde Année: Italie*, is a collection of ten pieces, all of which had been previously published under separate cover. Their titles are:

* With regard to the odd realism and evocation of these pieces, I am informed that the late Peter Warlock played the *Vallée d'Obermann*, the most extended and important piece in the Swiss book of the *Années de Pèlerinage*, to a friend who was under the influence of hashish at the time. He cried out: 'Don't stop! It's like the valleys I used to know as a child.' He was brought up in Switzerland. (Story told me by Constant Lambert).

1. *Sposalizio.*
2. *Il Penseroso.*
3. *Canzonetta di Salvator
   Rosa.*
4. ⎫
5. ⎬ *Tre Sonetti di Petrarca.*
6. ⎭

7. *Fantaisie, quasi Sonate:
   d'après une lecture de Dante.*
Venezia e Napoli:
8. Gondoliera.
9. Canzone.
10. Tarantella.

This second volume was published in 1848, but the three pieces called *Venezia e Napoli*, though written in 1839, were only included in the *Années de Pèlerinage* as appendix to an edition published in 1861.

Taken as a whole, there can be no doubt that this book is better than the volume of Swiss sketches. If the first two numbers, *Sposalizio* and *Il Penseroso*,* inspired by the picture of Raphael in the Vatican, and by the tomb of Giuliano de Medici by Michelangelo in the Cappella Medici at Florence, are but the devout or lofty impressions of a sensitive tourist, there are other pieces in this Italian volume that are among the very finest of the works of Liszt. This praise, indeed, may be applied to all the other titles in this collection.

The taste of the time is wholly reflected in the *Canzonetta di Salvator Rosa*. That artist still had a great name in Italy. He was a part of popular legend. Two pictures of harbours on rocky coasts, with great ships drawn up to be careened, or lying wrecked and deserted, hang in the Palazzo Pitti, at Florence, and show Salvator at his best. An indefinable romance of the ragged, tatterdemalion sort, attaches to them. The galleons are like great lutes, great melon shapes of wood and ivory. A century ago, these were among the most prized pictures in the Pitti; now they hang above a door and are hardly noticed. In the days when Liszt went on his Italian travels, Salvator Rosa was one of the names conjured up by the word, Italy. It was on the lips of every cabman, as Tasso was on the lips of every gondolier.

His name stood, especially, for Southern Italy, and Naples and Calabria were as nothing without him. Perhaps, in order to appreciate his contemporary importance it is necessary to read one of the most delightful minor things in the literature of Italy, the

* *Il Penseroso* ends with some curious harmonic passages of distinctively Wagnerian type, remarkable in view of their early date—and subsequent effect.

63

Life of Salvator by Lady Morgan. In that, the fullest account may be found of his sojourn with the brigands in the wild mountain valleys between Salerno and Amalfi, and every detail of his picturesque career is given with delight and emphasis. Brigandage had, in fact, become a decorative style, comparable to the chinoiseries or singeries, of a century before this. Romantic novels intensified this background, and operas, such as *Fra Diavolo* or *La Muette de Portici*, increased the audience still further. It must, also, be admitted that much of the material was falsely masquerading under Salvator's name. Pictures found in dusty corners, and only recognized in our own day as the work of Magnasco, were then freely attributed to Salvator. They were harbour scenes; storms at sea; bandits in Roman ruins; anchorites, more faun than hermit, in the wild woods; kitchen comedies; picnics of monks, or nuns, in grottos; and all the situations of the convent; the calefactorium, with the monks warming their feet before the fire; the refectory, showing the monks breaking their fast; and the parlatorio, with the nuns at their embroidery, talking to their friends or lovers, through the grill. There was this immense body of romantic and picturesque incident attaching to Salvator; and the authentic details of his life, when truly known, in no way diminished from this. For Salvator was an actor, a poet, and a musician, as well as everything else. He took part in the Commedia dell'Arte as Coviello, and as Pascariello; and so far developed the mask of Coviello that two characters of his invention, Coviello Formica and Coviello Patacca, remained in the repertory of Neapolitan Comedies until, at least, the time of Liszt. The conjunction of these facts, proven or otherwise, is sufficient explanation of the interest Liszt felt in him, and, as a mere dilettante, a cultured traveller, it is in no way remarkable that he should have set a poem, or song, by Salvator.

In its earliest form, it must, almost certainly, have been an actual song, as were the *Three Petrarch Sonnets* in this same collection. But, in the case of the *Canzonetta di Salvator Rosa*, there was, in all likelihood, the traditional melody attached to the words, which will have been of Salvator's own composition. The *Three Petrarch Sonnets* were written as songs during his stay in Rome, but they only appeared in their final form, changed into piano pieces, in time for the publication of this Italian album in 1848. They form the most perfect examples of Liszt's art. His genius was of the sort which has to act upon suggestion, so that, in this instance, the circumstances were most favourable to its fruition. In their earlier version, they form an astonishing transition into musical form of the atmosphere, the sentiment, the shape, even, of Petrarch's sonnets; while the transference of these finished songs into pieces for piano solo, an art of which Liszt was the supreme master, has resulted in an extraordinary fusion, for they have their own perfection as piano pieces, are as typical of Liszt, at his best, as are *Waldesrauschen* or *Les Jeux d'Eaux à la Villa d'Este*, and have, at the same time, the sunburnt and fiery romance of the rhymed words from which they took their origin. It might be remarked in parenthesis to this, that England, the home of Italian political refugees and the centre of the revived interest in Italian letters, was in a sense forestalled by Liszt, for Dante Gabriel Rossetti was only a boy of eighteen when Liszt performed this Pre-Raphaelite experiment. The *Three Petrarch Sonnets* have, indeed, the diction and the atmosphere of Swinburne, and they form an item to themselves, and are of no little importance in the crowded catalogue of Liszt's works. It is difficult to express a preference for any one in particular, of the three. But perhaps the most beautiful and successful of them is the second, in E major.

No less remarkable is the next number in the album, the *Fantaisie, quasi Sonate: d'après une lecture de Dante*. This is a piece of inordinate length, and of tempestuous, stormy character. It is among the most remarkable productions in the whole of romantic art; and were it possible, by some magical transmutation in time, to hear Liszt play, this is one of the pieces that every lover of Liszt would wish to include in the programme. Nothing like it had ever been attempted before in music. It was written at Bellagio, on the shores of Lake Como, at the time of the birth of his daughter, Cosima. We know, already, that he was an ardent reader of Dante, and he must have had, even at this time, the intention to compose a great work inspired by his favourite poet. This ambition was realized, many years later, in his *Dante Symphony*; but, for this piano piece, he adopted something of the same procedure that had resulted in the *Three Petrarch Sonnets*. He obtained his focus, that is to say, not by first setting some words and then converting the music into a piano solo, but by condensing and crystallizing his inspiration by means of a smaller lens.

For this purpose, he made use of the poem by Victor Hugo, called *d'après une lecture de Dante*. It is no part of our project to discuss Victor Hugo, and no more need be said, therefore, than that this is among the better of his poetic productions and that in the glare and dazzle of the Romantic Movement, for which Victor Hugo was so largely responsible, Liszt was no more to be censured for admiring him than was our own Swinburne, a generation later. This piece, in which he unwittingly assisted Liszt, is, at any rate, not Victor Hugo but Dante.* It does certainly give the impression that any sensitive person obtains on turning over the pages of the *Inferno*. It belongs to the same category in Liszt's music as the *Mephisto-Waltz*, or the *Totentanz*. The air of damnation hangs over it and the images are of the Vortex and the Whirlwind.

The last piece in this album of Italian sketches is very different in character. Under the title *Venezia e Napoli*, it contains three separate items, Gondoliera, Canzone, and Tarantella. They were derived from popular music. We know that Liszt was always noting down popular songs during his stay on the Italian Lakes and in Venice. The Tarantella, by far the most amusing of the three pieces, he must have taken down in Rome, or more naturally in Naples. There is no direct evidence that he visited Naples from Rome, but the probability of this may be taken almost as a certainty, in view of the easy journey and the invariable extension to Naples of every foreign traveller's trip to Italy. Besides, Liszt will have been especially eager to visit Naples because of its musical reputation. In any case, the Tarantella is a delightful epitome of the warm Italian south, not to be taken too seriously, except by the pianist who may have to wrestle with its appalling difficulties. For this, perhaps the most arduous of all the pieces in the *Années de Pèlerinage*, is essentially a concert finale and belongs to that class of Liszt's works which seem calculated to leave the executant paralysed, or struck down with tetanus, at the close of his performance. It may be taken as a study of the contemporary atmosphere of Naples under the Bourbon Kings,† and is therefore, equally, a virtuoso piece; a costume plate such as may be found in

*On a certain celebrated occasion in the United States this piece was called: *After a Lecture by Dante*!

†The fact that this piece was only added to the *Années de Pèlerinage* in 1861, the year that saw the downfall of the Kingdom of Naples, is the best proof of this contention.

A drawing of Paganini
in 1837

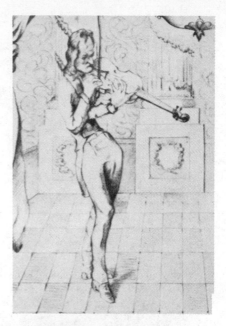

Liszt in 1856

Hector Berlioz, in about 1860

an old book of travels; and an essay in local colour, of the sort practised in their piano pieces by Debussy, Ravel, or Albéniz. It is gay and glittering, and not in the least profound.

This is all that concerns us with the *Années de Pèlerinage* for many years to come, since the third book was not written till the very end of his career, and the separate items that made it up were not collected and published as the final volume of his travel sketches until 1890, four years after he was dead. But, of those already mentioned, *Au Lac de Wallenstadt, Au bord d'une Source,* the *Three Petrarch Sonnets,* and *Fantaisie, quasi Sonate: d'après une lecture de Dante,* take a very high rank indeed among his compositions. They are written with all his impeccable skill, and they represent an entirely new direction in music.

CHAPTER XIII
The Soirées Musicales de Rossini—Soirées Italiennes de Mercadante—Nuits d'Été à Pausilippe de Donizetti

There is, now, a curious but most typical phase of Liszt's talent to be considered, and one which was found inexplicable by the serious school of Brahms and Clara Schumann. In fact, it has done more than anything else seriously to damage his reputation. If he was disliked on the one side for his sensational modernities, he was despised by the same trend of opinion for his retrograde tendencies, and he was accused of making music cheap and trivial. This trouble was connected with his liking for Italian music. His detractors looked with horror upon Italian opera. It was partly a question of nationality, and then, again, the dislike was tinged with jealousy. The great names of northern music, save for Handel and Haydn, had perished in poverty. The fate of Mozart, of Beethoven, of Schubert, made the affluence of Italian operatic composers an insupportable insult, and if they were so popular as that they were doomed, at any rate in the next world. No musician of serious intentions could have any concern with them. Great composers of different origin thought otherwise, so long as they did not come from Germany. That is why both Chopin and Tchaikowsky were not ashamed to admit their love for Bellini. And a man with the omnivorous musical interest of Liszt could not be blind to their merit. Their large, open melodies held a genuine appeal for his ear, and while it is freely admitted that his arrangements of Schubert's songs are surpassingly beautiful—to the extent that some critics would say they are the best, or even the only good things that Liszt accomplished—his fantasias upon Italian operas are lightly put aside and allowed no consideration whatever. If this is so, his arrangements of minor pieces by the same Italian composers are almost completely unknown to the public.

The best of these are the *Soirées Musicales de Rossini*. The reputation that Rossini then enjoyed, outside those stricter circles of German musical nationalism, was of a greatness that it is difficult to comprehend. He was an old Italian master in the authentic line; and no intelligent person was afraid to mention him in the same breath as Raphael, or Leonardo. His early retirement, due more to nervous exhaustion than to his reputed laziness, had increased the excitement attached to his name, so that his admirers lived in constant hopes that he would break his silence and produce another masterpiece. Therefore, the smallest trifles that fell from his pen were reverently collected and preserved.

He had written various songs which his friends, and sometimes himself, would sing, after the dinners which were his recreation. Copies of these were somehow obtained, and an edition of twelve of these songs was published in 1834, apparently without his knowledge, and at least without his consent. Instantly, they became the rage; and when Liszt was in Milan in 1839, and was so often the guest of Rossini, he completed his arrangements of all twelve of these. Their titles are:

1. *La Promessa.*
2. *La Regata Veneziana.*
3. *L'Invito.*
4. *La Gita in Gondola.*
5. *Il Rimprovero.*
6. *La Pastorella delle Alpi.*
7. *La Partenza.*
8. *La Pesca.*
9. *La Danza* (Tarantella).
10. *La Serenata.*
11. *L'Orgia.*
12. *Li Marinari.*

Liszt had skilfully blended the voice and the accompaniment, and made from them a whole that was completely satisfying and a finished work in itself. His uncanny pianistic cleverness made such things possible where any other musician would have failed; and, in the result, the *Soirées Musicales* remain both Rossini and Liszt, in a unity where they cannot be separated from each other, and in which each personality is present in all his idiosyncrasies. This was exactly the result that Liszt arrived at in his arrangements of Schubert's songs, and the transition in this instance is a no less wonderful proof of his cleverness and taste.

Certain of these songs had made their appearance in an arrangement from his hand previous to this. During his stay at Geneva he had published, as his Opus 8 (1), a fantasia based on the *Serenata* and *L'Orgia*, while Opus 8 (2) was a fantasia upon *La Pastorella delle Alpi* and *Li Marinari*. These four songs were now separated and reset, in order that they might appear in their proper order in the *Soirées Musicales*.

Of all Liszt's works which are unknown to the public these are among the most charming and delightful. It is scarcely necessary to say that they were played by Ferruccio Busoni, and that they had a place in his tremendous repertory. In their time, these songs were sung all over the world. They lay open on the piano in the drawing-room of every house in London or Paris whose inmates had ever frequented the opera; and they were carried by travelling opera companies to Mexico and to South America. Their popularity lasted for a generation and now they are, undeservedly, dead.

La Pastorella delle Alpi revived the echoes of *William Tell*, the last and final opera by Rossini; *La Regata Veneziana*, a favourite piece with Busoni, is a beautiful nocturne; while *La Danza*, which was written for the great basso, Lablache, became so popular at Naples, his birthplace, that its strains must have sounded out all over the town, as did *Funiculì-Funiculà* when the author first remembers Naples. In fact, *La Danza* became entirely identified with that city and was perpetually sung to the tinkling mandoline, below the windows of the hotels along the Chiaia, on gaily lit barges in the bay, and in front of every celebrated view of Vesuvius. Yet *La Danza* had completely faded out of existence when Diaghilev revived it, for the Tarantella in *La Boutique Fantasque*.

It is certain that these songs of the *Soirées Musicales* are Rossini at his very best; and, perhaps, there is no great name in any of the arts of whom it can be more truly said, as is the case with Rossini, that all his qualities and the full breadth of his personality appear in the very smallest trifles that come from his pen. This is the case with little piano pieces scribbled on the backs of menus, or in the albums of autograph collectors, little things that he improvised on the spur of the moment and completed in a few seconds. That some of the most successful ballet music ever performed should have been put together out of these minute musical scraps is a testimony to the prodigious gift of Rossini. In the case in point, these piano pieces were given no more than a straightforward and quite simple orchestration, so that the *Boutique Fantasque* relies entirely upon the melodies of Rossini and owes little, or nothing, to the arranger, Respighi. Yet the personality of Rossini dominates the whole affair; his generous, prodigal gift is omnipresent, and one is left with the impression that if Rossini did really leave three hundred and fifty such pieces behind him there must be material enough for a whole week of theatrical entertainment.

His genius had been formed in the Italy of Napoleon, among the ruins of the eighteenth century, that were lingering and slow to die. Yet his style had none of the characteristics of the French Empire; it was an involved and belated baroque, descending, in its worst moments, to the level of a photographer's painted background such as can be seen in the earliest photographs. It was the rococo of the fire grate and of the mirror frame. Once that has been said, it need not be added that the *Soirées Musicales* show him on the same plane as the *Barbiere* and *L'Italiana in Algeri*. The skill of Liszt has made the *Soirées Musicales* present in all their potency, and it is a pity that they should be entirely neglected in the modern concert programme.

During the same year, 1838, that saw his publication of the *Soirées Musicales*, Liszt issued a volume of song-transcriptions from Mercadante. It is difficult to glean anything beyond the mere bones of information about this forgotten opera writer, and the mystery is only deepened by a cryptic reference in Grove's *Musical Dictionary*, to the effect that in the opera buffa, *I Due Illustri Rivali*, 1838, Mercadante 'completely changed his style, marking the accents heavily with the brass'.* Be that as it may, the *Soirées Italiennes* consist of six numbers:

---

* Mr. Constant Lambert drew my attention to the manner in which Mercadante is mentioned in Joyce's *Ulysses*, where he keeps on returning as a curious 'idée fixe'.

1. *La Primavera.*
2. *Il Galop.*
3. *Il Pastore Svizzero.*

4. *La Serenata del Marinaro.*
5. *Il Brindisi.*
6. *La Zingarella.*

Of these, the *Galop*, the *Brindisi* (or drinking song), and *La Zingarella* should deserve, at least, a temporary exhumation out of the past. The volume is dedicated to Elizabeth of Austria, the Vice-Queen of the Lombardo-Venetian Kingdom, who with her husband, had entertained Liszt, that summer, at the Castle of Cattaio.

As a final contribution, Liszt afterwards added three songs by Donizetti to the collection. They are dedicated to Marchesa Sophie de Medici, bear the charming title of *Nuits d'Été à Pausilippe: Trois amusements*, and consist of three numbers:

1. *Barcarola.*   2. *Notturno.*
3. *Canzone Napoletana.*

It is more than probable that there is something delightful hidden away here, too. Anyone who has heard *Don Pasquale* will be eager to know what other things Donizetti could accomplish when he was free from the toils of 'opera seria'.

In all, then, the *Soirées Musicales*, if we group them together, contain some twenty pieces; and a selection from their number would certainly make a welcome change from the more hackneyed Liszt, or the Albéniz, with which every piano recital is expected to end. They contain some of Liszt's finest workmanship, and they present a delightful picture of Italy before it was united—when the Pope was still ruler of the Pontifical States and the Spanish Bourbons yet reigned in Naples and the South.

CHAPTER XIV

Operatic transcriptions—Partitions de piano—*Fantasias* on
Bellini and Donizetti—Don Juan Fantaisie

The operatic transcriptions, or, as he called them, 'partitions de piano', were responsible for much of Liszt's popularity with the public, and for a great part of his income from the publishers. This kind of music had a much surer sale than was the case with original compositions. But the demand and the necessity for this class of work have so completely disappeared that it is difficult to realize how important it once was.

His operatic transcriptions may be best compared, perhaps, in their effect and intention to engravings of famous pictures. These could be bought and hung on the wall and something of the original picture was preserved in them, while they may have been excellent and masterly engravings in themselves. If this comparison is at all accurate, then Liszt was the greatest and most temperamental engraver there has ever been. Indeed, this may be the clue to his whole character as composer. We may think of him as a black and white artist. His skill and taste in engraving other men's work were impeccable; many of his own drawings were original and interesting, but when he came to use the full colour of the orchestra, when he put down the pencil and took up the brush, the results were nearly always disappointing. He was full of ideas, theories that other men put into practice better than himself; but it was against his temperament, and, moreover, he had taken to it too late in life. He was thirty-six years old before he composed a big orchestral work. His years of virtuosity had wasted his time.

Even so, it would seem that the vast mass of his work that consisted in the writing of fantasias upon operas must have made cruel inroads upon his energy. But there is no evidence that he complained of the task. It secured him an income, which became valuable when he abandoned the concert platform, and it afforded opportunities for his skill which were too pleasant for him to grumble at. Operatic fantasias amount, indeed, to such a large body of his work that it is possible to divide them into several different classes according to the method and the form that he employed.

They differ, from the simple embroidery upon some operatic air, to the complete transcription of an entire overture, and from the blending together of two or more of the chief moments of an opera, to the evocation of its whole atmosphere by an introduction, by joints, and by a coda of his own invention and workmanship. There are instances of simple arrangements that any amateur could play, and examples of such virtuosity as only himself possessed in his generation. In all, he wrote fantasias upon some forty operas, and the part of this work which he had already accomplished by 1840, or a year or two after that, amounted to about one half of the total. It was most occupied, by necessity, with Bellini, Donizetti, and Meyerbeer. The later part of it was concerned with Meyerbeer, with Verdi, and, to an ever-increasing extent, with Wagner. Several of these latter pieces are still popular; so is his arrangement of the quartet from *Rigoletto*; the others are all forgotten.

The earliest of all is a Fantasia upon the *Tyrolienne* from Auber's opera of *La Fiancée*. This was written in 1829, when Liszt was eighteen years old. After this first essay there was a long interval till 1836, when he wrote his Fantasia upon the *Niobe* of Pacini. He played this, it will be remembered, during his contests with Thalberg, in Paris. About the same time, he published a Grande Fantaisie Brillante, *Réminiscences de La Juive*, a big parade piece, of a liquid, meretricious sort, upon the opera of that name by Halévy. There is, also, a tremendous arrangement of the overture to *William Tell*, written in the same year, but not published till 1846. This was a favourite concert piece with Liszt during his early career. But it is doubtful whether modern audiences could support it.

With the operas of Bellini, Liszt entered upon a task more worthy of him. All three of his famous works, *I Puritani*, *Sonnambula*, and *Norma*, were dealt with by Liszt. His Fantasia upon *Sonnambula* even appeared in two different versions. All the Bellini transcriptions are admirable; but his Fantasia upon *Norma* is a really beautiful work which has been unduly forgotten. It is a perfect example of Liszt's method. The whole beauty, the whole atmosphere, of *Norma* are caught and imprisoned for these few moments. The airs in *Norma* are of an exquisite beauty, and it would have seemed impossible that they could preserve their charm without a voice to sing them, but Liszt has contrived to accomplish this.

When it came to Donizetti, Liszt was on less certain ground, but he was unable to withhold his hand in *Lucia di Lammermoor*. He wrote a long and extended Fantasia upon this, called by his invented term of *Réminiscences*. In its way, this is one of the finest pieces by Liszt. He begins with the air of Raymond, one of the highlights of the opera, links it quickly and deftly to the finale of the second act, and then, quickening the pace to a kind of galop, subjects it to every trick and device of the highest virtuosity, changes and turns the theme about, works every kind of metamorphosis in its dead body, and with a most extraordinary display and parade of octaves brings the Fantasia to a conclusion in a mood of force and display that is more familiar in the *Rhapsodies*.

He also wrote *Réminiscences* of *Lucrezia Borgia*, another opera by Donizetti, which, if it were only called by some other name, might not have perished for ever. Liszt was at much pains over this, too; for the *Réminiscences* appeared in two separate parts, and the second of these had two separate editions from his hand. He wrote, as well, a Fantasia upon motifs from *Dom Sebastian*.

This was not all. He published, in 1842, a *Grande Valse à Capriccio*, taken from a theme from *Lucia di Lammermoor*; and in *Trois Caprice-Valses*, published much later, in 1852, this waltz again makes its appearance as one of the pieces, and its second motive is a theme from an entirely forgotten opera by Donizetti, called *Parisina*, to the poem of that name by Byron. This theme is practically identical, by some curious chance, with the charming adagietto in the Diaghilev ballet, *Les Biches*, the music of which was by Francis Poulenc.

The ascendant operatic genius of the day was Meyerbeer, whose contemporary importance must be taken practically for granted, since there is so much incontrovertible evidence to that effect, and our own generation is never given the opportunity either to confirm or deny it. Liszt wrote *Réminiscences* of both *Robert le Diable* and *Les Huguenots*, while he dealt at much greater length with *Le Prophète*, for his Fantasia upon that opera ran into four separate parts. His ornaments for Meyerbeer are much more heavy and solid. This was international grand opera, and not an entertainment put together in a few weeks for the Carnival in

Venice or Naples. They are, for that reason, redundant, showy pieces of a rather painful length and importance.

To close the list of his operatic transcriptions up to this time, there is his setting of the Hunting Chorus from an opera called *Toni*, written by the Duke of Saxe-Coburg. This was a piece of good manners, and nothing more.

There remains, however, his Fantasia upon the *Don Giovanni* of Mozart, a true masterpiece of its kind. He took the entire duet of 'Là ci darem la mano' for the subject of his variations, framed them, as it were, by means of an intrada derived out of the overture, and concluded with a final presto based on the Brindisi from the first act. This is a wholly admirable instance of his art. He also wrote, in 1843, but left unfinished, a Fantasia upon the *Nozze di Figaro*, which remained unpublished until Busoni took it in hand, worked it out, and brought it into a state in which it could be printed.

Out of all this mass of material there remain, perhaps, four things worth serious attention—*Norma, Lucia di Lammermoor, Don Giovanni,* and *Figaro*—and the only one of them ever played is *Don Giovanni.*

The enumeration of these different works of transcription has carried us two or three years beyond the stage to which we have taken the story of his life. But there is an essential continuity running through them all, and once the last of them, that upon *Figaro,* had been begun, we find him doing no more work of the same kind, save the Tarantella from *Masaniello,* until 1849, when the first of his Wagner transcriptions saw the light. That is, most obviously, the beginning of a new epoch, and the discussion of it must be postponed until that moment has arrived.

In the meantime, we have examined all his compositions, the *Grandes Études,* the *Années de Pèlerinage,* the *Soirées Musicales* and the Operatic Transcriptions, and the stage is ready set for his years of transcendental execution. We return, therefore, once more, to the moment when he left Madame d'Agoult at San Rossore, near Pisa. She was to go to Paris; and he was to journey, for the second time, to Vienna. There, his career as virtuoso may be said to have begun in earnest.

BOOK II

1839–1847

The Years of Transcendental Execution

CHAPTER XV

Liszt plays in Vienna on behalf of the Beethoven Memorial at Bonn—The beginning of his estrangement from Madame d'Agoult

Liszt has parted from Madame d'Agoult and is on his way to Vienna. The seven years of his career as virtuoso through nearly every country of Europe are at their beginning, and they start with the sort of flourish that is so characteristic of our hero, both in his shortcomings and in those finer qualities that make his personality unique and almost heroic.

The months of September and October, which were spent at San Rossore, must have been mournful and sad to an extreme degree. The emotional situation had to resolve itself with a gesture, if it was not to end on terms of reproach and embitterment. Now that he was to embark upon concert tours of the most extended description it was impossible for Liszt to drag round Madame d'Agoult and their three children, not to mention the two children of her former marriage, who had to spend part of each year with her. It was too expensive, and too scandalous. Again, if he left Madame d'Agoult, it was not only to fulfil his destiny, but also in order to provide his children with funds for their maintenance and education. The dwindling autumn days, despite the Italian sun, must have been a sad reminder of their youth together, only four years before.

The crack of the conjurer's pistol was nearly a necessity in their situation, and its report came with commendable promptitude just at the right moment. It appeared in curious and chivalrous form. The newspapers announced that an international subscription, set on foot by the town of Bonn in order to erect a statue to Beethoven in his birthplace, had been a complete failure. Donations to the French section of the fund amounted to no more than 424 fr. 90—about £17. Liszt determined immediately to make it his business to see that the scheme was successfully carried through. He wrote to his friend, Lorenzo Bartolini, a pupil of Canova, who lived in Florence and was reputed to be the finest sculptor of the day, to enquire what the cost of the statue would be. Bartolini replied that a monument in marble could be completed in two years and would cost from fifty to sixty thousand francs. Liszt then wrote to the Beethoven Memorial Committee at Bonn offering to take over the whole expenses of the project and only stipulating that the order for the statue should be given to Bartolini and to none other.

The Memorial Committee was of course delighted, while, for his part, Liszt's separation from Madame d'Agoult took on a purpose very different from that of mere sordid money making. Unkind critics might point out that, a year before this, Liszt had found a similar excuse to leave Madame d'Agoult in Venice and go off to Vienna. Then, it had been a question of Danube floods and ruined Hungarian peasants. But, if this occasion was even more propitious, the sternest of his detractors must admit the long and fatiguing work that it entailed upon him. It might also be advanced in argument that his years of virtuosity could not have been embarked upon with a greater advertisement than by this prodigal and unselfish act of generosity. But Liszt, of all people whoever existed, can surely be cleared of this charge. That it enabled him to leave Madame d'Agoult on terms that satisfied her idealistic nature and her aspirations may be conceded; but it is at least probable that his sentimental regrets and the serious side of his nature made him welcome this long spell of unrewarded labour. It was his sacrifice to the gods.

Nor was their separation to be one of permanence. They pretended that the necessities of his career had dictated it. Both of them, it need hardly be said, must have understood its full implications. The series of their letters, edited by M. Daniel Ollivier, contains more than a hundred and fifty pages that they wrote to each other in the first six months after their parting. Those that were written by Liszt immediately after she had left him in Florence are in terms of genuine sadness and regret. Both of them knew his weaknesses. 'Je crains pour toi les femmes' had been his father's dying words to him. Affectionate, faithful infidelity was in his nature. It was now to have full and unfettered play, but it did not prevent him from writing to her nearly every second day all through this period upon which we are embarking.

This was a time, it must be remembered, when people were given to romanticizing over their emotions to an extent that is quite outside contemporary experience. The full force of the Romantic Movement was in blast; and it would hardly be possible to discover two more formidable exponents of its rigours than Liszt and Madame d'Agoult. She had all the seriousness of her temperament; her forceful and dominant personality which found but ineffectual outlet in her writings; and the sense of the three children that she had borne to him in despite of all the conventions of her upbringing. She took everything seriously. Did she not, only a few months before this, note down in her journal, under the heading 'Au couvent de St François d'Assise', the following words: 'Depuis David, l'art de la danse est discrédité. J'ai toujours considéré la danse comme un art fort sérieux, fort religieux même.' It will be recalled also, how, while they were in Venice together, she and her lover read, on alternate days, Dante, Shakespeare, Goethe, and Tasso. All her emotions were tinged with these serious purposes; indeed, in all the pages of this voluminous correspondence there is, on her part, no single note of humour. This was a constituent that must have been altogether lacking in her character.

From a strictly ethical point of view Liszt should have stayed with her and have more or less abandoned his career, but few male readers of these pages, and still fewer female, would have found the possibilities of this alternative career interesting enough to follow. The truth is that Liszt was faced with the sort of dilemma in which there is only an apparent choice. His talents were insistent, and it was of no use for him to attempt to refuse the direction in which they pointed him.

And, at the moment, it was not a question of permanent separation. They were to live together at intervals whenever his concert tours allowed of it, and indeed their new association lasted for another five years. They had met for the first time, and exchanged letters, and begun to be an influence in each other's lives, in 1833. It was, now, October of 1839, and the final break in their relationship did not take place until April 1844.

They parted, so to speak, on the road, for Liszt's career of vagabondage had begun. For seven years it took him to every corner of Europe. It brought him prodigious, unprecedented fame, and much money. At the same time, as we shall see, it cultivated all the latent weaknesses of his character and talent. If these had not been developed, if he had stayed with Madame d'Agoult and embraced a life of ordinary, if irregular, domesticity, the self-sacrifice and self-effacement of his later career would have lacked their force and truth. For the interest of his life, artistic and episodic, is in his repentance.

CHAPTER XVI

Liszt in Venice—Byron's gondolier—He arrives in Vienna— He returns to Hungary—He is presented with the jewelled sabre—He is given a patent of nobility—He consults Madame d'Agoult about his coat of arms—He visits his birthplace—The Tziganes—He plays in Prague and Leipzig—He meets Mendelssohn and Schumann

The journey from Florence to Vienna in those days was a long one. Liszt did not arrive in the Austrian capital until the middle of November, and on their respective ways to Paris and to Vienna they wrote to each other from Genoa and from Venice. The railway was not yet built, so that he made the inevitable entry into Venice by gondola. This provoked him to memories of his first visit to Venice with Madame d'Agoult, and on this subject he writes her a letter the tone of which was certainly unexpected in the circumstances.

It is not all concerned with regrets. He mentions the unfinished palace on the Grand Canal; describes how he hurried to the Piazza San Marco as soon as he had arrived, as all travellers have done in every age; and then details his conversation with the gondolier during a voyage down the canals.

The gondolier showed him where Napoleon stood to see the fireworks on the lagoon, and pointed out to him the palace where Byron lived: 'Come? Lord Byron?—Sì, Signore—L'avete conosciuto voi?—Sì, Signore. L'ho servito cinque giorni perchè uno dei suoi battellieri era ammalato.' 'What do you say? Lord Byron? —Yes, Sir.—Did you know him yourself?—Yes, Sir. I served him for five days, because one of his gondoliers was ill.' After which conversation the gondolier recited to Liszt two poems by Byron which he had learnt by heart while the poet rode on the Lido, and gave Liszt the latest news of the Guiccioli, and of Byron's mistress Teresa, who kept a little shop at Dolo for the sale of coffee and liqueurs.

Byron had only been dead for fifteen years. He was no more distant in time than the beginning of the war is from ourselves. His fame was universal; so that England, who, in a sense, rejected him, had to share him with Italy. He was a part of Italian life and legend. Immediately after their conversation upon Byron the gondolier sang to Liszt a strophe from Tasso. It was a perfectly natural transition to the Italian poet of three centuries before from the English poet who would have been no more than fifty years old, if still alive. Liszt may be said to have brought the Italy of Byron down to contemporary times, and to have been the link between the old traditional Italy and our own day.

There is, for this reason, a singular interest in the picture of Liszt on the threshold of his fame, armed with such thrilling and compelling powers of conquest. No poet can ever have known such excitement from the publication of his verses as this unprecedented virtuoso drew from every audience to whom he played. During those few days in Venice he was on his way to his career. No person of more exciting potentialities can have stayed in Venice during those few years since Byron went from there to Greece. In more ways than one, Liszt was the heir of Byron; but these fine shades of his personality must be built up, touch by touch, during the chronicle of his successes.

Meanwhile, he went through Trieste to Vienna, arriving there about 15 November. It took three nights and two and a half days by diligence, to cover what is now accomplished by air in about two hours. Eventually, Vienna was reached in the early hours of the morning; and Haslinger, the impresario, came to meet Liszt at his hotel, at eight o'clock. A series of six recitals had been arranged; six hundred people had already been refused tickets, while another three hundred had engaged themselves, in advance, for any further concerts he might give. At this first recital there were three thousand people in the audience, an unprecedented number for those times, and the Dowager Empress was present in the royal box.

Liszt was immediately the 'lion' of Vienna, and it must be

admitted that his letters, at this moment, are written in a kind of intoxication of self-importance. He spares Madame d'Agoult no detail of his triumphal progress. When he enters his agent's office fifty people wait outside to see him come out; the doctor who looks after him—for he has arrived in Vienna with a fearful cold—has become a famous man within two days, and is consulted by his patients only in order to hear the latest news of the pianist.

The second concert was at an interval of ten days after the first, owing to the ravages of his cold, or influenza, but it was an even greater success. The proposed memorial to Beethoven was a certainty. It is a little disappointing, after this universal acclamation, to read his programmes. The *Hexameron* variations,* the *Ave Maria* of Schubert, the *Pastoral* symphony, and a concerto of Beethoven (probably the Fourth, in G major) formed his initial concert. They continued in the same vein, and each recital ended with his arrangement of the *William Tell* overture, a selection from the *Études Transcendantes*, or from the *Années de Pèlerinage*. The Tarantella *Venezia e Napoli* was a favourite of his, and so, of course, was the *Galop Chromatique*.

He writes to Madame d'Agoult that a certain Krauss has orchestrated the *Galop Chromatique*, the *Grande Valse*, and several of the *Fleurs mélodiques des Alpes*, the title under which the Swiss studies of the *Années de Pèlerinage* first made their appearance. These pieces were, obviously, as far as he could venture at the moment with the greater public, and their titles, it will be agreed, sound a little like the catalogue of a French perfumer of the time. *Fleurs mélodiques des Alpes* have too great a resemblance to 'Potpourri des Plantes Marines', to 'Amidine de Guimauve', or 'Ethiops Martial', by the French perfumer, Guerlain.

But in private, and to a more select audience, he played anything and everything. All that Chopin and Schumann had written, to date; pieces by Bach, Scarlatti, Beethoven, Hummel, Weber; his own 'parade pieces'; his transcriptions of Italian operas; his arrangements of Schubert's songs; his Hungarian melodies, the embryonic form of the future rhapsodies; the whole of a huge and varied repertory. Liszt was the first pianist to appear with the modern repertoire as it has lasted for the century that has elapsed

---

*The *Hexameron* was a set of variations by various composers upon the march from Bellini's *Puritani*. Liszt wrote the intrada, the connecting links, and the finale. Chopin's contribution was a little larghetto in E major.

since then; both the first pianist, and there can be no doubt of it—the best. The consummation of his genius had taken place in the two years since he last played in Vienna; and his programmes were now complete.

But the culmination of the tour was still to come; this was its extension to Budapest. He had not visited his native land since his tenth year. The fame of Liszt in the Western world was already well known to his countrymen. They were in a condition of wild and effervescent nationalism that was working up towards the disastrous rebellion of 1849, and in their welcome to Liszt they saw an opportunity to extol the only Hungarian who had, as yet, become known beyond the bounds of his native country. The only exception to this were the Hungarian Magnates, but the diamond suit worn by Prince Esterházy at the coronation of George IV could hardly be accorded a national welcome upon its return to its native country.

Hungarian literature was in its infancy, for the poems of Petőfi were not published until 1847. There was no Hungarian drama, no painting, and no architecture. The frescoes of Maulpertsch and the baroque palaces and convents might be described as distant, and provincial, Viennese. Two things distinguished the country; the extraordinary and varied dresses worn by the peasants, and the improvised and unwritten music. This was in their blood. It was their national sport and pastime. The return of Liszt has in it, in fact, something of the homecoming of a famous matador. All classes of the populace, every degree of opinion, were waiting to welcome him.

A deputation came as far as Vienna in order to invite him to Hungary. The first halt was at Pressburg, where he arrived on 18 December. An inscrutable Providence has awarded this town to Czechoslovakia, but this does not prevent its having been one of the chief strongholds of Hungarian feeling. It will be remembered that the first public concert at which he ever played took place in this same town of Pressburg. He came back to it as the most famous living Hungarian, but having almost, if not completely, forgotten the use of his native tongue. French had become his native language; German he was learning to speak slowly and with difficulty. He was received in Pressburg with an electrical excitement in which nothing else was of moment. The Prince Palatine of Hungary (brother of Francis II, the last Holy Roman

Emperor) had to postpone a levée he was giving, for it would have been empty. Nothing could keep the Hungarians from the concert that Liszt was going to give in Pressburg.

A day or two later he went in triumphant progress to the capital, arriving there on Christmas Eve. He travelled in a coupé with Count Casimir Esterházy, while three other carriages followed behind, bearing Baron Benckheim, two Barons Zichy, and Count Leo Festetics. It is described in a letter to Madame d'Agoult as 'toute une caravane aristocratique'. Liszt stayed as the guest of Count Festetics, and he writes that the hotelkeepers were extremely annoyed at this, one of them, especially, having made superb preparations for his reception.

It would be monotonous to recite his triumphs, but they were attended, need it be said, with a mass of amusing incidents. He was serenaded, immediately on arrival, by a choir of sixty voices, while a military band, of as many executants, thundered out Hungarian airs attributed to him in the courtyard of the palace. He had to go out on the balcony to be applauded, and coming back into the saloon found seven music desks arranged ready and the seven best amateur players in Budapest starting the first bars of Beethoven's *Septuor*.

But all this was as nothing compared to the excitement that attended the presentation of the sword of honour. The idea of it must have been broached at one of the many banquets offered to him, for at festivities of this nature almost anything might have happened. At one of them, the idea entered someone's head to propose a subscription for his bust. In less than ten minutes fifteen hundred francs had been offered. Liszt, in his letters, states that at Budapest all the richer classes, even the most elegant, were in bed by ten o'clock at night, with the exception of only five or six persons. (Who can these have been?) It may be easily imagined, therefore, that the occasion of these banquets gave an excuse for almost hysterical excitement and enjoyment. In some such atmosphere as this, the question of the sword of honour must have been discussed.

The actual presentation took place after a concert given in the theatre. He had played his Fantasia upon *Lucia di Lammermoor*, the inevitable *Galop Chromatique*, and his arrangement of the *Rákóczy March*, which he describes, appropriately, as a kind of 'Marseillaise aristocratique hongroise'. As he left the platform, Count Leo

Festetics, Baron Palffy and Count Teleky (all three of them, as he assures Madame d'Agoult, Magnates of Hungary), together with three other nobles, all in magnificent Hungarian costumes, advanced and presented him with a jewelled sabre. Count Festetics girded the sword to his side and read a short address in Hungarian, to which Liszt replied in French.

When he went home, after this, it was at the head of a torch-light procession, with a military band marching before him. The students would have unharnessed the horses and dragged the carriage, but someone reminded them that they had done the same, only a short time before, for a 'miserable dancing girl', Fanny Elssler. So, instead, Liszt and Festetics got out of the carriage and walked on foot, with the crowd all round them. Liszt, himself, it should be added, was wearing an expensive Hungarian costume which he had bought for a thousand francs, for the occasion. At eleven o'clock that night, the streets were full of people. The whole town stayed out of bed for the occasion.

The repercussions of this affair resounded all over Europe for years to come. A famous quatrain was written about it, as follows:

'Entre tous les guerriers, Liszt est, seul, sans reproches,
Car malgré son grand sabre, on sait que ce héros
N'a vaincu que des doubles croches,
Et tué que des pianos.'

In fact, the atmosphere reverted to what it had been, four years before, in Milan, when Liszt was forced to issue a general challenge to all and sundry, and had to drive round the town in an open carriage to provoke an assault upon himself. In this instance the arena, being the whole of Europe, was too large, so that he had to content himself with writing indignant letters to the news-papers.

Then there was the question, as well, of his being given a patent of nobility. He had already written from Vienna to Madame d'Agoult to the effect that in about six weeks' time he was going to be given letters of nobility by the Hungarian diet, a body which, it may be remarked, carried on its discussions in colloquial Latin until the Revolution of 1849. Later on, he announces that several of the Magnates have decided to make a special journey to Vienna in order to obtain these letters of nobility personally from the Emperor, for his consent, in person, was absolutely necessary. He adds that the idea of a petition signed by the Magnates and Deputies, which would have borne the signatures of an overwhelming majority, if not, indeed, unanimous, had been abandoned. This was because such an overwhelming demonstration of opinion would have aroused suspicion in Vienna, where Hungarian affairs were looked upon as fraught with dangerous and revolutionary possibilities.

But if he was to be granted the rank of nobility there was the question of what arms he was to assume. He writes to consult Madame d'Agoult upon this point. He wants her to invent them for him. As far as things had gone at present, Festetics agreed that the figure of an owl could be brought in; for the lyre, the harp, and the roll of manuscript paper were absurd. All the same, he felt that the owl was the important idea and that something else significant could be added. It must have been by something more than a coincidence that, in one of her letters that crossed his, Madame d'Agoult should have said that she had bought him a pin for his cravat, the design of which consisted of an owl. She added that perhaps it would not be to his taste; but at least it seems to have borne important results.

The end of his stay in Budapest was another series of banquets. A magnificent ball, for instance, given in his honour by the society ladies of Budapest. Two hundred people to supper, and sixteen hostesses carrying bouquets of ivy and immortelles. It was prolonged until 2.30 a.m.—a very late hour for Budapest. On another occasion, he himself gave a dinner party of twenty-two covers for his men friends, and a few days later a supper party, for fifteen ladies and thirty men, while the best singers from the opera were hired to sing to them.

These festivities finished his tour, and he returned to Vienna about the end of January, writing, on the way, to Madame d'Agoult, from Pressburg, to tell her of a way to cool champagne that he had only seen practised at the house of Prince Batthyány. It had to be put on the ice from early morning, until, by the evening, it was almost like a sorbet, having, incidentally, lost nearly all its alcohol in the process. He recommended this to her for her parties in Paris.

There was a repetition of the same scenes of enthusiasm when he came back to Vienna. Dinners were given in his honour, and he entertained his friends in return. He writes that he is giving a supper party. The chief guests are to be:

> Prince Pückler-Muskau
> Prince Fritz Schwarzenberg
> Count Apponyi
> Count Hartig
> Baron Reischach (aimable garçon)
> Count Széchenyi (l'illustre)
> Count Waldstein
> Count Paul Esterházy

and he adds, 'ce sera un peu froid probablement, mais du meilleur genre'. Prince Pückler-Muskau, one of the most eccentric characters who ever existed, was a new acquaintance of his. Liszt had dined with him, the day before, and been made to smoke four or five out of his collection of Turkish, Egyptian, and Chinese pipes. After that, he was shown his Arab horses, and, perhaps, his harem, for the Prince was an Orientalist of pronounced tastes.

Even now, one more Hungarian sensation was in reserve for him. This was his visit from Vienna to his native town of Raiding. The little house in which he was born had become the home of a gamekeeper, and he was escorted to it through the streets of the town by the usual concourse of people and by twenty peasants, in magnificent dresses and on horseback, who had ridden out two leagues to meet him on his way. The inevitable Tziganes made their appearance; but Liszt gives such a good account of this, himself, in his book on Hungarian Gypsy music, that his actual words must be quoted.* The Tziganes were one of the memories of his childhood; until his return to Hungary he had not heard them since he was ten years old. It was, therefore, with a singular excitement that he enquired for them and found their encampment on the outskirts of the little town.

'They had built their fire under a colonnade of ash trees and were sitting round it, violins in hand, on the piled sheepskins that were their only furniture. The women were crashing their tambourines, and uttering little cries of mimicry while they danced. In the intervals of this, there was the crepitous noise of the wooden axles of the waggons, creaking loudly as they were drawn back to make more room for the dancers.

*The Gipsy in Music.

'Meat and wild honey were being eaten. The children cut capers, turn somersaults, and utter wild cries, while they fight over a bag of peas, or crack nuts upon stones. The Gypsy hags sit with inflamed eyes, warming themselves and listening to the music. The men resemble each other like sons of one mother. Some of them have profiles in which sarcasm seems to be actually sneering. Their tawny skins and faces are framed in locks of hair which fall like snakes of a bluish-black tint upon their necks, the colour of which is a lively orange. Their eyes shine like sparks which seem to be illuminated and extinguished by some interior contrivance.

'They got up from the ground to look at some horses that had been given them in exchange that day. This pleased them and they put on quite a heavenly smile, showing off their teeth, which were as white as snow. After this, they started imitating castanets by cracking the joints of their fingers, which are always long and charged with electricity. Still uncertain, they began throwing their caps into the air, and followed this by strutting about like peacocks. Then, they looked at the horses again, and as if suddenly given the power to express their pleasure in the bargain, they flew to their violins and cymbals, and began playing in a fury of excitement. The Frischka, or quick Gypsy dance, rose into a frenzy of delirium till the dancers were breathless and fell to the ground.'

Liszt threw them handfuls of coins and they began playing again. 'This time it was the gentle and melancholy Lassan, the slow measure of the Gypsies, but as it quickened they grew more excited and led forward the prettiest of the girls for me to dance with. The orgy went on far into the night, while the clearing was lit by a dozen barrels of pitch, the flames of which rose up into the air like cylinders of fire.

'Next morning it was raining, and they rode off early to the fair. Some of the Gypsies were in long, narrow carts, holding about twenty of them standing upright. Those who rode on horseback wore their sheepskin pelisses, with the wool outside, because of the damp. This made them look like as many bears mounted on wild horses, for they kept their spurs so much in play that the horses jumped at every moment. The drivers of the waggons went at full speed, cracking their whips above the clatter of the old ironwork of their carts. They bumped against heavy stones in the road, all the Gypsies in the carts talked at the top of their voices and shrieked with laughter, and the children ran by the side begging from all they passed; while the young girls went up to every stranger, and even looked in through the doors of houses, to tell fortunes, blandishing and cursing their prey.'

After such scenes as this, the routine of giving concerts in any other country must have seemed rather an anti-climax. But, in Prague, he was as popular as in Vienna; and since the days of Mozart, when *Don Giovanni* was commissioned and produced there, Prague had the reputation of having the best taste in music of any town in Europe. His success, therefore, was particularly gratifying and he was compared, openly, to Paganini, to the latter's disadvantage. The concert hall was crowded at every performance. On one occasion, when the audience, in a frenzy, called for Schubert's *Ave Maria* as an encore, Liszt played them, instead, the *Hexameron* variations, the *Galop Chromatique*, and then, without any pause or stop, the *Ave Maria*.

Socially, he was as popular as ever. 'L'aristocratie de Bohème, la plus fière de la Monarchie, a été charmantissime pour moi. Ici, comme ailleurs, les femmes sont pour moi. Les hommes cèdent à cette influence quoique avec un peu d'humeur. Avant-hier j'ai eu à souper le Prince de Rohan (avec lequel je me suis quasi-lié) le Prince Lichtenstein, le Comte Schlick, les Comtes Thun, etc. . . . Nous étions une douzaine environ', he writes to Madame d'Agoult.

A bourgeois audience would be more difficult for him to conquer, and Leipzig was a disillusionment. The Leipzigers were determined not to lose their heads. Bach was the solid background to their musical history, and in Liszt they suspected a charlatan. His first concert was not a success. He took to his bed, and postponed his second appearance for several days. At his next concert in the Gewendhaus he played Schumann's *Carnaval*, but did not suceed in obtaining his usual applause.

In compensation, he gained the friendship of Mendelssohn and Schumann. The former came to his bedside eight or ten times during the two days that he was ill; while Schumann, who hated travelling, had taken the trouble to go all the way to Dresden to meet him.

All three of them were, at once, fast friends, and in his letters Liszt neatly characterizes them both in a few words. He pays tribute to the extraordinary culture and versality of Mendelssohn.

He played the violin and alto, could draw beautifully, read Homer in the original Greek, and spoke four of five languages with ease. As for Schumann, he notices how silent and taciturn he is; he would stay quietly in the room and listen to him playing for hours on end. Schumann, for his part, wrote to Clara Wieck to say that it was the greatest artistic experience of his lifetime. Liszt would play his Sonata to him, or his Fantasies, or the Novelettes, and he was astonished and spellbound by his own music as if he had never heard it before.

It is interesting to compare this with the sensations of Chopin on hearing Liszt play his Études. That was in Paris, some seven or eight years previous to this, and Chopin wrote to a friend, 'I write to you without knowing what my pen is scribbling, because at this moment Liszt is playing my Études, and transporting me out of my respectable thoughts. I should like to steal from him the way to play my own Études.'

Schumann, we are told, would get himself more or less lost in Liszt's rooms. The day would dwindle into evening; Liszt would write letters or play the piano, and after an unbroken silence a voice would come from a dark corner of the room. Schumann was still there. He regarded these long silences as charged with conversation, and, at the end, when a move had to be made, would close one of these imaginary dialogues by saying, 'There! We have been talking again with open hearts.'

If Schumann was a silent listener, Mendelssohn, by contrast, was most eloquent in his championship of our hero. In fact, he relieved the situation at Leipzig and rallied the audience. Not only this, but he organized an immense musical reception in honour of Liszt, to which two hundred and fifty professional musicians were invited. An orchestral and choral programme was given, and, for the final item, Liszt, Ferdinand Hiller, and himself played a concerto for three pianos by Bach. Eventually, his success at Leipzig, thanks to Mendelssohn, was complete. What had amounted to a dangerous apathy was turned into triumph. He had conquered the most difficult defences of criticism in Germany.

This was the close, for the time being, of his tour of Central Europe. It was the end of March, and he had been away for almost six months. If he set out to achieve fame, his projects had succeeded beyond his wildest expectations. Never had there been a sensation comparable to it, except the recitals of Paganini. But the concert season was now over, and towards the end of March he arrived in Paris to join Madame d'Agoult.

CHAPTER XVII

His situation with Madame d'Agoult—Her flirtation with Bulwer and Potocki—Liszt rejoins her, and leaves again for London—Lady Blessington and Count d'Orsay—Madame d'Agoult arrives in London

The emotional situation between them was one that would enthral the mind of any novelist or dramatist. Most certainly, from the point of view of romantic fiction, there has never been a 'hero' more blest with the faults and virtues of his rôle. The cast of the characters is perfection.

Liszt is not yet thirty years old. He has supreme fascination for women. He has been the hero of the Parisian salons since childhood, when he was welcomed as a second Mozart; his physical appearance, as we can see from his portraits, was of quite extraordinary beauty; and he had, which distinguished him all through his life, the manners and fine bearing of a courtier. His friends were the aristocrats of every country in which he played. With the distrust and dislike of any form of artist that is inherent in such society, in every land, Liszt would never have been admitted into their friendship if not an adept in all the elegancies and conventions of such a life. He is, indeed, the first musician who ever appeared in those circles on terms of equality. This fact must be taken into serious consideration, for it explains the tone of his letters and condones his conscious extravagances of dress and manner. He felt that he had raised the whole social status of his profession.

The aged clichés ring with a new brilliance in his letters, for they are written with the same youthful enthusiasm that makes *Mlle de Maupin* so delightful to read. Like one of the lovers out of that novel it was inevitable that Liszt should be in love with a Countess, and that the Countess should be a few years older than himself. He is, indeed, the personification of the youth and elegance of this book. He lived in the same atmosphere. There is the same romantic devotion to poetry, as if these cavaliers and their loves read nothing less ethereal than that, the same admiration of Arab horses, the same love of perfumes and *pommades*, so that it is an easy transition from *Bois de Santal des Îles* to the *Fleurs Mélodiques des Alpes*. The glitter of chandeliers, the smoothness of lovely shoulders, the strains of distant waltzes, the camellia for flower of the evening, all the amenities of the city alternate with a 'vie de château', a green, leaf-hid summer at the end of avenues, with the ripple of the lake and its answering statues seen through the branches.

Then, again, Liszt came from the great Eastern plains, from the edges of the civilized world, so that the background of this Chopinesque picture was filled in appropriately. Women, who have never excelled in their knowledge of geography, were easily satisfied with its aristocratic remoteness. Russia, Poland, or Hungary—it was probably all the same, even to the superior knowledge of Madame d'Agoult.

The theme of the novel, if we think of it in that way, is to be the extraction of our hero from the tangle of experience in which he is enmeshed. His present embarrassment, with a Countess who is a married woman older than himself, has to be resolved. Then he will be at the service of other and younger women; ready to pass on the benefits of his experience to them, for no woman wants too youthful and untried a lover. There is room enough for nostalgia in all this; and that, precisely, was the disease of the Romantics. Liszt was an acute sufferer from it, himself. After his final break with the Countess we shall watch him become more and more true to its precepts. Through a variety of romantic adventures we shall see him entering into a permanent liaison with a Russian Princess, even more remote in origin than himself; while his troubles, very late in life, with the Cossack Countess continue this aspect of his career almost to its conclusion in death.

If Liszt started out on his concert tour to proclaim his talents, and, at the same time, effect a partial break with the Countess in order to achieve the sort of semi-liberty in which he might have scope for intrigue, it is a necessary part of the plot that the

Countess, on her side, should try to make him jealous during his absence from her. This is exactly what did happen.

We see the first hints of it in her letters to her lover. She had two cavaliers in Paris: Count Bernard Potocki, scion of a famous Polish family, and Henry Bulwer-Lytton, brother of the well-known novelist. He was a diplomat, on duty in the French capital to negotiate a trade treaty between England and France.

'27 Novembre. Hier soir Monsieur Bulwer, encore Monsieur Bulwer, toujours Monsieur Bulwer! Il a l'air de s'amuser beaucoup avec moi', she writes to Liszt. A few days after this, our old friend the poet Ronchaud sends her 'une lettre brûlante' to announce his arrival. Soon afterwards, 'Avec Bulwer deux scènes, dont une scena patetica et l'autre quasi una farsa.'

She writes to ask him for 'une permission d'infidélité'; and, although she does not mention a name, he guesses that it is Bulwer of whom she speaks. A few days later, she describes in a letter a conversation with Bulwer in which he expressed a wish to adopt a daughter, but stipulated that she should be of good family. After a moment's silence he asked, 'Monsieur Liszt, aime-t-il les enfants?' so that it was evident that he was thinking of either Blandine or Cosima.

Bulwer would seem to have been the typical Englishman to perfection. Even the trade treaty that he was negotiating had in it something of the traditional eccentricity of our race; for, on its successful conclusion, Madame d'Agoult says that the only apparent result is that the French will be able to buy as much Wedgwood as they like.

A delightful instance of the point of view of a typical Englishman of good family occurs at this point in the correspondence; for he asked Madame d'Agoult in tones which expressed all his admiration for him, why Liszt had not chosen another career than that of pianist? It was an implied compliment, of the most lavish sort possible to so restrained a personality.

The Countess would seem to have preferred Bulwer to Potocki, but there were other aspirants as well. There was Ronchaud, who had now arrived safely, and there was Ponsard. 'J'ai donné une belle canne à Ponsard qui me comble de camélias: en général le cadeau réussit.'

Potocki, for his part, was in that agonizing situation where the position has been carried up to a certain point, in conversation, and there has been an interruption. Other guests have been announced, or a servant has walked in. The next morning she writes to Potocki to say that she is feeling unwell and cannot see him, that evening.

The following day, when he again makes his appearance, it is impossible to take up the conversation where they left it off, and the Countess puts up every obstacle in the way of his approach to it. He has to advance by indirect allusion, by means of a kind of abstract and impersonal dialogue. Madame d'Agoult writes to Liszt all the stages of this, with his eventual declaration that 'Si, un jour, vous deviez vous séparer . . . eh bien! je tacherais d'obtenir la succession.' She returned another evasive answer to his declaration, and once again the position was postponed. And as a final essay Potocki told her, not for the first time, how much she resembled his wife.

It was all an elaborate make-believe. The only person who mattered in the least to her was Liszt. No one who reads their letters can be blind to that, and its evidences are most pathetic. Her letters are filled with expressions of affection, mingled with her worries about his health. She entreats him to be more careful. 'Oh je vous en conjure à genoux, il n'y a plus à hésiter. Renoncez pour quelques semaines au café, au tabac, au vin. Faites cela pour moi.' And a few days later, 'Pourquoi le baron Eskeles vous donne-t-il des cigares? Vous refumez donc, déjà? Mon Dieu, n'obtiendrai-je donc pas de vous le sacrifice du cigare? . . . Vous avez bien renoncé à la prière et vous ne renonceriez pas au cigare.'

The one certain bond that they had in common was love of their three children. In nearly every letter there are references to the 'Mouches', as they called them; and the Countess was so sure of his genuine affection for them that there is never a maudlin appeal to his conscience or any call upon his sense of duty.

When they were together, once more, after this long separation, it is easy to understand the disillusionment that followed upon the first few days of their happiness. The Countess was the type of person who had to be either neglected altogether, or made the entire centre of attention. It was Liszt's idea for her that she should play the rôle of a sailor's wife, ready and anxious to receive him back whenever he returned to port after one of his long voyages. But her seriousness and her pride made this quite impossible, though it is evident that when she saw him again and came under the spell of his personality and of his physical attraction her love for him came back with greater force than ever before, for it was augmented by all her memories of what had seemed to be their irrevocable love for each other. Mutual promises of this nature become very poignant, in retrospect, even if made no more than four or five years before.

The beginnings of a fresh series of difficulties are to be seen as soon as their letters start again. They had spent a month together in Paris, and early in May 1840 he left for London. His first letter was written on the Channel-boat, but as soon as he reached London his accounts of his daily life are mingled with the old recriminations and regrets.

It is only natural that the more interesting side of their correspondence should be in the details that he gives of his life in London. He had not visited England since 1827, and in these early years of the reign of Queen Victoria it was a very different world from that in which he had played, as a child, to George IV at Carlton House. In fact, it was so different that, as we shall see, the new vitality infused into the moral code took such a stern view of the pianist and his irregular union with Madame d'Agoult that his concert tour was a failure. This would not have happened in the days of the Regency.

Its full force only broke on him later in the month when the Countess came to London to join him. Meanwhile, although his reputation had preceded him, he was welcomed in Society. Lady Blessington and Count d'Orsay, as it may be imagined, were among the first to receive him, and in their house he met Louis Bonaparte and Lords Castlereagh and Chesterfield. Soon he gives a return party to the above-mentioned gentlemen and to Lord Burghersh, a famous musical amateur and friend of Rossini. He plays his Tarantellas, and everyone, as they might well be, is astonished.

Lady Blessington was much struck with his personality and looks, and she, also, perpetrated that same classical remark which had already been voiced by Bulwer during his protestations to Madame d'Agoult. She said to Reeve, the biographer of Greville, and an old friend and admirer of our hero (see page 30), 'Quel dommage de mettre un pareil homme au piano!' It was almost like a request to him to assume English nationality, to become 'one of us'. Salaman, from whose reminiscences we have already quoted the story of Liszt and the gooseberry pie, in the early part of this book, has some illuminating remarks to make about his later recitals. Apparently the term 'recital' was unpopular with the critics. 'What does he mean? How can anyone recite upon a piano?' was the gist of their remarks. And Salaman goes on to tell us, 'At these recitals, Liszt after performing a piece set down in his programme, would leave the platform, and, descending into the body of the room, where the benches were so arranged as to allow free locomotion, would move about among his auditors and converse with his friends, with the gracious condescension of a prince, until he felt disposed to return to the piano.'

But, above all, Liszt was anxious to make the best impression on English Society. He writes to the Countess, asking her to send him, from his rooms in Paris, '1° la redingote hongroise avec fourrure (cela se nomme Séké); 2° la robe de chambre hongroise et une espèce de pantalon turc en bleu, plus un autre pantalon du matin dans le même genre, blanc, (étoffe singulière); 3° mon médaillon de Bovy (n'oubliez pas le portrait en robe de chambre et la statuette de Dantan); 4° mon surtout gris;' and the Countess, in a vein of humour most unusual for her, answers in English with the appropriate sentence: 'Pacha! to hear is to obey. Vos commissions seront faites.'

These accessories seem to have been a material aid to his success. He was invited to play to the Queen at Buckingham Palace, and signed a contract to play in the provinces at five hundred guineas a month, with all expenses paid, for himself and for his servant Ferco, an importation from Hungary. In the meantime he began to look for lodgings for the Countess. He went to Hampstead for this purpose, and writes to her about the purity of its air and the delightful excursions they could make, once or twice a week, to Richmond and to Greenwich.

His concert at Buckingham Palace was a decided success. The Queen and the Prince Consort were almost the only audience, and he says that she laughed a lot (as was her way) when he told her that his vanity was not in the least injured by her not remembering him. The Duchess of Kent asked him whether he had not played in her house before, fourteen years ago, but the Queen, who can only have been eight years old at the time, had no memory of it at all.

Count d'Orsay painted his portrait. Lady Blessington, for her part, said that he resembled both Bonaparte and Lord Byron, and regretted his profession as pianist. He must, also, remind Madame d'Agoult not to forget to bring with her his two Hungarian overcoats, the one made of velvet and the other one with fur collar and cuffs.

He played at the Royal Philharmonic Concerts three times, on May 11, June 8, and June 14; but the newspaper criticisms were far from polite, as may be seen from the following in the *Musical Journal*: 'Liszt has been presented by the Royal Philharmonic Society with an elegant silver breakfast service for doing that which would cause every young student to receive a severe reprimand—viz., thumping and partially destroying two very fine pianofortes.'

His search for lodgings at Hampstead failed, but he promised to meet her at the Tower of London, where she was to disembark; or, if he had a concert that day, and it was probable that he might have to play at two concerts, he would send Ferco to meet her. The Countess must have been looking forward eagerly to her visit, for, once again, she was in that unusual vein of humour. She writes to him, in English:

> 'Let us buy a maisonette
> Let us far idyll',

and it was decided that they should stay a few days in the hotel at Richmond. The Countess, indeed, was left at Richmond while he played at Lady Beresford's house to the Duchess of Cambridge and to Lady Jersey. D'Orsay took him to dine with the Duke of Beaufort, and an engagement to play at the Duke of Beaufort's house prevented him, again, from joining the Countess in her retreat at Richmond.

His continual absence was the cause of trouble. The last letter published in the volume begins with the quotation of a remark she had made to him: 'At the moment, and probably for always, I cannot do anything else except live alone.' So that, he continues, is what she has to say to him after six years of the most complete devotion. 'Yesterday, all the way from Ascot to Richmond, we drove along without your saying a single word to me that was not a wound or an insult. Bonsoir, dormez bien', and here, unfortunately, this volume of letters comes to an end, just where the situation, from the point of view of the novelist, is developing in the most interesting way possible.

But, if the Countess was jealous of his success, and it was impossible for him to take her into these circles of society where he was popular, the rest of his stay in England was marred by his failure in the provinces. He played to apathetic audiences in Manchester and Glasgow, and eventually cancelled his contract and refused to accept any of the fees. The impresario was compensated for all losses by this typical act of generosity on the pianist's part, who lost over a thousand pounds by his gesture.

His provincial tour was preluded by the following rather witless advertisement: 'Mr. Lavenu with his corps musicale will enter the Lists again on the 23rd instant, when it is to be hoped the Listless audience will Listen with more attention than on his last experiment, or he will have enListed his talented List to very little purpose.'

The tone of the newspapers, under the pressure, we may assume, of some considerable bribe, had altered proportionately. The *Musical World*, in an article full of superlatives and mixed metaphors, compared him to 'Some giant, some tiger-tamer, some new Niagara, some wingéd being (mental or bodily, and unclassed in the science of ornithology). Our obdurate faculties are roused into the consciousness that miracles do exist. Of the miracle genus is Monsieur Liszt, the Polyphemus of the pianoforte, the Aurora Borealis of musical refulgence, the Niagara of thundering harmonics. His rapidity of execution, his power, his delicacy, his Briareus-handed chords, the extraordinary volume of sound that he wrests from the instrument,' etc. etc.

But that the English public disapproved of him was the opinion he was forced to arrive at, and except for one more fleeting visit to London, in order to play at the Royal Philharmonic Society's concert (14 June 1841), he never ventured upon these shores again until the last years of his life. After 1841, he never played in England until 1886.

It is probable that there was a twofold reason for his unpopularity. There was the scandal of his association with the Countess, a scandal made more notorious still by the three illegitimate children born to them. And there were the affectations of his dress, manner, and deportment. Such things were more easily forgiven in an older man. Liszt was a young man at the height of his physical powers; all his English admirers agreed that it was a pity he had been 'put to the piano'. Eccentricity was expected, and pardoned, in Paganini. He was an old man, aged beyond his years, of skeleton figure, more like a corpse than a living body. He belonged to the past, while Liszt was too much a part of the present. His activities roused distrust and annoyance.

CHAPTER XVIII

He leases the isle of Nonnenwerth in the Rhine—He becomes less French and more German—Felix von Lichnowsky—Berlin 'en combustion'—Charlotte de Hagn—Bettina von Arnim—His first concert in St. Petersburg, described by Stassov—Serov and Stassov like two madmen—Liszt's travelling coach—His three three hundred and sixty cravats

It would be monotonous to follow the course of his concerts during the next winter and spring, but, apart from Paris, they lay chiefly in Germany. He was earning enormous revenues, and spending them as lavishly. He played in Hamburg, for instance, for the benefit of the Pension Fund for destitute musicians and gave the whole of the proceeds, nearly nine hundred pounds, to the Fund. It has been calculated that his income during these years amounted to at least three hundred thousand francs a year (fifteen thousand pounds), while the Countess had an allowance from her own family of twenty thousand francs (one thousand pounds). They were able to live in princely style, surrounded with luxury.

His concerts in the Rhine-towns, where he was largely occupied in raising funds for the Beethoven Monument at Bonn, drew his attention to a little island in the Rhine, called Nonnenwerth. It was in the district of the Siebengebirge, the Seven Mountains, near Bonn, and it was just large enough to contain a half-ruined convent, a chapel and a few fishermen's huts. This island, in the midst of the old German legends, made an instant appeal to his romanticism.* He rented it, at a small cost, and determined to make it into a summer home where he could repose himself between his tours. The Countess and their children should come there, and he would work and practise, undisturbed by the world, separated from it by the width of the waters.

They spent two or three summers together in this idyllic spot. It was the last home they had together; so that their romance ended, in a prosaic way, with the termination of the lease. Doubtless they read together, as before, and the subject of their reading, it may be guessed from their surroundings, is almost certain to have been German poetry. It was during this time that Liszt was occupied in arranging Schubert's songs; and, altogether, this stage in his life may be taken as marking his gradual transition from a French to a German mentality.

There can be no doubt that one of his links with Germany was his friendship with Felix von Lichnowsky. This young nobleman was nephew to the Lichnowsky who was a friend and patron of Beethoven. He was heir to immense estates in Silesia and East Prussia surrounding the feudal castle of Krzyzanowitz, and he had the liberal politics and outlook so often found in young aristocrats. As a direct result of this, for it put him in difficulties with his family, Lichnowsky found himself in financial straits and was glad to attach himself to Liszt, who, it may be added, lent him ten thousand francs.

The bond between them was their mutual elegance as much as anything else. Their friendship reminds one of the young poets and dilettanti in *Il Fuoco*, where D'Annunzio placed himself among imaginary disciples such as Stelio Effrena, all, of course, of noble birth. Lichnowsky was his boon-companion, his fellow-cavalier, and he became the inseparable friend of Liszt. He shared the romantic isolation of Nonnenwerth, and made himself agreeable to the Countess.

Where his services became more especially useful was during Liszt's visit to Berlin, for this city was the next sphere that he set out to conquer. In a letter written many years later, he describes himself at this stage of his career as 'une sorte de fantôme de célébrité, à Vienne, à Pesth, et un peu ailleurs'. He might have

---

* An interesting piano piece, *Die Zelle in Nonnenwerth*, is a souvenir of this island. It was in Busoni's repertory.

added 'à Paris et à Londres'; it would have been the truth, and his extraordinary fame had preceded him to Berlin to the extent that the whole city, to quote another phrase of his, was 'en combustion à mon arrivée'.

In the course of a couple of months he gave a series of twenty-one concerts. Frederick-William IV, the King of Prussia, and his family were present at most of these, and what can only be described as an attack of Liszt-mania overtook the whole town. Its symptoms were peculiar and sometimes displeasing. His women admirers made collections of his cigar ends and even carried phials into which they poured the dregs of his coffee.* His portrait was in every shop window and was worn on brooches and cameos by his audience. To some among them the concert hall was an elysium of poetry, to others it was a revivalist meeting, an agapemone, an abode of love. The modern world, it must be remembered, is satiated with a century of pianism. In those days the flood gates were just opened. Not only was this the first and greatest of pianists, but, also, the whole repertoire was new.

He was just at the height of his 'Glanz-Periode', his period of splendour. The disdainful arrogance of his manner is reflected in his letters in sentences of this sort: 'Le Roi a été très convenable pour moi'; and, a little after this: 'I have at least sixty waistcoats'.

There was certainly nothing to disappoint his public in the way he dressed. His answer to those brooches and cameos was his wardrobe of Hungarian clothes, his huge collection of cravats, and the long hair that he wore down to his shoulders. But in the very next phase of his life we have such an excellent description of his person, and of the atmosphere in which he played to his audience, that we will delay no longer over his triumph in Berlin.

It is only necessary to record that the end of his sojourn in the Prussian capital had been solaced, appropriately, and perhaps delayed, by his friendship with two women. One of these was Charlotte de Hagn, the finest actress and among the greatest beauties of her time, a typical Bavarian with blond hair and blue eyes. Their friendship developed into something more serious. She scribbled verses to him upon the leaves of her fan, and he

* 'Vieilles filles allemandes, dont l'une, dit la légende, portait sous sa linge, depuis 1843, le bout d'un cigare fumé par lui. . . . De là bien des cancans. . . .' (*Vie de Liszt*, by J. Chantavoine, p. 102, writing of Weimar in the 'eighties, forty years after this.)

carried it home and set her poems to music. This light-spirited beginning developed into a definite love affair.

His other friend was Bettina von Arnim, a woman nearly sixty years old, who had known Goethe well and shown condescending kindness to Beethoven. Their feeling for each other was on an intellectual and spiritual basis, and led to a perfervid correspondence. It was, therefore, perhaps more permanent than the other.

When, at last, the day came for him to leave Berlin he was driven out of that city in a coach drawn by six white horses. Thirty other carriages followed, drawn by four horses apiece, while an escort of students, in their uniforms, followed him for some miles on his way. Felix von Lichnowsky, in the character of aide-de-camp and boon-companion, rode at his side. By way of Warsaw they reached St. Petersburg, in the early spring of 1842.

His success was assured there from the start, for he had the direct patronage of the Empress Alexandra-Feodorowna, and had, indeed, come to Russia at her invitation, having been presented to her two years before at Ems, where she was taking the cure. He played to her, at Ems, every evening, for three days. He had other Russian friends, as well, whom he had met in Rome in the winter of 1839. A famous Russian musical amateur, Count Vielgorsky, whom we shall meet more nearly in a moment, had arranged a concert in Rome in the house of Prince Galitzine, the Governor-General of Moscow, who was wintering in Italy. This assured his success in Moscow, as well as in St. Petersburg. His visit began, therefore, under the best possible auspices.

His first concert in St. Petersburg took place in the Salle de la Noblesse before three thousand people, and the following delightful and naïve account of it is the best contemporary description that we have of Liszt in this phase of his career. It is written by the well-known critic, Stassov, who was then a young student but became, later in life, the chief upholder of the Nationalist school of music. It is translated from his memoirs by Mrs. Rosa Newmarch; and his companion and fellow-student Serov, whom he refers to in the course of it, also became celebrated in later life. Serov was an opera composer, and, later, a convinced and fanatical Wagnerian. Both were young men of twenty at the time; and the whole of this eulogy, indeed, is written in the state of infectious intoxication only possible at about that age.

'Liszt', we read, 'entered the hall on the arm of Count Viel-gorsky, an "elderly Adonis", and typical dandy of the 'forties. Vielgorsky was somewhat inclined to obesity, moved slowly, and stared at the elegant assemblage with prominent short-sighted eyes. His hair was brushed back and curled, after the manner of the Apollo Belvedere, while he wore an enormous white cravat.

'Liszt, also, wore a white cravat, and over it the Order of the Golden Spur given him by Pius IX' (Mozart had been given the same order by Clement XIV, in 1770). 'He was further adorned by various other orders suspended by chains from the lapels of his dress-coat. But that which struck the Russians most was the great mane of fair hair reaching almost to his shoulders. Outside the priesthood, no Russian would have ventured on such a style of hairdressing. Such dishevelment had been sternly discoun-tenanced since the time of Peter the Great.

'My friend Stassov was not favourably impressed at first sight. Liszt was very thin, stooped a great deal, and though I had read much about his famous Florentine profile and his likeness to Dante, I did not find his face beautiful. I was not pleased with his mania for dressing himself with Orders, and afterwards I was as little prepossessed by his somewhat affected demeanour to those who came in contact with him.

'There were three thousand people in the audience, Glinka among them. Liszt mounted the platform, and pulling his doe-skin gloves from his shapely white hands, tossed them carelessly on the floor. Then, after acknowledging the thunderous applause, such as had not been heard in Russia for over a century, he seated himself at the piano. There was a silence as though the whole hall had been turned to stone, and Liszt, without any prelude, began the opening bars of the overture to *William Tell*. Curiosity, speculation, criticism, all were forgotten in the wonderful enchantment of his performance.

'His Fantasia on *Don Juan*, his arrangement of Beethoven's *Adélaïde*, the *Erl-King* of Schubert, and his own *Galop Chro-matique* followed upon this. After the concert, Serov and I were like madmen. We scarcely exchanged a word, but hurried home, each to write down his impressions, dreams and raptures. But we both vowed to keep this anniversary sacred for ever, and never, whilst life lasted, to forget a single instant of it.'

The two friends, it would appear, stayed up the rest of the night, pen in hand. The next morning, there was an interchange of impressions. Stassov, our author, was able to read the eulogies of Serov; while Serov was sent something approaching what we have just read ourselves. And, both of them being Russian, we may take it for granted that they sat up, many subsequent nights, talking far into the morning.

Serov, at least, was not at all behindhand in his appreciation, but vied with his friend in the extravagance of his expressions. 'First, let me congratulate you on your initiation into the great mysteries of art,' he writes, somewhat condescendingly, to Stassov, 'and then—let me think a little. It is two hours since I left the hall, and I am still beside myself. Where am I? Am I dreaming, or under a spell? . . . Happy, indeed, are we to be living in 1842, at the same time as such an artist. Fortunate, indeed, that we have been privileged to hear him! I am gushing a great deal—too much for me—but I cannot contain myself. Bear with me in this lyrical crisis until I can explain myself calmly . . . what a festival it has been! How different everything looks in God's world to-day! And all this is the work of one man and his playing! What a power is music! I cannot collect my thoughts—my whole being seems in a state of abnormal tension, of confined rapture!'

Perhaps it is true to say that the impression left by this first appearance of Liszt lasted longer in Russia than anywhere else. The Russians were in a condition of peculiar receptiveness. They were so far removed from the rest of Europe that they may be imagined as listening with a strained attention to all the sounds they could catch over that great distance. The more remote vibrations of the Romantic Movement had just reached them.

But, to a Russian, there are not the same implicit differences between Classical and Romantic that there are to races who live nearer to Rome and to the Mediterranean. Both Classical and Romantic are equally remote from their experience and absent from their past. For this reason, at one and the same time, we find them enraptured by Liszt, and still in the midst of that period of building activity which changed St. Petersburg into a city of such classical architecture as never existed in Greece or Rome. Quarenghi of Bergamo, a belated Italian, and Rossi, the illegitimate son of a Russian ballerina, were the artificers of this last and final outbreak of the classical spirit. When Liszt visited St. Petersburg, the chief buildings were no more than ten or twenty years old, and many of them were, as yet, unfinished. Foreigners who saw the city were struck by its prodigal magnificence and its modernity; George Borrow, for instance, says repeatedly that its equal does not exist in the world.

If that was the external aspect, Byronic echoes had reached them, also. Pushkin had only been dead for five years; and his crescent fame raised a whole host of musicians and authors from its sparks. There had been nothing before; now, there was to be everything. The air was pregnant. Those years of the early 'forties, coming just after Pushkin's early and tragic death, are of peculiar importance in any history of the arts. Glinka was making his first experiments in national music. Russians of the young generation, men like Stassov and Serov, were ready to admire anything and everything. Taglioni, for example, met with almost as frenzied a reception as Liszt for her farewell performances during this same year of 1842. The doors of the theatre were besieged for days on end. Count Vielgorsky, as immaculately odd as ever, was conspicuous in the stalls; and we may feel certain that Stassov and Serov were in the gallery. The pitch of excitement was fantastic; life was suspended, as it were, while her season lasted.

It has been necessary to stress such peculiar sensitiveness on the part of the Russian audience because the enthusiasm that it engendered was to last until all the masterpieces of Russian music were completed. We are speaking of 1842, when Russian music consisted of Glinka and no one else, but its effects were to endure until the deaths of Borodin, Moussorgsky, and Balakirev, men who were scarcely born at the time of this first Liszt recital in St. Petersburg. So far as Liszt is concerned, that is a section of his life that must be dealt with at a far later stage of this book, and it is only needful to mention it here in order to excuse the prominence given to his first reception. Russia was his most appreciative and permanent audience.

Under the ægis of Prince Galitzine, the Governor-General of Moscow, he was greeted with as great a tumult of applause in that city as in St. Petersburg; he had to give six concerts instead of the one originally planned. And the contagion spread rapidly through Russia; the provinces, as well as the two capitals, were clamouring to hear him. If the size of his audience was unlimited so was the amount of money to be made from them. This was the reason why he returned to Russia, again and again, during the next few years.

It is to be regretted that his letters to Madame d'Agoult, written during this period, have not yet been printed, as they must contain so many of the lost details of his strange travels and still stranger audiences. Certain facts have, however, been preserved. There are records of the special travelling-coach that he had built to his designs. It must have been nearly as big as a Gypsy caravan, and was bedroom and drawing-room in one. We are told, also, that the number of his cravats had increased, by now, to three hundred and sixty, a different one for every day of the year. But the pace of his travels, even though the railways were not yet made, compels us to return from Russia to lands where his travelling coach was no necessity.

CHAPTER XIX

The Glanz-Periode—His Spanish tour—Liszt in Seville and Granada—In Lisbon and Oporto—Details of his arrogance— He rebukes Nicholas I—Liszt and the sculptor Dantan

From now, onwards, it will be impossible to follow Liszt in all his travels. With the solitary exception of England, there was hardly a country in Europe to which his journeys did not extend. We find him in Seville, in Lisbon, in Copenhagen, all over Poland and Russia, at Jassy in Moldavia, and at Constantinople. The scope of his voyages was without precedent in the history of music. He could easily have contented himself with concert tours in Germany, Austria, and France; but some strange impulse drove him from end to end of the Mediterranean.

He was to lead this restless, wandering life until its false splendours became unendurable to him. Meanwhile, his renown went from end to end of the Continent. There had never been a painter, a writer, or an actor, with such universal fame. He could command an audience wherever there was a piano, and very often a crepitous, out-of-tune instrument gave him his best opportunities.*

Nor were the countries nearer to home omitted from his travels. He toured Germany once more, and early in 1845 the Beethoven memorial at Bonn was, at last, unveiled. There had been many troubles connected with it; the sculptor Bartolini was forced to resign his commission, but, in the end, thanks entirely to the generosity of Liszt, a compromise was arrived at, and the statue was unveiled with great ceremony; a special Cantata written by Liszt was performed; and all was well, except that the presence of Lola Montez, who was in his company, put the final seal upon his broken relations with Madame d'Agoult.

His Spanish tour was in the winter of 1845. He gave a cycle of concerts at the Teatro del Circo in Madrid, from October till December of that year, and then he took himself, more by way of a holiday, to Seville and Granada. In Seville, he seems to have lingered for some weeks. It was too pleasant for him to leave, and he was in a condition of nervous uncertainty about the future. In the early months of the spring he went to Portugal, and then we find him at Gibraltar.

He writes from there to a friend, Franz von Schober,† in phrases which show that the idea of retirement from the concert platform was already in his mind. 'My Vienna journey, next year,' the letter runs, 'will pretty much mark the end of my virtuoso career. I hope to go thence (in the month of August, 1846) to Constantinople, and on my return to Italy to pass my dramatic Rubicon, or Fiasco. So much for my settled plans. What precisely is going to become of me this coming spring and summer I do not exactly know. In any case to Paris I will not go. You know why. My incredibly wretched connexion with —— has perhaps indirectly contributed more than anything to my Spanish-Portuguese tour.'

In a letter to George Sand, of about the same date, he mentions

* We find the following account of his last tour, in 1846–47: 'During this tournée, and upon his arrival at the various railway stations, crowds were in the habit of assembling, and it became the custom to have an instrument in readiness for him, in order that he might perform in the interval pending the arrival of the following train. This, however, he was ultimately compelled to discontinue!'

† Another letter to von Schober is extant, written by Liszt in 1840, from Stonehenge. This shows the wide scope of Liszt's travels.

the month's voyage from Lisbon to Barcelona, says that he cannot count how many bottles of sherry he drank to her honour and glory during that time, and offers her a cargo of camellias from Oporto. But such a month, even counting its pleasant convivial moments, was a waste of time, and he was beginning to feel the emptiness of his career of virtuosity. It was becoming fearful in its demands upon his vitality, and in its inroads upon his time.

Only a few months later he is at Constantinople. In view of the many painful experiences of the sort that he must have undergone, it is reassuring to read, in one of his letters from there, that Sebastian Erard, the great manufacturer of these instruments, had sent out a particularly good specimen of his handiwork to that city, in order that the pianist should appear to the best advantage. He played upon it, twice, to the Sultan Abdul Medjid,* in the Palace of Tcheragan, upon the Bosphorus; and at two more concerts, one of them in the Russian Embassy, the windows of which looked out, as he says, from the Bosphorus to the Sea of Marmora, from the Seraglio Point to Bithynian Olympus, in fact from Europe to Asia. Even then, the romantic destiny of this piano was unfulfilled; for it was sold, afterwards, to a Phanariot, M. Baltagi, for sixteen thousand piastres, as a present to his young and beautiful fiancée.

Here, again, we must call a halt and leave our hero against this Turkish background of minaret and cypress, though he returned from Turkey to Russia, or, at least, to the Ukraine. There, his fate was decided. He met the person who was to be the chief influence in his life for the rest of his days, and he retired, finally and irrevocably, from his life as virtuoso. This was so drastic a change in his career that the discussion of its details must be deferred for a little. Meanwhile, it is time to give some general picture of him in this zenith of his fame.

From one of the letters we have just quoted it would seem that it was his breach with Madame d'Agoult that prompted him to travel upon such ever-widening circles. But there were other reasons for it besides that. As one of the principal embodiments of the Romantic Age it was virtually impossible for him to keep still. He had to conquer the world. 'I have got a tremendous fit of

* There is a curious paraphrase, by Liszt, of the march written by Donizetti to the order of this Sultan, Abdul Medjid. It was published in 1847, and figured in the repertory of Busoni. It is by Giuseppe, brother of Gaetano Donizetti.

Byron on. Be indulgent and kind as ever!' he writes in another letter to von Schober; and it is, indeed, to this Byronic feeling that we must ascribe his wish to be found in the more remote parts of Europe playing to a barbaric audience as susceptible to music as the wild beasts and the serpents of legend. The traces of this remained with him all through his life, till, in his poverty-stricken old age, his feudal aspirations had to be content with an Albanian or Montenegrin bodyguard, his servant Spiridion.

At this moment, he could command everything he wished. And his vagaries of dress and manner have lasted for a century. To take the most simple of instances, long hair need never have become the necessary, and derided, prerogative of musicians had it not been for Liszt. He was a consummate actor, an inspired showman, in addition to all his other qualities, and his long mane of fair hair, that reached to his shoulders, was as necessary to him as the cloak of the Spaniard. He had a way, on the platform, of shaking back his hair, of running his fingers through it, that savoured of the finest gestures of the Romantic actor. As to this mannerism, we have the account of Legouvé, that 'Liszt's attitude at the piano, like that of a pythoness, has been remarked again and again. Constantly tossing back his long hair, his lips quivering, his nostrils palpitating, he swept the auditorium with the glance of a smiling master. He had some little tricks of the comedian in his manner.' His clothes; his green gloves (they were sometimes of that colour); his Hungarian pelisse; the Orders that he wore, dangling and clanking from the lapels of his dress coat, his thin, rather diabolical figure; the paleness of his hands; and, above all else, his quite extraordinary good looks;* all these things were contributory to his fame. He succeeded, where he would, otherwise, have been mocked at, for three reasons. Firstly, his tremendous and real genius as a pianist; secondly, his youth and good looks; thirdly, his fine manners and his wit which made him welcome wherever he went. But his fault, as it may be imagined, was his pride.

Here are some of the details of his arrogance. He refused to play before Louis-Philippe; indeed, he insulted Louis-Philippe, as if to settled plan. This was because of his Legitimist sympathies. It was

---

* The fiery and excitable Janka Wohl remarks of his portrait by Ary Scheffer that 'the eyes are like incandescent grapes'. Could adulation attain to more far-fetched images than this?

his opinion that if the French had a Bourbon King it should be the Comte de Chambord (Henri V) and not a member of the Orléans family. On another occasion, when Louis-Philippe said to him, 'Do you remember the time when you played at my house as a little boy, when I was still Duke of Orleans? Things have greatly changed since then!' Liszt answered, 'Yes, Your Majesty. but not for the better.' His reply cost him the Legion of Honour.

At other times he threw the diamonds given him by Frederick-William IV into the side-scenes; he refused to give the usual invitation to his concerts to Ludwig I of Bavaria (his rival in the affections of Lola Montez); he treated Ernest-Augustus of Hanover, that choleric letter-writer, in the same manner; he would not play to Isabella II of Spain because court etiquette forbade his personal introduction to the Queen; and we are told, for what it is worth, that he confronted, with defiant word, Nicholas I of Russia. Certain it is that the Tsar, who seems to have been his only obstacle in Russia, had said of him, 'As to his hair and his political opinions they displease me'. His revenge for this remark, which was repeated to him, came a few weeks later. He was playing, and the Tsar did not lower his voice but continued talking. Liszt, thereupon, took his hands from the piano and waited with bowed head, as if listening for a command. When, at last, the Tsar enquired the cause of this sudden hush Liszt replied, 'Music, herself, should be silent when Nicholas speaks!'

It was the first time that 'Music, herself' had rebuked a reigning monarch. This had never happened before. Liszt was determined that music should be listened to with proper respect. Incidents, such as the above, are more easily explained when the intolerable conditions under which musicians had to play are taken into consideration. When the reproof to these tiresome personages was administered by someone with so much more breeding and distinction than themselves the conditions were soon altered. Liszt was, in fact, performing a universal service in these social clashes.

So great were the effects of his personality that it is more easy to find accounts of his physical appearance than of his actual playing. But he can be found contrasted with his old rival Thalberg in these words: 'Liszt, compared with Thalberg, was the more artistic, more vibrant, more electric. He had tones of a delicacy that made one think of the almost inaudible tinkling of tiny sparkles, or the faint explosion of sparks of fire. Never have fingers bounded so lightly over the piano.' This impression corrects the notion of his violence. 'The young matadors of the piano', as Liszt, himself, calls them, were the pupils and disciples of Rubinstein. Our hero must be altogether absolved from blame for these.

But it is better to keep any attempted analysis of his effect as a pianist until later in the book when he comes within the memory of persons still alive. There is the more reason for that because it was in his later years that he formed the schools of pupils some few of whom played, till lately, to the public; and, also, because it is only at that stage of his career, even though he had retired some thirty or forty years previously, that he can be compared with the three other pianists whom it is permissible to mention with his name, Anton Rubinstein, Paderewski, Busoni. So we will retain this chapter for a discussion of his personal characteristics.

These can be seen, wonderfully portrayed, in the statuette by the sculptor, Jean Pierre Dantan (1800–1869), who had invented for himself a special genre of satirical sculpture. It was a thing unique of its kind, which has hardly had an equivalent in any other age. In the *Memoirs of Léon Escudier*, to the curious and discreet translation of James Huneker, a great Liszt enthusiast, we read, of this statuette, 'The pianist is seated before a piano, which he is about to destroy under him. His fingers multiply at the ends of his hands. I should think so (*sic*). Dantan made him ten at each hand. His hair like a willow floats over his shoulders. One would say that he is whistling.'

Liszt was, it would appear, displeased with the statuette, and Dantan made another. 'One only sees', resumes M. Escudier with Mr. Huneker's assistance, 'a head of hair. The pianist is seen from the back. The head of hair plays the piano. That is all!'

The second statuette is, indeed, perhaps the finer of the two, but both are incomparable in their kind. If we want to evoke the Liszt of the 'forties in our imagination, there is more of him retained in these caricatures than in all the portraits that are left. He is better, burlesqued, than idealized. Here we have his long, gaunt figure, his mane of hair, his long, thin fingers: he is more like a man riding a whirlwind than a person playing on a musical instrument. He is a man holding on for life to the flying hair of the whirlwind; and able to do so, with apparent mastery, seated on an ordinary dining-room chair.

This pair of statuettes are successful because they are in burlesque. But the ordinary art of the sculptor involved our hero in less romantic situations. There was the occasion, for instance, when another sculptor carved him as he sat at the piano, and, in a passion for complete accuracy, included the whole instrument in his work. When Liszt was shown this in the studio he remarked, 'Thus, thus shall I appear to posterity. You represent me as playing a music coffin. I shall be seen hanging by my nails to this funereal box.' The sculptor smiled at this, and said, 'I can substitute an upright!' 'Then I would seem to be scratching a mummy case', Liszt answered. 'They will take me for an Egyptologist engaged on some sacrilegious work.'

His personal mannerisms, his excessive vanity and egoism, the train of camp followers who followed him from place to place, and, to be frank, a great many of his pianistic tricks, had begun by now to discredit him in the eyes of serious music-lovers. Such different admirers as Schumann and Monsieur Ingres, his friend of the Villa Medici at Rome, felt a repulsion from so great a gift put to such base purposes. Schumann, at least, he could generally reconquer; but there is no doubt that his general reputation has never recovered from those seven years of indiscriminate popularity. He had spread his own fame from end to end of Europe. But it was no more fair to accuse him of being a charlatan than it would be to lay this charge against some great actor, for his genius was essentially histrionic in character.

CHAPTER XX

'One hope still remains to me; it is that after my death the calumny will have spent itself, and that those who have avenged themselves so cruelly for my success will let my ashes repose in peace.'—Extract from a letter written by Paganini to the newspapers.

The influence of Paganini upon Liszt—Declining health of Paganini—His visiting-card—Paganini as Baron—Miss Watson, Mr. Watson, and Miss Wells—Mr. George Harrys introduced—Sir Charles Hallé and a ghostly memory of Paganini—Famous incident of Paginini and Berlioz—Death of Paganini—He lies in state—He is refused Christian burial—Adventures of his corpse—Baron Achillino and the Czech, Ondriczek—Paganini in the Florentine Nights *of Heine— The deaf painter, Lyser—Paganini and his familiar, Mr. George Harrys—Account of Paganini's music, published and unpublished—Paganini at Shrewsbury, at the Lion.*

During these years of transcendental execution it is certain that Liszt had a definite objective before him. This concerned, equally, his public and his private life. He set out to conquer fame; by doing so he would free himself of the shackles by which he was bound; and, having done so, it was always his intention again to change his career and become composer. For the first two or three years he tried to combine both careers in one, and his lease of the isle of Nonnenwerth shows his intention to spend each summer, at least, with Madame d'Agoult and their three children. But these two or three months of each year, with all his concerts ahead to prepare for, and with the nervous tension of his increasing estrangement from the Countess, did not leave him enough time to accomplish anything more lengthy than the transcription of Schubert's songs. He resolved, therefore, to travel still further and further afield, to return no more to Nonnenwerth, and to make little or no attempt at serious composition for another two or three years. At the end of that time he would have collected enough money, and his situation with the Countess would be finished, once and for all.

His tours to Spain, to Turkey, and to Russia, are more easily explained when this is understood.

Time was slipping by, and his career as composer, however much aided by his extraordinary fame as an executant, would be none the easier for his embarking upon it when no longer in the first strength of his youth. In a future chapter we shall make some examination into the actual work that he accomplished during his years of vagabondage; but it can be said, already, that until he abandoned it, when thirty-six years of age, he had never fulfilled the promise of his early piano pieces and had written nothing of any moment for the orchestra.

In the meantime, while he waited, Paganini, Berlioz, Chopin, accomplished their destinies. Perhaps their genius, in its full development, was necessary to him before he could begin, himself. They must be considered, therefore, in relation to this. Paganini may be said to have been the model of his own early virtuoso pieces; Chopin was the material of his recitals; Berlioz was the pattern, to some little extent, of what he hoped to accomplish in the future. These three men might, indeed, be called the past, the present, and the future, of Liszt.

Of Paganini this is particularly true. He had been the inspiration of Liszt from 1830 onwards, and all his piano pieces published up till 1840 show the predominance of this influence. His seven years of concert tours were conceived of, and carried out, upon the same principles. From the age of nineteen, during the long months of incessant practice at his instrument, it was Paganini whom he had in mind. 'Je travaille de quatre à cinq heures d'exercices, tierces, sextes, octaves, tremolos, notes répétées, cadences', he had written, all those years ago, to a friend. It is impossible to exaggerate the impression that Paganini made upon him. The whole of his personality was transformed.

In an earlier chapter some attempt was made to describe the physical appearance of this extraordinary being, and, once again, it is the sculptor Dantan who has left the most lifelike portrait of him. Perhaps no person more odd and peculiar than Paganini has ever existed. When Liszt first heard him, in 1831, he was nearly fifty years of age, and it is only natural that his peculiarities should grow more marked with increasing years.

Within a year or two of Liszt first hearing him play, the health of Paganini began to decline. The tubercular disease of the larynx from which he suffered made it nearly impossible for him to swallow any food; and it also affected his voice. He could scarcely speak above a whisper. It would seem, as well, almost certain that he was the victim of syphilis. In addition to this, an unskilful dentist, whom he consulted in Prague, had removed all, or nearly all, his teeth. A macabre episode, this must have been, if ever there was one! And there could be no better background than the dark, twisting streets of Prague. Indeed, the most sinister of German films could hardly improve upon this situation.

Everything connected with Paganini participates in the cadaverous horror of his appearance. Even his visiting card, which can be seen reproduced in a recent biography, haunts the memory. It bears the words, 'Baron Niccoló Paganini, Commandeur et Chevalier de plusieurs Ordres'. He had been given his title of nobility by some German Court, most probably that of Saxony. And, somehow, as a Baron, Paganini is an even more terrifying apparition than as an ordinary individual.

Certainly every detail of his behaviour was calculated to increase his diabolical reputation. There are several accounts to be found of his concerts in England, and they tally exactly with all the descriptions of him from Continental sources. It is remarked again and again how he would never play his cadenza, while rehearsing a concerto, but would smile sardonically when the moment arrived and say, 'Et cetera, Messieurs', to the players in the orchestra. He would invariably collect the orchestral parts, the moment a concert was over, lest one of the musicians should have time to make a copy of the score. We read of him, at the start of a concerto, 'raising his foot and bringing it down promptly. This was his signal to begin. His glasses were dark blue, giving a ghastly appearance to his emaciated face; they looked like two large holes in his countenance.'

The story of Paganini and Miss Watson belongs to this time. It appears that, in London, Paganini lodged in Gray's Inn Lane with a Mr. Watson, an American. Mr. Watson, Miss Watson, and a Miss Wells are included in his printed programmes as assisting him at his concerts. They sang Irish and Scotch airs. No sooner had Paganini left London for the Continent and landed at Boulogne than the French papers published a story of his elopement with a girl of sixteen—Miss Watson. The scandal reached to enormous proportions and became most acrimonious. Paganini, meanwhile, stayed in an hotel at Boulogne; Mr. Watson and Miss Wells arrived in search of Miss Watson, and the local newspapers printed the fiery letters of the disputants. 'Now why does Mr. Paganini allow us to assume that Miss Watson might not have left London at his instigation when so many witnesses saw his agent, name Urbani, go to seek her at the boat and reclaim her with the most enthusiastic insistence!' Paganini replied to this that Miss Watson came of her own free will; that she was eighteen, not sixteen years of age; and that if he had wished to remove her from the protection of her father it was to spare her virgin soul the spectacle of her father's odious and illicit association with Miss Wells, a girl of the same age, but so much older in experience. And, on 10 July 1834, he writes to the editor of the *Annotateur de Boulogne*, 'Your official information is not fortunate, Sir, because it is positive that Miss Wells came to Boulogne with Miss Watson. I, myself, saw her leave the boat; she wore a hat of yellow straw and a green coat which I knew perfectly.' For a few days it must have seemed to the prurient-minded that Paganini's intention had been to secure possession of both Miss Watson *and* Miss Wells. How the dispute was eventually decided it is difficult to ascertain, but no doubt a payment of money took place; and, in a sense, the fortunes of Miss Watson were made, for when she returned to America she was able to tour that gullible continent as the partner and fiancée of Paganini. More than this we do not know.

These stories date from the actual years when Liszt heard him play. But, in 1834, having toured Europe for about six years, he retired once more to Italy and bought a considerable property called the Villa Gajona, near Parma. He lived there in obscurity for some time, according to his invariable custom, for all through his life he had alternated between the wildest feats of personal publicity and a hermit-like seclusion. As an instance of this we may mention that Rossini, who formed a deep friendship with him, and who accompanied his playing at concerts in the Palazzo Pignalver at Bologna, in 1814, when he was the rage and sensation of that town, found him again in 1817, at Rome, where he had lived completely ignored by the public for three years as the result of a long internal illness.*

* My acknowledgments for much of the detail in this chapter are due to Miss Lillian Day, for her book, *Niccoló Paganini*, New York, 1929. This work is a

How he occupied himself during these long spells of inactivity it is impossible to know. It is likely, though, that he spent the greater part of the time, if not the whole of it, in doing nothing at all. Even on a concert tour he never practised. The son of a German rabbi, George Harrys, or Harris, of Hanover, a young man who spent an entire year touring with Paganini as his private secretary, in order to write an account of him, says that during the whole of that period he never saw him open his violin case so much as once. His fingers, from long training, retained all their suppleness without it being necessary for him to exercise them.

In 1836 his old mania for gambling, or for the associations of gambling, returned to him, and he left Parma for Paris, where the Casino Paganini had recently been opened at his instigation and with his financial support. He was involved in endless litigation as a result of this project, lost large sums of money, and still further damaged his health. He is described at this time as 'hardly able to move, bent nearly double, like a half-opened penknife, and evidently in great pain. He had to be carried upstairs, even to the first floor.'

For the details of Paganini's life at this time we have the evidence of his diaries, little red books, entered for each day, dated in French, but written in Italian. The following is a sample:

Mai 1. Purgativo	5. Vomitivo
2. Riposo	6. Figlio prezzo
3. Purgativo	7. Purgativo
4. Riposo	8. Figlio purga
9. Vomi-purga:	

and they contain no more than this ghastly record, except that, occasionally, there appears the name of an hotel, with some derogatory comment. It continues like this for an entire year. On 4 June, Paganini took a spoon and a half of purgative, third grade. On Wednesday, 9 September, he was at Milan, and vomited. There is no more than that in these diaries, but, somehow, they bring Paganini close before our eyes.

He lived in Paris for the greater part of the next two years, and it was then that Sir Charles Hallé, a young student of nineteen, met Paganini and, many years later, wrote an account of it in his

mine of information, diligently collected from various sources, and without its help these pages could never have been written.

Memoirs that remains the best direct description of Paganini ever written.* Hallé was so excited by this strange memory of his own youth that the episode stands out from his Memoirs as the unique piece of literature in an otherwise uninteresting collection of anecdotes.

'To return to 1838, a year to me so rich in reminiscences. I must say a few words about a man, in his way the most remarkable of his time, Paganini. He was one of the wonders of the world to me, so much had I read and heard about him, and I deeply deplored that he had given up public playing and—so I was told—even chose his lodgings so that the sound of his violin could not be heard outside. The striking, awe-inspiring, ghostlike figure of Paganini was to be seen nearly every afternoon in the music shop of Bernard Latte, Passage de l'Opéra, where he sat for an hour, enveloped in a long cloak, taking notice of nobody, and hardly ever raising his piercing black eyes. He was one of the sights of Paris, and I had often gone to stare at him with wonder until a friend introduced me to him, and he invited me to visit him, an invitation I accepted most eagerly.

'I went often, but it would be difficult to relate a single conversation we had together. He sat there, taciturn, rigid, hardly ever moving a muscle of his face, and I sat spellbound, a shudder running through me whenever his uncanny eyes fell upon me. He made me play to him often, mostly by pointing with his bony hand to the piano, without speaking, and I could only guess from his repeating the ceremony that he did not dislike it, for never a word of encouragement fell from his lips. How I longed to hear him play it is impossible to describe, perhaps even to imagine. From my earliest childhood I had heard of Paganini and his art as something supernatural, and there I actually sat opposite to the man himself, but only looking at the hands that had created such wonders.

'On one never-to-be-forgotten occasion, after I had played and we had enjoyed a long silence, Paganini rose and approached his violin case when there passed in me what can hardly be imagined; I was all in a tremble, and my heart thumped as if it would burst my chest; in fact, no young swain going to the first rendezvous with his beloved could possibly feel more violent emotions. Paganini opened the case, took the violin out, and began to tune

* *Life and Letters of Sir Charles Hallé*, edited by his son. London, 1896.

it carefully with his fingers without using the bow. My agitation became almost intolerable. When he was satisfied, and I said to myself, "Now, now, he'll take the bow", he carefully put the violin back and shut the case. And that is how I heard Paganini.'

It will be agreed that this episode is complete in all its details. The young student and the alchemist, the old music shop, this classic theme, and every implication of it, is contained in these few vivid lines. It would be impossible to improve upon them.

Close upon this, but a year or two later, when Paganini was still more ill and haggard, there came the historic incident of Berlioz and Paganini. It is described, in the inimitable words of Berlioz, in his Memoirs. Readers of that book will remember how Paganini approached Berlioz after the concert; how he knelt on the platform to kiss the hand of Berlioz; how his son, his beloved and illegitimate son, Achillino,* then a child of ten, had to stand on a chair and put his ear to Paganini's lips in order to interpret his father's inaudible words; and how he presented Berlioz, nearly destitute as usual, with a draft for twenty thousand francs as commission for a piece of music.

The real truth of this curious incident is that the donor of the money was not Paganini but Armand Bertin, the rich proprietor of the *Journal des Débats*. Berlioz was on the staff of that paper. Bertin had a great opinion of his talents and was looking for an opportunity to help him. He thought that a gift of money would be more acceptable to Berlioz if it took the form of a presentation from some other celebrated musician. He, therefore, persuaded Paganini to act as donor. The concert was on 18 December 1838, and the programme included the *Symphonie Fantastique* and *Harold en Italie*. Only one or two of Bertin's friends were admitted into the secret, and it appears that the suspicions of Berlioz were never aroused and that he always remained in ignorance of the true identity of his benefactor.

Paganini never lived to see the completion of the work that he had commissioned. But Berlioz, thanks to the twenty thousand francs, was able to work in peace for seven months, and produced the symphony, *Roméo et Juliette*.

---

* The Baron Achillino, Achille Cyrus Alexander Paganini, Paganini's illegitimate son, was born at Palermo, in 1826. His mother was the ballet dancer, Antonia Bianchi. The child accompanied Paganini to all his concerts and was his inseparable companion.

His encounter with Berlioz on the concert platform was the last public act of Paganini. His disease developed so rapidly that it was evident he was dying, and the doctors advised his removal to the warmer climate of the south if he was to live through the winter. He spent some months on his way south living in the house of an Englishman with the curiously modern name of Douglas Loveday.* I have been unable to discover anything whatever about this individual, except the fact that his hospitality involved him in a lawsuit. He charged Paganini, who must have been part of the time a paying guest, with not contributing his full share of the expenses, and Paganini countercharged with an account for alleged violin lessons given by himself to Loveday's daughter. He also charged Loveday with introducing a doctor to him in order to run up a bill for his own benefit.

From this curious household Paganini removed to Marseilles, whence he was driven by his frayed nerves to Genoa, his birthplace; and from Genoa he fled, as before death, to Nice, where he spent his last few weeks on earth. Here, his love of economy, even in his ultimate moments, made him take up his lodging in two rooms in a mean street. He ate nothing, drank nothing, and had no need of luxuries.

His condition of debility became worse and worse. He was racked by a terrible cough and suffered from fearful spasms of pain. He died, at last, on 27 May 1840;† and, considering the strange rumours with which all his living acts were surrounded, it is no surprise to be told that, on the night before he died, Paganini stretched out his hand for his violin and played for a whole hour, or more. It is no surprise, too, to be told that a friend, the Comte de Cessole, who knew him well, declared that this improvisation during his last hours was the most remarkable feat of his whole life.

But death did not lay his soul to rest. His body led what can only be described as a tormented life, from the very moment that he died. It lay in state on a platform, with aquiline features and glassy eyes, pallid and horrible to behold. A white cotton nightcap, held in place by a blue riband across his forehead, decorated

* From another source it is reported that Paganini's sojourn in Loveday's villa was in 1834, not 1838.

† Paganini left his illegitimate son, the Baron Achillino, the equivalent of eighty thousand pounds.

his head; while a white cravat failed to conceal the bandage which kept his jaws closed. There are lithographs to be seen which show the features of Paganini in this ghastly travesty.

A few days later, when it had been embalmed, his body, dressed in the black coat and trousers in which he appeared on the concert platform, was put into a coffin which had a glass pane above his face. And a dealer in secondhand objects offered the Comte de Cessole, who had been appointed trustee for Achillino, the sum of thirty thousand francs in order to exhibit the corpse in England.

Meanwhile, the clergy had protested against Christian burial for the body. It was alleged that he had not died as a Christian, and that he had committed offences which put him outside the pale of the Church. The coffin was, therefore, taken directly from the house where he died and placed in the waiting-room of the Lazaretto of Villefranche. This was the leper-house where travellers who arrived by sea were forced to spend many weary weeks before they were allowed to enter France. The body remained here for a month, and so many complaints were received because of its state of putrefaction that another move was decided upon, and it was buried in the ground nearby. Once more there were complaints and, this time, Comte de Cessole set out to bury the body, himself. It was interred, by night, at the foot of a Saracen round tower, by the Cap St. Hospice, on the property of a friend of the Count. Hastily, so hastily that the burial was incomplete, the coffin was pushed into the ground by the side of a foetid rivulet formed by the refuse from a neighbouring olive-oil factory. A year or so later, the Baron Achillino decided to take his father's body back to Genoa, but there was an outbreak of cholera at Marseilles, whence it had to be shipped, and so his project could not be realized, and the vessel had to put back to Marseilles. It was, therefore, buried once more on the Ile St. Ferréol, one of the little Îles des Lérins, off Hyères, and to this day the ditch in which the coffin was laid is known as Paganini's ditch.

At length, in 1844, the Duchess of Parma, Marie Louise, the widow of Napoleon, gave permission for the body of Paganini to be brought into her dominions, and, Christian burial being still refused to it, the coffin was taken first to the Villa Polevra, a Paganini property, and afterwards, to the Villa Gajona, the estate that the Baron Achillino had inherited from his father. There it remained till 1853, when it was exhumed and subjected to a fresh process of embalming.

Many years later, in 1876, the Baron Achillino prevailed upon the religious authorities to allow a service to be held for his father in the Madonna della Steccata, a church which belonged to the Knights of St. George. They were an Order of Chivalry belonging to the Duchy of Parma, and Paganini had been a Knight of the Order. The ceremony was presided over by a nephew, the Baron Attila, yet another member of this sinister family of Barons.

Even now, the troubles of that poor shrivelled body were not over. In 1893, a Czech violinist, Ondriczek, who died as lately as 1922, persuaded the Baron Achillino, then an old man of seventy, to open the coffin in order that he might see the body. And finally, in 1896, what is described as 'urgent necessity' made the authorities open the coffin once more. It is said that fearful as was its state of decay and putrefaction the features of Paganini were still recognizable, but his black coat was in tatters, and the lower part of his body was no more than a heap of bones.

When the Baron Achillino died, and whether he has left any descendants, I have been unable to discover, but, at least, the body of his father has been left undisturbed since then. Fifty-six years had elapsed, by 1896, from the time he died and, as his age at death was fifty-six, it can be said that this kind of ghastly shadow life, these fearful and sinister adventures of his corpse, continued for just the same span of time as his life upon earth.

These incredible details have been given at great length, because the diabolist atmosphere in which everything connected with Paganini is steeped had a strong and deep influence upon Liszt—and also because the details are irresistible in themselves. Anyone who has ever had the curiosity to make any enquiry or research into the question of Paganini remains haunted by the thought of his personality. It is a delight, therefore, to find the effect that he left upon a person of exceptional sensibilities, and we have an instance of this in the case of Heinrich Heine. For that strange prose work, *The Florentine Nights*, contains a long impression of Paganini and of his playing, and when I referred to it recently for the purposes of this book, after a lapse of many years, I found, as well, that a little problem which had long puzzled me was solved in its pages.

There is an excellent and eerie portrait of Paganini, to be seen reproduced in some of the books upon him, which is invariably ascribed to a painter named Lyser. I had searched every dictionary and index of painters, and found no mention of him.* Nor was it possible to discover the whereabouts of the picture. This, in fact, still remains a mystery to me. But, in reading *The Florentine Nights*, the identy of the artist is immediately revealed, and it appears that Lyser was a friend of Heine and a native of Hamburg. He was deaf. He attended the concerts of Paganini, but never heard him. Perhaps his evidence is, for this reason, all the more reliable!

This curious figure comes into the first of *The Florentine Nights* as the cicerone and guide to Maximilian, the Scheherazade, so to speak, of the tales.

He is described as an intense lover of music, in spite of his deafness. He even acted as operatic critic to one of the leading journals of Hamburg. 'I believe there was but one man who ever succeeded in transferring Paganini's features to paper, and he was a deaf painter named Lyser.' And then Heine goes on to describe Paganini himself, as he heard him in the Alster pavilion at Hamburg, in company with this very friend of his, the deaf painter, Lyser. 'Paganini's strange features belonged to the sulphurous land of shadows. . . .

'And now it was indeed Paganini who approached us. He wore a dark grey overcoat, reaching down to his feet, and making him appear very tall. His long, black hair fell upon his shoulders in wild locks, and, like a frame, encompassed his pale, corpselike face. . . . A short, self-complacent person in plain attire tripped along at his side. His face, although florid, was full of wrinkles. He wore a light grey coat, with steel buttons, and bowed in every direction with most excruciating politeness, while he, now and then, cast half-fearful, half-insipid glances at the sombre figure walking at his side, serious and wrapt in meditation. It reminded

---

*Johann Peter Lyser, for at last I have discovered his identity, was born at Flensburg in 1803 and died at Altona in 1870. And, while dealing with dates, it may be mentioned that *The Florentine Nights* was published in 1837, within the lifetime of Paganini. This is another proof of the halo of mystery in which Paganini lived. A London bookseller, late of Leipzig, sent me a page from one of his pre-war catalogues, reproducing a drawing by Lyser of three persons he met in the street on the same morning in Vienna. They were Beethoven, Hofmann, and Paganini.

one of Faust and Wagner, walking before the gates of Leipzig. Lyser made me take particular notice of Paganini's long and measured step. "Does it not", he asked, "seem as if he still had the iron bar of the galley slave between his legs?* He will never get rid of that prison gait. Do you observe with what contemptuous irony he looks down upon his companion, whenever the latter annoys him with his dull and prosy questions? He cannot get rid of him. A bloody compact binds him to this servant, who is none other than Satan himself. The ignorant imagine his companion to be the dramatist and anecdotist Harrys of Hanover, and believe that Paganini carries him along in his travels that he may attend to the financial management of his concerts. They do not know that Satan has merely borrowed the form of Mr. George Harrys, and that, along with other trash, the soul of that poor creature will remain locked up in a chest in Hanover, until the devil returns its carnal envelope, when, in the nobler guise of a black poodle, he will accompany his master Paganini through the world. . . ."

'At last a sombre figure, which seemed to have risen from the dark regions, appeared on the stage. It was Paganini in full evening dress. His black coat and vest were of some such horrible cut as infernal etiquette prescribes at the court of Proserpine. The black pantaloons flapped about his legs most wildly. His long arms seemed still longer when he made his strange obeisance to the audience, and bent so far forward that the bow in one hand and the violin in the other almost touched the floor. There was something so terribly wooden and so foolishly animal in the angular bendings of his body, that his bowing produced a great desire to laugh outright. But his pale face, rendered still more deathlike by the glaring lights of the orchestra, seemed so supplicating and so full of shy timidity that shuddering compassion suppressed the desire.'

From this point Heine launches into an account of Paganini's playing which is too long and intricate to quote from.† But, already, enough has been said to transmute Mr. George Harrys

---

*This refers to the popular belief that Paganini had served twenty years in the galleys, or hulks of Naples, for murdering his mistress.

†It is of some interest that Hans Andersen seems to have attended this same concert at Hamburg in 1837. He describes Paganini, playing, and seems to have been amused by the audience. 'Near me, on a sofa, reclined a young Jewess, stout and overdressed. She looked like a walrus with a fan.'

of Hanover into a personage of sinister and diabolist repute. His association with Paganini was recorded in a small book of sixty-eight pages entitled *Paganini in seinem Reisewagen und Zimmer, in seinem redseligen Stunden, in gesellschaftlichen Zirkeln und seinem Conzerten. Aus dem Reisejournal*, or *Paganini dans sa chaise de poste et dans sa chambre, dans ses heures de causerie, dans les salons, et dans ses concerts*, published at Brunswick in 1830. It is not surprising, in view of Heine's theories, that there should be no trace of this book in the British Museum Library. Mr. George Harrys, in fact, remains branded as the familiar of Paganini, and it seems impossible to discover any more about his identity than the few facts already given.*

The description in *The Florentine Nights* of Paganini playing is no more than a general dissertation or fantasy upon his effects. It does not deal with any particular piece of music. We are left indeed, to draw our own conclusions about the whole question of his own compositions, for only a handful of them was ever published. Besides the *Twenty-four Capricci*, those pieces which had such an intense effect upon Liszt and so much influenced his career, very little of the music of Paganini was published during his lifetime. It had been his intention to arrange for their publication when he had retired from the concert platform, but it was a resolution that he never accomplished. Certain manuscripts were printed in Paris in 1851–2, after his death, but the great bulk of his manuscripts is, to this day, unpublished and likely to remain so.†

Published or unpublished it is all the same: they are never played. What, then, are we to think of such affairs as the violin sonata called *Varsovia*, a souvenir of Warsaw; of the *Balletto campestre*, variations upon a comic theme; of the *Ghribizzo vocale*, a Grille, or sketch for soprano voice with orchestra; or of the twenty variations called *Le Streghe* (*Les Sorcières*) written on an air taken from *Il Noce de Benevento*, an opera by Süssmayer, the friend of Mozart who completed the *Requiem*? These were some of the most famous pieces in his repertoire. The mystery about everything concerned with Paganini becomes still more strange

---

* I have not yet (1955) suceeded in tracing this book.

† The unpublished manuscripts were bought from the heirs of Paganini in 1910, and are now in the Museum of History at Cologne. See *Paganini* by Julius Kapp, Berlin, 1923, where these unpublished manuscripts are fully examined.

when we arrive at the Vingt Variations sur l'air Vénitien populaire, '*O Mamma*', in fact the famous *Carnaval de Venise*. And
there is, as well, his *Moto Perpetuo*, which contains 3040 double
stoppings, without pause. There is, also, one of the last works ever
written by him, the Soixante Variations en trois suites, avec
accompagnement de piano ou de guitare, sur l'air populaire
connu à Gènes sous le titre de *Barucaba*;* there are the Variations
called *St. Patrick's Day*, written for Dublin; and finally there is
the *Fandango Spagnuolo* with barnyard imitations, known under
the title of *The Vagaries of the Farmyard*. It is, in fact, impossible to
discuss these things because they sound merely ridiculous. But
we have only to read back to what was written of Paganini by so
acute an intelligence as that of Heine in order to realize that our
laughter would be quickly quelled were the ghostly figure of
Paganini to appear before us, bow in hand. There is something
exceptional about this ghost; for, as we have shown, his adventures continued into two worlds. From 1784 until 1896 there was
no peace for his spirit.

In fact, as we have said, everything to do with Paganini is
haunted by his personality, and something of the same interest
attaches to the places where he performed as that which surrounds
every house where Mozart ever lodged or gave a concert. I
cannot give a better instance of this, when closing this chapter,
than by mentioning the Assembly Room of the Lion Hotel at
Shrewsbury. It was here that Paganini played on his way to, and
from, Dublin in 1831.

The Assembly Room, at the back of the hotel, though not
actually designed by the brothers Adam, is a delicate and magnificent example of Adam decoration, as fine, in its way, as
anything in the country. The colour scheme is in green and white,
and there are splendid gilded mirrors upon the walls. At one end
of the room, supported upon pillars, there is a fine gallery where
the band would have played during dances. Though it now
appears stilted and old-fashioned, with Woolworth's and the
Cinema to either side of it, this Assembly Room is, of course, as
much a monument to civilization as the ruin of a Roman theatre
in the African sand. Shrewsbury, to this day, is a town of medieval
half-timbered houses belonging, mostly, to the early seventeenth

---

* *Barucaba* has been recently published (1954), but, I believe, has not yet been
performed.

century. It is a town like one of the medieval towns of Germany, like Dinkelsbühl or Hildesheim; and this Assembly Room, in its midst, strikes a remarkable note of gaiety and delicacy. It must have been just as much in contrast with its surroundings a century ago when Paganini drove through the streets. He will have arrived here, as likely as not, with Mr. George Harrys, whom Heine has revealed to us as his familiar; and we know, from the published account by this very familiar, that Paganini could never be induced to look out from the window of his travelling coach, however beautiful the bribe of scenery. All he would say was, 'Yes! Very pretty, very pretty!' On the other hand, Paganini, who would be generally taciturn and prone to silence, would never stop talking in the coach and seemed to find the rolling of its wheels to be a relief to his weak voice and aching throat. He would, therefore, lean forward in earnest conversation with Mr. George Harrys, regardless of the feelings and patience of his fellow-travellers.

We can imagine, if it pleases us, the supper of Paganini and his familiar. A cup of soup or camomile tea for Paganini, and something much more substantial, a beefsteak, perhaps, for Mr. George Harrys. They will not have stayed for more than a moment in the coffee-room because of the bucolic starings and nudgings of their fellow-guests, and of the natives of Shrewsbury, Salopians, come into the coffee-room for that purpose. They will have climbed upstairs to the high and damp bedrooms, and talked in Paganini's room, where the fire was lit and there was a warming-pan between the sheets, and the maidservant was so frightened of the peculiar gentleman that she could not speak when she came into the room. And everyone in the inn will have been listening, but they will have heard nothing.

Paganini would lie upon the sofa with many rugs over him. Their commerce would continue far into the night in low voices, with long intervals of silence. Eventually his familiar left him, coming back, once more, as though to be certain in his own mind. And by the light of a single, shaded candle, we can see Paganini undressing to his bones, for his ribs showed through the flannel of his shift, and he is more gaunt, still, in the cotton nightshirt that he passes over his long fingers and skeleton arms. He wears a nightcap, too, and looks once into the mirror, holding the candle to see himself.

As he does so, the cats strike up their concert upon the tiles. But, before we have time to see his expression, Paganini has blown out this one light and is huddled in bed, almost as if their music was the sign for darkness. He does not sleep soundly, and we hear him turning from side to side, rattling the sheets and pillows. Presently the clock strikes, and in a shaft of moonlight coming through the curtains we see him fumbling for the flint and tinderbox. He finds it and begins to scratch for a spark, but the music starts again, like the wailing of a violin, like a strong and bitter wind blowing through the strings, sighing and wailing, never-ceasing, blown suddenly nearer, close to the panes. And, then, as suddenly, it stops altogether: the serenade is over, and complete stillness and darkness take possession of the room.

CHAPTER XXI

Liszt and the Songs of Schubert—*The* Soirées de Vienne

During his eight years of incessant travels it is no wonder that Liszt accomplished little in the way of serious composition. Indeed, up till the end of 1847, he wrote practically nothing for the orchestra. With hardly any exception, all that he published consisted in adaptations of the works of other musicians. It seemed as if his own vein of originality was exhausted; no one could have foreseen the colossal activities of his next period when he abandoned virtuosity in order to become conductor and composer.

At present, it is the period of his transcriptions, of the 'partitions de piano', as he called them. And it brings us to a curious anomaly, because the most furious detractors of Liszt, the most severe critics of all his future works, are agreed that if he accomplished nothing else his transcriptions of Schubert's songs are masterpieces in their delicacy and appositeness. They do not hesitate to call these the one serious contribution made by Liszt to an art in which he, at least, covered more paper than any of his colleagues, past or future. And they will not pause at anything except these songs, although it is so clearly demonstrable that if these are admired there is a great deal more of his work that falls into the same category and should win their approval, the *Soirées Musicales de Rossini*, for instance.

In all there are fifty-three transcriptions of Schubert's songs, and all but one of these were written between 1838 and 1847. It is interesting to note that the first literary work ever done by Madame d'Agoult was in translating the words of some of these songs from German into French. That was in 1838 when she and her lover stopped some days at Lyon on their way to Geneva. It was, in fact, the beginning of her transition from the Comtesse d'Agoult into Daniel Stern, and this little fact is of moment for that reason.

The problem that Liszt set himself to solve in the Schubert songs was the fusion of voice and accompaniment into an entity that retained the atmosphere and the characteristics of Schubert while it kept the form and manner of his own interpretation, just as if he was a great singer, or some famous actor who had his own unmistakable way of rendering a part. Liszt had a particular devotion all his life long for Schubert, whom he called 'the most poetical composer who has ever lived', and he exercised a particular care and restraint where these songs were concerned. His customary magniloquence and his tricks of pianistic ornamentation are subordinated to the poetical directness and simplicity, the freshness and the free imagination of the songs. All their lovely qualities are transferred in a miraculous way from one medium into another, so that what was an impossibility without a singer became enlarged into the experience of many who had no other opportunity of hearing them. In themselves, they are miniatures of many different moods, inimitably expressed. Perhaps the transcription of *Auf dem Wasser zu singen* is the most beautiful of the lot, but then one remembers *Der Atlas*, *Ständchen* or *Meeresstille*, and it is hopeless to decide upon their merits. All the beauties of the Romantic Age are present in them, and they are impregnated with all the sensitiveness of this extraordinary virtuoso who, at the time that he was setting them for his instrument, was at the very summit of his powers of interpretation. A great part of this work was accomplished during the two or three summers that he spent with Madame d'Agoult on the islet of Nonnenwerth in the Rhine, while their passion waned. It should, also, be remarked about these songs that they show Liszt moving in spirit from France to Germany. Until he was thirty years old he had been to all intents and purposes a Frenchman; he was, now, in his years of travel, someone of undecided nationality; during his next phase, at Weimar, he became a German; it was only when that was over and done with that he became, again, a person of international creeds and beliefs.

Besides the songs, Liszt set four marches by Schubert for the piano, and reduced the famous *Divertissement à l'Hongroise* from its original version for four hands into an edition for solo instrument. This was done in 1846 when he was working at his own *Hungarian Rhapsodies*, so that it was a work supremely appropriate and congenial to the moment.

Finally, while we are dealing with his association with Schubert it is best to mention, here and now, the *Soirées de Vienne*, though, as a matter of fact, they were not published until 1852, a date which is outside the immediate period with which we are concerned. They may be described as an ornamental elaboration upon certain waltzes of Schubert so as to make them suitable for concert performance. The waltzes are nine in number, and as Liszt had been playing his versions of them for many years before they were published, they belong, rightly and properly, to this period of his virtuosity. They were, in fact, favourite pieces in his repertory, and he hardly gave a recital without including a number from the *Soirées de Vienne* in his programme. It is impossible to imagine anything more graceful and delicate than his setting of these delicious tunes; and, in themselves, they were the start of a whole series of piano pieces of the kind, the best example of which is the *Nouvelles Soirées de Vienne*, arrangements of Johann Strauss waltzes by the favourite pupil of Liszt, Karl Tausig. These were meant deliberately to be a pendant to his master's version of Schubert waltzes, showing the dance tunes popular in Vienna some half-century later.

Altogether, the coupling of the names of Schubert and Liszt is a particularly happy chapter in the immense chronicle of Liszt's works. His veneration for Schubert kept him within the strictest bounds, and none of the charges laid against him in his other piano arrangements are applicable in this instance. It was a music which recalled the days of his own earliest youth, when he left his native Hungary for Vienna and stayed there breathing the same air as

Beethoven and Schubert, studying from Salieri who had been the rival of Mozart. How much of Schubert's music he actually heard during those early days it is impossible to determine; very probably nothing more than Schubert's name and reputation were familiar to him. It is, at least, certain that they actually met, for he was introduced to him by Randhartinger. But there can be no doubt that the music of Schubert had an additional appeal to him because it spoke to him of the simplicities of an older world. There were no factories, no railway engines, no machines, when Liszt was a child in Vienna; the golden age of music was living before his eyes, albeit its end was so near. It is, in fact, easy enough to understand his admiration for Schubert and the light way in which his fingers touched upon those fragments of eternal youth.

CHAPTER XXII

The Partitions de piano—*Organ preludes and fugues of Bach —Liszt and the first edition of* Domenico Scarlatti—*Busoni and the operatic fantasias of Liszt—Mr. Sorabji and his theory of 'possession', or 'control'—The* Tarantella—*Two aberrations —Lucia di Lammermoor and the* Don Juan Fantaisie

We come, now, to the much more complicated question of Liszt's *Partitions de piano* as a whole. These took on many different forms, and are of varying merit. It is impossible, for instance, at this time of day, to take any interest in his *Variations upon God Save the Queen* written especially for performance in London, in 1841. This belongs to the old Thalberg School, to the kind of thing that he had, himself, defeated some years before when he vanquished that musician in open competition. His transcriptions, on the other hand, of Beethoven's Septet, and of Hummel's Septet, and of the nine symphonies of Beethoven, all completed during this period but not published in their entirety until twenty-five years later, belong to a very different category. So do his transformations of three of the Beethoven piano concertos into versions for two pianos. These were works, certainly as regards the nine symphonies, of supreme utility, making available for study works which in those days were but rarely heard in the concert hall. Their usefulness is now gone, with the invention of wireless and gramophone, but they served two or three generations of music lovers, and were worked upon by Liszt with the most scrupulous exactitude and care. They form one of his most important contributions to this class of music, but the credit due to him has passed him by, and their very faithfulness, as transcriptions, has almost dissociated his name from their publication.

Another work, of equal importance, is his piano edition of six organ preludes and fugues by Bach. These mark, indeed, the beginning of the cult for Bach, who had just begun to be rediscovered at that day. The credit for this is due, chiefly, to Mendelssohn and to Liszt, and both of them were the leading spirits in starting the *Bach-gesellschaft*, which took some sixty years to finish its labours of editing and publication. His edition of these preludes and fugues has never been improved upon in its principles. They are transferred from one instrument to the other with most telling effect and are magnificent in their splendour and sobriety.

In general, Liszt was too much interested in the music of his contemporaries, and in the future possibilities of the art, to take much share in resuscitating the old masters of music. Besides the practical form taken by his interest in Bach, almost the only other instance of his enthusiasm for older music is in the edition of Domenico Scarlatti published by Czerny at Vienna in 1839. It was Liszt who first drew the attention of the public to Scarlatti, and, but for him, this publication would never have taken place. Its inception is due entirely to Liszt, and the edition is appropriately dedicated to him.

But it is time, now, to speak of his *Fantaisies Dramatiques*, a class of composition in which he has been much despised, but never excelled. These must be distinguished from the *Partitions de piano*. The aim of the latter, as clearly expressed in the *Oxford History of Music*, vol. vi, was the reproduction of orchestral effects as closely as the pianoforte permitted and without regard to difficulties of execution. The idea of the *Fantaisies Dramatiques* was to combine the tunes and variations from some scene of an opera in such wise that the entire piece, from the introduction to the final climax, should consist of a crescendo of effects reproducing the mood of some dramatic situation, or condensing an entire act. They are something more, therefore, than the mere engraving of some particular scene; than the transference, as it were, of its colours into terms of black and white. In performance, these pieces demand the utmost skill and consideration, and, when thus given, never fail to produce the most magnificent effect. It was only necessary, indeed, to hear that veteran, Moriz Rosenthal, play the *Don Juan* Fantasia of Liszt in order to experience one of the most extraordinary feats of pianism imaginable. Had Rosenthal performed the *Norma* Fantasia or that based upon *Robert le Diable*, it is certain that we would have been equally surprised, for it is the truth that these despised works are among the most remarkable of Liszt's creations.

Some details of the *Fantaisies Dramatiques* have been given in an earlier chapter, for the reason that the bulk of those mentioned were written in 1841-2-3, and that, after that date, he composed nothing more of the kind until 1849 when the first of his Wagner transcriptions saw the light. But the performance, if not the composition of these pieces, is so essential a part of his years of virtuosity that it is entirely necessary to reconsider them. If well played, they are the most dazzling pieces imaginable, and the revival of many of them in the concert room is long overdue. The utmost ingenuity of which he was capable has been lavished upon them, and piano technique cannot be said to have moved forward in any degree since their composition. They have, in fact, an athletic appeal which is a definite part of their artistic merit. They are a wonderful vehicle for the virtuoso, and as an important part of the machinery of this extraordinary man's success they deserve a great deal more attention than they now receive. Certainly they are war-horses, but they are war-horses of a rare strain, swifter and more fiery of blood than any others. At least four of them, *Norma*, *Sonnambula*, *Robert le Diable*, and *Don Juan*, should be familiar to everyone who loves to hear the piano well played.

The enthusiasm of a mere amateur, here expressed, is also, it may be added, the conviction of a great many serious musicians. That great master, Ferruccio Busoni, edited no fewer than five separate editions of the *Don Juan* Fantasia, and he completed and published the unfinished *Figaro* Fantasia. His admiration for the *Fantaisies Dramatiques* of Liszt was well known and often expressed in dazzling fashion at the piano. But their best criticism in literary form is to be found in *Around Music*, a book of essays published by Kaikhosru Sorabji.* Speaking of the *Norma* Fantasia, he says: 'This is in some ways the most remarkable of all. Very nearly every conceivable musical and pianistic device of treatment is turned on to Bellini's themes, and it is here that one feels the power that was also Busoni's—that power of seizing upon extraneous themes and so charging them with his own peculiar quality that, without actual alteration, they lose all semblance of their original physiognomy, and become "controlled", to use an expression borrowed from the spiritualists, or "possessed". Bellini's themes never had, by themselves, the grandeur and magnificence that Liszt is able to infuse into them.'

The idea, here expressed, is a definite discovery in criticism. There is no other image than that of 'control', or 'possession', to describe the extraordinary process of transformation undergone by these themes as they come under the spell of Liszt's hands. The most remarkable of all the *Fantaisies Dramatiques* in this respect, and far more striking in effect and atmosphere than the *Norma* Fantasy, is Liszt's treatment of the waltz from Gounod's *Faust*. This, also, was a favourite piece with Busoni; but it belongs to a much later period in Liszt's life than the present, and so discussion of its almost unearthly merits must be postponed, more especially as an occasion will come to attempt some description of Busoni's effects.

In the *Fantaisies Dramatiques*, speaking generally, Liszt dealing with Donizetti or Bellini must be differentiated from Liszt at work upon Meyerbeer, or upon Verdi. These various shades of treatment it is better to reserve, also, until a later stage of the book, when all his Verdi and Meyerbeer arrangements were completed. Meanwhile, it may be said that the *Fantaisies Dramatiques* formed an important item in his programmes and constituted the major part of his compositions during these years.

Mention of them would be incomplete without attention being drawn to the *Tarantelle de Bravura* from Auber's opera of *Masaniello*. This was one of the latest of the present series, being written in 1847. The idea of this piece may sound an absurdity, but it was a revelation when played by a pianist of the calibre of Frederic Lamond. At the end of a concert Liszt delighted to

Around Music, by Kaikhosru Sorabji. London, The Unicorn Press, 1932.

dazzle his audience with a thing of this kind. He played this particular Tarantella when he came to England forty years later, a few months before he died, so that it was a composition of which he was, obviously, not in the least ashamed. It must be one of the most difficult, as it is certainly one of the most effective, of his virtuoso pieces.

Finally, in order to stress the strange ground on which we are treading, it is better to take this opportunity of mentioning two particularly glaring instances of Liszt's inconsistency. These are his transcriptions for piano of two popular pieces of the day, the *Russischer Galopp* of Bulhakov and the *Zigeuner Polka* of Conradi. Contradictions as strident as this are to be found attendant upon this extraordinary man through every stage of his career. What can have induced him to do such things? It is of no use to question his taste, because, at the same moment, in this and in exactly similar contingencies, he is to be found producing masterpieces of tact and delicacy by the very side of such trivial anomalies as the two salon pieces just mentioned. Neither, for this same reason, can his sense of porportion be disputed, for it can be argued that this was one of his pre-eminent qualities. But there was a want of discrimination in his vision. He was not French, or German, or Italian; he was a Hungarian, and his mildly barbarian origin, to use that word in its most complimentary sense, must account for these few discrepancies in his character. It gave him his brilliance and fire, with some of the penalities of that over-vehemence. Liszt, one of the chief histrions of the Romantic Age, was a consummate actor; it is only to be expected, then, that he should show some of the glitter of the footlights. The second of this pair of pieces dates from 1849, two years beyond the date to which we have followed his career. It is, therefore, the more striking as an illustration of his lapses and shortcomings, for it occurs in the middle of his great period of creation, when he was at work upon the Symphonic Poems.

But this chapter must not be ended upon a note of disillusionment. A pair of nondescript salon pieces cannot detract from the great achievement of the *Fantaisies Dramatiques*. His presentation of these Italian airs formed the bulk of his work as composer during the most sensational and brilliant years of his life, for the *Études Transcendantes* and the *Années de Pèlerinage* date from earlier years than these. It may be said with truth that the *Fantaisies*

Dramatiques are instinct with his grandiloquence, and that their old-fashioned manners and the perfection of their method are but the exterior shell to their inner, peculiar virtues. No better description of these could be found than in the phrases, just quoted, of Mr. Sorabji. The themes of Bellini, simple and beautiful in themselves, become absolutely transfigured as a result of the magical processes to which they are subjected. The *Don Juan* Fantasia has an indescribable and sinister virtuosity which is strangely in keeping with the cynical romanticism of its subject. Other pieces seem to interpret the opera house; the hard light of the stage, the chatter of the audience, the romantic trickery of the airs, so that in the *Réminiscences de Lucia di Lammermoor* we seem to be reading Flaubert's description of that opera in *Madame Bovary*. In the Tarantella from *Masaniello* the languor and light spirits of the old Kingdom of Naples are reproduced with a fidelity that is only matched in the delightful descriptions of that city given by Gregorovius in his *Siciliana*. In fact, in their way, the *Fantaisies Dramatiques* are so many expressions of mood and atmosphere.

Whatever their virtues, and whatever their defects, it would have been impossible to prophesy from this evidence the extraordinary developments that Liszt was to undergo. His whole life becomes transformed, now; he abandons his career, and embarks upon another. His fame as virtuoso, an empty title to someone with his ambitions, had spread from end to end of Europe, but he must have felt as if he had accomplished nothing, or less than nothing, in that sphere to which he was really drawn. A number of piano pieces, mere vehicles for his skill, and nothing more. Nothing that could compare with all the achievement of Chopin. It was time for him to begin; he was thirty-six years old, and would not be young for ever. It was late indeed, already.

BOOK III

1847-1861

Lizt at Weimar

CHAPTER XXIII

Madame d'Agoult turns into Daniel Stern—Liszt promises his services to Weimar—His last public concert tour—He plays in Kiev and meets Princess Carolyne of Sayn-Wittgenstein—Her history and origin—He is invited to Woronince—His last concert at Elizabetgrad

T he translation of Liszt into his new life was preluded by the usual emotional accompaniment, for a changed career and a fresh nationality meant no less than an alteration in everything. He ceased to be French and became, for the time being, to all intents and purposes, a German. Every one of his old shackles was broken; the Comtesse d'Agoult, after long probation in chrysalis form, had at last turned into Daniel Stern.* This masculine nom-de-plume was admirably suited to her temperament, and, henceforth, she was to console herself with literary projects conceived upon so immense a scale that they occupied all the rest of her long life and were only matched as feats of endurance, and, it may be added, in the quality of being completely unreadable, by the similar enterprises of the very person who was providing the new background for our hero's emotions.

The strength of this new character arrived into his life at just the right moment, for he had already, as is proved in his letters, decided upon his future. Its nucleus was to be the town of Weimar.

He had visited Weimar as early as 1841, when he played on three evenings to the Grand-Duchess Marie-Paulowna, sister of Tsar Nicholas I. He owed the success of his first Russian tour to her recommendations and he came back from Russia, the following year, for the marriage celebrations of her son, Karl-Alexander of Saxe-Weimar, with Princess Sophie of the Netherlands. The Grand-Duchess Marie-Paulowna at once urged upon Liszt that he should spend a part of each year at Weimar, and he entered enthusiastically into her plans.

Weimar had been the city of Goethe and of Schiller; and,

* His actual break with Madame d'Agoult took place in April, 1844.

indeed, we might say that no lover of the late Comtesse d'Agoult could regard this little German town without a spirit of reverence. The Grand-Duke Karl-August had been the Mæcenas of that age. What was to prevent its repetition under Karl-Alexander? And Liszt agreed, immediately, to sign a contract binding him to give his services every year for three months, as conductor and musical director, to the Grand-Ducal Court.

He entered upon his new duties in 1844, but the full realization of his ambition had to wait until he had finished his career of virtuoso. During his vagabondage all over Europe he must have thought with more and more longing of the opportunities and the leisure that were offered him at Weimar. For the greater part of each year he would be able to work undisturbed at his own music; while, during three months of the winter, he would be in complete control of the musical life of this small city and could produce any work that he pleased, in concert hall or opera house. He would have the full support of a Court without any of the distractions of a great capital. It seemed an ideal situation; and, at length, there were only his outstanding engagements to fulfil before he could give the whole of his time and energies to the enterprise.

His last public concerts took place in the Ukraine and in the south of Russia. In the early months of 1847 he gave a series of recitals at Kiev. Liszt gives a delightful sketch of this city in his book on Gypsy music, and it is obvious that he was keenly alive to its picturesque character and to the barbaric charm of its domed churches.

Kiev has been described by travellers as the most beautiful inland city in Europe. The fact that it was in the possession of Poland until the reign of Peter the Great has given its delayed Byzantinism a more decided architectural unity than is to be found in other Russian towns. This was augmented during the eighteenth century, under Russian rule, by many churches and convents built in a curious, bastard Rococo. These experiments in tinted stucco culminated in the church of St. Andrew, designed by the Italian Rastrelli, architect of Tsarsköe-Selo and the Winter Palace. It stands on a cliff above the city; and Liszt, who loved Rome, was the first to appreciate its Italian, but exotic, charm. The terrace, outside this church, gives a wonderful view over the whole city. Its golden domes sparkled in the sun, and the chanting of thousand of pilgrims in the town below mingled with the violin and cymbalon of the Gypsies huddled in the dust near at hand. These nomads had, in fact, an enormous encampment just outside the town. But they were no more wild and unlikely in their looks than the strange figures in all the streets. Barefoot pilgrims jostled with checked and embroidered peasants come in to market: bearded and black-hatted priests and monks rubbed shoulders with Circassians and with merchants from Isfahan and Bokhara. The Jews, repulsive and cringing where all other races were picturesque, were universal with their oily locks and stained gabardines; and there were Tartars and Cossacks, Monghols of the Kirghiz, and the pale men of the North with flaxen hair and fair beards.

Liszt had come to this curious city out of a remote distance. But, if it was another world compared to Paris where he had spent his youth, it showed at least some points of resemblance to his early memories of Hungary. The rich cornfields, or the dreary steppes of the Ukraine, these were not so far removed in appearance and in atmosphere from the plains and salt lakes of the Puszta. In the background there was the same contrasted life of peasant cabin and feudal mansion. And it was in this very contrast that he was to find his affinity.

The series of recitals that he gave in Kiev ended in a performance for charity, and a letter arrived for him on the morning of this final concert enclosing a hundred-rouble note with a message written in terms of the utmost enthusiasm. On the following day Liszt paid a call of ceremony on his correspondent, and from that moment his fate was sealed.

Her name was the Princess Carolyne of Sayn-Wittgenstein. She was twenty-eight years old, some eight years younger than our hero; the daughter of a great Polish landowner, Peter von Iwanowski and his wife, Pauline Podowska. She had been married, at seventeen, to Prince Nicholas of Sayn-Wittgenstein,* a Russian branch of the Westphalian family of that name; and her husband, who was a millionaire, was adjutant to the Tsar. They had one daughter, the Princess Marie, or Magnolet as she was called by our hero, but their temperaments were so ill matched that husband and wife agreed on a separation three or

---

*His grandfather, Prince Christian-Casimir, had emigrated to Russia and entered the service of the Empress Elizabeth.

four years after their marriage, and the Princess was left to live upon her estates.

The force of her masculine temperament was not likely to be long satisfied with this. She was in need of some outlet for her energies. Her solitude had been solaced by incessant reading, and the seriousness of her thoughts made it a necessity that she should meet every single person of interest who arrived into her sphere of life. Liszt was playing in Kiev. She must make his acquaintance.

For the first time Liszt was dealing with a woman who was younger than himself. Their acquaintance must have begun upon easy terms, for they had in Paris many friends in common. There was, for instance, the inevitable Countess Potocka who was the friend of Chopin and of Liszt. But they had much more serious bonds than these; and, indeed, this adjective best describes the whole tendency of their ripening friendship. The same literary tastes accounted for a good deal in it; and when the Princess heard of his intention to retire from the concert platform and devote himself to his own compositions and to furthering the works of other composers, it is certain that her curiosity about his character must have deepened into determination. Both of them were deeply religious: that was another, and a most important, link between them.

It was only a few days before Liszt received an invitation to stay with her at Woronince. This was the chief of her estates; and these were of immense size, as is proved by the fact that she had inherited no less than thirty thousand serfs from her father. Woronince was in Podolia, a region which is of permanent pianistic interest as having been the birthplace of Paderewski, who was born near the little town of Kurylowka. The whole of this region is now separated from Poland and submerged in Soviet Russia, Kurylowka being some hundred miles within that dread frontier. Woronince, too, has disappeared; and, indeed, the whole of this region of Podolia is mysterious to our age because so effectually lost from our sight.

The château of Woronince would seem to have been built early in the last century upon vaguely classical lines. It had great avenues, ornamental canals, and woods with long rides cut through them. There were more foresters than gardeners, and the lawns were swept with brooms by barefoot peasant women. The horizon was infinite, and lost in distance on the plain.

Inside, the atmosphere of the house was exactly what one would expect of its associations. Each room was a different colour; there was a library with Dante and Goethe lying open upon the table, and a music-room furnished with bearskin rugs on which the Princess would lie in oriental repose, listening. Near her, there was ever a little stool of Egyptian or Turkish workmanship, inlaid with mother of pearl. This was to support her box of cigars, for she was never without them. It was another taste they had in common.

The servants, who were legion, slept anywhere and everywhere, wrapped in a blanket, along the passages and outside the doors of the bedrooms. When it snowed, or during the long evenings, they sang together in unison, like a choir, and accompanied themselves on the balalaika and other stringed instruments. In fact, as an environment for this pair of lovers Woronince was both romantic and convenient.

By the time that Liszt left her, after a few weeks of this life, their plans for the future were all settled. He had only the very last of his public engagements to fulfil. The ultimate concert of all took place in October, at Elizabetgrad, in the extreme south of Russia, now rechristened Stalingrad by the Soviet.

After this, he never played again in public for money. In fact, as he wrote to his friend and biographer, La Mara, much later in life, 'Since the end of '47 I have not earned a single farthing by piano playing, teaching, or conducting. All this rather cost me time and money.'

And, after Elizabetgrad, he went back once more to Woronince for a holiday of some four months. He had to rest before proceeding to Weimar; though repose, to him, was anything but idleness, for he was already at work upon a new and vast scheme of compositions. And the Princess had made up her mind. She would divorce her husband in order to marry Liszt, and they would live together at Weimar.

CHAPTER XXIV

*From Woronince to Weimar—The Villa Altenburg described—
Miss Anderson, or 'Scottie'*

Progress from Woronince to Weimar took place by formal,
almost processional, stages, even if one of these, as we shall
show, was a little precipitate. Liszt was the first to leave;
and the Princess followed as soon as she realized the money from
the sale of some property.

It was difficult in those days for Russian subjects, even for the
aristocrats, to leave Russia without permission from the Government,
and the Princess, whose matrimonial intentions had become
known, and whose husband was adjutant to the Tsar, was not
likely to obtain the necessary police permit. It was essential to
think of some compromise, and eventually, for reasons of health
and on the grounds no doubt that Europe was a big place, she was
given permission to go to Carlsbad for a cure. Just at that moment
the troubles of 1848 reached their climax, and what must have
seemed like universal revolution broke forth. The Princess was
only just in time. The couriers of the Tsar reached the barrier at
full gallop, just behind her, and the frontier was closed to all
comers, whether for entry or exit.

Once safely in the Austrian dominions she proceeded by easy
stages to meet her lover. Their rendezvous was the castle of
Krzyzanowitz, lent to them by Lichnowsky, and what there was
of doom about this whole episode escaped them both and fell
upon their friend and protector, for Lichnowsky was soon to fall
victim to a mob of frenzied revolutionaries in Frankfurt.

Meanwhile, there was an idyllic peace, and Liszt was at work
again upon the orchestration of more than one of his Symphonic
Poems. When, at last, the time came to leave Krzyzanowitz they
went together, first of all, to visit the scenes of his childhood, to
Raiding and to Eisenstadt, places to which he had not dared to
bring his former love, the Comtesse d'Agoult. But their own
situation was very different, or so it seemed to them both, for no
doubt can have existed in their minds that they would very shortly
be married.

146

Princess Carolyne
Sayn-Wittgenstein
in 1876

Liszt playing at a concert in Budapest in 1872

Baudelaire, a photograph by Carjat, in about 1865

Liszt was the first to arrive in Weimar, and there was a passionate interchange of letters between them as the Princess came nearer and nearer to their new home. After many delays she arrived there, in February, 1849, and for the first few months they lived under separate roofs. Reports would be quickly carried back from Weimar to St. Petersburg and caution was necessary. They were sure of the friendship of the Grand Duchess Marie-Paulowna; but her brother, the Tsar, had already listened to the complaints of the Sayn-Wittgenstein family and had made up his mind to protect their estates from possible alienation by divorce. So, at first, Liszt lived at the Erbprinz Hotel, while the Princess installed herself at the Altenburg. But this arrangement was only temporary, and before many months had elapsed Liszt joined the Princess and shared the Villa Altenburg with her.

This is the moment, in fact, to attempt some description of their home, for they were to live there, together, during twelve years. The Altenburg is an unpretentious villa, but built on a scale large enough to hold the Princess and her daughter while Liszt was accommodated in a separate wing looking over the garden. This consisted of two rooms, his bedroom and his study. It was here that he worked, and there were only two pictures upon the walls: Dürer's engraving of Melancholia and a drawing of St. François de Paule walking on the waves, the latter being of interest to us because it was to inspire him to one of the most striking among his mature compositions.

All there was of interest in the Altenburg was contained in the main rooms of the villa that he shared with the Princess. These consisted of at least four large drawing-rooms or libraries, unless we call them all music-rooms, for this was their reality. The biggest of these rooms held his concert piano, and the walls were decorated with medallions of Berlioz and of Wagner and with the death mask of Beethoven. A smaller room, leading out of this, contained Liszt's collection of swords of honour given him in Hungary, in Russia, and in Turkey; and, chief among these, the jewelled sabre which provoked the quatrain we have quoted on page 87. The decorations of this room were oriental tables inlaid with mother of pearl, Turkish coffee-trays, rugs, and pipes.

The floor above consisted of the library with all his collection of autographed first editions and manuscripts of the great composers. There was, also, the Broadwood upon which Beethoven had last played. The actual music-room was next door to this. It contained his favourite Erard; a small, early piano said to have belonged to Mozart; and the giant instrument built to his own design, with three keyboards, sixteen registers, and stops which reproduced the tones of every wind instrument. This was long in the making, and final delivery did not take place until Liszt had been living in the Altenburg for some eight years.

As if to complete the Altenburg in its Victorian furnishings we must report the presence there of Miss Anderson, a Scotch governess. Her charge was Magnolet, the daughter of the Princess, and quite a little history can be read into the mention of her in Liszt's letters. She appears in them as 'Scotch', as 'Scottie', or just 'Scotland'. 'Tell Magnolet to give my "shake-hands" and accolades de tendresse to Scotland.' 'Tell Magnolet to give my respects to Scotland, à laquelle je pense souvent et doucement.' When the family are away he dines alone with Scotland, and plays 'cinq parties de sixty-six avec Scotch, dont j'ai gagné trois et une double'. On another occasion he sends messages to Miss Anderson and to the nightingale in the garden. Miss Anderson was a slight distraction to his thoughts, it would seem.

In fact, Miss Anderson apart, the interior of the Altenburg sounds very practical and very ugly. But this was the decade of the 'fifties, the years of the Crimean War and the Indian Mutiny. Take away the pianos, and it is the exact background in which an artist like Flaubert had to work! Take away the pianos and put in their place still more bric-à-brac, and it is the background of Balzac! Make it all uglier still, hang it with pink satin and spray it with Rose de Bengale, and they are rooms worthy of Wagner!

So here is the pianist, firmly, and it would seem finally, established at Weimar. All his virtuosity he had cast aside: his new career had begun. He was reborn, but with all the experience of his former life, and had nothing to learn of the world, at least. His career, for the next twelve years, was to be an epitome of the most extreme energy to be found in the career of any musician, or, indeed, any artist, in history. But the details are so profuse and so interesting that we must enter, at once, upon their discussion.

CHAPTER XXV

*Magical prestige of Liszt described by Saint-Saëns—The operas produced by Liszt at Weimar—His literary works—*The Life of Chopin

'It is impossible to believe the force and the magical prestige that attached to the name of Liszt in the eyes of all young musicians during the first years of the Imperial epoch of Napoleon III. This name of Liszt, sounding strangely enough, in any case, to us Frenchmen, sharp and whistling in its sound, like a sword cutting the air, traversed and sliced in two by the "z" of the Slavs, as if by the furrow of the lightning. . . . Both as man and artist he seemed to belong to the world of legend. After having been the incarnation at his instrument of all the flourish (le panache) of the Romantic Age, while he left behind him the glittering trail of a meteor, Liszt had vanished behind the curtain of clouds which hid the Germany of that time, so different from the Germany of our own day: a Germany made up of an agglomerate of little kingdoms and autonomous duchies, bristling with battlemented castles, and preserving, even in the Gothic character of its handwriting, the imprint of those Middle Ages which had vanished for ever from our midst, in spite of the efforts of our poets to restore them and keep them living. The majority of the pieces that Liszt had so far published seemed impossible of execution to anyone but himself, and were, in very truth, if one considers all the processes of the old method of pianism which prescribed absolute immobility, elbows touching the body, and all action of the muscles limited to the fingers and the forearm. We knew that at the Court of Weimar, disdaining his former principles, Liszt occupied himself with the highest forms of composition, dreaming of a rebirth of the art of music, and being, for that reason, the subject of the most disquieting rumours, as is always the case with those whose intention it is to explore a new world and to break with accepted traditions.'

This passage, which has been freely translated from the *Portraits et Souvenirs* of Saint-Saëns, gives, one may think, the fair measure of Liszt's renown at this new beginning of his life.

Saint-Saëns, who lived to the age of eighty-seven, and was conducting the opera season at Algiers as short a time ago as 1920, the
year before he died, had become almost a legend himself, not, it is
needless to say, because of his own music, but for his association
with the giants of sixty years before, with Liszt in the height of his
fame, and with Berlioz. This old and lonely ghost remembered
everything but had no means of expressing himself in speech. In
the two or three volumes of memoirs that he wrote there is not a
single anecdote worth quoting, not a scrap of atmosphere. All he
had to say of moment in these several hundreds of pages is this
passage that I have just translated concerning Liszt. Except for that
there is nothing. But Liszt had moved him so powerfully that he
found the phrases, and we are reminded of that one other incident
of literature in the *Life and Letters of Sir Charles Hallé*, where
Paganini is mentioned. It was, also, a phrase with Saint-Saëns that
his memories of Liszt, playing, were his one consolation in
growing old.

The prestige and the renown of Liszt were, in fact, enormous,
and all the force of his personality was, from now onwards,
directed upon unselfish ends. This greatest of all virtuosi, who
had been earning thousands of pounds a year, and whose financial
prospects may be said to have been unlimited with another forty
years of public career still before him, gave all his services and all
his energy to Weimar for the paltry salary of £200 a year. He
was, also, in possession of a very small private income secured
from certain sums that he had invested with his cousin, the
Chancellor Eduard Liszt,* who was, throughout life, his friend
and financial adviser. After these twelve years, when Liszt resigned
from Weimar, his income was smaller still from the loss of that
emolument; but it is safe to say that for the next forty years his
income never exceeded the equivalent of some three or four
hundred pounds a year. And most of this he derived from his
publishers; not through the sale of his own compositions, which
were never a financial success, but through his *Partitions de piano*.

He had his liberty; he was untrammelled by money and had
broken the fetters that bound him to his instrument. He effected,
in this way, a complete alteration in his own life, and must have
had the sensation, as much as any human being can ever believe in

---

*The death of Eduard Liszt, in 1879, removed one of Liszt's dearest friends
and exposed him to much financial worry in his last years.

its truth, that he had changed his own destiny. His concern, or the reason for this sacrifice and these ambitions, was the music of the future. This meant, first and foremost, and to an ever-increasing degree, the music of Wagner; but so important was their association that it must be kept for separate discussion. And, when that has been said, we must follow his own unvarying precedent and talk of the music of others before we come to music of his own.

His activity in the production of opera was formidable, for he rehearsed with endless patience and supervised the most minute details. It was no small feat, in itself, to produce at that day, four operas by Gluck: *Orpheus, Iphigenia, Armida, Alceste*; *Don Giovanni* and the *Magic Flute* of Mozart; the *Euryanthe* of Weber. Indeed, the revival of Gluck's operas amounted to a real resuscitation, for they were absolutely unfamiliar to a contemporary audience. The *Alphonso und Estrella* of Schubert was another complete novelty; in fact, this opera received its first performance at his hands. *Fidelio*, also, was nearly unknown to the public. In grand opera, he mounted and produced on a lavish scale *Le Pré aux Clercs* of Hérold and *La Juive* of Halévy, several operas by Cherubini and Spontini and the most elaborate and spectacular operas of Meyerbeer. Much of Rossini, Donizetti, and Bellini figured, as well, in his programmes, including the comic operas, *La Gazza Ladra, L'Italiana in Algeri*, and *Le Comte Ory* of the former; also, *Ernani* and *I due Foscari* of Verdi. In addition to all these he produced, despite the growing and unreasonable hostility of the composer, *Faust, Manfred, Geneviève*, and *Paradise and the Péri* of Schumann. Works of minor importance: *King Alfred* by Raff, the *Barber of Baghdad* by Cornelius, can have given him scarcely less pains than such troublesome productions as the *Benvenuto Cellini* of Berlioz. Yet it is certain that all this vast display of energy was subservient, in his mind, to what he considered to be the true function of his operatic activities, the first production of the operas of Wagner.

In the concert hall, his programmes were no less comprehensive. All of Beethoven's Symphonies, including the, then, rarely heard Ninth; much of Mozart and Haydn; the Symphonies of Mendelssohn and Schumann; in Oratorio, *The Messiah* and the *Samson* of Handel; these are but to name the more obvious items upon his programmes. On occasion, he would give a programme devoted to the works of one composer. An entire week of Berlioz was, perhaps, the most ambitious of these undertakings. It included performances of *Benvenuto Cellini*, *Romeo and Juliet*, the *Damnation of Faust*, the *Symphonie Fantastique*, *Harold in Italy*, and the overtures to *Waverley*, *King Lear* and the *Corsair*.

But this is not the only importance of his concert work; for it may be said that with his orchestra at Weimar we have reached the foundation of the first modern orchestra as it is understood to-day. The first standards of modern orchestral playing were achieved under his direction. Not this alone, but Liszt was the first modern conductor; and, in leaving the concert platform in his rôle of pianist and taking up his new post at the conductor's desk Liszt was pointing the way towards that new kind of virtuosity which has been the discovery, and, in some ways, the unfortunate discovery, of our own century, when the virtuoso at the conductor's desk has a more sensational part to play than the solo player in a concerto. It is only necessary to look at the Royal Philharmonic Orchestra in the background of Maclise's drawing of Paganini playing (in the Victoria and Albert Museum), in order to see the extent to which an orchestra had altered during the score of years between 1831 and the years of which we are speaking. Their casual and listless attitudes argue ill for orchestral discipline, and it is probable that their ensemble would sound out of place, to-day, in a provincial theatre. It was a matter of choice, even, as to whether a conductor used a bâton or led the orchestra with a violin. The composer Spontini, who was by repute the best conductor of his day and who bore, in rigour of discipline, in method, and in point of physiognomy, an extraordinary resemblance to Toscanini, was in the habit of conducting his orchestra with an ivory, jewel-mounted bâton, which he grasped in the middle.

The reform and the progress of orchestra are due in the first place to Liszt. Given equal opportunities, perhaps the genius of Berlioz would have achieved even greater, if more selfish, results; but Berlioz was never in the position of having a permanent orchestra at his command, and certainly, at his hands, the music of his contemporaries would have suffered a purposeful eclipse. Liszt was the first, therefore, of the race of great conductors. Even so, it is certain that the orchestra at Weimar must have been very far from satisfactory, for expenses were strictly limited. But the extraordinary extent of his personal experience, compared with that of any other practising musician, gave Liszt an authority which was possessed by no one else and his inspiration, or his dæmon, must have secured some most remarkable performances.

In pursuance of his plans for making Weimar a capital of all the arts Liszt inaugurated the Goethe Foundation, which was intended to be an annual contest and international reunion of musicians, painters, and poets. But, after a great deal of trouble, this scheme collapsed, when only one or two of the meetings had been held. The project was, obviously, impossible of realization. Music was in its heyday; but where were the artists? In all Central Europe there was not one painter deserving of that name. The scheme could take no practical form and had to be accounted a failure. The Goethe Foundation must have occupied, none the less, a great deal of his time and attention during the first few years at Weimar.

In addition to all this Liszt was busily engaged upon various literary projects, some of them of no more than a journalistic importance, though even these must have taken much time and trouble to prepare. Others were of some literary pretension. His essays upon the early operas of Wagner, and similar works dealing with the operas *Fidelio*, *Orpheus*, and *Euryanthe*, were works of pioneer importance in musical criticism.

There was, also, his big book upon Chopin, written soon after the composer's death, and published in 1852. It is customary to deride this as being emotional and superficial. There is, certainly, nothing of technical discussion to be found within its covers, and it is possible, perhaps, to trace the helping hand of the Princess upon certain of its pages. Without her assistance, it is difficult to to see how Liszt could have written in such detail upon the use of consonants in the Polish language, while the touch of the typical Polish aristocrat is evident whenever any event in Polish history is mentioned. And it must be conceded that the book is so loosely written that its quality, almost, may be said to exist in its irrelevancies.

But it is the last document of the Romantic Age from the pen of one of the greatest actors in that period. It establishes, once and for all, the imaginative atmosphere in the way that it is presented in no novel and in no other work of criticism. The chapters on the polonaise and the mazurka, on their own literary merits and without considering that they are written by Liszt, to the memory of Chopin, are no less important in the history of romanticism than the finest pages of Trelawney or Borrow, of Beckford or of Gautier. They throw much light upon the history of taste in that day, and should not be neglected by anyone who loves the music and the poetry of that period. They give a new force to the phrase quoted at the beginning of this chapter where it is said that Liszt had been 'the incarnation of all the panache of the Romantic Age'. It is the man who played Chopin better than Chopin himself, and closer to the composer's intentions, who wrote these pages. As a young man, still in his twenties, he had been, as virtuoso, the rival of Paganini; since then, he had been the impersonation of the Romantic Age and had carried its fame from end to end of the civilized world; his life and his actions were wholly without precedent. This book is his postcript to the Romantic Age.

The period was dead, it died with the Revolution of 1848; and Chopin, who died the year after it, and Liszt, who abandoned his career the year before it, may be said to have dealt, in their different ways, death blows to the whole movement. The frantic energies shown by Liszt during these ensuing years were his attempt to organize upon a new basis. His immense programme of work was intended to consolidate the past and display the present. It might be, though, that he would have time for nothing else during these years, but we shall see in the next chapter that his true importance as composer had but just begun.

CHAPTER XXVI

The Twelve Symphonic Poems

Above all else, these were the years of his Symphonic Poems. In the twenty years that had elapsed since the death of Beethoven almost the only contribution to symphonic music had been due to Mendelssohn. His *Italian* and *Scotch Symphonies*, his incidental music to the *Midsummer Night's Dream*, are the proofs of his new orientation, though his early death, and, perhaps, his facility, ruled out the possible ultimate developments of which this form was capable. But Mendelssohn had broken the silence; and, after the death of Beethoven, there was necessarily an interval of pause. A new direction had to be given, and the person behind this had to be possessed of sufficient genius and enough force of character to make effectual this change in musical form and material.

The most interesting facet in this transformation of Liszt that we are about to witness lies in the fact that at thirty-six years of age he was almost completely inexperienced in orchestral writing. It would seem inconceivable that a man who had spent his life at the keyboard of a piano should be able to develop above that technique—and what a technique!—into the vaster regions of a complete orchestra. Yet he was to present the future and all its possibilities in a series of symphonic pieces that, if they are very uneven in merit, show nearly every range of possibility as regards both subject and treatment. Even the very term, Symphonic Poem, was an invention of Liszt, who was ever an adept in nomenclature. He devised the piano recital, and had now arrived at the Symphonic Poem.

They are actually twelve in number, and these are their titles:*

1. *Héroïde Funèbre.*	7. *Prometheus.*
2. *Tasso—Lamento e Trionfo.*	8. *Festklänge.*
3. *Les Préludes.*	9. *Orpheus.*
4. *Hungaria.*	10. *Hunnenschlacht.*
5. *Berg-Symphonie.*	11. *Die Ideale.*
6. *Mazeppa.*	12. *Hamlet.*

The first of these, *Héroïde Funèbre*, had been sketched out as long ago as 1830, and was, at that time, intended to form the first movement of a *Symphonie Révolutionnaire*. In execution, it was postponed until the next revolution, that of 1848, and his political views, which had changed during this score of years, made it assume a very different character, in which it can be interpreted as an elegy upon the death of Chopin, and upon the murder, by a revolutionary mob, of his friend, Lichnowsky. It begins with a prolonged and terrible fanfare, in which the tocsin of the revolution, the throbbing of drums, the pealing of bells, the universal

---

*This is the order in which the Symphonic Poems are mentioned in Grove, but it does not tally with the order in which Liszt arranged them for the published edition.

sobbing and wailing, are maintained until they become un-endurable. The effect of this opening of the piece is remarkable.

Of the other Symphonic Poems, the familiar *Les Préludes*, the *Berg-Symphonie*, *Prometheus*, and *Die Ideale* can be classed together as being less interesting and those in which Liszt had the least to express. Their inspiration, perhaps, comes too directly from literature. Music founded upon Lamartine's *Méditations Poétiques*, *Les Préludes*; upon *Ce qu'on entend sur la montagne*, the *Berg-Symphonie*; upon a poem by Schiller, *Die Ideale*; music from such sources as these is only too apt to betray its own limitations. The holes and patches show too clearly. It is, therefore, not the actual results but the working of the system that is interesting in the pieces named, for they are remarkable in their progeny. This need be specified in no more detail than by the mention of Richard Strauss. If, indeed, *Till Eulenspiegel, Don Quixote, Don Juan, Tod und Verklärung, Heldenleben,* are not the descendants of these other symphonic poems of fifty years before, it can only be said that all the originality of Strauss consisted in the greater violence with which he gave expression to these voices of a generation earlier than his own. Unfortunately, with the exception of *Les Préludes*, these pieces by Liszt are so seldom performed that it is difficult to form any clear idea of their faults or merits. And this has always been the case, even in the lifetime of the composer, as is proved by his *Hamlet*, which was published in 1861 and never performed until 1886. In fact, his period of neglect had already begun, even in the very height of his fame at Weimar. It still continues. Neither *Hamlet*, nor the equally interesting *Orpheus*, ever appear in any programme.

We will turn, now, from this forgotten *Hamlet* to the more sensational of his Symphonic Poems. *Mazeppa* has never been denied a hearing, and is still to be found in programmes at fairly frequent intervals. Liszt took this directly from his *Étude Transcendante* of that name and adapted it for orchestra, adding the Tartar March at the end. It is easy, nevertheless, to prefer *Mazeppa* as a piano piece. The orchestral web is too thin and, even, the programme too obvious. Yet there have been Tartar Marches ever since. Tchaikowsky and Borodin are convincing proofs of the importance that *Mazeppa* must have possessed in its day.

After this flat and shallow music it is more interesting to come to *Tasso*. This, again, had been conceived in the first place as a work for pianoforte; but it was eventually produced, during these years at Weimar, as an introduction, or overture, to Goethe's *Tasso*. It continued, though, to occupy the composer's thoughts to a much greater degree than most of the other Symphonic Poems. In fact, *Tasso* came to assume, almost, the dimensions of his great *Dante* and *Faust Symphonies*, for he added an Epilogue, *Le Triomphe Funèbre de Tasso*, finished as late as 1878 and only published after his death.

Tasso must have become identified in his mind with the sorrows and the resignations of his own old age, when no one would listen to him, when his own music was never performed. The matchless brilliance of his early career had spoilt everything. His incomparable gift as interpreter and executant had prevented the recognition of his own genius as composer. Therefore, as he had broken his career in order to give his talent the time and the opportunity it needed, and the world still refused him a hearing, he found himself living in a peculiar loneliness in which he was still allowed his early fame and renown but anything more than this was refused to him by public opinion. This was like the fearful isolation of Tasso's later years. Tasso, too, had been the sensation of civilized Europe when he was a child. When only some twenty-five years of age, the strain of his nerves from overwork, the ravages of an unhappy love affair, and the effect of these different forces upon his too nervous and febrile constitution, brought on a dreadful collapse of all his sensibilities. His mind was impaired and the brain so injured that his faculties were crippled. Legend has it that he was imprisoned by the Duke Alfonso of Ferrara because of his attachment to the Duke's sister, the Princess Lucrezia.* Certainly their letters to each other breathe something more than mere friendship, even if it is more probable that his detention by the Duke at the villa of Belriguardo was an act of kindness and that the state of his mind made it necessary to keep him under restraint. The actual cause of Tasso's imprisonment was when he recited his sorrows, one day, to the Princess Lucrezia and, imagining that a servant was listening, rushed upon him, knife in hand. He was removed under armed guard to Belriguardo and afterwards to a Capuchin convent.

* She was granddaughter to Lucrezia Borgia. This princess, with her sister Leonora, and their brother Duke Alfonso, made Ferrara the most cultured Court in Europe.

When, eventually, Tasso was able to leave Ferrara, the details of his life become yet more extraordinary. He wandered from Court to Court, received everywhere with the marks of respect due to his genius, but treated by his hosts with a sort of amused kindness. As a chronicle of life, the later years of Tasso are as romantic and pathetic as anything to be found in history. He could do no work and was a penniless wanderer, the living ghost of his own achievement.

Liszt must have seen the parallel between his own life and that of Tasso. Both careers were wrecked by their early genius. The life of Tasso, after, so to speak, his own death, is one of the romances of history. But he was assured a posthumous fame, a Triomphe Funèbre, such as has not been accorded to Liszt, whose greater works are still neglected in favour of the cheapest and most trivial of his compositions. In one of his letters, written at a much later date, we find an indication of the material employed by Liszt in his Epilogue to *Tasso*. He made use, in fact, of a melody to which, three centuries after the poet's death, he had heard Venetian gondoliers sing the first strophes of *Gerusalemme Liberata*.

'Canto l'armi pietose e'l Capitano
Che'l gran Sepolcro liberò di Cristo.'

'This song', says Liszt, 'once made a profound impression upon me. The motive, itself, was a slow plaintive cadence of monotonous mourning; the gondoliers, however, by drawling certain notes, give it a peculiar colouring, and the mournfully drawn-out tones, heard at a distance, produce an effect not dissimilar to the reflection of long stripes of fading light upon a mirror of water.' And, it may be added, in parenthesis, that the above sentence by Liszt is of interest in itself, for it is typical of his prose style and it proves that the flamboyant images in his writings, in, for instance, his books on Chopin and on Gypsy music, are of his own invention and not the creation, as has been too often assumed, of the Princess.

In spite of all this, I believe it to be the fact that the *Tasso Symphony* is not really successful in performance. It suffers, apparently, from those faults of obviousness that were the bane of all Liszt's orchestral writing where he was not inspired and carried away by his subject. In all the Symphonic Poems so far mentioned, there are, indeed, the failings of the amateur. Liszt had come to the orchestra too late.

But three of the Symphonic Poems still remain for discussion, and they redeem the others. The subject matter of *Hungaria* is clearly indicated by its title, and, in performance, this symphonic poem is magnificently to the point. Its quality is the quality of Chabrier, open and glittering, immediately effective, with some appeal to every taste in the audience. And in the introduction to the larger and more extended version of *Hungaria* a distinct anticipation of Siegfried's Funeral March is to be found.

Festklänge is quite another type of composition. The French title, *Bruits de Fête*, is a second indication of its nature. Mr. James Huneker assumes, and he was probably right, that this piece was written to glorify his coming marriage with the Princess. 'The introductory allegro', we quote Mr. Huneker's vigorous words, 'is devoted to some tympani thumps—à la Meyerbeer—and some blaring fanfares which terminate in a loud blatant theme. Then comes the andante with the principal subject. Eventually it launches into a polonaise, and, until the close, Liszt busies himself with varying the character and rhythms of the foregoing themes. Finally, the martial prevails again, decorated with fanfares, and thus the composition closes.' *Festklänge* is, in fact, part Meyerbeer, part Rimsky-Korsakov.

Variants and additions to *Festklänge* were published posthumously, and may have been written by Liszt as late as 1886, the year of his death, so that this piece, also, was one which preoccupied his attention. This makes it the more to be regretted that, so far as the writer knows, no performance of *Festklänge* has been given of recent years.

We come, finally, to *Hunnenschlacht*, the Battle of the Huns, the finest of the whole series of Symphonic Poems. It was suggested to Liszt by an immense picture painted by Kaulbach, an extremely bad painter, famous in his day. But the inspiration might have come, just as well, from Verestchagin, from Meissonier, or even from Lady Butler. The music has nothing whatever to do with its original inception. In fact, in its way, *Hunnenschlacht* is something unique in music; and, if it remains extraordinary now, what must its effect have been in 1861, when it was first performed? It is the first half of the music that is most striking; though an extraordinary effect is achieved in the final chorale on the wind instruments, accompanied by bell-like scales on the strings, which is reminiscent of Moussorgsky's 'Great Gate of Kiev'.* But the beginning of *Hunnenschlacht* is magnificent and terrifying. It has to be heard to be believed. The opening moments are one of the most extraordinary sensations in music, reminiscent in quality and in timbre, and shall we say, in calibre—though not in any respect directly comparable—to the most inspired Berlioz. And the orchestral writing is so masterly, its effects are so peculiar and so extreme, that it is impossible to believe the same hand is responsible that wrote the banalities of *Mazeppa* and *Les Préludes.* This is the great Liszt—the Liszt of the *Faust Symphony*, the *Mephisto-Waltz*, the *Thirteenth Psalm*.

Liszt wrote one more Symphonic Poem, not included in the twelve here mentioned. This was called *Von der Wiege bis zum Grabe* (From Cradle to Grave). It was in three parts and was published and, it would appear, written, as late as 1883; but the fact that it is another, if belated, member of the same family of his music makes it more easy to name it at this point of the narrative. This piece appears to be completely unknown, and no performance of it can be traced. It is quite short, the full score only extending to twenty-five pages. The three sections into which it is divided are concerned, it is hardly necessary to explain, with the three stages of life. It is the Victorian three-volume novel, all over again; but the last section, with its very original use of simple diatonic harmonics and poetic reminiscences of the trumpet call in the middle section, is by far the best part of the work. And it displays the extreme economy of notes that characterizes the late, and unknown, works of Liszt. This last of his Symphonic Poems should most certainly be given a performance. It may turn out that this is no unfitting conclusion to the whole series. At least three of them are of extreme musical importance. Thus prepared, it is an easy transition to Liszt in the finest moments of all his achievement.

---

* 'The Great Gate of Kiev' is the finale of Moussorgsky's *Pictures from an Exhibition*. The pieces were written for piano, but the effect to which I refer is in the orchestral version scored by Ravel.

CHAPTER XXVII
The Faust *and* Dante Symphonies

There were three books that Liszt never allowed out of his sight. These were his Breviary, Dante, and Goethe's *Faust*.* They were in every room that Liszt occupied, on the shores of Lake Como, in Weimar, and by the fountains of Villa d'Este. They accompanied him, in early days, in the diligence, from his parting with Madame d'Agoult, at San Rossore, to Vienna and to Budapest; they had their place in his specially constructed caravan, while he toured Russia and the Ukraine; and, in his last years, when he spent nights in the train from Rome to Budapest, in those smoky tunnels between Florence and Bologna; or on that longer journey still, from Rome to Weimar, while the train toiled through the mountains and the gaslit carriage became damp with steam, the old priest, who was sleepless, would be reading one or other of these books until the dawn. Dante and *Faust* were as much a part of his life as Shakespeare and Virgil were to Berlioz. His personality and his whole thoughts were moulded by them. His very identity became inseparable from their atmosphere, so that, physically and mentally, he was part of their legend.

As he grew older, this became more and more true of him. If he felt some affinity of the spirit, some parallel between his own life and that of Tasso, there were points of resemblance still more striking that made his own middle age like that of Doctor Faustus. The more conscious he became of the failings of his own genius; the more disappointed he was with the neglect of his music; his ever-increasing sadness and disillusionment; all these things but make the likeness more apposite. He had all the resources, and not the supreme gift. He had all his skill and the matchless brilliance of his technique; he could enchant any audience and lift them out of their senses; in his own compositions he had opened up new

---

* The original copy of Goethe's *Faust* that belonged to Liszt, with many pencil-marks in his writing, was one of the treasured possessions of the late Sir Alexander Mackenzie. I have held it in my hands. This romantic relic was bequeathed to him by Miss Constance Bache.

regions never before touched by music; but the gift of life, the absolute secret of creation was never his. It was denied to him.

No alchemist, no Doctor Faustus had ever such opportunities as Liszt. Fortune had showered her presents upon him so profusely that he had thrown one half of them, one half of his life, away. He had left the stage and locked himself in the study. He would work, no longer for his own advantage, but for others, and he laboured unselfishly, denying himself his gifts of gain, ceaselessly experimenting. And all his researches brought him nothing but loss and disappointment.

If Liszt is established in history, for ever, as the equal and rival to Paganini: if he is, for always, the virtuoso, the magician, personified: then how much more applicable to his personality and to the truth of his life is that remark of the poet Heine, quoted in a previous chapter of this book, who, when he saw Paganini and his mysterious secretary, Mr. George Harrys of Hanover, compared the pair of them to Faust and Wagner walking before the gates of Leipzig. For Liszt was haunted and obsessed by the real Wagner. The greatest material success during his lifetime, ever vouchsafed to any artist, was granted to this extraordinary being, whose destiny was bound up with that of Liszt to such an extent that they are for ever associated together. And his very success was due in large measure to the efforts of Liszt, who had thrown away of his own will, half of his own talents and could achieve no success with the other half. It was Liszt who worked the hardest for his cause; nor, in the arrogant assurance of his own genius, did he scruple to make use of Liszt to his own advantage, to depend upon his energies for the furtherance of his own works, to obtain money through his good offices, and to help himself liberally to Liszt's discoveries. Liszt, indeed, was to be put in the shade for ever by the overweening selfishness, the violent ambitions of his friend and companion, but he resigned himself willingly to this eclipse. For it was Wagner, in the eyes of Liszt, who was the supreme creator, the supreme artist.

If Liszt was thrown, by the many circumstances of his life, into some likeness to Faust, he was Mephisto, as well. Such a lover of music in its more pure, Mozartian form as his friend, Monsieur Ingres, who was the greatest admirer of his genius as a young man, could only consider all the tricks and mannerisms of his later life as the results of his commerce with the false gods;

Rossini, a photograph by Carjat in about 1865

The Wagner family at coffee,
Weimar

Cosima Wagner
with parasol

and, to be sure, that worship led him nowhere. His sins had spoilt him for ever in the eyes of many men. His uncanny skill had that diabolist dye in which the talents of Paganini were so deeply dipped. He had learnt his technique with the powers of evil to help him: this was why so much of his life was spent in repentance.

The rôle of Mephisto is played by Liszt to an ever-increasing extent, at this period of his life. In old age, he had the physical appearance of a magician. This was noted by all who have left any account of him, and, no doubt, it amused and occupied his histrionic talents to be wearing a priest's robes and to look like a wizard, a Merlin.

This character, to use that word in its theatrical sense, was responsible for a great deal of his creation. Nowhere is it more apparent than in the *Faust Symphony*, where he may be said to have given rein to every emotion of this kind, to have postulated, wilfully and of set purpose, his failure in the supreme realms of music and to have shown every device and all the frantic strivings by which his spirit hovered so near to creation and yet failed. It is, in fact, the final touchstone of this alchemist's experiments; and his processes are of such astounding interest and so absorbing as a spectacle that they achieve something absolutely parallel to a work of art of the first water. Yet it is only a parallel: it has not the free and unfettered flight of genius. That, in its supreme sense, was never his.

✶ The *Faust Symphony* was undertaken by Liszt over a long stretch of years. It was begun in 1853 and not completed until 1861.✶ The three movements of which it consists were given the title of character portraits: Faust, Gretchen, and Mephistopheles, and these names are sufficient indication of what should be expected from the music. This characterization is, in fact, his aim much more than the illustration of any particular episodes in the story. He achieves a much greater unity and strength by this method than could ever have been accomplished by means of an episodical treatment of chapter and verse. Richard Strauss, who employed that system forty years later in his *Don Quixote*, for all his

---

✶ Mr. Constant Lambert pointed out to me that there are two editions of the *Faust Symphony*; and that the miniature score does not quite tally with the parts used for concert performance. The orchestration has been touched up, and a short episode of about twelve bars has been added just before the end of the slow movement.

cleverness, has burdened his structure with a weight of imitative detail that is more reminiscent of a patient triumph of Teutonic craftsmanship than of any work of art that springs to life out of its own volition. *Don Quixote* is, in fact, on the vastly larger scale of this musician's accomplishment, something more of a parallel to one of those elaborate clocks where the wonder of the ordinary mechanism is surpassed, at each hour, by the puppets and the marionettes in their motions, or by the work of the Augsburg silversmiths who could perfect the image of a galleon in full sail with every detail of its rigging and the crew alert and at their posts. Perhaps the fact that the music of *Don Quixote* is enclosed within its form of variations heightens the impression that it gives of soulless, mechanical perfection.

The *Faust Symphony* is, then, musical dramatization, not musical illustration. The music plays, or acts, the chosen rôles and does not imitate them. In manner, if we must name the style and atmosphere of the whole work, it is only possible to mention Delacroix as being in any sense an equivalent, in another art, to this orchestral masterpiece of the greatest solo player, or virtuoso, who has ever existed. It is impossible to listen to the *Faust Symphony* without being reminded of the lithographs drawn by Delacroix for Goethe's *Faust*. These drawings have the same weirdness and the same fire that are implicit in this music. And, indeed, they belong to an earlier date; they were made in 1830, just before Berlioz had finished the *Symphonie Fantastique*. It might be said, almost, that music for orchestra had made no progress during these thirty years, for the *Symphonie Fantastique* and the *Faust Symphony* represent the two highest achievements of the Romantic Revival in music. That this statement amounts to some diminishment of Liszt's originality of conception cannot be denied, but the force and the pristine invention of Berlioz are as extraordinary as anything to be found in the history of the arts.

The *Faust Symphony*, meanwhile, can be compared to its rival without shame. It does, at least, seem to be a work of absolute sanity, and raises no doubts in the listener's mind as to the nervous equilibrium of the composer. Not that its machinery is any less extreme in the manner of its functioning, but the issue is never in any doubt. This cannot be said of Berlioz. The *Symphonie Fantastique* only reaches its end, without collapsing, by sheer force of genius. The *Faust Symphony* at the outset has that simplicity, even blatancy of theme, that is to be associated with all the Symphonic Poems of Liszt. In particular, the Faust theme in the first movement is broad, ordinary, incapable, it would seem, of any subtlety of treatment. It seems impossible to form any mental association between this short, bare tune and the character it is meant to display. But it is the processes to which it is subjected, the shapes into which it is driven, that give it similarity and truth. The theme is no more than the length of material that some consummate actor might use for his cloak, his vehicle of expression, twisting it this way and that, altering its whole appearance by his manœuvres as much as he developed his fictitious, his stage personality with the aid of its lifeless, dull ends, for it is just any material that came to hand, not silk, or anything precious in its own workmanship.

The second movement, in which simplicity and guilelessness are implied in the very title, is, in itself, the least impressive of the three, except in so far as it is interesting as portraying a picture of innocence. It is, therefore, sentimentally, the most dated part of the whole symphony. Its innocence is so different from sophisticated inexperience. Even so, its childish, Victorian domesticity is accentuated on purpose so as to give a foil to what is to follow.

For it is the third movement that makes the success of the *Faust Symphony*. Here, wildness and hysterical excitement run riot; the simple, blatant themes are tortured and twisted out of all semblance to themselves. They are given sneering, sarcastic shape: are corrupted and made evil and embittered: are presented in triumphant, exultant loudness: they sound forth in the guise of sardonic laughter: they mock and imitate: they travesty and burlesque the truth until the original themes can hardly be recognized behind their derision, until it seems as if they will be coloured for ever in the memory by these distortions of their true shape.

The themes are now recalled into their original forms, and, like the dispersal of the ghosts at cockcrow, the whole atmosphere changes; darkness becomes light, and the magnificent choral ending brings the *Faust Symphony* to a close. It is a setting of the last chorus from Goethe's *Faust*, and the effect is splendid and thrilling to high degree. Even the fact that on the rare occasions when it is performed in entirety, with the chorus, they are forced to sing in unison, and to reiterate again and again, in the English translation, the words 'Eternal Feminine', 'Eternal Feminine', with the accent on the last syllable of the second word, pronouncing it to rhyme with wine and nine, even this does not detract from the marvellous force, the blaze and glitter of the finale.

The author recalls that memorable occasion at the Queen's Hall, when the *Faust Symphony* was conducted by Ferruccio Busoni.* Though it cannot be said that Busoni was much more than extremely competent as director of the orchestra, his association with this work of Liszt, for whom he had such deep and comprehensive sympathy, and the fact of his own well-known predilection for the subject of Faust, produced a performance of exceptional, phenomenal kind. The theme must have attracted him so much because it was as appropriate to his own character of magician (and magician he certainly was), as to the person of Liszt. Both of them, with their exceptional, magical powers, were for ever searching for a secret that was never revealed to them, or was only suffered to live in flashes before their eyes for the space of a few moments. Both of them were weary, weary to death of one half of their powers, weary of the public, weary of their cheap applause, tired of stupidity. This performance of the *Faust Symphony* was what can only be described as a ghostly occasion. Such a combination of unearthly, superhuman personalities working together upon such a subject can have occurred but rarely. It would, perhaps, be impossible to hear the *Faust Symphony* under better auspices than these; a performance much more meticulously correct, with an orchestra, more efficiently conducted, and rehearsed to a much finer degree of precision and finish, could not have produced anything to approach the spectral qualities of this alliance between Liszt and Busoni.

The *Faust Symphony*, then, represents Liszt at the summit of his powers, in the acme of his achievement. The Romantic Revival —such shades as those of Ossian, Byron, Alfieri, Hoffmann, Delacroix, Berlioz, Paganini—attains its culmination in this work. After this, the Romantic Age is dead and produces no more.

But another work by Liszt, considered by him to be of an importance at least equal to the *Faust Symphony*, remains to be described. This is the *Dante Symphony*; and it is so rarely performed that it is outside the experience of the majority of concertgoers.

*June 1920.

166

The composition of the *Dante Symphony*, based upon the *Divina Commedia*, was completed by Liszt in 1856, after many years' work. It is a commentary upon that age, and one that in its strictures upon their taste could, perhaps, be applied indiscriminately to all artists of that period, that this project, when first conceived of by Liszt, took the very curious form that is about to be described. The first idea of the Symphony came to him during the year 1847, when he planned to make musical illustrations from certain scenes of the epic with the aid of the newly invented diorama, or magic lantern. This shows his resourceful, inventive brain suffering, for a moment, from the same childlike malady that besets some of the minor intelligences of our own day, who think that all the arts, and poetry more especially, must share the influence of the aeroplane. It may be remarked, in parenthesis, that the railway train, which in a shorter time wrought much greater changes in the lives of many more millions of people than aeroplane flight, cannot be traced in its effects upon poetry. Since then, the motor car! Why, now, the aeroplane? So we see, at this moment, Liszt foretelling, by a few years, the drawings of Gustave Doré and leaning out of his own age towards the cinema of ours, and our equivalent to Doré, Walt Disney.

But we must come back to the *Dante Symphony*, in its eventual form, when the idea of the diorama had been dismissed. It is in three parts, *Inferno*, *Purgatorio*, and *Paradiso*; but it is better described as a symphony in two movements. The first movement is a triptych, and the second movement, a diptych, ending with a choral Magnificat for finale.

The whole symphony opens with a terrifying whirlwind of sound, a sort of crescendo of fanfares. The words of the *Inferno*:

> 'Per me si va nella città dolente;
> Per me si va nell'eterno dolore;
> Per me si va tra la perduta gente.'

These words, read by Dante, as he looked at the gates of Hell, are thundered out by trombones, tuba, double basses; and, immediately afterwards, trumpets and horns make the proclamation:

> 'Lasciate ogni speranza, voi ch'entrate.'

There are two motives, two themes, to be taken for Liszt's conception of Hell. A descending chromatic passage in the lower

167

strings against a roll of drums, and a theme given to the bassoons and violas, of hollow, awful sound, having the effect of a male-alto voice.

From now, onwards, the tumult intensifies again. The air is rent with shrieking voices. There is a Babel of sound and a mighty, tearing whirlwind, in illustration of the lines:

> 'Languages diverse, horrible dialects,
> Accents of anger, words of agony,
> And voices, high and hoarse, with sound of hands,
> Make up a tumult that goes whirling on
> For ever, in that air for ever black,
> Even as the sand doth, when the whirlwind breathes.'

Once again, the words 'Lasciate ogni speranza, voi ch'entrate' are blared forth by the brass, and the whole orchestra has a tremendous passage, fortissimo, depicting the madness of despair and the rage of the damned.

The next movement portrays the lovers, Paolo and Francesca. The motives for this section, which is tender and gentle in character, in contrast to what has gone before, are given to the harps, flutes, and violins. Later on, there comes a recitative for two clarinets and bass clarinet to depict the lines:

> 'There is no greater sorrow
> Than to be mindful of the happy time
> In misery—'

and this is followed by a harp cadenza, until the whole forces of the orchestra are let loose again, the whirlwind bursts forth, the words 'Lasciate ogni speranza' are thundered forth, once more, together with the two Hell motives, sounding together in combination. The orchestration is grotesque and infernal; and, in the score is written: 'This whole passage should be understood as sardonic, blasphemous laughter, and most sharply defined as such.'

Following on this, for there is, unfortunately, a happy ending, there comes a choral Magnificat. But it brings the *Dante Symphony* to an impressive, triumphant close; and there are, in truth, exceptional, extraordinary passages in it. If it has not the conviction, the unity of conception of the *Faust Symphony* it is because the work, as a whole, is too long. The loudness and the blaring, clanging effects of terror, in which lies its excellence, have been balanced and compensated for by stretches of weakness and humility, resignation and patient suffering. This is, perhaps, always a fault with Liszt. It was part of his good manners, his sense of balance. It never entered the head of Moussorgsky that it was necessary to do this, or *Boris Godounov* would be twice as long and half as effective. This fullness, this unnecessary redundance, is the weakness of the *Faust Symphony*; and, in just the same way, Liszt spoils the effect of the *Hunnenschlacht*. The first half of that, with the battle of the Huns, with the Hungarian plain thundered upon by a million hooves, with the terrible, strident trumpet calls, the menace and the military thrill of the brass, are balanced by the second half in which the *Crux Fidelis* sounds forth on the organ and the *Hunnenschlacht* comes to a conventional optimistic end. The *Dante Symphony* suffers from the same weaknesses. If it was much shorter, and was confined to the Infernal Regions, it would be among the most extraordinary originalities in music. In comparison with the *Faust Symphony* it fails, for that is the summit of his achievement and stands with the three masterpieces of Berlioz, the *Symphonie Fantastique*, the *Requiem*, and the *Grande Messe des Morts*.

CHAPTER XXVIII

Liszt and Chopin—Chopin in Scotland—His death—The genius of Berlioz—Berlioz and Estelle—Childhood under Napoleon—The Te Deum—Les Troyens—*The last Russian journey of Berlioz—The banquet at Grenoble—Death of Berlioz*

It has been part of the method of this book to describe the influence of other composers upon Liszt in terms of their individual lives and works. This process was maintained until the death of Paganini, and it is time to resume the narrative. Liszt was, by now, quite removed from the influences of that particular virtuosity, unless we like to conclude the whole of that period with the final revision and publication of the *Paganini Études* and the *Études d'Exécution Transcendante*, in 1851 and 1854 respectively.

They amount, indeed, to an extraordinary corpus of correction and re-invention, coming, as they do, in the middle of his most energetic period of creation. How he can have found time for this work, with all his other activities as composer and conductor, passes comprehension.

But, during the decade after 1840, and for a year or two after that, there was also Chopin; and Chopin had a very powerful effect upon Liszt. He was, indeed, not free to assert his own individuality until Chopin was dead. The solid attributes of the later Chopin, his masculine strength, the architectural qualities of his late works, once he had forgotten Bellini, were not slow in dawning upon Liszt's appreciation.

The character of this unique and wonderful artist is, perhaps, best caught in the little reflections of him, a mere line or two at a time, to be found in the Letters and Journals of Delacroix. His consumption can be traced, month by month, with mention of his terrible coughing and his pale, or hectic countenance. Yet, during these last two years, he was able to produce the *Polonaise Fantaisie*, the *Barcarolle*, and the most lovely of his mazurkas, Opus 59. But his final rupture with George Sand (and what a nuisance she was in the lives of how many men!) together with the outbreak of the Revolution of 1848, broke up his resistance, once and for all.

If Chopin is typical, for ever, of the consumptive artist, so true to type that he is like one of the paler masks of Italian Comedy, there is, also, an extraordinary resemblance to be traced between Chopin and Watteau. Not only are their works the creation of exactly the same spirit of poetry and fine elegance, but the circumstances of their last months of life are precisely similar. For both of them finally ruined their chances of health by a visit to England. In the case of Chopin, he allowed himself to be dragged round from place to place until, as he says in one of his letters, he was incapable of composing, not because he did not wish to, but for purely physical reasons, and because he had to move about from one house to another, every week.

The instigator of his incessant journeys was his Scots pupil, Miss Jane Henrietta Stirling. She had lived in Paris for some years, and Chopin had dedicated his two *Nocturnes*, Opus 55, to her, as long before as 1844. She brought Chopin to London, in April 1848, where he lodged in Dover Street, gave several concerts, and played at the Duchess of Sutherland's, before Queen Victoria. From London he went to Edinburgh, and stayed at Calder House with Lord Torphichen, the brother-in-law of Miss Stirling. He also stayed at Keir, the home of the Stirlings, and at Johnston Castle. It was his fate, too, to play at Glasgow and Manchester, in the failing autumn, and by the time Chopin returned to Paris, in January 1849, he was nearly dead.

In a sense, it was the tour of a suicide. Chopin knew he was doomed and took no precautions. He did not care. But some competent essayist, who is in a position to verify the personalities and expatiate upon the places, should examine the letters written by Chopin from Scotland. They paint a curious picture of the strange characters whom he met; of persons who boasted to him (for the centenary of 1745 was only just past) of their descent in ten or fifteen generations from the Stuarts, but spoke of Mary Queen of Scots and of the Pretender as if they were still living, breathing persons; his descriptions of feudal, intoxicated gloom in turreted castles; of the Scots Sabbath—these things could be the ingredients of a delightful book.

On his return to Paris, we have more news of him in Delacroix's Journal. He moves from lodging to lodging, never satisfied, exactly as Watteau, that other consumptive artist, had done a century before, during his last months. In fact, the death agony of Chopin has begun. From lodging to lodging, always finding fault; until, at last, he reaches the last of his apartments, 12 Place Vendôme. And soon he writes the last of his letters, a little note scribbled in pencil, when he was too ill to speak. 'I think my cough is strangling me. Will you please see that I am not buried alive?' He rallies, once more, and speaks those pathetic words to Princess Czartoryska, confiding his pupil, Franchomme, to her care. 'You will play Mozart together, in my memory, and I will hear you.' Early in the next morning, before dawn, he was dead.

When Chopin died it was utter finality, the end. There was nothing more about him to discover. He was no Schubert, leaving so many unpublished manuscripts behind him that it was difficult to believe they were the genuine creations of one, unknown man. The scrupulous care and finish of Chopin made that an impossibility. Nor was his music a thing which could be continued by pupils or imitators. As a person, and as an artist, Chopin could never occur again. And, after he was dead, time after time Delacroix comes back to Chopin in his Journal, for he made the greatest impression on him of anyone he had ever known. He writes of him on anniversaries, and mentions him on occasions when he wishes Chopin had been there. His person, and the memory of his playing, could never fade.

That Liszt felt exactly the same upon this subject is proved by his book on Chopin, which speaks in the most touching terms of his affection for him. He died just at the turn of Liszt's career, when the pianoforte as a solo instrument had ceased to be his interest and his livelihood. It is probable, therefore, that Chopin had more influence in the way of reforming the exuberance of Liszt's personality than in the way of exercising a direct pressure upon his music. Chopin had no need for the conjurer's tricks, or the actor's cloak; the strength and grace of his poetry were enough in themselves.

The erratic, unequal genius of Berlioz was the greatest influence in the life of Liszt, after Paganini, until Liszt came into contact with Wagner. It might even be said that Berlioz was his true direction, and that his worship of Wagner, and his self-effacement before him, were his eclipse and ruin. In every art, the character from whom there is most to be learnt is the artist who is not wholly complete in himself. Chopin and Wagner, within their different limitations, attained to such a pitch of fulfilment that there was nothing left over, no shred of their talent that they had not turned to the best advantage. On the other hand, the most transitory acquaintance with Berlioz will show the latent and undeveloped possibilities towards which he was reaching. His whole life was a striving after the impossible, the unattainable; whether in dimension or in point of execution.

There was nothing normal in Berlioz; he was extreme in everything. We are dealing with a character as fantastic in action and in appearance as Paganini; a being set apart, physically and mentally, as much removed from ordinary mankind as was the poet Swinburne; unmistakable, never-to-be-forgotten when once seen; and apparently made different, physically, from other men in order to adapt him better to his purposes. The auburn hair of Swinburne, his curious throat, his sloping bottle-neck shoulders, his short arms and small white hands, these belonged to no one but this poet.

Berlioz was no less peculiar, but his genius was not of that inward-looking, introspective order.* His whole bent was towards the creation of things never yet attained. He had given the measure of his talent in the *Symphonie Fantastique* and in the *Grande Messe des Morts* (Requiem). These are the early Berlioz, and some details of that part of his career have already been given in a previous chapter.

He was like no one else who has ever existed.

Legouvé, who saw Berlioz at a rehearsal of *Der Freischütz*, writes of 'a young man trembling with passion, his hands clenched, his eyes flashing, and a head of hair—such a head of hair! It looked like an immense umbrella of hair, projecting like a movable awning over the beak of a bird of prey. It was both comical and diabolical at the same time.' In another place Legouvé says that the hair of Berlioz was like the edge of a precipice. It gave him vertigo. This was Berlioz in his youth, before disappointment and the fatigues of journalism had broken his health.

If this was his enthusiasm on hearing *Der Freischütz*, it may be imagined that he was less calm, still, if it was an opera of Gluck, his idol and god. And when it came to a performance of his own music he was like a madman. What must the scene have been, in 1840, when Berlioz conducted his *Symphonie Funèbre et Triomphale*, in the open air! There was a full orchestra and a military brass band of two hundred musicians, whom Berlioz conducted with a drawn sword. And when it was all over, Berlioz lay stretched out across the kettledrums, weeping.

But the receipts, after so much excitement, amounted to nothing. It was always the same. A most successful concert of his works, organized that year at the Opéra, had been ruined because two journalists, complete nonentities, had boxed each other's ears and distracted the attention of the public. Something always went wrong.

The effects of these alternate efforts and failures, spread over a number of years, coupled with the incessant journalism that was the bane of his life, and with the futile labour of conducting seasons of opera, when his one ambition was to write and produce

* In the Journals of Delacroix there is a sort of recurring refrain whenever the author met Berlioz at a dinner-party, or had to spend the evening with him. 'Berlioz, insupportable.' 'Comme toujours, Berlioz insupportable.' His faults were egoism and ceaseless argument.

operas of his own, all these things contributed to a breakdown of his nervous resistance. His health was impaired, and it is the sad fact that, after 1840, Berlioz was no longer capable of the excessive flights of genius that might have been expected of him. The whole future of music might have been thought to lie within the grasp of the man who had written the *Symphonie Fantastique* and the *Grande Messe de Morts*. But, if this did not happen, if these exceptions were left unfulfilled, he remains not the less isolated as a phenomenon. In this country, if nowhere else, he is still regarded as an unsettled and arguable problem, a sort of equivalent in music to the position in painting occupied by El Greco. His virtues are altogether denied, or he is given extravagant praise.

When Liszt was engaged with his problems of orchestra, while he was writing his Symphonic Poems at Weimar, the only example he had before him was that of Berlioz. And Liszt, in the 'fifties of last century, was shaped to a great extent by the Berlioz of twenty years before. Now, by contrast with the music of Berlioz, all of the classical symphonies, from Haydn to Beethoven, can be grasped, readily and quickly enough, from the piano score. With the advent of Berlioz, both the solo qualities of the separate instruments, and their massed and tremendous tonality, have become increased to such an extent that it is no longer possible to form any idea of them in terms of the pianoforte. A symphony of Haydn or Beethoven, even the *Eroica* or the Ninth, can be played and understood on the piano. But such a comparatively simple work of Berlioz as the *Carnaval Romain* is more or less inarticulate, and conveys nothing of itself in the piano score.

The reason is that Berlioz is the greatest virtuoso of all time for the orchestra. Instruments had never sounded before, and have never sounded since, as they were made to sound by Berlioz. In this respect, he is the exact historical equivalent to Paganini and to Liszt.

In order to realize this, it is only necessary to hear a first-rate performance of *Carnaval Romain*, or even of the *Corsair* overture. Whatever his merits or shortcomings may be from point of theory, in practice there is nothing to compare with him. This applies, of course, only to good Berlioz. There is bad Berlioz, just as there is bad Mozart and bad Beethoven. A great deal of *Harold in Italy* is bad; and so is much of *Romeo and Juliet*; but, in the midst of that, comes the *Queen Mab Scherzo*. And this breathes the poetry of Shakespeare to an extent that is unimaginable. It shows Berlioz, whose forte was the stupendous and colossal, dealing with a world of subtle, gossamer delicacy. The *Scherzo* takes place in a kind of enchanted stillness, like that of a wood on a summer evening. The throbbing and buzzing of a million wings becomes audible, and the sylvan enchantment flutters and hovers on the air.

But we must proceed to his Babylonian, his Ninevean side. His expectation was for successes upon this scale. We find him writing from Weimar, where Liszt had mounted his *Benvenuto Cellini*, of his 'succès pyramidal'. It was a favourite phrase with him. In his incessant striving after the overwhelming, the stupendous, certain things in his psychology must be considered, for they give the key to these mysteries of his nature.

Berlioz was a person of early maturity. He was precocious; his talent was fully developed, in all its characteristics, at an early age. He was, therefore, extremely receptive of early impressions. This is proved by the famous story of Berlioz and Estelle. It was the year of Waterloo, Berlioz was twelve years old, and during his summer holiday he fell so passionately in love with Estelle, a young girl of nineteen who lived next door, that the impression remained with him all the rest of his life. He never saw her again until 1864, when as a lonely old man (so lonely that the very thought of him raises pity) he sought her out again, engaged in a passionate correspondence with her, the frenzied tone of which seems to have alarmed more than it amused this old lady of seventy, and travelled as far as Lyon, and, later on, Geneva, in order to see her.

If the strength of his susceptibilities at an early age is proved by this story we may imagine the other impressions of his childhood. For it is, perhaps, impossible for us to understand what childhood, during those years of Napoleonic triumphs, before Waterloo, must have been like for a boy of abnormal sensitiveness. Théophile Gautier, who was of the same age, says somewhere that the feelings of the generation born at that time could never be recaptured.

The whole world was in French hands. France stretched from Danzig to Cadiz. The forces of the Revolution, carrying military glory and Imperial splendour behind them, had spread from end to end of the Continent. The thrilling words of the proclamations of French victories pasted on the village walls, and worded, very often, by that consummate journalist, Napoleon, in person, were not the less intoxicating, if untrue. And who was to tell whether they were true or not, for the frontiers of France had been extended to the furthest shores of Europe?

Napoleon encouraged every conceivable device by which to stimulate military ardour. The great reviews on the Champ de Mars, the parades before the Tuileries; the echoes of these Roman triumphs must have penetrated to the most remote villages of France. The dazzling uniforms of his troops, the effort (so different from the ethics of modern war) to make soldiers as conspicuous as possible, all these attempts to float military glory before the eyes must have produced a most violent impression upon the ambition and the imagination of a child. Where was it to end? It could only finish when the whole world was conquered and a Roman peace, the Pax Romana, reigned once more upon earth.

Such was the Imperial epoch. When it fell, the collapse came with disastrous rapidity. The Empire tumbled like a pack of cards. These rumours were like distant thunder to the ears: they rumbled at the back of the horizon, to all sides at once, in every direction. The rattle and the roar of battle came nearer and more near. The Emperor was a flying fugitive. And, when the peace came, men could not believe it.

We can see the picture of those strange times in the Diary of Benjamin Haydon. He had gone to France, and found himself in Paris on a certain Sunday morning, just after the Emperor had abdicated, at Fontainebleau, and set sail for Elba. 'This was the first Sunday since the Revolution on which the shops had been shut. As I sat down in the gardens a respectable old gentleman said, while he mopped his forehead: "This is a Sunday, at last, after twenty years' disturbance." '

Later in that day—it was the Fête Dieu—Haydon betook himself to Fontainebleau, to see the scene of Napoleon's abdication. The troops of Louis XVIII had not yet taken over from the Imperial Guard. In the evening Haydon strolled to the parade. He noted the large, tall, and bony veterans of a quarter of a century of war; their black moustachios, their gigantic bearskin caps. 'The evening was delicious; the fountain worthy of Armida's Garden; the poetry of my mind unearthly, for the time, when the crash of the Imperial drums, beating with a harsh unity which stamped their voices as those of veterans in war, made my heart throb with their stormy rattle. Never did I hear such drums before, and never shall I again: there were years of battle and blood in every sound.'

If we can establish the childhood of Berlioz to the tune of such distant military echoes, such reverberations of the brass, there is, also, one other circumstance to be considered. When his livelong adoration for Virgil is mentioned, it is never stressed that this may have been brought about by the associations of his own name, Hector. That was enough, in itself, to frame the whole direction of his interests. The antique heroes had a kind of ghostly companionship for him. They were bound up with him. They became a fixed idea. He was as inseparable from this ghostly contact with them as a prisoner in his cell is from the remembrance of former times. In the long years of imprisonment, the age of all these ghostly shadows remains the same. It is unaltered; it is only the prisoner who grows older. The strange, the haunting, descending mournfulness of his opera, *Les Troyens*, may be traced to these causes.

But, before we reach *Les Troyens* the first part of our argument about the mental origins of Berlioz is exemplified in the *Military Te Deum*. The fall of Napoleon dissipated the atmosphere of his youth. Martial glory had departed. But, with a personality like that of Berlioz it is only natural to find that this dead actuality should live with a still more violent sort of life in his imagination. It lay dormant. Its echoes would burst forth when their moment came. The opportunity was the *Military Te Deum*.

No words can describe the magnificence of the effect that this makes in performance. The senses are intoxicated by its splendid triumph. It is the re-creation of military glory: the Napoleonic legend seen through an imagination that lifted it to the highest planes: an ode to victory of Pindaric force and poetry. The history of this masterpiece but supplements the little that can be said of it in description.

It was written in 1849, and was first performed in 1856, at one of the few successful concerts ever organized by this unhappy genius, in the Church of Saint Eustache at the opening of the Universal Exhibition. Nine hundred executants, and what Berlioz terms 'une organisation Babylonienne', took part in the performance. It is, therefore, late Berlioz, when Berlioz was turning from the Romantic tendencies of his youth into the Classical mood of his mature age.

The first idea of the work came to him in 1832, with his project for a symphony upon a Napoleonic theme, *Le Retour de l'Armée d'Italie*. It will be remembered that this year, 1832, was made memorable by the death of l'Aiglon. At the time when the *Te Deum* was performed in its eventual shape, for the Exposition Universelle, it is interesting to find an article, obviously inspired by Berlioz himself, and written in explanation by his friend Maurice Bourges, in the *Gazette Musicale*, 6 May 1855. 'In the composer's mind', we read, 'the *Te Deum* was intended to form part of a composition conceived of on colossal lines, half epic, half dramatic, intended to celebrate the military glory of the First Consul. It was originally called "Le Retour de la campagne d'Italie". At the moment of General Bonaparte's entrance under the arches of the cathedral, the *Te Deum* bursts forth from all directions, the standards are dipped, drums beat, guns sound, and the bells ring out in great peals. This is what explains the altogether warlike atmosphere ("la physionomie toute guerrière") of this work.'

The reader need now only be reminded that the French Empire had just been restored, in the person of Napoleon III, for him to grasp the meaning of this resuscitation of military splendours. As such, it is without parallel in art. It is, in fact, possible to prefer the *Te Deum* to the *Requiem* of Berlioz. Here, all is accomplishment, and not experiment.

The *Te Deum* is in six pieces, and is written for two choirs of a hundred each, and a third choir of six hundred children, accompanied by an immense orchestra and by the booming of the organ. The last piece of all, the 'Judex crederis', brings the work to such a pitch of triumph that it is intoxication itself. For sheer sound there can never have been anything to equal this, whether by thunderstorm or explosion. Any nation that could ever produce an individual capable of this symbol of war and victory can most obviously never hope for peace. It will be war after war, as long as history lasts.

The excitement wrought by the 'Judex crederis' is carried to an even higher degree of intoxication by the actual last movement of the *Te Deum*, which is nearly always omitted from performance, even on the very rare occasions when the *Te Deum* is given. It is an orchestral march for the presentation of the colours, a veritable epitome of military feeling and excitement.

The *Marche Troyenne* is just another emblem of War, inevitable War. If this march can be heard, in the concert version of 1864 that Berlioz prepared, with the brass instruments doubled, it is the greatest excitement, the greatest physical thrill, that music can bring.

And here, with this mention of *Les Troyens*, we are brought back to Liszt himself. For the opera would never have been written had it not been for the persuasion of Liszt and the Princess. Berlioz had paid two visits to Weimar in 1855 and 1856, when the talk had been of nothing but Wagner. It may have been his habitual good manners that made Liszt urge Berlioz to set to work upon his long-cherished scheme for an opera based upon his beloved Virgil. If that was its true origin, the Princess, who loved great projects, musical or literary, in ratio to their length and difficulty of presentation, became so enthusiastic that she is said to have bidden Berlioz never again to come into her presence unless *Les Troyens* was near to accomplishment. She must have relented, at least, when Berlioz sent her the complete manuscript of the poem six months later. And it is not impossible that it would have suited the secret purposes of the Princess to be able to raise up a rival to Wagner in her lover's estimation.

During the years to come, Berlioz was occupied with it during all his spare moments. It became, in his own words, his 'tâche phrygienne'. The immense scale of the work, for it occupied two entire evenings, made the question of performance so unlikely that it was necessary to secure the patronage of the Emperor. It is typical of both Berlioz and Napoleon III that after six months of intrigue, when the composer at last received a summons to the Tuileries, he should find Napoleon, 'qui avait son air de 25 degrés au dessous de zéro', and who took the manuscript from his hand with the empty promise that he would read it when he could find a moment of leisure.

It was, of course, after an interval of five years that *Les Troyens* was first given at the Opéra, and, then, only in mutilated form. Only the second part, *Les Troyens à Carthage*, was performed.* Its failure was complete. The truth is that *Les Troyens*, in its

*The first part, *La Prise de Troie*, was not performed at the Opéra until 1899. An abridged form, condensing both the operas into one evening, was restored

complete edition, is nearly impossible of performance, but is, in places, one of the grandest things in the whole of musical creation. It could be given, under ideal conditions, in the Roman Amphitheatre at Verona, and perhaps nowhere else. For it is of Imperial, processional splendour: an opera for a restored Empire, for a modern Cæsar.

Some incredible things are contained in it. There is the opening of *La Prise de Troie*, with the Trojans feasting and rejoicing in the deserted encampment of the Greek armies. The *Marche Troyenne* sounds forth with unbelievable splendour. There is the scene of Cassandra's prophecies, and the entrance of the wooden horse into the town of Troy. In the third act the city is in flames. The shade of Hector appears on the battlements to warn Æneas, and all the ghosts of Troy are seen. The scene in which these phantoms appear is without precedent for the way in which it chills the blood. There is something spectral in its accents, and the whole episode of these ghostly heroes is a conception on the highest planes of the imagination. At the end of the opera, Æneas is shown leaving Troy at the head of his soldiers, carrying the treasures and the gods of Ilium to Italy.

Les Troyens à Carthage opens with the loves of Dido and Æneas. There is a remarkable episode, where Dido, as Queen of Carthage, and founder of the city, receives deputations of workers, sailors, and peasants. The differences of musical treatment are most remarkable in their separate choruses. After a while, Æneas and the Trojans arrive, and offer Dido their services to drive away the Numidians. There is a scene of feasting and triumph in the palace gardens, by the sea. A beautiful septette is sung, and the atmosphere of the music is soft and gentle, to suggest the love of Dido and Æneas and the peaceful scene in the garden, with the sun setting.

The next act is the parting of the lovers; while, in the fourth act, in two tableaux, we see the death of Dido and the foundation of Rome. The Capitol is shown in an apotheosis, and the destinies of Rome and its Imperial fortunes are thundered forth in vast choruses, with the *Marche Troyenne* resounding in different

to the repertory of the Paris Opéra in 1921, and is still given, very occasionally. The present fashion in French musical taste continues to ignore this masterpiece. It was the intention of Liszt to produce *Les Troyens*, complete, at Weimar; but his resignation put an end to the plan.

phases and in the 'mode triomphale'. It has been, in a sense, the leit-motif of the whole opera, treated in various styles to suit the mood of the separate acts, and now appearing, in full force and splendour, with triumphant, heroic effect.

Such, briefly narrated, is the opera of *Les Troyens*. But it has other and wonderful features. There are, for instance, the 'pantomimes expressives', a device made use of by Berlioz, in which a symphonic interlude by the orchestra is interpreted on the stage by the miming of actors. The scene in which Andromache, the widow of Hector, leads her son Astyanax by the hand is an instance of this. And there is the famous *Chasse Royale et Orage*. This is familiar from concert performance, and hardly needs description. Dido and Æneas are hunting in the forest. They lose themselves, a fearful storm of thunder breaks, and they have to take refuge together in a cavern. This short interlude is, in itself, a veritable masterpiece. The flourishes of the hunting horns, the crashes of deafening, frightful thunder are portrayed as nowhere else in art. Mention should be made, also, of the ballet music, which is most original in conception. There is a most effective *pas des Nubiennes*, a little conventionally oriental, perhaps; a *pas des lutteurs*; and another jeu athlétique in the form of the famous *pas du ceste*, the details of which are left to the flutes; but, in the end, it becomes a sort of saltarello, finishing rather in the measure of the *Carnaval Romain*.

It is time that this opera of *Les Troyens* was performed for the English public. The orchestration is masterly beyond words; the brass instruments, more especially, being written for with most exciting, thrilling effect. *Les Troyens* is unlike anything else in music. It is absolutely and truly individual. Perhaps, if we knew *La Vestale* of Spontini, we might recognize in it some of the accents and the method of *Les Troyens*, but, in ignorance of the music of Spontini, it is only possible to be amazed and stupefied by *Les Troyens*.*

After this enormous undertaking, written in failing health and in the teeth of every kind of disappointment, Berlioz had only the

* If the accent and the mood of *Les Troyens* remind one of anything at all it is of Flaubert's *Salammbô*. This was published just at that time; and it is not without interest that Berlioz wrote of it in enthusiastic terms in the *Journal des Débats* for 21 December 1862. *Les Troyens à Carthage* was first performed on 4 November 1863. The music had been practically completed in 1858.

energy for one more enterprise. This, the last of all his compositions, was the little two-act comic opera, *Béatrice et Bénédict*, on a
libretto taken from Shakespeare's *Much Ado About Nothing*. This
was produced at Baden-Baden, in 1862, and has hardly been
given since,* though the delightful overture is fairly familiar
from concert performance.

We must follow the fortunes of Berlioz, or his ill fortune, to
the end. From this moment, he seems to have been determined to
die. He finished his Memoirs, bringing them up to 1 January
1865. His visits to Estelle were the one consolation of his life,
and then, as a final blow, in 1867 he heard of the death of his son
Louis, who died of yellow fever on naval service at Havana. His
son was the only person left to him.

The nervous energies of this extraordinary individual were
capable of one more effort. He spent the four winter months of
1867–8 in Russia, conducting great concerts at St. Petersburg and
Moscow. He was so ill, and so racked with pains, that he had to
spend nearly the whole time in bed, when not conducting or
rehearsing. The details of this desperate concert tour are extremely
difficult to discover, but it is certain that he met with outstanding
successes and that his music and his personality made the most
profound impression upon the younger Russian musicians.
Balakirev, whom we shall meet again later on in this book, was a
great deal in his company; and it is probable that Moussorgsky
was much influenced by this dying man.

His return from Russia, in the ill-lighted, ill-heated trains of
the day, with no sleeping car, and travelling absolutely alone and
unattended, took three days and four nights. It is interesting to
think of his departure from the railway station; of the droshky-
drivers in fur coats and fur hats; the porters in smocks and peaked,
military caps, as in the opening chapter of *Anna Karénina*;
of the dreary light of the gas-lamps; of the crowd of passen-
gers; and the group of his young disciples come to see him off,
headed by Balakirev. Moussorgsky and Borodin may well have
been there, too, on the platform. In the midst was the haggard
form of Berlioz, fur-coated and top-hatted, a tragedian in face
and figure and in his tempestuous hair; as curious a sight as it is
possible to imagine; having to be helped up the steps when the

---

*It was in the repertory at Weimar from 1862 onwards, owing to the
recommendations of Liszt.

horn blew, and never looking back, we may be sure, at the young men whom he would never see again, and of whose youthfulness he will have been jealous. What must his thoughts have been during those four nights in the train?

His condition of fatigue at the end of such a journey can be imagined. But this Russian tour had given him the sad satisfaction of hearing the music of his youth, of his days of genius, played for the last time. After this, he had only one desire, for the sunny heat of the South. He had written from the snows of St. Petersburg, some months before, of his wish 'to be bathed in violets and to sleep in the sun'.

Still alone, in utter solitude, he went down to Nice in order to enjoy the heat and to solace himself with the scenes he had loved in his youth, thirty years before, when the world was full of promise. It had been warm, then, and the shores were coasts of romance. It was the Mediterranean, the Virgilian sea. The airs were at fever heat, and his imagination was in a ferment. Nice, itself, he had always loved. It had a place in his music. His overture, *The Corsair*, was called in those days *Ouverture de la Tour de Nice*, or *Ouverture du Corsaire Rouge*. He must have dwelt long upon these things in his mind, and have thought of Paganini, who died at Nice, and whose phantom had come up to him in the concert hall, after *Harold in Italy* was played. And, could he have foreseen the future, his cynical mind would have found sardonic amusement in the statue of himself set up, further down that coast, on the terrace at Monte-Carlo, near the Casino. It commemorates the success of the *Damnation of Faust*, first given in opera form at the theatre a stone's throw away. Produced to amuse the gamblers, and paid for with their money. This was how his success came, half a century after the music was written!

But, now, Berlioz was not strong enough even to walk along the shore. He stumbled and fell. He was so ill that he had to come back to Paris, still alone.

He was already like a ghost, himself, and this extraordinary apparition made one more appearance, at Grenoble, the capital of Dauphiné, his native province, on 16 August 1868, where he went to preside at a banquet in aid of a choral society. An eyewitness describes how Berlioz, the guest of honour, came into the banquet-hall of the Hôtel de Ville supported by a friend on each side of him. His appearance struck the assembly with horror. The climax came when a wreath, a coronet of enamel, was placed on his head and, being too weak to make a speech himself, he motioned to Bazin, his deputy, to do so for him. Berlioz rose from his chair to leave the hall, and, all at once, an appalling storm rushed down the whole valley of the Isère; it burst in through the windows, it filled the folds of the velvet curtains, and blew out all the torches in the hall. And Berlioz had to be helped out of the building by the flickers of the lightning.

This extraordinary occasion, which reads like a parody of an orgy scene from one of Offenbach's operas, for these always end with a crowning with a wreath of roses in the midst of an uproar, a tornado of waltzes and redowas, was followed by a solitary railway journey of twenty hours, back to Paris.

Even this fantastic scene at Grenoble, the climax, the apotheosis of this old and dying Romantic, was not the end. He existed through the winter; he even appeared in the streets, so ill that he could no longer recognize his oldest friends*; and always alone. At last this terrible, dragging agony of death came to an end, and he died on 9 March 1869. Few persons, perhaps, can have been more pleased with oblivion.

CHAPTER XXIX

Liszt, Rubinstein, and the Fishwives of Rotterdam

The details of the last chapter are so unbearably, so poignantly sad that it is pleasant to turn from them to a lighter topic. We leave Berlioz and come back to our hero, Liszt. During these years at Weimar he seldom left Germany;

*An appalling theory about Berlioz's last months is advanced by Bertrand, who had seen him in St. Petersburg. It is supposed that the memory of Berlioz was beginning to fail, but Bertrand says of him: 'Il n'y avait nullement chez Berlioz, éclipse d'intelligence, comme on le croyait généralement, mais il se complaisait dans la silence et la désespérance, pour que ce fût complet, absurde, et fatal.' *Cf.* Gustave Bertrand, *Nationalités musicales étudiées dans le drame lyrique*, Paris, 1872.

but on one occasion we find him at Rotterdam, attending a musical festival held there in 1854. An occasion in itself of some importance, because it introduces a new figure into our story. No less than Anton Rubinstein, the only rival to Liszt in his lifetime as a pianist. And this anecdote, for what it is worth, we copy down, word by word, from the original.*

'In 1854, at Rotterdam,' we read, 'Liszt and Rubinstein had a curious experience. Both artists were engaged for the musical festival there, and, living together in the same hotel, they were in the habit of driving out together. On one occasion, having some business at one of the shops near the quay, they drove there; but, the business ended, they returned to their carriage only to find it had gone off and was nowhere to be seen. There was nothing, therefore, to be done except walk home, and this they started to do.

'At that time both were young men; Liszt, tall, stately, dandified, although disordered in attire, wearing light kid gloves, and with long golden hair thrown back on his shoulders; Rubinstein with his lion head and Beethovenish cast of features, was no less striking in appearance. The appearance of both, however, awoke the sense of the strange, and to the vulgar mind, therefore, the ludicrous in the minds of the fisher-women—brawny, red-armed Amazons—loitering about the quays with their creels of fish, and they gathered in considerable number about the two artists.

'Liszt, aristocratic to his fingertips, was in despair and as the women, gathering closer about him, observed this they became more and more hilarious and rude, till finally the two unhappy artists had to come to a dead stop, the women forming a ring and dancing around them, plucking them by the sleeves and coattails and laughing uproariously.

'At length matters became insupportable, and Rubinstein, in one of his sudden passions, broke through the ring, Liszt following; and taking to their heels the two artists fled to their hotel, followed by the derisive shouts of their tormentors till they got safely under cover.'

*Anton Rubinstein, by Alexander Macarthur, London, 1889.

CHAPTER XXX
Liszt and Hungarian music—The Rhapsodies—*The* Spanish Rhapsody

The final transformation of Liszt, his appearance as necromancer in the black cassock of a priest, is not far off now. With the mass of evidence gathered in every concert hall, it must already be obvious to the reader that, in addition to his other talents, Liszt was a consummate actor. He had the genius, and many of the actual attributes, of Henry Irving. In his final rôle as a priest it was as if the actor in him had decided to live permanently in character, to feed and sleep, as it were, in the theatre, on the stage, to be never out of his actor's clothes. The part he had chosen for himself was that of active resignation. He had to prove this by contrast, by alternations of energy; just as he had to contradict the obvious goodness and benevolence of his looks with a flash of Mephisto, so as to show he had only arrived at goodness through resolution, so as to prove that he had a past. Meanwhile, his character is not complete unless the boldness of his rôle, the clear-cut profile of his part, can be established with all the necessary contrast that came before it. Liszt, as Hungarian, played no mean proportion in this.

When Liszt returned in triumph to Hungary, in 1839, at the beginning of his career of virtuoso, he had nearly forgotten the use of his native tongue. He had left Hungary when ten years old; the naturally strong flavouring of his native land must have struck him with redoubled freshness. It is hardly necessary to say that music was an integral part of this. He listened to Tzigane bands and diligently collected their tunes. This was no original idea, in itself; nor, where Hungarian music in particular is concerned, was Liszt the first person to make use of Zigeuner music. Haydn, who had lived for so many years in the actual district where Liszt passed his childhood, on the estates of the Esterházy, had done this before him. And, in more recent times, Schubert, who passed one or two of his summer holidays giving lessons to Countess Caroline Esterházy, at Zeliz, had allowed the music of the Tziganes to colour his own works. There are the finales of several string quartets, there is the famous *Divertissement à l'Hongroise*, there are the books of Hungarian airs. And Liszt had already, at this time, written piano versions of Schubert's Hungarian marches and melodies, while his arrangement of the *Divertissement à l'Hongroise* followed these after a brief interval. At about this time, too, Liszt made the acquaintance of Reményi, a Gypsy violinist of extraordinary quality, to whose influence and playing Brahms was, later on, indebted for his Hungarian moods.*

But, if his interest in Hungarian music is not without precedent, his craze for technical experiment made his study of Gypsy airs assume an extremely ambitious form. They were no mere arrangements of melodies, but evidently had for their aim the reproduction of all the effects of a Tzigane band. And, perhaps, if they are considered from this point of view, they become less obvious and hackneyed to the modern ear.

The tapping and rattling of the cymbalon is embodied, in the *Rhapsodies*, equally with the chorus of violins and with the solos of the leader. It cannot be denied that this has been done with extraordinary success; and, in its day, as an innovation in music, these new effects must have been of immense originality. If some contemporary pianist of tremendous skill was to achieve the apparently impossible by producing the tricks and effects of a good Negro band, of Duke Ellington or of Louis Armstrong, not as the piano in the band but as the whole band itself, we should, perhaps, be able to form some idea of what must have seemed the revolutionary innovations of the *Rhaposdies*. And the Rhapsodist, himself, was about to become a priest in Holy Orders!

There must, also, be taken into consideration the excessive cleverness of Liszt in finding titles for his new inventions. The name, Rhapsody, was a particularly clever hit in the art of nomenclature. But for their title, the *Hungarian Rhapsodies* might have remained as ignored by posterity as many other, more derserving compositions of the master. As it is, their fame has been universal for a hundred years and they have played no small share in sullying the composer's reputation, for the *Rhapsodies* are over-familiar and over-played.

*Liszt intended to write a violin concerto for Reményi. He made the preliminary sketches in Rome, in 1861-2, but the work never progressed beyond that stage. Had the project matured we may feel certain that it would have taken Hungarian rhapsodical form.

Their final publication in mature form, after earlier editions of several had been withdrawn, took place between 1851 and 1854, in the midst of all the activities of his Weimar period. The *Rhapsodies* were fifteen in number; a series sufficient in themselves for it to be possible to choose less hackneyed examples than the eternal Second or the Twelfth. It is not easy to say anything new about that pair of Rhapsodies. Their influence on popular music during the last hundred years has been vast, and generally disastrous. The proletarian, non-Aryan modernities of American music, in particular, are indebted to the Second Rhapsody.

It is pleasant to turn from them to the Third, which is given the sub-title of *Héroïde Funèbre*, or to the Ninth, the *Carnaval de Pesth*; the latter, a delightful, if less ostentatious, example of Liszt in his mood of nationalism. There are, also, the Tenth, in heroic style, and a splendid, magniloquent instance of that; and the Thirteenth, of which the first half, or Lassen, is singularly fine and restrained. These four less well known of the *Rhapsodies* give, indeed, a different conception of the whole set, the balance of which is thrown out by the more banal, over-popular specimens.

Much later in his life, Liszt extended the series of *Rhapsodies* beyond the Fifteenth, which is the *Rákóczy March*, and added four more Rhapsodies to the set. A final, or Twentieth Rhapsody, is still in manuscript, unpublished. These pieces, dating from his old age, are interesting examples of his mature style, and are almost unknown to the public. And, some years before this, Liszt, with the assistance of an apt pupil of his, Döppler, orchestrated six of the *Rhapsodies*, giving them an effective concert form. And one or two of them, notably the Sixth, are definitely improved in the process. The three latest of the series, the Seventeenth, Eighteenth and Nineteenth, are among those thus available for orchestra.

This is the occasion, also, to mention the *Hungarian Fantasia* for piano and orchestra arranged from the Fourteenth Rhapsody. It is effective, but tawdry, and of noisy, melodramatic Mestrovic feeling, the airs being like the heads of frowning heroes by that Yugoslav sculptor. The descent of many Jazz composers, and George Gershwin not least of these, can be traced to it.

Finally, and for a change of atmosphere, this account of Liszt's *Rhapsodies* must be completed with a note upon his *Spanish Rhapsody*, written in 1845, during his Spanish tour. It is based upon La Follia, an old Spanish dance made famous by Corelli, and upon the Jota Aragonesa. A version of this for piano and orchestra was arranged by Ferruccio Busoni, and, when played by his pupil Egon Petri it is a fine piece of pyrotechnics. It is a curious fact that Liszt seems to have paid no attention, while in Spain, to the Flamenco music, although he spent the greater part of one winter in Seville and Granada. There would be every reason to think that he might have been deeply interested, but, apparently, it altogether escaped his notice; and he characterizes the Spanish Gypsies, in his writings, as being utterly devoid of all musical talent.*

The *Rhapsodies*, taken as a whole, have lost much of their appeal in recent years. Their place, at the end of a piano recital, has been usurped by Albéniz. They have been charged with all the faults they possess; and with a few, of which they can, perhaps, be held exempt. The chief of these is that they do not represent the true music of Hungary, but only the depraved, debased music of the Tziganes. In support of this argument, such composers as Bartók have assembled many hundreds, or even thousands of tunes, in their original, unadorned simplicity. But the answer to this is that, however wrong Liszt may have been, his *Rhapsodies* have lasted for more than a hundred years, and have carried the fame of Hungarian music from end to end of the world. Liszt is the greatest, if not the only great, artist that the Hungarians have produced. His contribution to their fame is better left unchallenged.

Some years after the appearance of the *Rhapsodies*, Liszt published his book on Gypsy music. It had been maturing over a long period, and was finally printed in 1861, coming out simultaneously in German and Hungarian. Once again, the helping hand of the Princess is visible, and perhaps its great length, for it runs to four hundred and fifty pages, was due to her example. The arguments it contains are unconvincing: his attempt to show the whole of the *Rhapsodies* as a kind of national epic will not bear the weight of any close scrutiny.

But the interest of the book lies in its picturesque phrasing and imagery. He gives accounts of his own adventures in Gypsy

---

*Liszt's only other contribution to Spanish music is his arrangement of a Spanish song, *El Contrabandista*; *Rondo sur un thème espagnol*, published in 1837. This was, in reality, a song by Manuel Garcia, made famous by his daughter, Malibran. Anton Rubinstein, as we shall see, was an *aficionado*.

encampments which are as fine as anything to be found in Borrow. His metaphors are strikingly modern. When he says, of a forest of thick brushwood, that 'it lay against the horizon like a huge rhinoceros, or the hide of an elephant asleep', his prose has taken a leap into modern poetry. And we come to sentences like the following: 'They shook the wild-growing trees and brought the fruit down like sweet hailstones. . . . Seeing a young willow tree covered with frost, and looking like a huge bird in some sacred Indian vale, they shook the boughs and reduced it again, for nothing, to its native ugliness.' Or, for a whole paragraph, we find: 'All this time, the quicker tunes were playing with wild varieties of rhythm. Sometimes like leaping asclepiads, which progressing by unequal steps imitate the slow reptation of the serpent, or throw themselves forward in a bold curve quickly reaching to some distant support. The path is strewn, as it were, with drops of blood, to which certain notes in the Gypsy rhythm bear a definite metaphorical resemblance, and the best players were those who, having syncopated their theme so as to give it a light swinging effect, restore it to the normal measure as if preparing to lead a dance, after which it appears, as it were, casting sparks in every direction by clusters of small shakes.' In short, Liszt can claim, on the strength of a good many episodes in this book, to be considered as the equal of George Borrow. It lacks construction: it has the faults of the inexperienced writer: but he excels in imagery and metaphor, and in *The Gipsy in Music* he has written the best book extant on the Tziganes.

In this trend of his music, and in the book we have just described, we see Liszt asserting his claim to nationality. Until he was forty years of age it might have been forgotten that he was a Hungarian. He may be said to have recovered his nationality by these means. If, to our day, the *Rhapsodies* are one of the least interesting phases of his music, it is because they were the precursors of so much bad music of the popular sort. The longest, most drawn-out agonies in restaurant and cinema, the worst and noisiest thunders of the concert hall, are laid to the door of Liszt. But this does not diminish the original importance of the *Rhapsodies*, it merely proves the truth of that; and, to this day, at the hands of the greatest players, they make strong testimony to the pyrotechnics of a century ago.

CHAPTER XXXI

The B minor Sonata—*Many other works*—*The* Glanes de
Woronince—Chanson Bohémienne

Even now, in order to present the stature of our hero in all
its proper achievement, some of the most important of his
compositions during these years of amazing fertility remain
to be discussed. First, and foremost, the *Sonata in B Minor*. In the
opinion of many, this is the finest of all Liszt's piano compositions.
And it has never suffered eclipse. Published as long ago as 1854,
the Sonata still keeps its pristine originality and force. In writing
it, Liszt thought that he was breaking the bonds of Sonata form
and was preparing the way for a whole new development in piano
music. It was one of his supreme attempts, but the Sonata has had
no progeny. He must certainly have intended to follow it up with
more inventions of his own along the same lines, but the Sonata
met with such a storm of abuse that it remains isolated in his
work. Nearly every critic attacked it; and, in musical circles, as we
learn from one of Liszt's letters, it was called 'the invitation to
stamping and hissing', after the ponderous joke of Gumprecht,*
a deservedly forgotten critic. It struck their minds as a display of
empty force and rhetoric.

Lack of interest in the Sonata was universal. Brahms, then a
young man of twenty, and a protégé of Liszt, is said to have fallen
asleep while the master played it to him. It was the beginning of
their coolness to each other, and they ended in open hostility. All
their followers took sides. Twelve years later, and still because of
this, we find that ardent disciple of Liszt's, Hans von Bülow,
writing: 'Que m'importent les Brs? . . . Brahms, Brahmüller,
Brambach, Bruch, Bragiel, Breinecke, Brienecke, Brietz? Ne
parlons plus d'eux . . . le seul qui m'interesse est Braff.' It is
curious, after this criticism, to realize that von Bülow ended as the
greatest admirer and supporter of Brahms, the pioneer of his
symphonies.

*It is interesting to find this same Otto Gumprecht, in the *National Zeitung*
17 September 1878, attending a concert of Tchaikowsky in Berlin and stig-
matizing his *Francesca da Rimini* as 'madness', 'musical contortions', etc.
Gumprecht was fortunate in his dislikes!

Perhaps the soft opening of the Sonata lulled Brahms into his slumber, for it begins in a vein of gloom; it is, in fact, very much like the opening bars of *Les Funérailles*. But more energetic strains follow soon, even if the mood is, now, a little tinctured with that of *Liebesträume*. Eventually, the close of the Sonata, a fine open tune magnificently laid out for the hands, makes its appearance. This tune has to be fought back for, once again, till it returns, all obstacles vanquished, in a kind of apotheosis; and the Sonata ends, as it began, as if to the tapping of muted and funereal drums.

The *Sonata in B Minor* is not a favourite piece with the writer of this book, even if it is admitted to be a proud passage of Romanticism. In the hands of Busoni, or even of Horowitz, it sounds magnificent; but, in the opinion of the writer, always empty; and, unless it is played by such pianists as these, the awkwardness of the pauses and the jerky, staccato sentiment render the Sonata painful and irritating to the nerves. This is a mere personal opinion; in the minds of most critics, the Sonata is either the masterpiece of Liszt and one of the finest things in the whole of the piano repertory, or it is hollow, pretentious bathos. Perhaps it is neither the one nor the other.

The famous Sonata apart, there are other notable things to be indicated. There is the seldom played *Ab-Irato*, an *Étude de Perfectionnement*. This was a long time in maturing. It had first appeared in Fétis and Moscheles' *Méthode des Méthodes* in 1842, where it is called *Morceau de Salon*. The second edition, entirely rewritten and revised, came out, in Berlin, in 1852, and another and final edition was printed two years later. These details show the ceaseless care for correction and improvement that characterized all Liszt's compositions. The title, *Ab-Irato*, means in a rage, or in a fit of temper, and this gives the mood of the piece. It is, in reality, a delayed and rather special *Étude d'Exécution Transcendante*, and dates, in style, from his earlier, Paris period.

Several piano pieces, appearing at about this time, seem to show Liszt in a frame of mind engendered by the death of Chopin. These pieces, that is to say, have titles which Chopin used; and if there are, in reality, great differences in mood and in execution it is because of the distance in temperament and style. A polonaise by Liszt could not be the same as a polonaise by Chopin. It is possible, for instance, that it might be more reminiscent of the polonaises of Weber. And, as if to prove this, there are the two well-known polonaises of Liszt published just at this time. There is, also, belonging to exactly the same genre of music, a *Mazurka Brillante*, quite unknown to the concert public. When we come to the *Trois Études de Concert*, still played occasionally, we are again on the same ground; but these *Études*, which are much longer and more complicated than those of Chopin, can be described as being lacking in fire compared with their prototypes. Their mood is that of the Polonaises. None of these pieces, in fact, is first rate.

The same stricture applies to the *Scherzo and March*, and the *Grand Solo de Concert*, in E minor, afterwards arranged as a concerto for two pianos. They are inferior examples of Liszt. There is much more besides; but where could space be found for more than the mere titles of the *Consolations* (six pieces), the *Harmonies Poétiques et Religieuses* (ten pieces), the notorious *Liebesträume*, with its two innocent companions, guiltless only because they have escaped publicity. Nevertheless, there are delightful things hidden away in the *Consolations* and the *Harmonies Poétiques*, such as the splendid *Bénédiction de Dieu dans la Solitude*, the third piece in the latter collection; and, to close this list in a happier vein of appreciation, there is the *Berceuse*, an exquisite little piece, one of the most lovely in fact of his smaller works, as near perfection in its way as the Eglogue of the *Années de Pèlerinage*. The little *Valse Impromptu* is delightful, too. This is Liszt in his most detailed, miniature manner; and, finally, and best of the lot, there are his two fine *Ballades*, of which the second, in B minor, is a really magnificent thing, not to be confused, by its title, with the *Ballades* of Chopin, for they could not be more different. It is less passionate and more full-blooded; concerned, as it were, less with personal suffering than with great happenings on the epical scale, barbarian invasions, cities in flames—tragedies of public, more than private, import.

Such, with reservation always of one or two special things for separate mention when their occasion arises, is a mere note of his compositions during the incredible years that he spent at Weimar. It was little more than a decade in length, but it might have been the lifetime of several different composers. Even now, many delightful things have escaped notice. There has been no space, for instance, for the *Glanes de Woronince*, three transcriptions of Polish melodies written down during those first romantic months when Liszt began his love affair with the Princess. They are the relics of his stay at her château. The first of these tunes is the same as that of one of Chopin's Chants polonais, the *Mädchens Wunsch*, but it is differently treated. The third is a Dumka, a Slavonic rhythm used so often by Smetana and Dvořák in their chamber music. These are pieces of an exquisite delicacy and finish; the time and place in which they were written giving them an exceptional place among his numberless trifles. That they are nostalgic and sentimental is no detriment to this.

But his extraordinary personality pervades even the smallest efforts of his pen; and, as with every great artist, he can often be recaptured more easily in the smallest sketch than in the most ambitious of his works. Take, for instance, the *Chanson Bohémienne*, a Russian Gypsy song, which must be entirely unknown to all but the most omnivorous of his admirers. This is a complete virtuoso piece, in miniature. There could be nothing better with which to end a recital. It has all the parade of the most ambitious Rhapsody, and not the Rhapsody's length or redundancy. It has all his mannerisms, and no room for bathos and rhetoric. Within its limits, this *Chanson Bohémienne* must be a perfect epitome of his ornament or arabesque. It is ornament for ornament's sake, and is, indeed, of complicated mechanism; only to be played ideally in the precision of a musical box, or by the hands of a pianist of rare competence. If we are ready to admit its perfection when rendered by mechanical means, it belongs to a whole category of little pieces by Haydn, by Mozart, by Liszt. All of these share the same requirements; they must be rendered mechnically, in perfect gradation. And, to close this chapter, no better illustration of our meaning could be found than in the mechanical pianos to be heard in Seville, in the wineshops. These play Spanish dances of the utmost complexity, and their perfection could only be bettered by the most skilful hands imaginable. So it is with this *Chanson Bohémienne*; it must be played consummately, or not at all. And this is true of the greater part of Liszt's piano music.

CHAPTER XXXII
Liszt and Wagner

In these early days, before his piano-pupils absorbed so much of Liszt's time and attention, when it was still a question of making Weimar the musical centre of the future, it was only natural that his entourage should consist of many of the names that were to be famous in Europe for the next fifty years, until the end of the century. Von Bülow, Richter, Joachim, are sufficient indication of that. But, with increasing strength, the assembly of these forces for the music of the future began to mean one thing above all others—the advancement of Wagner. We have arrived, in fact, at the name that is linked eternally with that of Liszt.

Their first meeting had been in Paris, in 1842; and it is better, perhaps, to let the story of their encounter be told in Wagner's own words. 'I met Liszt for the first time during my earliest stay in Paris, and at a period when I had renounced the hope, nay, even the wish for a Parisian reputation, and, indeed, was in a state of internal revolt against the artistic life I found there. At our meeting Liszt appeared to me the most complete contrast to my own being and situation. In the midst of this Parisian world, into which it had been my desire to flee from my sordid surroundings, Liszt had grown up, from his earliest age, the object of general love and admiration, at a time when I was being received with universal coldness and lack of sympathy. In consequence, I looked upon him with suspicion. I had no opportunity of disclosing my aims and ambitions to him, and therefore the reception I met with from him was altogether of a superficial kind, as was indeed quite natural in a man to whom every day the most diverse impressions claimed access. But I was not in a mood to look with unprejudiced eyes for the cause of his behaviour, which, friendly and obliging in itself, could but gall me in my then state of mind. I never repeated my call on Liszt and, without knowing or even wishing to know him, I was inclined to consider him as strange and hostile to my nature.

'My repeated expression of this feeling was afterwards reported to Liszt, just at the time when the performance of my

Rienzi, at Dresden, attracted general attention. He was surprised to find himself misunderstood with such violence by a man whom he had scarcely known, and whose acquaintance now seemed not without value to him. I am still touched at recollecting the repeated and eager attempts he made to change my opinion of him, even before he knew any of my works. He acted, not from any artistic sympathy, but led by the purely human wish of putting an end to a casual disharmony between himself and a fellow-creature; perhaps he also felt an infinitely tender misgiving of having unintentionally hurt me. Those who realize the terribly callous selfishness of our social life, and especially the lack of sympathy in the mutual relations of modern artists, cannot but be struck with wonder, nay, delight, at the treatment I experienced from this extraordinary man.

'Liszt soon afterwards witnessed a performance of *Rienzi* at Dresden, on which he had almost to insist, and after that I heard from all the different corners of the world, where he had been on his artistic tours, how he had everywhere expressed his delight with my music, and had indeed—I would rather believe unintentionally—biased people's opinions in my favour. This happened at a time when it was becoming more and more evident that my stage works would have no outward success. But just when the case seemed desperate, Liszt succeeded by his own energy in opening a refuge to my art. He ceased his wanderings, settled down in small and modest Weimar, and there took up the conductor's baton, after having shone so long in the splendour of the greatest capitals of Europe. At Weimar I saw him for the last time, when I rested a few days in Thuringia, not yet certain whether my pending prosecution (for revolutionary activities) would compel me to continue my flight from Germany. The very day when my personal danger became a certainty, I saw Liszt conducting a rehearsal of my *Tannhäuser*, and was astonished at recognizing my second self in his achievement. What I had felt in composing the music, he felt in performing it; what I wanted to express in writing it down, he proclaimed in making it sound. Strange to say, through the love of this rarest friend, I gained, at the moment of becoming homeless, a real home for my art, which I had longed and sought for always in the wrong place.

'At the end of my last stay in Paris, when ill, broken down and despairing, I sat brooding over my fate, my eye fell on the score of my *Lohengrin*, totally forgotten by me. Suddenly I felt something like compassion that this music should never sound from off the death-cold paper. I wrote two lines to Liszt; his answer was that preparations for the performance were being made on the largest scale the limited means of Weimar would permit. Everything that men and circumstances could do was done in order to make the work understood. . . . Errors and misconceptions impeded the desired success. What was to be done to supply what was wanted, so as to further the true understanding on all sides, and with it the ultimate success of the work? Liszt saw it at once, and did it. He gave to the public his own impression of the work in a manner the convincing eloquence and overpowering efficiency of which remain unequalled. Success was his reward, and with this success he now approaches me, saying: "Behold, we have come so far; now create us a new work that we may go still further".'

The famous letter contains, if not the whole truth, that part of it which suited Wagner, and as much of it as would have met with the approval of Liszt. Wagner, for all his genius, and because, in fact, of the confines of that, was incapable of taking even the smallest interest in anything that would not lead to his own personal advantage. Liszt only becomes a person worthy of any consideration in his eyes when *Lohengrin* or *Tannhäuser* is in prospect of performance. Then, without further delay, he recognizes in Liszt his second self; and, since even his second, or shadow, self must be a person of interest, it follows that Liszt is a composer of surprising talents.

The energies of this extraordinary man were so entirely concentrated upon his own career that a benevolent interest in that of any other composer was something quite outside his capacity. He will express himself upon Mozart or Beethoven, in order to establish his own stature beside them. Even then, he almost grudges them their achievement, and seems only to be recalled to a sense of their greatness by the recollection that they were the persons nearest to himself. And they were dead, safely dead. If that was his view of the past, while the present, the immediate present, was himself, and himself alone, the music of the future was no less egoistic in its prospects. The success of Bayreuth, and the ever-increasing life of his operas during the seventy years that have passed since his death, have justified his egoism. His career, to which there is no parallel in art, unless it is that of Rubens, who was as universally famous in his lifetime and whose works have never suffered the eclipse of fashion, this Wagnerian fame and omnipotence could never have been brought about had Wagner been less selfish and less self-seeking. He cannot, therefore, be reproached with that—but it may, at least, be remarked upon.

The intervention of Liszt on his behalf, at this early stage in his career, was at least as important as the later patronage of Ludwig II. His support, in the first place, fortified Wagner's tenure of the post of second Kapellmeister to the Royal Opera at Dresden. The production of *Rienzi*, *The Flying Dutchman*, and *Tannhäuser* was thus accomplished, even if the circumstances were not ideal to the composer's tastes, and these, it will be admitted, were difficult to satisfy. The revival of *Tannhäuser*, at Weimar, with Liszt conducting, must have been more near to his approval.

Within two months of this, the disturbances of that eventful year broke forth and Wagner had to flee from Dresden because of his revolutionary activities. He arrived at Weimar as a fugitive, carrying with him the manuscript of *Lohengrin*. Our hero welcomed him with enthusiasm, procured him a passport and contrived to delay his order of expulsion for as long as possible. He was even given time to visit the Wartburg, and, indeed, it would have been hardly fair to prevent his access to a spot he had made so famous with his music. But, in the end, Wagner had to go; and he went from Weimar to Switzerland, and then to Paris. From the latter city he wrote to Liszt, as he describes in the letter we have quoted, imploring Liszt to put *Lohengrin* into rehearsal. This was, therefore, the one opera by Wagner that Liszt actually produced, and it was given for the first time on 28 August 1850.

A period of ten years followed during which Wagner indulged in literary work and prepared himself for the immense and unprecedented labours that he had promised. No one but Wagner could have had the tenacity to put these promises into execution, but this lull in his actual operatic production extended until it was too late for Liszt to take any active part in their performance. The Weimar period was, in fact, over and finished before it could be a question of producing any more of his operas.

During these ten years Wagner lived, for the most part, in Switzerland. Liszt did not see him for four years until they met at Zurich, in 1853; and, in the autumn of the same year, they met again, at Basle, and went from there to Paris, together. Three years later found them together at Zurich, whence they went to St. Gall, but these sporadic meetings only stimulated their correspondence with each other, and Liszt must have been acquainted with *Tristan*, with the *Meistersinger*, and with *The Ring*, in every single stage of creation.

Their letters, which occupy two whole volumes, are the proofs of this intimate association between them. It is easy enough to criticize the one-sided nature of the communion together. 'I have just undertaken the publication of my three operas (*Rienzi, The Flying Dutchman*, and *Tannhäuser*). . . . The sum of money in question is as much as five thousand thalers. Have you got it; or has someone else, who will give it you for their friendship with you? Would it not be very interesting were you to become proprietor and editor of my operas? Besides, do you know what would be the result of it? It would be that I should become again a man, a man for whom existence would be possible, *an artist who for the rest of his life would never ask another penny* and would be content to work with joy and with pleasure. My dear Liszt, with this money you would buy my freedom from servitude. Do you think, as your slave, that I am worth that sum?' Or again, 'Find me someone who will buy my *Lohengrin* outright; find me someone who will order my *Siegfried*; I shan't ask too much!' Or: 'When you have brought *Lohengrin* into the world to your satisfaction, then I will complete my *Siegfried*, but *only for you* and for Weimar. Two days ago I shouldn't have believed that I could arrive at such a decision! It is to you that I owe this.' He will write, on the other hand, to von Bülow* (7 October 1859): 'There are many matters which we are quite frank about among ourselves (for instance, that since my acquaintance with Liszt's compositions my treatment of harmony has become very different from what it was formerly), but it is indiscreet, to say the least, of friend Pöhl to babble this secret to the whole world.' It was the discovery of this letter that prompted such a partisan of Liszt as Busoni to say that it suggested the morality of a fraudulent bank and accounted for Wagnerite standards of truth. Admirers of Wagner are agreed that the results justified the means. In the face of this

---

* Quoted from *Ferruccio Busoni* by Edward J. Dent, p. 233. Oxford University Press, 1933. Letters of Wagner translated in *Letters of Richard Wagner*, ed. W. Altmann. J. M. Dent & Sons, London, 1927.

triumphant genius no more can be said, therefore, than that this whole correspondence shows fidelity and disinterested enthusiasm contrasted with extravagant expressions of affection, constant requests for money, and a praiseworthy determination to succeed at all costs. The credit side are his operas; and they have been the delight of many millions—a great proportion of whom may be said not to care for any other music.

The one aspect of this whole question over which there can be no doubt is as to the genuine and wholehearted admiration felt by Liszt. He was content, and more than content—it was almost a relief to his feelings—to take second place and allow Wagner all the limelight. His letters to Princess Wittgenstein can be read, in vain, for a single ill-natured reference to Wagner. Nothing worse can be found than when he writes (on 30 August 1864), just after Wagner had accepted the offers of Ludwig II: 'Let us return to Wagner, whom I have called The Glorious, (der Glorreiche). Actually, there can be nothing changed between us. The great good luck, which he has at last encountered, will soften as much as possible a few asperities in his character.' This was in the nature of an extreme utterance; he could be induced to say no more than this, and that only to his most intimate friend.

It is idle to reproach Wagner with the tone of his letters. Had they been the absolute models in nobility of character, instead of betraying his selfishness and the weaker sides of his nature, it would make no difference to his music. But they form a psychological index to perhaps the most complicated character that ever existed. His superhuman labours and colossal ambitions could not be expected to leave Wagner an ordinary person. In order to achieve his purpose he had not an ounce of energy to waste upon anything else, it had all to be directed towards this one end—the advancement of his projects.

Their immensity, and the crushing weight of his personality, with its Teutonic disregard of other people's feelings, invaded the domains of the old opera with as little mercy as the Germans invaded Poland. Nothing could withstand his force. But, all along, it has been possible to prefer both the older methods of warfare and the older opera.

Liszt, at any rate, had no scruples as to the greatness of his friend. He proclaimed it at every opportunity. The pair of them are linked together by their friendship for all time; and Liszt, it is easily apparent, considered that any steps he had taken to advance Wagner's career were of more importance than all the compositions of his own hand.

If more space is given in these pages to Paganini and to Berlioz than to Wagner, it is because the giant shadow of Wagner has obscured other persons whose lives were less fortunate, if no less interesting and worthy of study. The history of Wagner is too well known; perhaps there is, now, too much light shed upon it. And this book, which is an attempt to depict Liszt in his true colours, cannot claim to show the influence of Wagner upon Liszt. The truth is in the other direction. The influences of Liszt upon Wagner, and his conscious or unconscious assistance, whether by word of mouth or through the lessons of his pen, must find their rightful place in the life of Wagner.

CHAPTER XXXIII

Liszt and his pupils—Hans von Bülow—Anton Rubinstein— Liszt resigns from Weimar

Perhaps there is something that belongs essentially to the Nineteenth Century in this ceaseless production, on the part of Liszt, during the Weimar period. We are in the years of the three-volume novel; and before long, for culmination, we shall have the three-volume opera, with an extra or fourth evening thrown in, even then. We are thinking of Dickens, of Balzac, and of Wagner.

This fullness of life was at its climax between the 'forties and 'sixties of last century. The masculine qualities were at a premium, as could be expected of a period that led up to the greatest dominance of the white races. And it is not without point that this period is the most hirsute in modern history. Beards had not been seen for two hundred years, so that the smooth manners of the eighteenth century would have been horrified at the appearance of their immediate descendants. Youths of twenty were as rough and unkempt as the tramps or swineherds of their grandfathers. The crinoline made women's fashions as artificial as in the time of Velázquez, and more material must have been employed in their dresses than at any period in history. Women writers, George Sand and George Eliot, were as much like men as possible, and their novels were as long or longer. All these things are symptomatic of that mid-century. It is possible to find its parallel in the truth to Nature preached by Ruskin and practised by the more realistic of the Pre-Raphaelite painters, and, alike in the huge orchestras of Berlioz and in the poetic vehemence of Swinburne.

We find our hero, during these years, incessantly preoccupied with work. In addition to everything else, he was planning an opera. He writes from Weimar, in 1851: 'As far as concerns my opera, allow me to thank you for the interest you are ready to take in it. For my own part, I have made up my mind to work actively on the score. I expect to have a copy of it ready by the end of next autumn. We will then see what can be done with it, and will talk it over'; and, later on, we learn that the subject of this projected opera was to have been Sardanapalus. This opera was one of the few things that Liszt never found time to accomplish. There were moments for everything else; even for giving lessons, which he did frequently, on the harp and trombone.

The generosity of his ambition made Weimar the centre of musical life. It was, therefore, only natural that he should come into contact with every single person of interest. It was indeed a galaxy of musicians that gathered round him. If this was the happiest period of his life, occupied, as he was, with so many projects for the helping of others, and of the art of music in general, and not yet disappointed with the reception of his own works, the credit is due in great measure to Princess Wittgenstein. The strength of the Wagner legend, so much of which is due to Cosima Wagner, has tended to obscure the part played in Liszt's life by her in order to put the Comtesse d'Agoult, her own mother, in place of the Princess. The descendants of the Princess Wittgenstein have been silent in this respect, while the family of Madame d'Agoult have had their say without contradiction.

The ring of satellites by whom he was surrounded at Weimar may be regarded, in a sense, as the fortification of his whims and mannerisms, some of which may be said to have descended, through two generations, to the concert platforms of our own day. This is true, not only of the piano-virtuoso, but of the orchestral conductor, as well. Von Bülow and Richter were his two chief disciples in this latter vocation, though they must have owed as much to the example of Wagner.

Hans von Bülow had come to him with a letter from Wagner as early as 1851.* He was a native of Berlin; one of those agile personalities, small in physique, with an enormous aptitude for work, great fires of conviction, deep loyalties, and a nervous system that gets strained beyond endurance. His musical talent was at once recognized by Liszt, who accepted him as a piano-pupil. Within two years he had developed into a pianist of formidable powers, who was likely to overwork himself by the scope and exactitude of an immense repertory.

Soon after his two years were accomplished, von Bülow was appointed professor at the Stern Conservatoire, in his native Berlin, and he left Weimar for his new post, where his mother kept house for him. It was at about this time that Princess Wittgenstein, who must have received gloomy reports from Paris, which Liszt had recently visited, put into operation her plan to remove Liszt's daughters, Cosima and Blandine, from Paris and bring them nearer their father's influence. Weimar itself would not do, but Berlin was close at hand, where the most loyal and ardent of Liszt's disciples was conveniently established with his mother. It was decided, therefore, to put Cosima and Blandine in her charge, as duenna, while Hans von Bülow would see to their education in matters of music.

Cosima wrought havoc in the household from her first arrival. 'You ask me, my dear master,' writes Hans to her father, 'for news of the Mlles Liszt. Up till now this would have been impossible for me, in view of the state of stupefaction, admiration, and even exaltation, to which they have reduced me, more especially the younger of the two. As to their musical capabilities, it isn't talent, it is genius that they have got! Yesterday evening, Mlle Blandine played a Sonata of Bach, and Mlle Cosima a Sonata

---

*The letters of von Bülow are one of the chief sources of information about Liszt during this period. A selection of them was translated by Miss Constance Bache in 1896. The whole series opens amusingly enough at a time when von Bülow was nearly mad with boredom and ennui as tutor to the daughters of Count Mycielski, at the Castle of Chocieszewice, near Posen. Boredom of this kind, l'ennui du château, can seldom have been better expressed than in the outpourings of this exile, who longed to be with Liszt, at Weimar. He was soon, we are glad to relate, restored to his friends.

of Beethoven. I am, also, making them work at piano-arrangements of orchestral works for four hands. I shall never be able to forget the delicious evening when I played, and replayed them, your Psalm. The two angels were as if on their knees, plunged in adoration of their father. They understand your masterpieces better than anyone, and you have really got in them a public given you by nature. How moved and touched I have been in recognizing the ipsissimum Lisztum in the playing of Mlle Cosima!' After this outburst, it will be no surprise to learn that, during Liszt's next visit to Berlin, Hans von Bülow announced his engagement to Cosima; and they were married eventually, on 14 August 1857.*

If von Bülow was the chief of his pupils, and the most energetic of his disciples at this time, Liszt had also the support and admiration of such men as Richter and Joachim. That they were drawn away from him by Wagner and Brahms, respectively, is a sign of the trend of public opinion, which, having refused to recognize anything but the interpreter and executant in Liszt, failed to show interest in his career as composer when he abandoned his concert fame for this purpose. The period of his neglect is, indeed, beginning; and it starts, typically enough, at the very zenith of his activity, both as original composer and as the pioneer of the musical future.

As if to intensify his difficulties, this was the very moment when his one rival appeared in that region where he had reigned to the exclusion of all other men. Only a few years before there had not been a single pianist to compare with Liszt; there had been no one who dared to challenge his absolute supremacy.

Anton Rubinstein is the only artist who has ever been mentioned in the same breath with him, even, if on every occasion that they have been contrasted together, Liszt has been allowed the mastery. This meteor made his appearance from exactly the quarter that might have been expected, from the region, in fact, of pianism; which, in nearly every instance but that of Busoni, has come from what might be termed the Marches of Russia. The Moldavian Colossus, as he was announced in those early days, was born at Wechwotynetz, in Moldavia, in 1829. This is on the

*In this same year, Liszt's elder daughter, Blandine, was married, at Florence (on 22 October, Liszt's birthday), to Émile Ollivier, the French statesman and minister of Napoleon III.

borders of the modern Rumania, near the Danube Delta; but his family moved to Moscow, when he was only a few years old, and his musical education was accomplished in that capital. In 1840 he presented himself to Liszt, whose soul, we can only imagine, was completely incapable of jealousy, for from childhood Rubinstein was a very near rival to his fame.

This tremendous executant and artist, born of Jewish parents in the Scythian steppes, was not by any means the sort of product that might have been expected of his place of origin. Instead, his tastes were of severely classical description. He liked to deny all music since the death of Chopin, and, in distinction to Liszt, was of entirely retrograde tendencies. This did not prevent him from being more prolific himself than almost any composer who has ever lived. He was a fountain of bad music. Very little of it has survived; but at the time we are speaking of, when he had attached himself to some extent to Liszt, he was surrounded by what must have been an almost frightening accumulation of mostly unpublished manuscripts.

Liszt recognized his true qualities at once. We find him writing to Dr. Brendel, 2 July 1854: 'That is a clever fellow—the most notable musician, pianist, and composer, indeed, who has appeared to me from among the younger lights. He possesses tremendous material, and an extraordinary versatility in handling it. He brought with him about forty or fifty manuscripts (Symphonies, Concertos, Trios, Quartets, Sonatas, Songs, a couple of Russian operas which have been given in St. Petersburg) which I read through with much interest during the four weeks which he spent here.'

A few months later, Rubinstein is again mentioned (December 1854). 'I am glad that you, dear friend, after some jerks and wrenches, have come together again with the pseudo-Musician of the future, Rubinstein. He is a clever fellow, possessed of talent and character in an exceptional degree, and therefore no one can be more just to him than I have been for years. Still, I do not want to preach to him—he may sow his wild oats and fish deeper in the Mendelssohn waters, and even swim away if he likes. But, sooner or later, I am certain he will give up the obvious and the conventional for the organically real, if he does not want to stand still. . . .'
Rubinstein did not have it in him to fulfil these expectations. As a composer, if we complete the simile that Liszt applied to all his

multiform efforts, he may be said not even to have swum away but to have spent his lifetime caught among the weeds.

But, as a pianist, he was to achieve unheard-of fame, carrying his conquests to America, and being the first great virtuoso to give concerts from ocean to ocean across that continent. This was a fatigue which the fates kindly spared to Liszt. In some sense, therefore, Rubinstein was successor to Liszt, and he may, certainly, be described as taking the fortunes that were waiting for our hero. But Liszt did not want them. He had retired, indeed, especially to avoid them.

If we take stock of Liszt's position in the closing years of the Weimar epoch, we are bound to admit that the rise of Rubinstein into such eminence as a pianist must have been but another of the forces closing in upon him to make his present situation impossible. It was not that he can ever have had any desire to return to that career, but the fact that he was now supplanted, and that his feats of pianism, already become legendary, were being matched by the achievements of a younger man, cannot but have had the effect of driving him still further into purposeful isolation.

This was but one of the threefold forces that were working against him. It cannot, even, be called that, for it is ridiculous to suppose that it had any effect whatever upon his decisions. But there was also the disappointing reception of his own works, whether for piano or for orchestra. And then, as well, there were the difficulties always attendant upon schemes such as those he had tried to put into practice, and actually sustained with his efforts for more than ten years, at Weimar. He did not have the support of the Grand-Duke to anything like the extent to which it had been promised. A note of this creeps into a letter he wrote, some years later, to the Princess. It was at a time when von Bülow, sharing in the favours with which Ludwig II had overwhelmed Wagner, had been invited by the King to the Starnberger See, had seen the King four times, and been invited to dinner with him tête-à-tête, without Wagner. 'His relations', Liszt writes (30 August 1864), 'are of a nature as exceptional as they are flattering to him. In fact, he finds himself more advanced in the Royal favour in a few days than I was at the end of ten years at Weimar. As to the position of Wagner, there is something prodigious about it. Solomon was wrong—there is something new under the sun!'

This is clear enough evidence of the sense of neglect with which his memories of Weimar were tinged.

Ten years is a long time; and, towards the end of this decade, the deaths of several persons occurring close together much affected the circumstances of his life. The death of the Grand-Duke Karl-Frederick, his original patron, in 1853, altered the whole outlook of his projects. Soon afterwards, the Grand-Duchess Marie-Paulowna died and his strongest supporter and partisan was thus removed. The young Grand-Duke, Karl-Alexander, had different intentions with regard to Weimar. It was his wish to revive the theatre; and, in his enthusiasm for Goethe and Schiller, the musical reputation that Weimar had gained owing to the efforts of Liszt was of little moment to him. He grudged the unnecessary expense.

It was in vain that Liszt appealed to him to mount the first performance of the *Nibelungen*. 'It is my duty, Monseigneur, once again to fix your attention upon a great matter, and I enter upon it without further prelude. For the honour and interest of that protection which Your Royal Highness has given to the fine arts, as for the honour of being the initiator, and for the prescience that I venture to ask you to display on behalf of Weimar in these matters, so far as it is possible, it seems to me not only suitable, but necessary and even indispensable, that the *Nibelungen* of Wagner should be given for the first time at Weimar. It is certainly nothing simple or easy; exceptional measures must be taken—for instance, the construction of a special theatre and the engagement of a personnel strictly according to the intentions of Wagner; difficulties and obstacles will certainly be encountered, but, in my opinion, all things considered, it will be sufficient that Your Royal Highness should seriously wish it to be done for these matters to accomplish themselves. As to the moral and material result, I am not afraid to guarantee that they will be at all points such as to give satisfaction to Your Highness. The work of Wagner, of which half is completed and the whole will be quite finished in two years, will dominate this epoch as the monumental achievement of contemporary art; it is undreamt of, marvellous, and sublime. How much, then, is it to be deplored that the evil forces of mediocrity, which in certain circumstances reign and govern, should prevent him from shining and giving light on the whole world!'

But it was no use. His proposals met with no success. The *Nibelungen* had to wait until their production at Bayreuth in 1876, and Weimar lost this honour which Liszt had tried to secure for it. As the first production of *The Ring* was the greatest ambition of Liszt, it may be imagined that his disappointment was personal and acute; and, while he met with this opposition over the most important of his projects, he began to be subjected to every kind of small and petty annoyance. His curious situation with regard to the Princess still remained the cause of scandal in this little provincial capital, even after it had been regularized by ten years of existence. They had to endure the slight, but irritating, impertinences of the wives of officials and of Protestant burghers.

The crisis came when Karl-Alexander appointed a person named Dingelstedt to be director of the theatre. Acting, no doubt, on the Grand-Duke's orders, this individual soon contrived to strike out of the State budget all new credits asked for on behalf of music. He reduced the musical programmes, as far as possible, and put on in their place a series of indifferent plays. The one novelty that Liszt had down for production was *The Barber of Baghdad*, a harmless opera by his pupil, Cornelius. When the curtain fell on this, Liszt was met, not with applause, but with hisses. He wrote immediately to resign his post. His retirement, at first, was only gradual, but we may date the end of the Weimar period, in effect, from that evening in the opera house. It was 18 December 1858.

CHAPTER XXXIV

Liszt begins to be deserted by good fortune—The Princess goes to Rome to plead her cause—Liszt in Paris—He lunches with Daniel Stern and dines with Rossini—His friendship with Baudelaire—'Plon-plon' and Count Walewski—Wagner comes to Weimar to hear the Faust Symphony *and bid farewell to Liszt—He brings the completed copy of* Tristan *with him. Liszt sets sail for Rome—Dramatic postponement of his marriage at the eleventh hour—An operatic dénouement*

A new pattern of life was beginning to shape itself, but at first the differences were not so apparent. Two more seasons at Weimar were to pass before he actually left the town. But his heart was no longer concerned for its future; he was more careless of its destinies, now that he knew how small was their scope. Weimar had been given its opportunities and had first neglected, and then refused them.

These dead possibilities had been centred in Wagner more than in any other personality. If *The Ring* could not be given, he would produce *Tristan*; but even this, simple as it was compared with *The Ring*, was not allowed him. Wagner, then, was his ambition, but it would not be just to lay all the blame for the failure of Weimar upon Karl-Alexander, for this Prince had the highest regard for Liszt and a genuine love for music. He was to show this, again and again, until many years later, by repeated attempts he managed to recall Liszt to Weimar for a part of each year, but in different, in, as it were, reduced circumstances, and without Princess Wittgenstein. It was this same Prince, who, forty years later, in 1901, invited Busoni to Weimar, to hold a Meisterklasse, and made the remark to him that 'Liszt *was* what a Prince *ought to be*!'*

If Karl-Alexander had, then, a great admiration for Liszt, the difficulties in his position with regard to him were over the Princess and over Wagner. Karl-Alexander was young; he had only just succeeded to the throne and he wished to make his own

* *Ferruccio Busoni*, by Edward J. Dent, p. 128. Oxford University Press, 1933.

reign different from that of his predecessor. He wanted to find self-expression for himself. The Princess, who was a woman of forty, was perhaps to some extent the Queen, if the notoriously uncrowned Queen, of Weimar. She could only be described as reigning at the Altenburg.

And then there was Wagner, one of the most difficult and exacting characters that have ever lived. It is, also, only fair to say that the expenses involved in producing *The Ring* would have been on an enormous scale for so small a town. Eighteen years later at Bayreuth, with the resources of all Bavaria behind him, and with a generation better educated in Wagner, *The Ring* could not be made a financial success. And it is conceivable, too, that Karl-Alexander may have been one of those music-lovers who do not appreciate the music of Wagner.

It must be remembered that Liszt only really cared for the music of his own time. He was interested, hardly at all, in old music. We find him, not long after his resignation, writing as follows to Agnes Klindworth, his female devotee and clandestine confidante: 'If I have stayed as much as a dozen years at Weimar, I have been sustained by a sentiment which is not lacking in nobility—the honour, the dignity, the fine character of a woman, to uphold against infamous persecution—and, more than that, a great idea: that of the renewal of music by its more intimate alliance with poetry. The idea of its more free development, more adequate, so to speak, to the spirit of our times, has always kept me fascinated. . . . If, since I fixed myself here in '48, I had wished to attach myself back to the posthumous side of music, to associate myself with its hypocrisy, to keep on good terms with its prejudices, nothing would have been more easy for me, considering my previous liaisons with the "big-wigs" of that body. I should certainly have gained in worldly consideration and in the niceties of life; the same newspapers that cover me with abuse would have vaunted me to the skies, without my having to give myself much trouble about that. They would willingly have pardoned and made innocent some of the peccadillos of my youth, in order to raise up and praise in every manner possible the zealot of good and healthy traditions, from the time of Palestrina down to Mendelssohn. But that could not be my lot: my convictions were too sincere, my faith in the present and in the future of art too ardent and too positive, at the same time, for it to be possible for me to accommodate myself to the vain formulas of objurgation with which our pseudo-classics like to cry out that art is losing itself, that all art is, indeed, lost. . . . All the time I have never concealed from myself that my position was most difficult and my task most awkward, for many long years at least. Wagner, having made such brave innovations and accomplished such admirable masterpieces, my first care must be to conquer a foundation, a root, for his works in German soil at a time when he was an exile from his country, and all the little theatres of Germany were afraid to risk his name on their programmes. Four of five years of hard work, if you like, on the part of myself, have been sufficient for what has been accomplished, in spite of the exiguous means that were at my disposal. Indeed, Vienna, Berlin, Munich, etc., for five years have done nothing but follow what little Weimar (at which they mocked, at first) showed them ten years ago. . . .'

It was, in fact, impossible for a person of Liszt's character to console himself in the past. He had to find present comfort in his art; and, if it failed, his consolation was in his religion. The blows of life were beginning to fall upon him. One by one, he lost his children. His two daughters, of whom he had become passionately fond, now that he saw more of them, were both married; and then tragedy came with the death of his only son Daniel, a boy of nineteen, who was studying law in Berlin.

Yet another blow was the marriage of the Princess's only daughter, Marie, to Prince Constantine Hohenlohe. This happened in the same year 1859. Liszt was devoted to this only child of the Princess; and her marriage, which took her away to live in Vienna, meant that they would hardly ever see her. It is probable that he was more fond of Princess Marie than of his own children, and his letters are full of affectionate references to Magnolette, as she was called. And not only Magnolette, but Magne, Magnet, Magnolet, Farfadet, Furet, l'Infante, Mux-Blanc, and Schahatte! Such was the extent of List's affection for the person whom we might as well call his stepdaughter.

In these accumulating troubles he could not even feel secure in his friendship with Wagner. He was no longer in a position to get Wagner's operas produced at Weimar, even though he continued to conduct the orchestra and to hold his classes for another couple of seasons; nor was he able to send a satisfactory answer to

Wagner's appeals for funds. He must, in fact, have begun to feel deserted on all sides, and even by his friends.

The effect of these sorrows and disappointments was to draw him nearer to the Princess. She was the one person who had a constant belief in his powers and who encouraged him to work; for, from the outside world, it would have mattered little had he given up his music and made that one more sacrifice of his talents. They were still hoping to marry: the question of the Princess's divorce had been constantly before the Russian ecclesiastical courts, and at last, in the spring of 1860, word arrived that her divorce had been made absolute by the Russian authorities. It now remained for the Roman Church to give their consent to the marriage. This time it was the Bishop of Fulda, the local Catholic dignitary, who raised objections, and so the Princess set off for Rome to carry her case, in person, before the authorities of the Roman Church.

Liszt, meanwhile, after finishing the season at Weimar, went to Paris. Perhaps the fact that his marriage was coming so near made him feel that, far from retiring from the world, he must get as near to its heart as possible. Another incentive may have been the chance that Wagner might at last conquer the French public with *Tannhäuser*, in the new version specially revised for the purpose, though, in the end, Liszt did not attend this performance and arrived in Paris to find Wagner in disgrace and despair at its bad reception.

During this visit to the French capital he was unable to avoid Daniel Stern. He had not seen her for sixteen years, and hardly any communication had passed between them over this long period. In 1855, for instance, we know that he refused to answer a letter from her about the education of their children. But, on this occasion, he went twice or even three times to her rooms in the Hôtel Montaigne, and she even gave a luncheon-party in his honour. But whether alone with her, or before her guests, and more when alone than in company, conversation proceeded only upon the stiffest and most conventional lines and the subjects discussed were all politics or literature. Daniel Stern had become a sort of literary machine, and her emotions were not in the least stirred by this encounter with her former lover. Or she dissimulated most successfully.

It must have been more pleasant to dine with Rossini. This

aged epitome of the Rococo had recovered his vein of melody and was pouring out ceaseless streams of little pieces of music, no longer in length than an anecdote or an epigram, written on the backs of menus and in autograph albums. The foremost musicians and singers of the day used to forgather in his house in order to perform these. Rossini had a genius for comic titles, and we find in the programmes, which were printed as souvenirs of these occasions, such titles as:

> *Ouf! le petit pois.*
> *Des Tritons s'il vous plait!* Montée et Descente.
> *Un mot à Paganini.*
> *Une larme*, pour basso.

Rossini lived in his house in the Chaussée d'Antin, gourmandizing, incessantly gourmandizing, and writing his music between the courses. It was said that he had recently invited the critic Caraffa, an admirer of Wagner, to his house, and to have served him with fish without sauce at dinner, explaining, in so doing, that Caraffa liked music without melody. But Rossini apologized to Wagner, publicly in the press, and Liszt must have felt himself at liberty to visit his old friend.

He was given a reception entirely typical of Rossini. 'Ces beaux cheveux, sont-ils à vous', and, as he said this, the old curiosity ran his fingers through Liszt's hair, which fell like a mane upon his shoulders. Liszt replied that his hair was his to do what he liked with; that it was his personal property to use or get rid of as he chose. And Rossini pointed sadly to his own wig and explained that, soon, he would have neither teeth nor even legs of his own.

During this visit to Paris, Liszt made the acquaintance of Baudelaire, who was an enthusiast for Wagner and had written a pamphlet in defence of *Tannhäuser*. The record of this is to be found in Wagner's own *Mein Leben*.[*] 'Another day', we read, 'we met for lunch at Gounod's, when we had a very dull time which was only enlivened by poor Baudelaire, who indulged in the most outrageous witticisms. This man, "criblé de dettes", as he told me, and daily compelled to adopt the most extravagant methods for a bare subsistence, had repeatedly approached me with adventurous schemes for the exploitation of my notorious

[*] *My Life*, by Richard Wagner, vol. ii. p. 780. London, Constable & Co., 1911.

fiasco (*Tannhäuser*). I could not, on any account, consent to adopt
any of these, and was glad to find this really capable man safe
under the eagle wing of Liszt's ascendancy. Liszt took him everywhere where there was a possibility of a fortune being found.
Whether this helped him to anything, or not, I never knew. I only
heard that he died a short time afterwards, certainly not from an
excess of good fortune.'*

There was, also, of course, Berlioz to visit; and Berlioz was in
an awkward position about Wagner, whose music he cordially
detested, and of whom he was desperately jealous. Berlioz looked
old, and ill, and hopeless. And, for contrast, there was Meyerbeer,
who was older still but overwhelmed with fortune.

It was a long way from Baudelaire to the restored glories of the
Bonapartes, but we find Liszt visiting Count Walewski, son of the
great Emperor, and dining in the famous Pompeian villa of Prince
Napoléon, 'Plon-Plon', who bore such a marked resemblance to
his uncle. This Cæsarean society was incomplete without Prince
Napoléon's sister, Princess Mathilde: but she had the tactlessness
to insist upon Liszt playing to the assembled company. As the
niece of a great soldier, she was accustomed to obedience.

We hear of Liszt, too, at the Tuileries, but Napoleon was an old
acquaintance of his. They had met in London, under the auspices
of Count d'Orsay, when Louis-Napoleon was a needy adventurer.
Liszt owned to an intense admiration for Napoleon III, whom he
considered as the greatest monarch of his time, extolling him for
his transformation of Paris into a magnificent modern town. In
conversing with Liszt, Napoleon must have dropped something of
the icy reserve, of the '25 degrés au dessous de zéro', noticed by
Berlioz. 'L'Empereur Napoleon', Liszt writes to the Princess, 'eut
presque un moment d'abandon, et me dit, avec quelque émotion,
"il me semble, que j'ai cent ans!" ' Liszt's reply to this: 'Sire, vous
êtes le Siècle', shows how much of the courtier there was in him.

At the end of his visit to Paris, Liszt went once more to Weimar.
It was for the last time, or so he thought. His mind, which was
always much occupied with anniversaries, was haunted by the
prospect of his fiftieth birthday.

He had begun to think about this as early as the year before,
when, on 14 September 1860, he drew up his will and testament
in the most solemn terms. 'All that I have done and thought in

* Baudelaire, as a matter of fact, did not die until 31 August 1867.

the last twelve years, I owe to her whom I have so ardently desired to call by the dear name of wife—against which happiness, human malignity and the most deplorable intrigues have opposed themselves obstinately up till now—to Jeanne Elisabeth Carolyne, Princesse Wittgenstein, née d'Iwanowska. . . . I cannot write her name without a trembling of the soul. All my joys are hers, and my sufferings all go to her to be appeased.' And, then, it is hardly necessary to add, he speaks of Wagner. 'There is in the art of our day a name already glorious, and which will be more and more glorious still: Richard Wagner. His genius has been a lighted torch to me; I have followed in his footsteps, and my friendship with him has had all the character of a noble passion. At a certain moment (about twelve years ago) I had dreamed of a new period for Weimar comparable to that of Karl-August, where Wagner and myself should have been the leading lights, as, in former time, Goethe and Schiller. The wickedness, not to say the villainy, of certain local circumstances, all sorts of jealousies and ineptitudes, both from within and without, have prevented the realization of this vision.' A few lines later, Liszt comes to the subject of his first love, Caroline de Saint-Cricq, now become Madame Caroline d'Artigaux, and living in the French provinces, in Béarn. She is to be given a ring in memory of him, when he dies.

This mood, this atmosphere of last will and testament, was the spirit in which he spent his last stay at the Altenburg. He read through old letters, packed up his belongings, and burnt old papers. Fourteen years of happiness were finished and over.

Meanwhile the Weimar Festival was in progress, culminating in the first performance of the *Faust Symphony* under von Bülow, who had developed into a magnificent conductor, the finest of his day. While the work was being rehearsed, a dramatic incident occurred. A thrill of excitement ran through players and audience, the doors of the theatre opened, and Wagner made his appearance. The musicians stood up to acclaim him, and he walked down the length of the theatre towards Liszt, whom he embraced. He had come specially to Weimar to hear the *Faust Symphony* and to bid Liszt farewell. He brought with him the completed copy of *Tristan*. It was a climax, an apotheosis of Liszt; and, after this, there can have been little more in his thoughts than that end to which he had been striving for so long, and which was, now, so near at hand.

His letters to the Princess take on the tone they had fourteen years before, when, as lovers, they had fled from Russia and Liszt was waiting for her to join him. He had waited for her in Weimar. Now he was to leave Weimar, in order to join her in Rome.

'It is impossible for me to reassemble on a single threshold', he writes to her, 'all the emotions of my last hours at the Altenburg. Each room, each piece of furniture, down, even, to the steps of the staircase and to the green lawns of the garden, all was illumined by your love, without which I feel myself annihilated. I could not keep back my tears. But, after a last prayer at your prie-dieu, where we used to kneel side by side before I set off on one of my journeys, I felt a feeling of liberation that comforted me again. In bidding the Altenburg farewell I feel I am coming nearer to you, and I breathe more freely.'

A few days later he has reached Marseilles, where he takes the steamer for Italy. 'These are the last lines that I shall write to you. My long exile is nearly over. In five days, I shall find my country, my hearth, and my home again in yourself!'

1861

✗ On 20 October he arrived in Rome. The wedding was to be two days later, on Liszt's fiftieth birthday, at six o'clock in the morning, as soon as day dawned. The church of San Carlo al Corso was already hung with flowers.

They spent the eve of their wedding day together, in her apartments. They must have prayed together before it was time for him to leave her. It was late, but not yet midnight, for superstition forbade that he should stay with her beyond that hour. But the moment of drama came, with a knocking upon the door. There were footsteps, and a servant with a lighted torch brought in a man in black.

The folds of his toga muffled him to his chin. He was nervous, and held in one hand a paper sealed with a great wax seal, while, with the other hand, he fingered the rolled brims of his Spanish hat.

The priest bore a letter for the Princess, from the Vatican. Her husband's family demanded a fresh enquiry into the case. The Wittgensteins refused to admit that she had been in any way forced into marriage with her husband. The Pope had no choice but to examine, once more, the whole argument for annulment. She was, by law, still married to Prince Nicholas. She could never marry Franz Liszt, her lover.

It was to these extraordinary circumstances that night dawned into day for the fiftieth birthday of Liszt. An ill-shaven priest had brought in a dénouement to the whole of his drama. It changes, now, and takes on fresh shape.

It is by such devices that the most skilful of operatic plots are sustained. The gardener comes in with a broken flower pot, and Count Almaviva has fresh evidence against Cherubino and the Countess. Susanna and Figaro must prolong the play, or it will end.

Or else it is Don Basilio, who interrupts the music lesson. Rosina is singing, while Count Almaviva disguised as another priest, as the very semblance, the shadow, of Don Basilio, plays the harpsichord for her song.

In the plot of *Il Barbiere* there is, indeed, more than a mere resemblance to our own. The priest comes in and interrupts the musician. If it is too late for him to adopt disguise, now, we may expect that in the next act. And, once again, the musician will become priest; we shall see him in his soutane for the rest of the play.

So, next morning, at what should have been their wedding hour, men on high ladders are taking down the garlands of flowers in San Carlo al Corso. The wedding has been countermanded and the flowers are not needed; the flower sellers take them back, soiled, to their stalls.

But, while all Rome ran with rumours, Liszt and the Princess stayed indoors, in their separate houses. There was nothing to be said, and nothing to be done. They were to continue the same course of life together. During some years they were hardly separated for a day; and, if Liszt becomes priest, we shall find the Princess a priestess, too. Only, were that possible, with more conviction than her lover.

BOOK IV

1861-1869

The Roman Period

CHAPTER XXXV

Last days of Papal Rome—Account of Liszt by Gregorovius—
He revisits Weimar—Returns to Rome and gives farewell
concert—The piano-centaur—Liszt becomes a priest—He is
lodged in the Vatican—The 'end of Lovelace'

The curtain for this fourth act rises upon a perspective of
Roman churches and convents. Every street is black with
priests and bells sound from every corner. Statues, beyond
number, stand on columns and upon the parapets of churches,
while as many beggars in their rags dwell below in the dust and
shadows. There is blue sky, a yellow, ochreish light along the
earth, and the shapes of cypress or stone pine, still, quite still
against the air.

In those last years of Pontifical Rome, the fountains of the
Piazza played, as now, while the shifting spectrum flashed from
out their spray to the striped Switzers, halberd on shoulder, in
the open windows at foot of Bernini's stairs; Pio Nono, himself,
could be seen at evening taking the cool with his prelates in the
Pincio gardens, and the Cardinals, in violet and purple, drove past
in their mule-drawn carriages, or walked, each with his Cauda-
torio, or attendant secretary, his sombre clothes, his half-incognito
only betrayed by black tricorne and scarlet stockings. It was still
the Rome of Pannini's paintings, of Pinelli's engravings; it was the
city of the priests. A town of Roman ruins and Baroque fountains,
peopled by monks and nuns who could not propagate and by
beggars who pullulated in the dust. Beyond Rome, the campagna
was a malarial plain; tumbled aqueducts ran for miles along its
length, and it was uninhabited except by herdsmen living in
conical, beehive huts. Rome could not be seen, but away in the
distance the dome of St. Peter's stood tethered to the ground, or
it might have risen into the Alban hills. There, close beside that
dome, dwelt the Pope, come down out of a remote antiquity,
childless, with his childless court, and drawing his very strength
from out that weakness. The different Orders of monks and nuns,
like companies of actors, played their sanctity and their devotions

in all the chapels; altars smoked with incense; church bells rang; and there was no purpose on earth but religion.

These professions have been joined, since the end of the last chapter, by two more acolytes or novices. The Princess had been the first to arrive in Rome, and during the eighteen months until Liszt arrived, while she was waiting for the annulment to be pronounced, it is probable that her latent religious interests came under the spell of this celibate city. When, therefore, her marriage to Liszt was forbidden by the Church, her scheme of life was not effectually altered by the decision. It was not necessary to change her plans; they would go on living in Rome.

We are not told where they would have settled, had they been married in the church of San Carlo al Corso. Weimar was impossible; so was Paris, owing to Daniel Stern; London was out of the question; Liszt had experienced too much, alike of big capitals, and of the petty jealousies of little towns like Weimar. It is quite likely, then, that their idea, in any case, had been to continue in Rome for some time. Her growing religious enthusiasm would account for this. As for Liszt, it will be remembered that he had already passed a winter in Rome, with Madame d'Agoult, in 1839. Rome was the city of his predilection.

He had undergone phases of deep religious experience as a child and—at intervals, and with interludes—all through his life. It was no new conversion with Liszt. One of his bonds with the Princess was the bond of prayer; a sentiment so nearly beyond the comprehension of the twentieth century that the mere mention of it is a curiosity. He had the conviction of his own worthlessness, and all his feelings of charity and generosity were aroused in its teachings. His religious feelings were of genuine force and fervour; there was nothing false in them. The Christian religion was his philosophy, his rule for making palatable the difficulties and hardships of life. Besides, the Church had been one of the greatest patrons of art. Music had been its handmaid. His own ambition, now, was to write music which would be the true picture of his faith. And, as we shall see, he had been writing church music since the middle years of the Weimar period.

He arrived in Rome having already sacrificed money, fame, his career, and, for the moment, every stimulus but that of faith. At the same time, Liszt was, at heart, too much a part of the Romantic Age, and, by disposition, too wilful and disdainful, to accept all the humility of religion without some show of rebellion against himself. Liszt was an actor, we must remember, a very great actor; and, had it been in our power to persuade Irving, for instance, never to be seen except in his stage clothes, to live permanently, as it were, in his stage part, we should after a time expect to find him returned, momentarily, to ordinary life just in order to point the contrast. The diabolist, it comes to this, will be displayed again in Liszt; that side of him is not dead.

In the meantime, he certainly presents a weird picture. It was not for nothing that Busoni, in his opera of *Die Brautwahl*, wanted the character of Leonhardt, 'a mysterious personage who had apparently lived for several centuries and was possessed of magical powers and uncanny arts',★ to look like Liszt at the age of fifty. This aspect of him certainly impressed intelligent observers of the time. The great Gregorovius writes of him in his Roman Journal, under date 13 April 1862: 'Have made Liszt's acquaintance, a striking, uncanny figure—tall, thin, and with long grey hair. Frau von S. maintains that he is burnt out and that only the outer walls remain, from whence a little ghostlike flame hisses forth.'

This was before he became a priest. He still occupied his rooms at 113 Via Felice and went, every evening, to see the Princess. She gave frequent receptions; and, with Cardinal Bonaparte, the Duca di Sermoneta, and his Italian pupil Sgambati, we find another name which was, henceforth, to play a large part in his life, that of Mgr., the future Cardinal, Hohenlohe, brother of Prince Hohenlohe, who had married the only daughter of the Princess. After a few months, Liszt, who was drawing nearer and nearer to priesthood, took advantage of an offer from the Pope's Librarian and went to live in the Madonna del Rosario, on Monte Mario. This took him out of Rome and makes his letters to the Princess more frequent, for he no longer saw her every day.

After he had been three years in Rome, living more and more in seclusion, never issuing forth except to see the Princess, but having received Pio Nono in his cell and played his harmonium to the Pontiff, Liszt came out of his retreat in answer to an appeal from von Bülow and set off for a musical festival at Carlsruhe. He writes to the Princess that his own works had a complete success, and adds: 'C'est quasi la première fois que pareil accident m'arrive.'

★ *Ferruccio Busoni*, by Edward J. Dent, pp. 175-177. Oxford University Press, 1933.

5 September 1864, finds him back again at Weimar, in the Altenburg. 'Les murs gémissent et pleurent. Je pleure, et pleure, et pleure encore, et ne puis que pleurer, prosterné devant vous, mon bon ange.' But let us hear of his arrival in Weimar, for nothing could be more typical, or more in keeping with the man and the circumstances. On this occasion he reached Weimar at three o'clock in the morning, and writes that he could not find a place in the only cab at the station. When he tried to get in, three men were already seated inside. So he preferred to profit by the dark night ('la nuit noire') to make the ascent from the station to the Altenburg on foot. 'Que de fantômes n'ai-je point rencontrés? Le Doppelgänger de Schubert sera le cousin le plus rapproché de cette famille spectrale.'

This was a scene absolutely in accord with one side of his nature. And we find this truly extraordinary character, who, it should be remarked, had in his power to possess himself of every luxury, writing back to Rome that in spite of all his efforts he could not economize, though he always travelled second class on the railway, never asked anyone to dinner, and could not even afford a carriage in the town. Immediately after Weimar, Liszt went to Paris, and it is no surprise to hear that he arrived there at five o'clock in the morning. But it was only a brief visit, the end of October found him back again in Rome.

He was preparing himself for what he must have considered the greatest event of his life, his reception into the priesthood. Prince Nicholas of Sayn-Wittgenstein had died the year before, in March 1864, but the question of Liszt's marriage to the Princess, who was now a widow, does not seem to have arisen again. They were both decided in their courses, and Liszt was, by now, deep in his devotions.

But, first of all, he gave his farewell concert. 'Liszt gave his farewell concert in the Palazzo Barberini,' writes Gregorovius; 'amateurs played and sang. He played *L'invitation à la Valse* and the *Erl König*, a curious farewell to the world. No one suspected that he had the Abbé's stockings already in his pocket.'

The next day he retired for a few days' preparation to the monastery of the Lazzaristi. He writes from there to the Princess to tell her how his days were passed. He rose from bed at half-past six, meditated alone in his cell, had coffee in his room, attended Mass at half-past eight, and, on Sundays, High Mass at half-past nine. This was succeeded by solitary scripture readings, visits to the Holy Sacrament, and dinner in the refectory at midday, where he was placed alone at a little table but could not follow what was read aloud by a monk from the pulpit. Then a siesta for an hour and a half, more scripture readings, walks in the garden, solitary meditation for an hour, supper at eight o'clock in silence, a talk with the Superior, P. Guerini, till half-past nine, and lights out at ten o'clock.

The actual ceremony of his admission took place on 25 April 1865. 'The following Sunday', we quote again from Gregorovius, 'Liszt received the tonsure in St. Peter's and first consecration at the hands of Mgr. Hohenlohe. He now wears the Abbé's frock, and, as Schlözer told me yesterday, looks well and contented. This is the end of the gifted virtuoso, a truly sovereign personality. I am glad that I heard him play again; he and the instrument seem to be one, as it were a *piano-centaur*.'

Liszt had, in fact, received four of the seven degrees of priesthood. He could not celebrate Mass, or hear confession. He could leave the priesthood when he wished, and it even left him at liberty to marry, did he so desire. But he was door-keeper, reader, acolyte, and exorcist. And an honorary canon, as well.

Immediately after the ceremony was over, on the very day of his reception into the Church, Liszt took over his new apartment. It was in the Vatican, opposite the Loggie of Raphael. Mgr. Hohenlohe, his friend, was next door. After dinner, that first night, he sat and smoked cigars with Mgr. Hohenlohe, with Prince Nicholas Hohenlohe-Waldenbourg, and with the d'Arenbergs. He offered them his private salon as a smoking-room, and the offer was accepted. But it is difficult for his biographer to think of Liszt in the Vatican without a memory of, for instance, Lola Montez. Few more peculiar characters than Liszt can ever have slept in such holy precincts. We find Gregorovius writing of him a few days later, on 7 May: 'Yesterday I saw Liszt clad as an Abbé. He was getting out of a hackney carriage, his black silk cassock fluttering ironically behind him. Mephistopheles disguised as an Abbé. Such is the end of Lovelace'; while Liszt is writing to the Princess, from the Vatican: 'Après demain votre très petit et infirme Abbé vous arrive avant 1 h.' This was Leonhardt or Mephistopheles, if you like. The new doorkeeper and exorcist was still himself, in fact, even in the Vatican.

CHAPTER XXXVI

*The Vatican and the Villa d'Este—Jonglerie Indienne de
l'Africaine—He revisits Hungary and plays Rhapsodies at an
open window—Two Episodes from Lenau's* Faust*—The*
Mephisto-Waltz*—The* Totentanz*—The* Faust-Waltz

So far as taking up lodgings in the Vatican is concerned this
palace is as inaccessible to ordinary mortals as the Potala at
Lhasa. There, also, a supreme Pontiff lives, surrounded by
his court of ecclesiastics, including, if the stories are true, a good
proportion of wizards and magicians, none of whom, we may
safely believe, for all their mitres and yellow robes and Homeric
helmets, were possessed of half the magical powers that were
present, beyond dispute, in the person of Liszt. He remained for
some months in the palace of the Hermit-King, if we like to make
use of this Tibetan title for Pio Nono, who still reigned in Rome.
And then a garden retreat was placed at his disposal that it would
be difficult to better. It was the cave of a wizard, the grotto of a
Merlin, transcendentalized.

Once again it was Mgr. Hohenlohe who was his friend and
patron. This prelate, who about this time received the red hat and
became a Cardinal, was in charge of the very important Austrian
interests at the Vatican. The Villa d'Este, at Tivoli, that had
descended to the Habsburgs, was at his disposal, and at the end of
this very month he furnished a suite of rooms at Villa d'Este and
installed Liszt in them. It is true that Liszt maintained a lodging
in Rome, but he left the Vatican when his friend became Cardinal
and moved from the Madonna del Rosario to the cloister of
Santa Francesca Romana. Here he had a view of the Forum, and
it is even possible that his windows may have looked out upon the
Temple of Venus. But the Villa d'Este became, more and more,
his place of choice, and he was to spend at least a part of each year,
for the remaining twenty years of his life, at Tivoli.

The Villa d'Este is one of the three or four most beautiful
gardens in the world. Perhaps there are only Capr22ròla and Villa
Lante to compare with it. The view of the Roman campagna
from the terrace is the landscape of Claude made permanent and

limitless, while the giant cypresses in the garden and the voices of all the waters could not be improved upon for poetry and music. It was amid this enchantment that he grew into old age, and it is certain that he worked more at Villa d'Este than anywhere else in those years.

Mephistopheles, or Lovelace, had not changed. He was still the magician, with a little of Satan and a little of the charlatan in him. His first letter to the Princess from the Villa d'Este, only a fortnight or three weeks after his priesthood, is completely in character. 'Ma journée d'hier s'est passée à lire une cinquantaine de pages du catéchisme de Persévérance en Italien—et à chercher quelques traits sur le piano pour la jonglerie Indienne de *l'Africaine*, dont je serai le coq d'Inde, autrement dit, le dindon de la farce.' *L'Africaine* was the last opera of Meyerbeer, corrected, revised, and postponed by him for twenty years, until it could only be produced the year after his own death. It was the newest sensation of theatrical music. The heavy, brassy Rococo of its strains, its military ensembles, the number of its figurants, as numerous and diverse as a circus train met with upon the road, these worldly contrasts were such a delight to Liszt that his fantasia upon the opera assumed double form and took up two volumes.

He was not still for long. By the beginning of August he had set off again upon his travels, this time to his native Hungary. He goes to stay in the country, near Pécs, with a rich friend, Baron Augusz, taking with him von Bülow and Reményi, the Tzigane, probably the most extraordinary and inspired violinist there has ever been. Here, there occurred a scene worthy of Leonhardt, the hero of Busoni's opera. On the Sunday evening he was serenaded and a crowd of seven or eight thousand people collected in the square outside the house. Instead of making a speech, Liszt, who appeared in his soutane, had his piano dragged to the open windows and played a Rhapsody to the crowd, with Reményi; and, after that, the *Rákóczy March*, for four hands, with von Bülow. After this episode his next letter to the Princess is addressed once more from the Vatican; and it is not improbable that *l'Africaine* may have occupied his attention within those sacred walls.

A week or two later he was in retreat once more with his friend Hohenlohe. They were woken at six, attended Mass at seven, and the day was passed in meditation and pious exercises till it came to supper at eight o'clock, in silence; at nine o'clock examination of conscience in the chapel, and at ten o'clock they were in bed and asleep.

It was in such extreme contrasts as this that his days were spent. He was accomplishing, as well, an enormous amount of work, chiefly in the form of religious music. But, before this phase of his life is mentioned, and while we have those words of Gregorovius still in our ears, the moment has arrived to show Liszt practising the rôle of Mephisto in more tangible form, in a shape that has long survived his own death. During the very year, 1862, in which Gregorovius made that first entry in his Roman Journal, Liszt published the finest instances of his work in this vein. I refer to the Two Episodes from Lenau's *Faust*.

These are entitled *Der nächtliche Zug* and *Mephisto-Waltz*, known in English as 'The Night Ride'[*] and 'Dance in the Village Inn'. They are, perhaps, his orchestral masterpieces; and, though the second of them is fairly familiar in the concert hall, the first is, for some reason, never performed, though it is a most dramatic subject rendered by the hand not only of a master but, almost, we might say, by that of the actual actor in the drama.

The title of the episode is not meant to depict a wild ride, but a stately, pompous procession. The piece opens with an evocation of a dark gloomy night, starless, we may suppose, but broken by warm breezes and by rustlings in the leaves and branches. It is, in short, a spring night, and the nightingales are singing. Faust enters on horseback, not pressing his horse into a gallop, but letting it saunter. Lights show of a sudden through the trees, there is distant singing, and the Chorale 'Pange Lingua' is heard, which rises to a great climax as a religious procession passes. The episode ends with Faust, alone again in the darkness, crying bitterly into the mane of his horse.

The weirdness of this scene and its romantic content are wonderfully portrayed in the music; and in the letter that we have quoted, written by Liszt to the Princess upon his return from Rome to the Altenburg, we must have the conscious echo of this scene. 'I preferred to profit by the dark night ("la nuit noire"). How many phantoms did I not meet? The Doppelgänger of Schubert would be the nearest relation one could find to this spectral family.'

[*] Translated in Breikopf and Härtel's catalogue as 'The Nightly Ride'.

The *Mephisto-Waltz*, which is the second of these pieces, is a thing really haunted in its own atmosphere. The scene is supposed to be a village inn which Faust and Mephisto enter, in search of love, on hearing the music from inside. The peasants are dancing, and the attention of Faust is taken by the landlord's daughter, who comes in to carry drinks to the dancers. Mephisto seizes the violin and his playing intoxicates the audience, who completely abandon themselves to love-making under the influence of the music. As the dancing reaches its climax, the singing of a nightingale is heard in the starlit woods, through the open doors. Mephisto goes on playing, while, two by two, the dancers disappear into the night. The village maiden throws herself into the arms of Faust, and on the wings of music they, too, vanish into the woods.*

This is one of the great documents of Romanticism, more akin to Hoffmann, perhaps, than to anything else in art, but having more than a mere resemblance to as unlikely a relation in this ghostly family as the *Eve of St. Agnes*. Certain lines in that poem:

> The boisterous, midnight, festive clarion,
> The kettle-drum, and far-heard clarionet,
> Affray his ears, though but in dying tone.
>
> . . . .
>
> . . . meantime, the frost-wind blows
> Like Love's alarum pattering the sharp sleet
> Against the window-panes;
>
> . . . .
>
> The arras, rich with horseman, hawk, and hound,
> Flutter'd in the besieging wind's uproar
> And the long carpets rose along the gusty floor.
>
> . . . .
>
> And they are gone: aye, ages long ago
> These lovers fled away into the storm.
> That night the Baron dreamt of many a woe,
> And all his warrior-guests with shade and form
> Of witch, and demon, and large coffin-worm,
> Were long be-nightmar'd. . . .
>
> . . . .

Such immortal lines, I maintain, find their parallel and equivalent in the Two Episodes from Lenau's *Faust*. This is praise,

---

*My attention was drawn by Mr. Constant Lambert to the fact that there are two alternative finales to the First *Mephisto-Waltz*. The first is the familiar working up to a climax, as in the piano version. The second, which is perhaps indeed, but it is deserved. The *Mephisto-Waltz* puts the powers of evil on to a plane from which they have been for too long dispossessed. The very tone of the music is haunted and evil; and, as we hear it, we remember that the person who wrote it was one of the most remarkable characters that have ever lived, beating his wings continually, if generally in vain, against the very highest summits, the topmost peaks of his art.*

Another piece of his music belonging to this same category, and so demanding mention at this moment, though written as long before as 1855, in all the turmoil of Weimar, is the *Totentanz*. In its original version, as edited by Busoni in 1918, it dates from as early as 1849. It is in the form of Variations, or a paraphrase, upon the *Dies Iræ*. This used to be splendidly performed by Siloti, his pupil; and in its occasional title of *Danse Macabre* it is not to be confused with the unfortunate efforts of Saint-Saëns to catch up with Liszt in this mood of his. The *Totentanz* was inspired in Liszt, apparently, by the frescoes of Orcagna in the Campo Santo at Pisa. Its shuddering, clanking rhythms, its sounds as of dancing bones, are of the weirdest achievement possible. It is, somehow, a piece admirably adapted for piano and orchestra; the piano has a real causus vivendi, a real reason for its presence in the orchestra. Although highly thought of by Liszt himself, this work, written so long before, had to wait for its first performance till Siloti played it at Antwerp, in 1881. One of the most original and effective works of the most famous pianist who ever lived; and it was more than thirty years before anyone could be induced to present it to the public!

If, in order to complete this chapter upon a fitting note a slight anachronism, or lapse in chronology is committed,† the fault lies in the fact that it is irresistible to include the work that is about to

---

finer, starts off with a terrific crescendo which quickly fades away into a shuddering, pianissimo chord. It is prefaced with German words which could be translated: 'They noisily swallow the ocean of their bliss', or 'They sink in the ocean of their own lust'. Both these finales come in the same place in the score, after the harp cadenza and the passage which depicts the singing of the nightingales heard through the open door of the inn.

*The *Mephisto-Waltz* was also published for piano solo. It is one of the masterpieces of Liszt. The three other *Mephisto-Waltzes* and the *Mephisto-Polka* are noticed later in this book.

†The *Faust-Waltz* was not published until 1868. It may have been written as early as 1863.

be mentioned with those that have gone before. The piece in question is Liszt's arrangement of the Waltz from Gounod's *Faust*. This is, perhaps, one of the most formidable instances of virtuosity achieved in any of the arts; and it is something more than that. We are concerned, once more, with that question raised by Mr. Sorabji in his book *Around Music*. This is, in his words, an absolutely clear instance of 'possession in music'; that is to say, the 'theme is so charged by Liszt with his own peculiar quality that, without actual alteration, it loses all semblance of its original physiognomy and becomes "controlled", to use an expression borrowed from the spiritualists, or "possessed".'

Liszt must have seized upon this tune from the most popular opera of the day, determined to make its worldly success his excuse for committing every kind of sacrilege with its body, and yet lifting it, in doing this, on to a higher spiritual plane than it could ever aspire to upon its own merits. The opening of the piece is most impressive. The tune of the waltz breaks out of the rumbling and the thunder of the preluding bars, as if it were floating over the city, over the Paris of Napoleon III, between the blackness of some tremendous storm and the million glaring lights of the town. It is possible to hear in this extraordinary moment a sort of epitome, not only of that particular gilded opera, but of all the slangy waltzes escaping out of the opened doors of theatres, with the gaslight still upon them from the stage. It is the music, by predilection, of a whole town, and of the re-stored Empire. The waltzes of Offenbach are implicit in it and we are reminded in its strains of those saturnine figures, those haters and commentators upon their own age, Baudelaire and Constantin Guys. Such eyes as these are in the streets, to-night, in that curious throng of crinolines, among the glistening carriages, dressed, as all the others, in black, and wearing the stove-pipe hats that were so much a part of the sinister ugliness of that age. It was to fall, doomed to fall; and perhaps there is the note of that, too, in this music. When the waltz comes back, once more and for the last time, it is decked out in devilish and fiendish finery like the goddess of prostitution, and it vanishes in thunder, or is, in effect, danced off the stage and into the wings, where thunder is waiting for it, whether real or feigned.

I wish it were possible to give some faint indication of the effect of the *Faust-Waltz*, as it was played by Busoni, and of the curious expression of his face during the performance. We must regard this waltz as one of Liszt's farewells to the world, and this old magician had appeared often enough before the public for him to appreciate their weaknesses. In this piece he is giving them their delight and mocking them in that. If it was a wonderful experience to hear Busoni play this, what would one not give to see and hear it played by Liszt, his black silk cloak fluttering ironically behind him! Mephistopheles disguised as an Abbé! Lovelace's Farewell! But we must return with him to the Vatican.

CHAPTER XXXVII

Liszt hopes to direct the Lateran and Sistine Choirs—The Messe de Gran—The Thirteenth Psalm—Christus—The Legend of St. Elizabeth—The Bach Fugue upon the name B.A.C.H—Ad nos ad salutarem undam. Weinen, Klagen Variations—Santa indifferenza—Death of Liszt's mother— He revisits Paris—A new joke by Rossini—Francis Planté— Liszt, Wagner, Cosima, and von Bülow—Liszt returns to Rome and goes into retirement at Grottammare with the Abbé Solfanelli—They read vespers while sitting in a fisherman's boat—Santa indifferenza

From the point of view of his own music, Liszt had still got definite intentions in coming to Rome. His ambition was not dead in him yet, however much of the world he had renounced. Though he appears to deny it in his letters, there can be little doubt that he hoped for a position at the Papal Court similar to that which he had occupied at Weimar. But he was never made music director of St. Peter's, and must have been disappointed in any hopes he had cherished of being put in control of the Lateran or Sistine choirs. 'Having, so far as I could, solved the greater part of the Symphonic Problem, I now mean to attack the Oratorio Problem', he says, in one of his letters, and in default of definite employment in Rome he set to work upon church music on the largest possible lines. The Papal Court neglected their opportunity to secure the services of the foremost musician of the day, but it certainly cannot be advanced against Liszt that he wasted any of his own time. His projects were planned upon an enormous scale, and during the first few years in Rome, before he resumed what might be called his international life, he accomplished those schemes, nearly in their entirety.

He had begun writing church music, as we have said, during the Weimar period. His chief composition at that time was the *Graner Mass*, or *Messe de Gran*. This was completed in 1855. It had been commissioned by the Prince-Primate of Hungary for the consecration of the immense new cathedral built in Gran, or Esztergom, as it is called in Hungarian. This was a very important occasion, and Liszt made the most of it. It is in six great divisions, Kyrie, Gloria, Credo, Sanctus, Benedictus, and Agnus Dei. The Kaiser Franz-Joseph and many of the Archdukes came to Gran specially for the ceremony, and the proceedings ended in a banquet for sixty guests and the health of Liszt proposed in ceremonial Latin by the Primate himself. As to the Mass itself, opinions differed. It met with the Primate's cordial approval and the Kaiser's intense dislike. It has been performed, ever since, to the same contrasted effects.

It is more easy to speak with conviction of the Thirteenth Psalm for tenor solo, choir, and orchestra, written at Weimar in 1855, and not published until 1863. This is of touching and dramatic sincerity, containing, as it does, passages which, in Liszt's own words, were 'written with tears of blood'. It is sincere in a way that was never possible with Berlioz, or it would be more correct to say that the spirit of this work is really religious and that Berlioz in his *Te Deum* or *Requiem* was concerned with anything but that side of the problem. His religious works, in the words of Sir Henry Hadow, are more reminiscent of some ceremony of human sacrifice, some pagan rite, than of the consolations of religion. In the Thirteenth Psalm, Liszt is writing in an entirely different spirit from this.

In all, no less than five psalms were set by Liszt; but the Thirteenth is by far the most important of the lot, and there is only space here for a mere enumeration of Psalm 116 for choir and pianoforte, and Psalm 128 for choir and organ. None of these, but the first mentioned, have claims to be considered as in any way sensational.

His interest in the Oratorio problem was concerned with two works carried out upon a truly gigantic scale, *Christus*, and *The Legend of St. Elizabeth*. The first of these was originally conceived from a poem by Rückert, but, in the end, Liszt took the words, himself, from the Bible. The first part of the work is the Christmas Oratorio. There is a symphonic introduction, the apparition of the herald angels, the coming of the shepherds to the manger, the arrival of the three Magi, and at the end a Stabat Mater for full choir.

The second part is entitled 'After Epiphany'. It begins with the Beatitudes (a project that had occupied the composer's mind for many years), followed by a magnificent Pater Noster, and an orchestral interlude of the Miracle of the Storm which takes a very high place among the finest of his achievements. This is succeeded by a Hosannah to celebrate the entry of Christ into Jerusalem.

The third section, which is devoted to the Passion and Resurrection, is preluded by an orchestral introduction in which the orchestra accompanies and comments upon the 'Tristis est anima mea' which is pronounced by the voice of Christ. A long choral Stabat comes after this, a Hymn, 'O Filii et filiæ', and the final Resurrexit.

In performance, this work is almost too long and complicated to be given in entirety, taking, as it does, some four and a half hours to accomplish. But isolated sections out of its huge length must be among the most important things in all his contribution to music. It occupied most of his time for five years.

The Legend of St. Elizabeth of Hungary, on a book by the poet Otto Roquette, attracted Liszt for a twofold reason, that St. Elizabeth was the patron saint of his native Hungary, and because of her historical connexion with Thuringia, in which Weimar is situated, and with the Wartburg. This also is upon a formidable scale, being in two parts and six episodes, and taking not less than two and a half hours in performance. It contains a good many tawdry pages, such as the Crusaders' March, and a few beautiful passages like the Miracle of the Roses. It was more often performed than *Christus*, being only about half the length, but it cannot be described as having met with much success. Both works

234

must, in fact, have been a grievous disappointment to the composer; and it is to be noticed that after the terrific effort involved in their composition his energy somewhat subsided and his remaining works are much more modest in scale. If he did not hope for preferment in the Church, he certainly aspired to play a prominent part in the reform of church music, and the disappointment of his hopes in this direction seems to have removed the last of his ambitions.

We have arrived, indeed, at another stage of his life, at which we may place the date of 1866, the year in which *Christus* was finished. But, in order to complete the picture of him at this period, it is necessary to delay our narrative in order to draw attention to the terrific *Bach Fugue* for organ, based upon the name of B.A.C.H. It was published, also, in a splendid piano edition. This dates, in reality, from 1857, but it somehow belongs in spirit to this later time. The *Bach Fugue* is one of the most tremendous things in all contrapuntal music; it must be considered as something apart in Liszt's music, and as a composition more important even than the *B minor Sonata*. It is one of those moments when Liszt confounds both his haters and his admirers by appearing in absolutely unexpected guise. There had been no classical architecture upon this scale since Beethoven in his highest achievement. And, as if to prove his magical powers of transmutation, Liszt accomplished something almost as extraordinary in the organ fantasia and fugue, *Ad Nos ad Salutarem Undam*, based upon a chorale from Meyerbeer's opera of *Le Prophète*, and taking more than half an hour in performance. This, also, belongs to the greatest things in organ literature; and a superb version of it, prepared by Busoni, has enriched the piano with one of the greatest curiosities in all music. Finally, in connexion with this group of his works, it is necessary to mention his variations for piano upon a Bach theme, the prelude *Weinen, Klagen*.* This, too, is magnificent, and dateless, as all works of this classical purpose should be, of necessity. But its effect is achieved in a curious manner: the Gothic structure is encrusted, so to speak, with Baroque decoration, in exactly the manner in which so many church interiors were treated in Italy and in Spain. A music student of serious principles could, indeed, 'restore' the *Weinen, Klagen* Variations.

*There is, also, an edition of the *Weinen, Klagen* Variations for organ.

Sufficient evidence must, by now, have accumulated of the serious religious principles at back of this strange mind. And, from just this point that we have arrived at, from the year 1866, a definite change in his character is to be noticed. He had become convinced of the futility of so much effort on his part. This feeling continued in him for some time, reaching its climax, perhaps, two years later, and making way, then, for another change in his character. We shall see him attaining the state of what he calls 'santa indifferenza'; and then rousing himself out of that lethargy in order to place his knowledge at the disposal of others, as if he felt this was a duty. But his own music became, henceforth, not a purpose but a recreation.

Meanwhile, in this very year, whatever his inward spiritual feelings may have been, his contact with the outer world was far from severed, for in March he once more visited Paris. His immediate purpose was to attend the performance of the *Messe de Gran* in St. Eustache, but there was, also, the additional reason that his mother had just died, in January, and that he must attend to her affairs. Liszt had always been most devoted to his mother, but she hardly occurs in the story of his life, and except for purely sentimental reasons her death cannot have made much difference to him. She had lived for many years past in the house of her grandson-in-law, Émile Ollivier. An old friend, the poet Ronchaud, who it will be remembered, may, or may not, have been the lover of Madame d'Agoult, years before, was one of the chief mourners, and the widow of Spontini,* the composer, was also among their number.

The *Messe de Gran* was given before an enormous concourse, but the results were far from successful. His old friends of thirty years before did not rally to his side, as he had hoped. Berlioz, indeed, left the church, saying that the Mass was the negation of art. In his letters to the Princess, Liszt seems to find a more naïve pleasure in the fact that he had been lent a carriage, by his friend M. Courzon, drawn by an English horse which he says runs like a tiger. For the rest, he had two interviews, *tête-à-tête*, with Daniel Stern, and it cannot have been at all pleasant to him to learn that she proposed to publish her memoirs. There were, as well, the

---

*She was the niece of Sebastien Erard, a very early friend and patron of Liszt. Mme Spontini survived her husband's masterpiece *La Vestale* for more than seventy years, only dying in 1878.

dinner parties of the Rothschilds, and with Prince Napoléon, and more than one invitation from Rossini, who had made a new joke to the effect that Liszt was only writing Masses in order to accustom himself to saying them.

And, in the midst of all these dead names, it comes upon one with a shock to see the name of Francis Planté. He is first mentioned in a letter of 10 May 1866, where he is described as playing Liszt's *Tasso* at a matinée in Rossini's house. Frequent mention of Planté follows upon this, and Liszt meets him again at the house of Princess Marceline Czartoryska, who had been the great friend and patroness of Chopin. For the interest is this, that Francis Planté died in 1934! It is scarcely credible that this veteran, whose gramophone records, made only twenty-two or -three years ago, are of memorable, exceptional quality, should have won his first prize for piano in the year 1850, but it is true. He became a magnificent player, second only to Rubinstein in the opinion of many critics, and was still playing, in his retreat at Mont-de-Marsan in the Landes in 1934, at ninety-four years of age. In truth, the house of Rossini, in the Chaussée d'Antin, seems as remote from our time as anything in history!*

The matinée of Rossini is succeeded by a party given by Gustave Doré, 'a séance dantesque', at which Planté and Saint-Saëns played Liszt's music, and then the next letter in the series is dated, once more, from the Vatican. A few days later he attends a banquet of thirty ecclesiastics given by Cardinal Antonelli in the Quirinal; and, after this, he seems to have remained for as much as a year working quietly at his music at the Madonna del Rosario, and finishing his *Christus*.

This unwonted peace was broken, at last, in 1867, by the *Hungarian Coronation Mass*, written for the crowning of Franz-Joseph as Apostolic King of Hungary. It was composed at break-neck speed in three weeks, and, on its completion, Liszt had to hurry off to Budapest to attend the ceremony. This is the last big work ever written by Liszt; and it was of an experimental nature, being written in Hungarian rhythms, alternately languorous and fiery, and containing a splendid Hungarian March. The Mass was well received by his fellow-countrymen, but unfortunately, until

---

* It is probable that the great violin teacher, Leopold Auer, who died at Dresden-Laschwitz on 15 July 1930, was the other last survivor of those who visited Rossini in his apartment in the Chausée d'Antin, or in his villa at Passy.

there is a restoration of the monarchy in that country there is little or no chance of hearing this work, which was a favourite with its composer.

A rush back to Rome for a few days, and this indefatigable traveller was off again, this time to Weimar where they were holding one of their perpetual anniversary festivals. This time it was for the eight hundredth anniversary of the Wartburg, and an occasion, therefore, for *The Legend of St. Elizabeth* to be performed. There was, also, a festival at Meiningen to be attended, and an immense amount of petty business seems to have taken up his whole time. In the end he was able to get away and remove to Munich, where the mysterious amours of his daughter Cosima with Wagner had caused a complete breakdown in the health of von Bülow, her husband. The actual happenings are of a complication that it is almost impossible to unravel, while it is equally certain that a great deal of the truth will for ever remain a mystery. It can only be said that the most extraordinary events had been taking place, and that it must have been an extremely difficult position for Liszt, who was devoted to all three persons concerned in the tangle. His immediate care seems to have been the health of von Bülow, who was, after all, the sufferer in the tragedy; but it was impossible for him to feel the slightest note of censure towards Wagner, whom he considered the greatest artist and the most important human being alive. And von Bülow had exactly the same sensations towards Wagner, which must only have increased the agony of his position. Neither of them, therefore, husband or father, could blame Cosima for her conduct; but it was certainly a most extraordinary situation for them all. Not least for Liszt, for seldom can anyone in the Catholic hierarchy, however humble or however proud their position, have been forced to take a decision of this sort and morally countenance the adultery of their own married daughter. It might have happened in the fifteenth, but could hardly happen in the nineteenth, century. These were things of which he could not well write to the Princess, if indeed she was ever in full possession of their import, any more than we are ourselves, and so we find little mention of these occurrences in his letters beyond allusions to his concern about von Bülow's health and to his general anxiety about Cosima.

When he came back to Rome for the winter Liszt must have felt the need for peace and tranquillity. His desire for 'santa indifferenza' grew more and more upon him. He lived, this winter, in Santa Francesca Romana, and his visits to the Princess were his one distraction. He was working upon various small pieces of church music, and, it is not improbable, upon the *Faust-Waltz*. His big ambitions had left him.

The climax of this mood came in the summer of 1868 with his retreat to Grottammare, a little town upon the Adriatic. It is not the least curious passage of his life. His companion was the Abbé Solfanelli, and they travelled by way of Assisi and Loreto, visiting all the religious sites upon the way. They remained for two months at Grottammare, staying with a cousin of Solfanelli, passing the entire day, together, in religious exercises, for, as Liszt avers, his one aim in undertaking the journey was to make himself familiar with the breviary. This they did walking together along the sands of the shore; and sometimes they read vespers and compline sitting in one of the fishermen's boats that had been hauled up on to the sand, mingling, as Liszt says, the flow of biblical words with the rumour of the waves.

Liszt was losing faith in everything but the consolations of religion. And it must be admitted that after all the efforts he had made in music, and on behalf of music, it was only reasonable in him to expect something more than the neglect with which he was treated. Excepting always his piano-fantasies, the elaborate nature of his compositions ran away with any small profits there might have been, and the sales of his original music grew smaller and smaller. At the same time, his true humility would let him do nothing to prevent this, or to push forward his own claims to consideration. He writes in 1859 to von Herbeck: 'In case von Bülow should make his appearance at the Vienna Philharmonic Concert he will on my advice not play my A major concerto, nor any other composition of mine, but just simply one of the Bach or Beethoven concertos. My intimate friends know perfectly well that it is not by any means my desire to push myself into any concert programme whatever.' And, five years later, in a letter to the same person, we find him writing: 'von Bülow will be the best one to arrange things, and to conduct. I wrote to him, the day before yesterday, to advise him again to be strictly moderate with regard to the number of my compositions. The half of what is given in your sketch of the programme would be amply sufficient. People do not want to hear so many of my things, and I do not care to force them upon them. With regard to performances of my works generally, my disposition and inclination are more than ever completely in the negative. My friends, and you more especially, dear friend, have done their part fully and in the kindest manner. It seems to me, now, high time that I should be somewhat forgotten, or at least placed very much in the background. My name has been too frequently put forward; many have taken umbrage at this, and been needlessly annoyed at it. While paving the way for a better appreciation, it might be advisable to regard my things as a reserve corps and to introduce new works by other composers.'

There is much more in the same vein in his letters. He writes to Mme Jessie Laussot, in 1865, as follows: 'Knowing by experience how little favour my works meet with, I have been obliged to force upon myself a sort of compulsory disregard of them and a passive resignation. Thus, during the years of my foreign activity in Germany I constantly observed the rule of never asking anyone whatsoever to have any of my works performed; more than that I really dissuaded many persons from doing so who showed some intention of the kind, and I shall do so elsewhere.' And, in another letter to her, he says: 'You know that I usually dissuade my friends from encumbering their concert programmes with compositions by me. For the little they have to lose they will lose it the more by waiting. Let us, then, administer F.L. in homoeopathic doses, one to be taken only occasionally.' A few years later he writes to Servais: 'Will you please tell M. Brassin that I thank him very much for not having been afraid of compromising his success as a virtuoso by choosing my concerto. Up to the present time all the best-known French pianists—with the exception of Saint-Saëns—have not ventured to play anything of mine except transcriptions, my own compositions being considered absurd and insupportable.'

No one who reads these letters can believe for a moment that Liszt was a seeker after publicity. But he had such a strong character and so remarkable a personality that he was certain to attract attention, as much when he was purposely trying to avoid doing so, as in his early virtuoso days, his Glanz-Periode.

Even in his mood of 'santa indifferenza' he is remarkable and conspicuous. The circumstances are, in their way, as dramatic as any in his experience. We leave him, then, for this moment, reading vespers and compline in the fisherman's boat, with the Abbé Solfanelli; the same, who, in the Vatican, only ten days after his reception into the priesthood, had made Liszt practise his genuflexions for close upon three hours. Thus they passed the heats of July and August, walking along the sandy shore, or high and dry upon the sands, in the fishing boat. The painted sail was furled, for the boat was inactive and wanted no motion. It had only to be pushed down into the waves, and when the sail was hoisted away it would go. So it was with Liszt. His mood of 'santa indifferenza' would not last for ever. A breath of wind, and he would take advantage of it and be gone. Meanwhile, he would appreciate this evening lull, while it lasted.

CHAPTER XXXVIII

New access of energy—A fugal curiosity—The Princess and her cigars—Agnes Klindworth—The Deux Légendes—His two piano concertos—More operatic fantasias—His appearance during the Roman period—He returns to Weimar

If, from what has just been said, we expect a fresh access of energy on the part of Liszt we shall not be mistaken. We find him resigned, but not to a life of inactivity. That was not in his nature. Perhaps the best description of his whole attitude in becoming a priest is contained in a letter written to an unknown correspondent, just after his ordination: 'Yes, Sir, it is true that I have joined the ecclesiastical profession—but not a bit through disgust of the world, and less still through lassitude for my art.' This is not the letter of a person who is without hope. It is, on the contrary, instinct with energy; and this was the mood to which he returned after his trip to Grottammare. He was more than ever determined to keep himself away from the sordid struggles of the concert world, and only wished, now, to place his prodigious gifts at the disposal of others, by way of teacher. Also, the instinct in him to write music was too strong to be resisted; but, if he indulged in this, it was more to please himself and to occupy his spare moments than with any view of adding to his own fame.

His religious duties, from now onwards, accounted for a considerable number of his best working hours. We have it on his own authority that at least two or three hours of every morning were occupied in reading the breviary. He complains in his letters of the slow, laborious process it involved, as he had never been a quick reader, and had often to read a verse of the Psalms over and over again before he could grasp its meaning. For the rest of his life, from now onwards, there are constant references in his letters to the burden of the enormous correspondence in which he was involved, all of which had to be answered, personally, in his own hand, as he could never afford the services of a secretary. When his duties with an ever-increasing train of pupils are added to this, it is no longer a matter for surprise that his later compositions are of more moderate length. His two hours with his breviary every day were, in all likelihood, more than the daily total of his working hours during these later years.

But we have not yet quite arrived at that period, for during the years to which we are limited by this chapter his pupils were comparatively few in number, and we find him on at least one occasion living in peace at Rome for as much as a year on end. The Oratorios of *Christus* and *The Legend of St. Elizabeth* were his occupation at this time, and it is certain that he was deeply immersed in studies appropriate to the new world of music in which he was engaged. Palestrina and Vittoria were scarcely to be heard anywhere except at Rome, ninety years ago; and in his ambition, clearly expressed in his letters, to have the Sistine Choir put into his charge and to effect a renaissance of church music, the study of these old masters must have been a recreation near to his heart. It was, indeed, if we except that edition of *Domenico Scarlatti*, of which he initiated the publication many years before in Vienna, the only trace of archæology to be found in all his manifold musical interests. Johann Sebastian Bach was barred, at Rome, by his Protestantism; for Mozart and for Haydn there are but few traces of his enthusiasm, their music was, perhaps, but the faded finery of a dead century in his eyes. His taste was for the old masters in their purity, for Palestrina and Vittoria, or, as ever, for the music of his own contemporaries.

This latter aspect of his taste was difficult enough to satisfy in

Villa d'Este, Tivoli

Liszt in his study at Weimar in 1875

Anton Rubinstein

the present; for, even had the Sistine Choir been put completely in his power, it is hard to believe that he would have ventured to present Berlioz, for example, to the Papal satisfaction. The *Stabat Mater* of Rossini, perhaps; but not the *Requiem* or the *Te Deum* of Berlioz! Nor, even, it is probable, the *Requiem* of Verdi, a work which he admired enormously.*

But, in the course of his insatiable quest for something new in music, Liszt had already, some years before at Weimar, discovered what can only be described as the last curiosity of the Italian classical school; and this particular oddity is so completely forgotten, now, that it is pardonable to give the details some little prominence. Not that Liszt can be said to have in any way discovered him, for his fame was widely spread in his lifetime, but its boundaries were Southern Italy, and he was never heard of outside Rome and Naples. His name was Pietro Raimondi; he was born at Rome in 1786, and he died there in 1853. Raimondi started life as an operatic composer, chiefly for Palermo, writing, in all, sixty-two operas, and excelling, so it is said, in comic opera. He then returned to Naples and wrote no fewer than twenty-one grand ballets for the San Carlo Theatre, mostly in two or three acts. After this more than sufficient prelude he devoted his attention to his real interest, church music.

It will scarcely be credited that this man wrote four masses for full orchestra; the whole Book of Psalms for four, five, six, seven, and eight voices; two books of ninety Partimenti, each as a separate bass, with three different accompaniments; four fugues for four voices, each independent but capable of being united into one fugue for twenty-four voices; a fugue for sixteen choirs; sixteen fugues for four voices; twenty-four fugues for four, five, six, seven, and eight voices, of which four and five separate fugues will combine into one; a fugue in sixty-four parts, for sixteen four-part choirs; and an opera seria and an opera buffa, which went equally well, separately, and in combination.

But worse is to follow! In 1852, Raimondi was made Maestro de Cappella at St. Peter's, and in that year he produced his masterpiece. It consisted of three Oratorios, *Potiphar*, *Pharaoh*, and *Jacob*, which were not only designed to be performed in the usual manner, but to be played, afterwards, all three in combination as

---

* Liszt published a transcription from the *Agnus Dei* in Verdi's *Requiem* in 1879.

one work, under the generic name of *Joseph*. Three orchestras were employed, and there were more than four hundred performers. So great was the composer's emotion that he fainted dead away, and, since he died a few months later, we may conclude that his own work had fatal results upon him.

Liszt tried to interest himself to get performances of some of Raimondi's works in Germany, but it seems to have amounted to nothing, and, in the end, our hero himself remarks that the idea of Raimondi gives him a headache. It will be agreed, though, that Raimondi would have been a difficult person to succeed as music director at St. Peter's. In the end, however, Liszt never received any kind of official appointment whatever at Rome, and the only music that he wrote of Papal instigation is the *Hymne du Pape*, published in the year that he entered the priesthood. This is not the most fortunate specimen of his talents. It breathes of the harmonium that Liszt played to Pio Nono when the Pontiff visited him in his cell at the Madonna del Rosario.

The evening of that very same day Liszt paid his usual visit to the Princess in the Via del Babuino. Their relationship, for its past inferences, at least, must have presented a curious contrast with most other clerical friendships. There cannot have been many other newly ordained priests who brought with them to Rome someone whose name had been so closely associated with their own for fifteen years. And, as well, he was the father of three children by another woman whom he had not married. There was, therefore, some reason for the lack of Church preferment shown to Liszt; and, all things considered, it can only be said that he was treated with the greatest sympathy and indulgence by the Church.

In truth, the communion of these two masculine souls was, by now, of touchingly innocent description. The Princess was involved in literary work, almost upon the scale of a Raimondi. The twenty-four volumes of the *Causes intérieures de la faiblesse extérieure de l'Église*, or at least the first of the series, were nearly ready to appear. She had installed a small printing press in her house, so as to supervise the most minute details of correction and production. Her tables were littered with papers, and there were more books and papers on the floor. It will be remembered that she was an inveterate cigar smoker, and as time went on and her tastes became less easily satisfied in this respect she was forced to smoke stronger and yet stronger cigars. Eventually, through political influence, she had special cigars manufactured for her by the Roman tobacco monopoly. They were of the Minghetti type, still familiar to Italian travellers, but of special length and double strength, dipped in iron filings, so it was said, to impart a special metallic tang to their flavour. Her rooms, therefore, were charged incessantly with cigar smoke, and it may have been difficult through that blue haze to see all of the fourteen busts of Liszt with which her drawing-room was ornamented.

The Princess was so immersed in her studies, having only that one other interest, the welfare of Liszt, that from the point of view of the outside world she must have begun to be lacking in the more human qualities. Liszt, for all his devotion to her, may have begun to feel this, too. She was hardly feminine any longer, except in her curiosity as to all her lover's movements if ever he was away from her. It was a curiosity tinged with something more than ordinary anxiety about his health. She was jealous of his friendship with other women. Before they had been settled long at the Altenburg Liszt had begun to show a particular interest in one of his pupils, Agnes Klindworth, an unusually pretty girl who came from Hanover. She quickly became his confidante, and the object at the end of his daily walks. When they were away from each other they corresponded together; and his letters to her, which have been published in a separate volume, are the proof of this romantic friendship. In spite of his entry into the celibate state Liszt could never dispense with feminine society for longer than a few days at most.

But it was exactly the charms of feminine society that were lacking in the Princess, as she grew older. He was devoted to her, he depended upon her strength of mind and set purpose, but it was more like the affection of two old soldiers, who have been through the same campaigns together, than the communion of two ardent souls. He loved a measure of retirement in his life, and to be able to dispense with the sordid considerations of gaining money, but it is apparent that what he dreaded was a static condition. His nerves were too highly resilient to let him stay still for long. He had not, as he says, entered the Church because of his distaste for life, but, in a sense, for exactly the contrary reason. It was because he wanted to live, walled round with his own standards, according to his own conditions.

He must have seen the changes that were taking place in the Princess. There are a hundred proofs of this in his letters. He apostrophizes her as 'Bon ecclésiaste', so that he seems to have realized the point we have raised that the Princess was as much of a priest as he was. And her cell was permanent. She had no intention of leaving Rome. The *Causes intérieures* was enough to keep her there for a lifetime, or more. And we find Liszt writing to her, on his way to the retreat at Grottammare, that he had just read in the *Moniteur* a story that reminded him of her. She was, in fact, threatened with a rival in literary fecundity. It concerned a Japanese novelist, Kiotze Bakin, who had just completed his novel in one hundred and six volumes, a task which had taken him thirty years to accomplish. Anyone who has made the acquaintaince of the Princess in her correspondence will wonder whether she even smiled at this pleasantry; it is more likely that she took the warning seriously and contemplated adding a twenty-fifth volume to her lifework.

In another letter, Liszt returns to his Roman disappointment, and remarks that even though he once made a setting for Mignon's song he never really admired Italy for its orange and citron trees. His energies were beginning to find there was no outlet for them in Rome. The consummate actor in him had to return to the stage for a little part of each year, if only to point to his absence from it during the rest of the time.

Meanwhile, if we have seen Liszt in some of the many facets of his personality, the picture that we hope to present would not be complete if we did not take notice of a few things not yet described, for, as Gregorovius remarked, Liszt and his pianoforte seemed to be one, as it were a piano-centaur.

The pick of them are the *Deux Légendes, St. François d'Assise prédicant aux Oiseaux* and *St. François de Paule marchant sur les Flots.** There is nothing more original in the whole piano-repertory than these two pieces. The second of them, especially, is a truly extraordinary production. They seem to belong, both of them, to the art of the Jesuits, to the painting and architecture of the Seicento. We are reminded of Padre Pozzo and of Longhena. The second of these pieces, taken from the life of the Calabrian saint, founder of the Mendicant Order of Minims, was a frequent subject with that wild and fantastic painter, Alessandro Magnasco,

* St. François de Paule was the patron saint of Liszt.

who seems to hover between El Greco and Salvator Rosa. The mention of his name will, perhaps, give an indication of the strange atmosphere of *St. François de Paule marchant sur les Flots*. As pictorial suggestion, as direct interpretation of the story into music, as creation of immediate visual effect by that means, this piece of music is without precedent.

Two other well-known piano pieces date from this time, *Gnomenreigen* and *Waldesrauschen*. They are called *Études de Concert*; and, of the two, it is possible to infinitely prefer the latter, which is a really beautiful and evocative thing. The piano writing is admirable beyond description. Its effect is really that of the wind in a pine wood; in one of those German or Bohemian woods where the lines of straight stems are like an army of lances, and the boughs droop down, not so much as leaves but as tassels, which the wind sways and dashes to and fro. One of the forests, in fact, of Altdorfer, with the prospect of a knight in armour to ride by, or an anchorite at the mouth of his cave.

There are, as well, his two piano concertos, in E flat and in A, one of them composed in Weimar and the other probably in Rome. The First Concerto is disappointing, though it has beautiful moments in the scherzo and in the mountainous, open-air finale; not exactly like a gallop, on the piano, through hilly country, but as if the eyes ranged wildly over an immense tumbled landscape of hills and woods. And, all the time, it does not seem as if Liszt, himself, was particularly interested. The Second Concerto is based, throughout, upon the same tune, which is introduced in most subtle and interesting way at the beginning. After terrific and varied career, this tune eventually becomes a march, decked out with every device of fanfares and of glissando passages for the piano, which instrument appears rather in the guise of a circus horse in the circus procession, wearing too elaborate a harness. It is an excessively curious thing, this concerto; pompous and pretentious in contemplation or in retrospect, but magnificent enough if played by, say, the late Moriz Rosenthal, the pupil of Liszt. Then, it appears sufficiently weighted, not overbalanced and toppling over in its own stride. It should be added that the balance of this Second Concerto is often spoilt by the omission of the accompanied cadenza, which comes after the rather tawdry march and restores the haunting and distinguished mood of the opening of the whole work. Properly given, and properly played, this concerto is a remarkable thing.*

A certain number of the *Fantaisies Dramatiques* date from this period, too. The best of them is the *Faust-Waltz*, that has already been described; while his fantasias based upon the *Reine de Saba* and the *Roméo et Juliette* of the same composer do not bear mention in the same breath. Young ladies, beyond number, must have suffered from these at the hands of their governesses, and vice versa. We will leave Gounod, then; and it is safer, perhaps, not to discuss the conjunction of Wagner-Liszt, for his transcriptions from *Lohengrin* or *Tannhäuser* are exceedingly painful to the ear and rouse lingering doubts, the nature of which we do not feel ourselves at liberty to disclose. But, in the case of *Tristan*, or of *Rheingold*, the circumstances are very different, and Liszt has produced an admirable piano score, which is beyond criticism.

His association with Verdi is more interesting. The Italian operatic airs were better suited for his alternate dissection and embellishment. His arrangement of the quartet from *Rigoletto* is, of course, well known and still popular; and, perhaps, his Fantasia from *Trovatore* would be a welcome change and prove no disappointment. *Ernani* and *I Lombardi* are other forgotten things upon which his fancies were allowed their run; as, also, upon *Aïda*, but it may be considered doubtful if this would be endurable. Two Illustrations from *Don Carlos*, the *Coro di Festa* and *Marcia funebre*, are, however, of great merit, and those chosen moments of the opera live again in exactly their right environment at his hands. Finally, there is an interesting late piece, written in 1882-3, *Réminiscences de Simone Boccanegra*, an opera by Verdi thought so highly of by the composer that he revised and edited it, not long before his great *Otello* was given to the world. In *Simone Boccanegra* Liszt may be said to give an excellent account of a musical curiosity that some few people would like to be acquainted with in this country. The magnificent, slow opening of this piece, altogether transforming and exalting the actual prelude of Verdi, is an admirable instance of Liszt's powers of 'control' or 'possession' where operatic themes are concerned.

*Other works by Liszt for pianoforte and orchestra are the *Hungarian Fantasia*; a Fantasia on themes from Beethoven's *Ruins of Athens*; an arrangement of Weber's *Polacca in E major*; the *Totentanz*; the *Concerto Pathétique*; and the recently discovered *Malédiction* for piano and strings.

Another piece that should be worth the trouble is his Fantasia upon *Zep Ilonka*, a Hungarian opera by Mosonyi, still famous in its own country, but quite unknown outside that; based, as it is, on the characteristic Hungarian rhythms, with the Czárdás, as it were, carried to excelsis. Liszt found time, also, to orchestrate the *Mazurka Fantaisie* of his friend and pupil von Bülow; and it is probable that this is worth, at any rate, a performance on the wireless.

We have not yet mentioned Liszt's songs. A collection of fifty-five of them was published in 1860, but not arranged in any chronological order. The most famous of these are his setting of Mignon's song; *Die Lorelei*; and the well-known *Angiolin da biondo crin*, which dates from his romantic period and was written when he lived on the shores of Lake Como with Madame d'Agoult. But it is certain that several others out of this collection must be interesting, for Liszt wrote some beautiful songs, and his contribution to this kind of music is not sufficiently known or admired. As a song writer he is almost ignored by the public, though his songs are an integral part of the German lieder, and the body of them is not complete without him, even if they are a little flavoured by the Parisian salons of his youth.

Last, and far from least of all these diverse things, are Liszt's exquisite settings for piano of Chopin's six Chants polonais. Two of these, at least, are well known and familiar to nearly everyone. Coming out in 1860, some years after the publication of all Chopin's complete and posthumous works, they make a sort of supplement in which his traits of character are resumed and given expression. No one could have done this better than Liszt. These small trifles are of absolutely perfect workmanship, unsurpassable in their delicacy. Chopin is present in them, but seen through the focus of the artist who played Chopin's *Études* better than he could play them himself, and to whom he dedicated those *Études*, in consequence. If his setting of Schubert's songs is praised even by the sternest of his detractors, the Chants polonais claim the same rights to universal appreciation.

One of these six pieces is a Polish song noted down by Liszt years before, during his first elopement with the Princess, and appearing in the *Glanes de Woronince*. Whenever he touched any music of Poland, or had any thoughts of that country, Liszt was apt to associate it in his mind with his affection for her. Mention of the Chants polonais brings us back, then, once more, to the Princess. For there is to be another parting: it is San Rossore come back again, thirty years later. Liszt is taking to the road, once more.

Three or four months of each year spent in Rome would be enough for him, in future; and even these he would pass in the solitude of Villa d'Este. Never again did he and the Princess sleep under the same roof. That time was nearly ten years past. Instead, he must have felt that a new life was opening for him, at nearly sixty years of age.

He is, by now, the Liszt who is familiar to us in all the photographs. In an Abbé's long black robe, with straight white hair falling to his shoulders. With long hands, and long thin fingers. Himself, tall and thin, with the bony frame of his body showing through his priest's robe. The cassock, itself, being part of the strangeness of his appearance, like the wizard's gown. He is, in fact, dressed for the magician, but anything sinister in him is dispelled by the expression of his features, which is benevolence personified. And anyone of greater distinction it would be impossible to imagine.

He was already a legend. It was more than twenty years since he had given a concert; and, during that space of time, the number of occasions on which he had appeared in public to play his instrument could be numbered, almost, on the fingers. He was the object of universal curiosity; the survivor, already, of a dead generation, the friend of Chopin, the rival of Paganini, and, at the same time, just as far removed into the future by his championship of Wagner.

He is taking to the road, once more, but not in the stagecoach that carried him from San Rossore, nor drawn in a carriage by six white horses and followed by thirty other carriages and a cavalcade of students, as when he left Berlin, in triumph, for Russia. He is, in fact, travelling second class in the railway-train, unable to afford greater luxury than that, compelled to sit up all night in the compartment, elbowed by his fellow-passengers and reading all night through, by the flickering oil lamp, some volume he has bought at the last moment from the bookstall. This is Mephisto, leaving Rome by the night train. But, when it was possible, he chose to travel by sea from Civitavecchia to Marseilles, though he can have been scarcely more comfortable upon the small packet-steamers of the day. On this occasion, though, it was by train. He had to wait some hours in Florence, missed his connexion in Padua and had to stay the night there; had a long wait, next day, at Verona, and reached Munich at five in the morning. The next day he left Munich at six o'clock in the morning and arrived at Weimar just before midnight. One wonders whether he had to walk home again from the station, profiting, once more, by the dark night, and meeting spectre after spectre on the way. Or whether he was met at the station by the servant, at least, of Mme de Moukhanoff-Kalergis.

BOOK V

1869–1886

Rome, Weimar, Budapest

CHAPTER XXXIX

Liszt is welcomed back to Weimar—The Hofgärtnerei—*The* Vie trifurquée—*The Academy of Music at Budapest— Franco-Prussian War—His admiration for Napoleon III— Madame Moukhanoff-Kalergis—A new Princess: Princess Gortschakoff; alias the Baroness Olga Meyendorff; alias the Baroness M. . . or the Countess X. . .—More serious situation of Liszt with Olga Janina, the Cossack Countess— Her childhood described from her novels—She marries, and deserts her husband—Her introduction to Liszt—His account of her to Princess Wittgenstein—She enters Villa d'Este disguised as a gardenboy—He flees to Weimar, she leaves for New York, but returns and pursues him to Budapest—The story told in the words of Janka Wohl—A disastrous piano recital—The Cossack Countess tries to shoot Liszt, and disappears from history after publishing two novels*

A good deal of diplomacy must have been exerted on both sides in order to open this last and final phase in Liszt's career. The Grand-Duke Karl-Alexander had been negotiating his return to Weimar for some years; and, while it may have been hinted politely that his presence there would be more welcome if he came alone and without the Princess, the burden of responsibility was upon Liszt to make the offer effective by contriving to do so with the least possible offence to her feelings. But she did not want to leave Rome: it interfered with her celibacy and with her literary work. She preferred the Via del Babuino, and her manuscripts and cigars.

The next step was to welcome Liszt back to Weimar as the honour and pride of the town, making special provision for his comfort, and handing over for his use a small house, furnished by the Princesses themselves, but so limited in accommodation that he could neither incur much expense, arouse local curiosity, nor involve the jealousy of the Princess Wittgenstein from her cell in

Rome. This little house was the Hofgärtnerei and he transferred to it in a few days from his hotel, the Erbprinz, for truth compels us to relate that our speculations as to the manner of his arrival in Weimar are set at rest in his letters. He had allowed himself, for once, the luxury of a first-class ticket on the railway, and passed the whole day from Munich at six o'clock in the morning till he came to Weimar, at midnight, alone in the compartment. He did not walk from the station; nor was he met by the servant of Mme Moukhanoff-Kalergis; but he stayed up talking to four men-friends in the Erbprinz till half-past one, and was at Mass, the next morning, at eight o'clock.

Of the Hofgärtnerei, itself, there is no lack of description. Liszt writes to the Princess, at once, to tell her of his new home. It had been the chief gardener's house; there were four rooms; a servant's room, his own bedroom, dining-room, and the music-room. This had four windows and was divided into two by an Algerian hanging, of red and green. There were good carpets, four Berlin stoves, three bronze clocks, several bronze wall-lights for three candles, six or eight lamps, a pair of mirrors, and table services of glass and porcelain for six persons. The Grand Duchess and the Princesses had chosen it themselves. It was, in fact, of a 'luxe Wagnérien', the sort of thing that the inhabitants of Weimar had never seen before.

We find a good account of it, also, by Miss Amy Fay, a young lady from Chicago whose acquaintance we must make at any moment now. 'It is *so* delicious in that room of his!' she writes. 'It was all furnished and put in order for him by the Grand Duchess herself. The walls are pale gray, with a gilded border running round the room, or rather two rooms, which are divided, but not separated, by crimson curtains. The furniture is crimson, and everything is so *comfortable.* . . . A splendid grand piano stands in one window (he receives a new one every year). The other window is always wide open, and looks out on to the park. There is a dovecot just opposite the window, and the doves promenade up and down on the roof of it, and fly about, and sometimes whirr down on the sill itself. That pleases Liszt. His writing table is beautifully fitted up with things that all match. Everything is in bronze; inkstand, paperweight, matchbox, etc., and there is always a lighted candle standing on it by which he and the gentlemen can light their cigars.'

The Hofgärtnerei was to be his home, during at least a part of each year, for the next seventeen years. At Villa d'Este Liszt was more or less inaccessible, but in the Hofgärtnerei he received his pupils and was visited by most of the leading musicians of the time. For he is emerging, now, into the knowledge of people still living to-day, who can remember that music-room and can recall the figure of Liszt in the summer afternoons.

And now, indeed, this new pattern which his life was forming begins to take on its final shape; and since he made the same journeys every year we can no longer set out with him each time he leaves Villa d'Este for Weimar, but must consider all his remaining years as the more or less punctual fulfilment of his settled plans. It was at Villa d'Este that he found most opportunity for his own work, and he stayed there, as a rule, from July till November, or December. April, May, and June were spent in Weimar, where he gave lessons, free of charge as always, to the most brilliant young pianists of both sexes and every nationality. But Weimar and Villa d'Este have to share his activities, in future, with a third home. For his fellow-countrymen had, at last, realized the expediency of retaining his services in their midst.

For this purpose a new Academy of Music was formed, with Government support, and Liszt was persuaded to pass two or three months of each year to give tuition and advise and set the new institution upon its feet. He spent the first three months of each year at Budapest, from 1872 onwards, and after much labour, due almost entirely to his own efforts, the Academy was at length opened, in November 1875. This side of his life is much less familiar than any other phase of his old age; chiefly because his correspondence concerning it was in Hungarian, and very few of these letters have been translated. But, in his concern for his native country, he was reasserting his nationality. He had never been, and never could be, a German. He was, mentally and physically, more of an alien in Weimar than in Rome. As friend and ally of Wagner, Liszt was, indeed, no more of a German than he had been a Frenchman when he was associated with Chopin and lived in Paris. On the contrary, he remarks in more than one letter that the German mentality was odious to him.

Before his 'vie trifurquée', as he called it, his threefold life, attained to its plentitude, the Franco-Prussian war broke out, and it is plain enough that his sympathies were entirely upon the side of France, as were those of the Princess. At the news of Sedan he writes to her: 'After the terrifying blow of the surrender of the French Army and of the Emperor we must resign ourselves for a long time ahead to give up the hopes we were discussing in your last letter. Providence has pronounced against the sovereign whom I admired as the wisest, the most able, and the best of our epoch. The prediction of Voltaire has come true—the century of Prussian dominance has at last arrived.' He speaks of Napoleon III, in other letters, in exactly the same terms of admiration and regret. When, indeed, Napoleon III died, three years later, he wrote no less than an apotheosis of his virtues to the sympathetic ears of the Princess. His heart was magnanimous, his intelligence universally comprehensive, his wisdom was tried and proved, his character was mild and generous; he had the breath of the divine Cæsar in him, and was the ideal personification of terrestrial rule. The day of justice would come when the French nation would place his body in the Invalides, beside that of Napoleon I. And he speaks in eager terms of the prospects of the Prince Imperial.

The fall of Rome to Vittorio-Emmanuele, which was the direct outcome of the war, was another event regretted by Liszt, who had so many associations with the last years of Papal rule. The Princess felt it much more deeply still, and it very nearly ended in her retreat from Rome. Liszt offered to come to the frontier and meet her, but eventually she stayed in the Via del Babuino, much, it may be feared, to Liszt's relief. For the 'vie trifurquée' had brought with it some liberation of his spirits. It is to be noticed that for nearly three years, from November 1871 till June 1874, Liszt never went back to the Villa d'Este. The new régime in Rome, his activities at Weimar, and the negotiations for his return to Budapest were the excuses for this absence. But there were other reasons, no less important.

Already, in Weimar, he may be said to have preluded upon his new life of freedom, and to have tried, as it were, the effect of such interludes upon his bonds with the Princess. Some few of these interruptions were already of long standing. There was Agnes Klindworth, the most charming of his pupils; and there was Mme de Moukhanoff-Kalergis, *née* Nesselrode, whose rhapsodical admiration for Liszt found vent in conventional form in letters to her daughter. This affection was, perhaps, distant and sedate, however deep and pressing. For Mme de Moukhanoff, as member

Ferruccio Busoni

Liszt in old age, 1886

of a family famous in the annals of diplomacy, will have tempered her Russian blood with mid-Victorian formality, and she was of mature years. If fire there had been, it had flickered in the past.

But Liszt, the creature of environment, had actually found at Weimar a new Princess with whom to wound those local susceptibilities that he had already pained before. She was the Baroness Olga Meyendorff, who had been a Princess Gort-schakoff before her marriage to a Russian diplomat stationed in Rome. She and Liszt had met each other at the evening receptions in the Via del Babuino. Just at the time Liszt returned to Weimar her husband, by coincidence, was appointed Russian Minister to that Court, but he died in 1871, and his widow established herself permanently in Weimar. The ardent sentiments of this woman of thirty must have renewed his youth. For the time being, at any rate, we no longer find so many of those expressions of 'très uniquement chère' in his letters to Princess Wittgenstein. He begins, indeed, to quarrel and disagree with her, but only in the slightest, mildest of forms; and if it is an anniversary, a Christmas Day or his birthday, her presents to him touch his sentiment and regain his affections in a moment. Nevertheless, the Baroness M., as she is to be found mentioned in mysterious contemporary accounts, was a person of supreme moment to him, and the inspiration of his days.

But the latent flames that her good looks had awakened spread beyond the parochial confines. They were not limited to Weimar, or even to the Baroness M. It is clear that after those few years of Roman seclusion the strength of his personality had received a new access of force. The black silk cassock was an aid to his hypnotic powers; it was the conjurer's robe, beyond a doubt, and all who beheld him were struck by the magician's air that it imparted to him. In the words of Henri Maréchal, who saw him at this time: 'En rectifiant ceci on pouvait décemment servir la messe, en corrigeant un peu cela, on était prêt pour le concert.'

Once established in his native Hungary, away from the vigilance of either, or both, Princesses, it was obvious that there would be trouble. And the disturbance arrived, with disconcerting rapidity, in the form of the Cossack Countess. The story is complicated because both actors in the drama give their own accounts of it. We have Liszt's own, rather halting, mention of it to Princess Wittgenstein; the Countess's narrative in the form of fiction.

spread over two novels; and the account of an eyewitness, Janka Wohl, an ardent Hungarian who had her own admiration for our hero and a dislike for all possible rivals.

We will begin with an abridged description of the youth of the Countess, culled from her two novels, *Souvenirs d'une Cosaque*, and *Souvenirs d'une pianiste*. These were published, to revenge herself upon Liszt, under the pseudonym of Robert Franz. But her real name was Olga Janina, a Christian name of fatal propensity to Liszt, when we remember Baroness Olga M. . . . But we must continue with our précis, because it gives such a complete picture of this new danger in his life.

She was born in the Ukraine. An old soldier dipped her spirit, or we could translate it better, in fox-hunting language, as 'blooded her', making a Cossack of her, by reciting the old heroic national epics to her attentive ears. Precocious reading transformed her into a revolutionary when about eight years of age ('vers l'âge de huit ans'). A frantic physical activity did not suffice to calm her fevered nerves. She killed horses under her. She improvised wolf-hunts of mad temerity and folly. She wanted to be a genius. One of her friends affirmed that, when a little older, she imagined herself to be the reincarnation of Saint Cecilia. The picture she presents of herself is complete in every detail; not one gadget of romance is lacking in it. We are treated to an immense description of the Oriental and Turkish arms belonging to her home, yataghans, scimitars, blades of Damascus and Toledo. We are told of her rides through the 'irritante électricité de la steppe'! We are taken to the stables and shown her coursers: 'des Arabes de pur sang, une jument aux crins d'or', and 'des étalons d'un blanc immaculé'. Horses were her mania—'j'étais folle de mes blancs coursiers'.

But all her spirits, all her élan, were held back and repressed in her by a reactionary stepmother, so she married, at fifteen years of age, having been promised her complete and absolute liberty in order that she might become a great artist. On the morrow of her wedding, when they woke up, she horse-whipped her husband, who tried to deprive her of her freedom—and left him. After having tried to kill herself with her daughter (a new phenomenon, whose appearance upon the scene casts a still more lurid light upon the activities of the Countess), she lets herself be calmed down for a while by the savage beauty of the landscape in the Ukraine, and by the music of Chopin. At this point, in her own words: 'L'infortuné directeur du Conservatoire de Kiev', who had saved her from despair by this musical revelation, was well punished: 'il en fut, d'ailleurs, bien puni. Il mourut de gangrène, mordu par un tigre que notre Cosaque promenait toujours à son côté.' But, before he died, he had time to introduce the music of 'L.' to her. She wrote to him, and 'L.' took her as pupil. She went to see him in Rome: 'traversant la Toscane en frissonnant de plaisir'. At their first meeting, in Santa Francesca Romana, 'j'étais vêtue en crêpe de chine blanc, lamé d'argent. C'était une de ces toilettes comme Worth seul possède le secret.' He received her in an oblong room, in the middle of which was the customary table with an open box of cigars and a lighted candle. She accepted the offer of a cigar and they both smoked, walking up and down the room. At one end was a figure of Christ, and, at the other, the Virgin of the Seven Sorrows. She felt a scruple of conscience at smoking, and asked Liszt if the odour of the tobacco did not inconvenience such august personages. His reply was: 'Mon Dieu, non, pour eux c'est comme une variété d'encens.' This first interview was followed by frequent visits; and she speaks of the complicated sentiments which were inspired in his heart by 'cette petite sauvage de 18 à 19 ans'. On one occasion, she was waiting for him when he came home from an evening party, probably one of the receptions in the Via del Babuino, and she lit his cigar for him. They spent most of the night in talking.

We find the first mention of her in Liszt's letters in February 1870. She has come to see him with an enormous bouquet of flowers brought from Nice, and after meeting her a few times he has given her some of his music to copy. She wrote such a lovely hand that he says she could send her manuscripts to an exhibition of calligraphy.

A year after this, when he had safely left Rome behind him, he writes to Princess Wittgenstein from Weimar, on 10 May 1871: 'You know that Mme Janina has been in Rome for a fortnight. Your reflections upon her are extremely just; and I am afflicted to see a woman so gifted with intelligence, with talent and with artistic sentiment, pursue her way with such fury in the road that can only lead her to ruin, material and moral. Unhappily Gregorovius's unfortunate opinion of her still seems to me to be moderate, compared with the truth. For years, she has been feeding her spirit upon the most perverse theories and sophisms. The blasphemies, imprecations, the extravagances of Proudhon and of the new Atheist school, and of the Asamistes and Anarchists, are her familiar litanies. George Sand seems faint and timid beside her! In the way of poetry, she has gone quite mad over the *Fleurs du mal* of Baudelaire ... whatever will happen to her? The ruin of her fortune, and several attempts at suicide, are not happy precedents for her future. But please, for Christian Charity's sake, keep all that I have said to you to yourself alone.'

His next letter on the subject betrays the seriousness of the situation. It was written from Budapest, on 29 November. 'My letter to you to-day is rather late. Besides, I have had a terrible disturbance, last Saturday, and I have only been able to settle it, on the evening of the day before yesterday. Mme la C^{sse} Janina— this title appears, now, upon her Austrian passport—has been spending these three days here. Forgive me the recital of her violences and furies—and have the kindness not to mention her to anyone at all. My guardian angel upheld me in this danger. After a new attempt to poison herself, carried out in my apartment, Mme Janina has left for Paris, where she will probably stay. But, again, I ask you not to speak of it to anyone—not even to me—as I want, as much as possible, to forget this crisis, which, thanks to my guardian angel, did not end in catastrophe or in public scandal.' And he continues, tactfully: 'Your beautiful views on the development of music and the pre-eminence of religious music especially have deeply interested me. . . .'

But Princess Wittgenstein was not satisfied, and Liszt had to write her fuller details of the occurrence, though he contrived to delay his reply until 3 February. 'In obedience to your request, I add some further details to the exact recital that I gave you, the next day, after the horrible incident of Mme Janina. She telegraphed to me from New York to Rome, in the middle of October, "I shall leave this week, in order to answer your letter personally." ... I understood immediately what she intended by answering me personally. In the middle of November, two letters from Schuberth in New York, and from Hébert in Paris, warned me to be on my guard against the vengeance of a hysterical madwoman. It seems that Mme Janina had told her friends of her resolution to come to Pest and kill herself and me. In fact, she came into my room armed with a revolver and with several phials of poison—ornaments which she had already shown me twice, last winter. I said to her quietly: "What you are intending to do, Madame, is wicked. I ask you to desist—but I will not try to prevent you." Two hours later Augusz (his host at Budapest) found her with me. She again repeated that she had no other object in life except to kill me and commit suicide. I protested firmly against the intervention of the police—for Mme Janina is quite capable of firing her revolver before they have time to handcuff her. Enough, and more than enough upon this subject. The next day she left for Paris. . . . I ask you, once again, not to mention this to anyone. Do not write it to Augusz—your silence will do me honour.'

The truth of the story would appear to be that she had introduced herself to Liszt, in Rome, at Santa Francesca Romana, and had become so dangerous to his susceptible heart that he fled from her to the Villa d'Este. During a whole year he saw her intermittently, and must have, it is obvious, fallen more than slightly in love with her. She was, we must remember, extremely beautiful and only nineteen years of age. Even his retreat at Villa d'Este was of no avail; it had, indeed, exactly the opposite result, for the Countess gained admittance dressed as a gardenboy, carrying another bouquet of flowers, probably also from the Riviera. The immediate results of her escapade would seem to have been fatal; for, having surrendered to her, once more, Liszt fled from Rome to Weimar, and, in desperation at her lover's desertion, she left Rome for New York.

The episode described in his letter occurred, therefore, after these Roman scenes; but the best account of them is in the book, already mentioned, by Janka Wohl,* and this is so entertaining that it is irresistible to quote a little from it. The account is written, be it remembered, by a Hungarian lady who was, herself, more than a little interested in the Master.

'One of his pupils, a Cossack lady, had followed him amongst others, when he left Rome. She was a Countess, still fairly young, but painfully thin. She had a pale, intelligent face, large black eyes, pleasing manners, and was altogether very "comme il faut".

'She read Kant and Schopenhauer, and to amuse herself had

---

* *Franz Liszt, Souvenirs d'une compatriote*, par Janka Wohl, 1887. An English translation by B. P. Ward was published the same year.

studied the microscope and vivisection, and now she wanted at any price to become a pianist. We found out, afterwards, that she had had relations with the master for several years.

'Liszt was living in a delightful suite of rooms in the house of his friend, the curé Schwendtner. Every Sunday afternoon all the fashionable world of Budapest went there to visit him. At one of these matinées the Countess played Chopin's Grande Ballade in G minor, and she played it with such bravura and fire that the master publicly congratulated her.

'She had promised to play at a charity concert which was to take place shortly, and we all advised her to play this Ballade which she played so admirably. But we none of us knew that we were giving her the worst kind of advice.

'On the evening of the concert a brilliant audience assembled. The Countess arrived, on the arm of Liszt, wearing a violet velvet dress buttoned up to her throat. He got her a seat in the little drawing-room with open colonnades facing the audience, which was reserved for the artists.

'When her turn came she was very graciously received, and she commenced her Ballade, of course playing by heart. All went well until the sixth page, when she hesitates and gets confused. In desperation she begins again, encouraged by indulgent applause. But, at the very same passage, her overwrought nerves betray her again. Pale as a sheet she rises. Then the master, thoroughly irritated, stamps his foot, and calls out from where he is sitting: "Stop where you are." She sits down again, and, in the midst of a sickening silence, she begins the wretched piece for the third time. Again her obstinate memory deserts her. She makes a desperate effort to remember che final passage, and at last finishes the fatal piece with a clatter of awful discords.

'I was never present at a more painful scene. Going out, the master upbraided her more than angrily, as she clung to his arm. He had been severely tried, and he at last lost all patience with the freaks of his pupil. And, this breakdown confirming, as it did, his oft-expressed opinion that she was not of the stuff that artists are made of, he no longer spared her.

'The Countess went home, took a dose of laudanum, and slept for forty-eight hours. They thought she was dead, but she woke up again.

'After letters had passed between them, the master insisted on her leaving Budapest immediately. They say she went to his apartments, one morning, with a revolver. She deliberately took aim at him. "Fire", said Liszt, advancing towards her. The unhappy woman dropped her hand, and fell at his feet, but all her entreaties were in vain. Liszt was inexorable, and she was obliged to leave Budapest.'

The subsequent history of this stormy petrel is unknown to us. She arrived in Paris, burnt several of his manuscripts which he had given her to copy, and brought out in rapid succession the two novels from which we have quoted.* Then she disappears from history, and no more is heard of her.

CHAPTER XL

Liszt and his pupils at Weimar—Miss Amy Fay's account of life at Weimar—Miss Amy Fay and the Baroness M. . .—Karl Tausig—Sofie Menter—Liszt returns to Rome—His visits to Budapest and contributions to Hungarian music—Death of Madame d'Agoult—Liszt mentions Miss Cecilia Gaul of Baltimore—'This is how I play when I am suffering from a cold'—Liszt at the Château of Loo—The cypresses of the Villa d'Este—Miscellaneous works—Liszt is made a Canon of Albano

I f we return to Weimar in this chapter, and more especially to that city considered as a school of pianism, it is to find a tradition established there to which the schools of the Renaissance are the only comparison. There could be nothing more delightful in the imagination than the atmosphere of those months of spring in this little town. Young men and women of talent, and of the most impressionable age, were gathered together here round this person of legend. He had given no concerts for thirty years, he would not play for money; but his counsel and advice,

---

*Someone else, under the pseudonym of Sylvia Zorelli, published two more novels, *Les Amours d'une Cosaque: par un ami de l'Abbé X*, and *Le Roman du pianiste et de la Cosaque*.

and the wonderful stimulus of his personality, were at the service of the young. No one came away from seeing him who was not the richer for that experience. He would criticize, he would comment, and there was always the hope that he would play. The magic of his technique was unimpaired, and it will readily be believed that those who heard him in such circumstances could never forget the impression of even a few bars played by his hands. His pupils, of whom there were sometimes twenty or thirty in the town, would bring him their pieces to play every afternoon, while on Sunday mornings, between eleven and one o'clock, there were regular concerts amounting sometimes to a whole piano recital by Liszt, according to his mood.

Every side of the life at Weimar must have been delightful. Besides the afternoons spent with Liszt, there were the excursions he made with his pupils to Sondershausen and Meiningen, where there were excellent orchestras to hear. And, of course, many of his pupils, and not the least talented among them, were a prey to the affectations of the adolescent. This must have made the streets of Weimar a most amusing sight. At any moment, for instance, one might pass by Arthur Friedheim, who, we are assured by a contemporary, 'in his street dress with a bronze-velvet cloak, great soft felt hat, and gold medallion portrait of Liszt worn as a scarfpin, looked the typical musician'.

His actual entourage was the agglomeration of hero worship. We have the testimony of Grieg, who took his piano concerto to show to Liszt. The young Norwegian composer could not but be flattered, for the veteran played through his concerto, at sight, with thrilling, magnificent effect, giving vent to the warmest expressions of enthusiasm and singing some of the tunes at the top of his voice as he played. In the background sat the entourage, listening attentively. 'Sgambati and Winding were there, and a German Lisztite whose name I do not know, but who goes so far in the aping of his idol that he even wears the gown of an Abbé. Add to these a Chevalier de Concilium, and some young ladies of the kind that would like to eat Liszt, skin, hair, and all.'

The assembled company, in this instance, amounted to no more than a handful of the 'jeunes matadors du piano' as Liszt delighted to call them. But, before we come to a detailed mention of any of their names, we must pause for a moment over the delightful picture of life in Weimar presented by Miss Amy Fay, a young lady from Chicago, in her book *Music Study in Germany*. She arrived in Weimar, hoping to take lessons from Liszt, in May 1873, and writes as follows: 'Last night I arrived in Weimar, and this evening I have been to the theatre, which is very cheap here, and the first person I saw, sitting in a box opposite, was Liszt, from whom, as you know, I am bent on getting lessons, though it will be a difficult thing, I fear, as I am told that Weimar is overcrowded with people who are on the same errand. I recognized Liszt from his portrait, and it entertained and interested me very much to observe him. He was making himself agreeable to three ladies, one of whom was very pretty. He sat with his back to the stage, not paying the least attention, apparently, to the play, for he kept talking all the while, himself, and yet no point of it escaped him, as I could tell by his expressions and gestures.

'Liszt is the most interesting and striking-looking man imaginable. Tall and slight, with deepset eyes, shaggy eyebrows, and long iron-grey hair, which he wears parted in the middle. His mouth turns up at the corners, which gives him a most crafty and Mephistophelian expression when he smiles, and his whole appearance and manner have a sort of Jesuitical elegance and ease. His hands are very narrow, with long and slender fingers that look as if they had twice as many joints as other people's! They are so flexible and supple that it makes you nervous to look at them. Anything like the polish of his manner I never saw. When he got up to leave the box, for instance, after his adieux to the ladies, he laid his hand on his heart and made his final bow—not with affectation, or in mere gallantry, but with a quiet courtliness which made you feel that no other way of bowing to a lady was right or proper. It was most characteristic.

'But the most extraordinary thing about Liszt is his wonderful variety of expression and play of feature. One moment his face will look dreamy, shadowy, tragic. The next he will be insinuating, amiable, ironic, sardonic; but always the same captivating grace of manner. He is a perfect study. I cannot imagine how he must look when he is playing. He is all spirit, but half the time, at least, a mocking spirit, I should say. All Weimar adores him, and people say that women still go perfectly crazy over him. When he walks out he bows to everybody just like a King!'

A day or two later she meets him. 'The door suddenly opened and Liszt appeared. We all rose to our feet and he shook hands with everybody without waiting to be introduced. Liszt looks as if he had been through everything, and has a face seamed with experience. He is rather tall and narrow, and wears a long Abbé's coat reaching nearly down to his feet. He made me think of an old-time magician more than anything, and I felt that with a touch of his wand he could transform us all.

'. . . As soon as Leitert had finished, I slipped off into the back of the room, hoping Liszt would forget all about me; but he followed me almost immediately, like a cat with a mouse, took both my hands in his, and said in the most winning way imaginable, "Mademoiselle, vous jouerez quelque chose, n'est-ce pas?" I can't give you any idea of his persuasiveness, when he chooses. It is enough to decoy you into anything. It was such a desperate moment that I became reckless and, without even telling him that I was out of practice and not prepared to play, I sat down and plunged into the A flat major Ballade of Chopin, as if I were possessed. Liszt kept on calling out "Bravo" every minute or two to encourage me, and made one or two little criticisms. He is just like a monarch, and no one dares speak to him until he addresses one first, which I think no fun.'

She is accepted as his pupil and goes to him three times a week. 'At home Liszt doesn't wear his long Abbé's coat, but a short one, in which he looks much more artistic. . . . I think he hates the trouble of speaking German, for he mutters his words, and does not half finish his sentences. Yesterday when I was there he spoke to me in French all the time . . . the more I see and hear Liszt, the more I am lost in amazement! I can neither eat nor sleep on those days that I go to him. . . . He goes far beyond all that I expected. Anything so perfectly beautiful as he looks when he sits at the piano I never saw, and yet he is almost an old man now. His personal magnetism is immense, and I can scarcely bear it when he plays. He can make me cry all he chooses. . . . Liszt knows well the influence he has on people, for he always fixes his eye on some one of us when he plays, and I believe he tries to wring our hearts. . . . Liszt is a complete actor who intends to carry away the public, who never forgets that he is before it, and who behaves accordingly. He subdues the people to him by the very way he walks on to the stage. He gives his proud head a toss, throws an electric look out of his eagle eye, and seats himself at the piano with an air.'

She gives charming accounts of their excursions. 'Weimar is a lovely little place, and there are most beautiful walks all about. Ascension being a holiday here, all we pianists made up a walking party out to Tiefurt, about two miles distant. The walk lay through the woods, and was perfectly exquisite the whole way. As we came back in the evening the nightingales were singing. There were cuckoos, too. Metzdorf and I danced on the hard road, to the edification of the others.' Another day they went to Sondershausen. 'Liszt himself, the Countess von X., and Count S. were to lead the party. The morning we started was one of those perfect autumnal days when it is a delight simply to live. Liszt and his titled friends travelled in a first-class carriage, by themselves. The rest of us went second-class in the next carriage. We were very gay, indeed. . . . After dinner, Liszt said, "Now let us go and see Fräulein Fichtner". She is a well-known pianist in Germany, and is both pretty and brilliant, a sparkling brunette with a face full of intelligence. We started in a procession, which is the way one always walks with Liszt. . . . It reminds me of those snowballs the boys roll up at home—the crowd gathers as it proceeds! I do not think he is the same when he is with aristocrats. He must be among artists to unsheathe his sword. When he is with "swells" he is all grace and polish. He seems only to toy with his genius for their amusement, and is never serious. The presence of the proud Countess von X., that day at Sondershausen, kept him, as it were, at a distance from everybody else.'

By this time it can be read between the lines that Liszt had begun to show traces of interest in this young American girl. They make an excursion to Jena with all the young musicians. 'After dinner Liszt said, "Now we'll go to Paradise." So we put on our things and proceeded to walk along the river to a place called Paradise, on account of its loveliness. This walk along the river was enchanting. The current was very rapid, and the willows were all blowing in the breeze. The way was under a double row of tall trees, which met at the top and formed a green arch over our heads. It was all breeze and freshness, and the sunlight struck picturesquely aslant the hillsides. I started to walk with Liszt, but he was so surrounded that it was difficult to get near him. At seven we were all invited to supper at the house of a friend of Liszt's. The tea was all laid on tables in the garden. . . . We sat down, pell-mell, anywhere—I, next to Liszt, who kept on putting things on my plate. We had new potatoes for dinner, boiled with their skins on, and Liszt threw one at me, and I caught it.'

This mild flirtation brings the mysterious Countess X. into the story. 'This haughty Countess, by the way, has always had a great fascination for me, because she looks like a woman who has "a history". . . . She is such a type of woman as I suppose only exists in Europe. . . . She is a widow, and in appearance about thirty-six-or-eight years old, slight to thinness, but exceedingly graceful. She is always attired in black, and is utterly careless in dress, yet nothing can conceal her innate elegance of figure. Her face is pallid and her hair dark. She makes an impression of icy coldness and at the same time of tropical heat. The pride of Lucifer to the world in general—entire abandonment to the individual. I meet her often in the park, as she walks along trailing her "sable garments like the night" and surrounded by her four beautiful boys. . . .

'I shall never forget the supercilious manner in which the Countess took out her eyeglass and looked over me as I passed her one day in the park. Weimar being such a "kleines Nest" (little nest), as Liszt calls it, every stranger is immediately remarked. She waited till I got close up, then deliberately put up this glass and scrutinized me from head to foot, then let it fall with a half-disdainful, half-indifferent air, as if the scrutiny did not reward the trouble. . . . She always seems to me to be gradually going to wreck—a burnt-out volcano, with her own ashes settling down upon her and covering her up. She is very highly educated, and is preparing her eldest son for the university herself. What a subject she would have been for Balzac!'

This mysterious Countess X. is, of course, none other than the Princess Gortschakoff, alias the Baroness M. . ., who, like her rival Princess Wittgenstein, was ever on the alert where Liszt's amours were concerned. Princess Wittgenstein, indeed, had a special spy stationed at Weimar, in the person of Adelheid von Schorn, whose duty it was to keep her 'au courant' with the latest fancies of this protean heart. Their correspondence on this topic fills a good-sized volume. At Weimar it was easy enough to keep him under observation; at Villa d'Este he was far enough removed from harm; but it is to be feared that at Budapest, escaped from the jurisdiction of both Princesses, and the adored idol of the fiery and volatile Hungarians, events may have occurred which would have brought both Princesses into temporary alliance together.

After the Olga Janina episode, Liszt, as we have said, kept away for some time from Rome. He was, in fact, fresh from those experiences when Miss Amy Fay fell under his spell at Weimar. And that atmosphere of youthfulness, as we have shown in the extracts from her book, was not all on her side. Liszt, also, had the spirits of a young man. We are reminded in so many pages in her book of the trip to Chamonix, undertaken thirty-five years before. Then, as at Weimar, every day was an unforgettable experience. Everyone was young, and the world was full of promise.

Perhaps the hand of death is never so near as in days like these, which held so much of the symbolism of life in their bright promise and early achievement. For death had just struck down the first, and perhaps the best of Liszt's pupils, Karl Tausig. This was the youth whom Liszt had prophesied would inherit his playing. He had been brought to the master when only fourteen years of age, in 1855, during the great years of the Weimar period, already a finished and most formidable player. He became the most devoted of Liszt's disciples, and a pianist of colossal powers who could perform the most difficult feats with an appearance of absolute ease. His excesses of industry must have ruined his health, for many accounts of him as a teacher at Berlin show Tausig tormented almost beyond endurance by his state of nerves. It was due, no doubt, to this reason that he fell an easy victim to typhoid fever, dying, when barely thirty years of age, in 1871. With the example of Liszt before our eyes it is bold to prophesy what a man of Tausig's powers might have accomplished, had he lived longer, though it may be doubted whether he would have proved to be a great composer. He left some piano transcriptions from Wagner, superior, perhaps, to those of his master; the *Nouvelles Soirées de Vienne*, delightful arrangements of Waltzes by Johann Strauss, intended as a pendant to Liszt's *Soirées de Vienne*, which were based upon waltzes by Schubert; and a set of *Ungarische Zigeunerweisen*, eleven in number, and said to be the equal of those by Liszt, to which on occasion they would certainly make a welcome alternative.

If Tausig, who had died by the date to which we have arrived, was the chief of his early pupils, there were, also, in those days, men of the importance of Hans von Bülow and Richter. The future of music in the last quarter of the nineteenth century lay largely in their hands. Richter was among the strongest partisans of Wagner, responsible, perhaps, more than any other man for the survival of Bayreuth as a place of pilgrimage after Wagner's death. Von Bülow, who, as a pianist was almost on the level of Tausig, and who became a member of Liszt's family by his marriage to Cosima, developed into a world-famous conductor.* Having been the apostle of Liszt and of Wagner, he then became the protagonist of Brahms and producer of his Fourth Symphony, and ended as protector of Richard Strauss. Nor were Hans von Bülow and Richter his only pupils of promise, for that word is certainly deserved in the case of his organ pupil Julius Reubke, who died, aged only twenty-four, in 1854, leaving an organ sonata which has survived to show the early fulfilment of his gift. And if they were not actually the pupils of Liszt, such men as Joachim, César Franck, Smetana, Dvořák, Vincent d'Indy, Grieg, and MacDowell, owed the first publication of their music to his good offices and were the recipients of his advice and counsel.

But, by 1870, these musicians were already established. The return of Liszt to Weimar was associated with a new lot of names: Klindworth, Nikisch, Felix Mottl, de Pachmann, Moszkowski, Scharwenka, Sofie Menter, among them. Of these, leaving aside Nikisch, whose fame needs no mention, we will particularize the conductor Felix Mottl, for an orchestration of Liszt's Legend, *St. François d'Assise prédicant aux Oiseaux*. Sofie Menter, too, must be given brief notice for she was the best of Liszt's women pupils, and the object of his constant praise. She made an unhappy marriage with the cellist, Pöpper, did not die until 1918, and left a curious contribution, or appendix, to the music of her master in the form of *Ungarische Zigeunerweisen* for piano and orchestra, the intrumentation of which was entrusted to Tchaikowsky. This should be a minor curiosity and possibly deserves a hearing. There were other women pupils, Martha Remmert, Milie Merian-Genast, Jessie Hillebrand Laussot, Elpis Melena, Caroline Unger-Sabatier, Nadine Helbig, Vera Timanova, Adela Aus der Ohe, who blossomed into prominence under his tutelage and then

---

*Von Bülow was, as well, a composer, but is never heard of in this connexion. He wrote a *Mazurka Fantaisie* for piano (of which Liszt made an orchestral arrangement), and the *Carnevale di Milano*, also for piano, and also never played.

disappeared from history with a rapidity that is really disconcerting. It is probable that they attracted the interest of Liszt in ratio to their charms, and we are inclined to think of them in the terms by which he had characterized his piano pupils at Geneva, forty years before: 'très petites mains', 'jolis doigts', 'beaux yeux'. Certain it is that their careers offer nothing further of interest to his biographer. They became music-teachers, or they married—that is all. It is sad to think of that climax to those walks to Paradise, along the river by the blowing willows.

Meanwhile, during these three or four years, Princess Wittgenstein had to be kept at bay and her curiosity must be satisfied, or soothed, until Liszt felt a desire to return to Rome. In order to do this he had to show an exaggerated interest in her literary works. Just at this very time, in July 1873, he writes wishing her success to her forthcoming volumes of a thousand pages each. A few months later, from Hungary, he describes a special visit to the douane in order to secure the third volume of the *Causes intérieures*, a book which the customs officials regarded, apparently, with suspicion. 'Quel volume—1149 pages', he exclaims. Another day he writes in answer to her, agreeing that a thousand pages upon the Episcopate, her next instalment of the work in progress, was a long and grave task; and he commends her industry in correcting proofs from half-past seven in the morning till half-past five at night. He even allows himself a joke at her expense, using the title of one of her books, 'La Simplicité de Colombe', as his motto for extricating himself from some musical entanglement to do with a forthcoming concert.

When, eventually, he did come back to Rome, and returned to his custom of passing two or three months of each year there, nearly all his time was spent at the Villa d'Este. When in Rome, he stayed in later years at the Hôtel d'Alibert, where he occupied two very modest rooms and there were always one or two of his disciples, or one of his granddaughters, the daughters of Blandine Ollivier, to keep him company. The routine of his life was most arduous. He rose at four a.m. and composed till seven a.m. After a second breakfast he attended Mass in San Carlo al Corso, and despite an afternoon siesta his day never ended till late at night.

At Villa d'Este he worked even harder. This must have been where he was most happy in his old age, left at peace and able to make progress with his own works. Villa d'Este, in his own words, was his 'El Dorado'. In those days it had to be reached from Rome by carriage and the journey took not less than four hours. On first arriving for his winter stay he was often serenaded by the municipal band, but, apart from this, was left to his own musical devices, except before Christmas, when the shepherds from Calabria, the zampognari, or pifferari, came down from the mountains to play their bagpipes before every household shrine. He listened to their traditional airs and made use of them in his own sacred music. His host, Cardinal Hohenlohe, was often at Villa d'Este with him, and his needs were attended to by the Cardinal's servants, Ercole and Fortunato. He had, besides these, his own servant Spiridion, an Albanian. When at Villa d'Este he wrote more often to the Princess, but did not see her except during his short stays at the Hôtel d'Alibert. Then he dined with her every night, and it is on record that the meal consisted always of cooked ham and red Hungarian wine, Szezgarder, procured for him by his friend, Baron Augusz.

This personage was often his host at Sexard, his country house in Hungary, near Pécs. His letters to Baron Augusz, written chiefly in French, have been published in a separate volume, but they are not of much interest except for the evidence they contain that Liszt was trying slowly to build up a body of Hungarian compositions. His Hungarian rhapsodies and marches, the *Hungarian Coronation Mass*, his transcriptions of Hungarian operas by Mosonyi, such as *Zep Ilonka*, and of pieces by the same composer, such as his *Puszta-Leben*, or of a *Nocturne dans le style hongrois* by Abrányi; these were his contributions to their national music. There are also some curious pieces that he wrote for his friend Count Géza Zichy, a brilliant virtuoso who lost his right arm through a shooting accident but developed a fantastic technique with his left hand alone. Liszt prepared various concert-arrangements for the left hand exclusively for his use.

But, in general, as we have said, it is difficult to discover much information about his annual visits to Budapest. His letters written from Hungary are, from this very lack of information, among the most interesting that he wrote, and many of them contain references to Count Albert Apponyi, whom Liszt considered as the ideal of the 'jeunesse dorée' of his native land.*

* The *Memoirs* of Count Apponyi, Heinemann Ltd., contain many references to Liszt.

This very eminent nobleman, who pleaded his country's cause so eloquently at Geneva, before the League of Nations, only died in 1933. He is first mentioned in the correspondence as long ago as 1869; but, Apponyi apart, there are few references to any persons who have come down into living memory.

Another feudal atmosphere in which Liszt delighted to stay, was with his friend Prince Hohenzollern-Hechingen, at Trachenberg in Silesia. He mentions the hundreds of guests in the castle, the five cooks who were at work, day and night, and the stud of sixty English horses. The Silesian plain may well have recalled his native Hungary to him, as the life at Trachenberg will have reminded him of his early memories of Eisenstadt and Esterházy.

During all these years, it may be said that his incessant interest was the production of *The Ring* at Bayreuth, which he considered to be the most important artistic event of the century and 'the miracle of German art'. Many are his references to the countless rehearsals and the years of preparation that this entailed, and his enthusiasm when it was eventually performed knew no bounds. Wagner was two years younger than Liszt. There was certainly, by now, a marked contrast in their respective situations.

Shortly before this, Liszt read casually in a newspaper of the death of Madame d'Agoult. But he had reached the age when such things fall softer on the heart; it is certain, indeed, that he felt the recent death of Mme de Moukhanoff much more acutely. He wrote an Elegy to her memory and organized a special concert at Weimar in her honour. The death of Madame d'Agoult, the mother of his three children, did not move him to any such effort; she died, unwept for and unsung. In a few days a letter came from the Princess enclosing an account of her last moments from the poet Ronchaud. Perhaps Liszt hardly felt himself to be the same person who had once loved her. All he said of her in his reply to the Princess was a remark about the falseness of her character. 'Elle avait éminemment le goût et même la passion du faux, excepté à certains moments d'extase dont elle n'a pu supporter le souvenir plus tard.' This is not the remark of someone who has forgiven his old injuries.

In fact, what sentiment there was left in this faded love affair had long ago settled itself in the breast of Madame d'Agoult, and this is not altogether to be expected of her demonstrably cold heart. She betrayed these emotions in drawing up her memoirs which she dedicated to Ronchaud who had been, at least, an aspirant to her heart. In these, for she knew they would not be published in her lifetime,* she was able to confide to herself and to a distant posterity in these words: 'Relu à Saint Lupicien, le 15 octobre 1866, Vingt-huit ans après! Qu'a-t-il fait de ces vingt-huit années; et qu'en ai-je fait? Il est Abbé Liszt et je suis Daniel Stern! Et que dé désespoirs, de morts, de sanglots, de larmes, de deuils, entre nous!' But the memory of their quarrels still rankled in the mind of Liszt. He could not forget; and we find him, only a very few months before her death, writing from Weimar where grand celebrations were in progress and the King of Sweden was the guest of honour, that 'on ne me m'a pas traité en Guermann de Nélida'. His resentment had lasted for thirty years.

Princess Wittgenstein, who may have mourned more sincerely for Madame d'Agoult than did her lover, must have laid the blame for Liszt's partial estrangement from herself upon Wagner and upon the Bayreuth festival. Nor can Cosima have been to her liking. Liszt's excitement over *The Ring* was a heretical, a pagan tendency in her eyes. It was at the opposite extremity from Rome, and its influences were calculated to undo all the good of ten years spent among the priests. But her fears, as to Wagner, were ill founded. As if to prove this, Liszt came back to Rome for a long stay in 1875, the year before the Festival, and now that it was over, now that the 'miracle of German art was accomplished', he came every autumn, almost without exception, to Rome.

But he had broken some of his shackles. Eight years had elapsed since he resumed his life at Weimar, while the school of music at Budapest was an established reality that took up another third of his time. He was no longer the recluse, but was accessible to the world.

He has arrived, indeed, into modern times. The child who saw Beethoven and Schubert, the young man who was part of the Italy of Byron, who was the companion of Chopin, now meets citizens of the U.S.A., and, in speech, they belong to the Twentieth Century. Miss Amy Fay is old-fashioned in comparison with them. We have the proofs of this in an interview at Weimar, in 1877, with the anonymous B. W. H. 'How much more some of us get than we deserve! Very graciously the Master mentioned Miss Cecilia Gaul of Baltimore. . . . He gave us roses. At last he

*Her *Memoirs* were first published in 1927.

276

stood up, took our hands kindly, and said "That is how I play when I am suffering from a cold, as at present". We asked if he had been improvising, or if what he played was already printed? "It was only a little nocturne", he said. It sounded like a sweet remembrance. "And was that", he replied cordially.'

We have said that Liszt was more accessible in these years, and another proof of it was the extension of his travels into Holland, which he visited several times, generally during May, as the guest of King William, staying at his country château of Het Loo.* The company consisted exclusively of musicians and painters, Saint-Saëns, Ambroise Thomas, Wieniawski, Vieuxtemps, Bouguereau, Gérôme, indeed nearly every minor celebrity imaginable. Dinner, it may be noted, was still at six o'clock. The fair sex was excluded, but, in compensation, the actresses and ballet dancers of the royal company performed during every evening of the fortnight that the visits lasted; and we gather from Liszt's letters that the château of Loo was not exactly a place of rest and retreat. In fact, in his words, the extreme amiability of the King towards his guests restrained their hours of leisure. Boredom could hardly be more courteously expressed.

If he only went back to Het Loo once or twice more, his wanderings in a general sense are to continue, now, until his death. But we will leave him in Rome for the end of this chapter, because his return to that city signifies the beginning of the new and ultimate phase in his life. To Rome, therefore, we come back once again, and note the relief expressed by Liszt at the opening of the new tramway to Tivoli, which absolved him from that long drive of four hours in a public diligence from the Piazza di Spagna to Villa d'Este. And he is awaited in Rome by his biographer, Lina Ramann, the creature, or very soon the creature, of the Princess. He writes from Villa d'Este to introduce her. He must explain her character. She has not come to Rome to amuse herself. The diversions of the Corso, the 'confetti and mocolletti' were not at all her affair—even the Colosseum and St. Peter's would hardly interest her. She was altogether absorbed in her task. Hers was a character which fitted in admirably with that of the Princess; and very soon they were in conclave together, behind locked doors,

---

*King William III of the Netherlands was the brother of Princess Sophie of Orange-Nassau who married the Grand-Duke Karl-Alexander of Saxe-Weimar.

preparing his biography from what might be described as the anti-Wagnerian standpoint.

The autumn days at Villa d'Este inspired him to some of the most interesting of his later creations. For three whole days, in September 1877, he spent every hour of sunlight and as much of night as was made visible by the moon in admiration of the cypresses. They obsessed his thoughts to the exclusion of all else, and two of the piano pieces in the third volume of the *Années de Pèlerinage* are the results of this. A third piece, *Les Jeux d'Eaux à la Villa d'Este*, an evocation of the fountains and the noise of waters in that lovely garden, is perhaps even better than its two sisters. It is an extraordinary anticipation of Ravel's *Jeux d'Eau*; and so remarkable is its prophecy of the future that no one, in ignorance of its true origin, on hearing the opening pages, would hesitate in ascribing it to that French composer, or even to Debussy.

His other compositions during the ten years that this chapter traverses are notably few in comparison with all other periods of his production. There had been too many disturbances, actual and emotional. He had begun a new oratorio, upon a vast scale, to a libretto by Princess Wittgenstein, the subject of which was St. Stanislas of Poland. This was planned to be the equal of *Christus* and of *St. Elizabeth*, but Liszt never found the time and energy to complete more than half of the work projected.* But it is certain that the interlude *Salve Polonia*, for chorus and orchestra, which is an extract from this immense torso, deserves revival. His other big work of this epoch was, also, written to the suggestion of the Princess. This is the *Glocken des Strasburgen Münsters*, for baritone solo, chorus, and orchestra, a setting of Longfellow's *Golden Legend*. This work, which is very little known, has an additional interest because of its influence upon Wagner. It is said that the liturgical motive of the prelude is to be found echoed in the overture of *Parsifal*, and elsewhere in that work. Besides these two works he was engaged upon the Epilogue to his *Tasso*.

These things apart, all that Liszt accomplished during these years was upon a small scale. We must mention his *Impromptu in F sharp*; the *Via Crucis*, a set of piano pieces; and the *Seven Sacraments* for chorus, solo voices, and organ; also, the *Legend of*

---

* Another oratorio, *St. Stephen of Hungary*, which was to be the pair to this, was never actually begun by Liszt, but its details were often discussed with Princess Wittgenstein.

St. Cecilia, a beautiful little work for mezzo-soprano, chorus, and orchestra; and an antiphony for the name-day of the same saint, written for similar combination.

The *Fantaisies Dramatiques* are conspicuous by their absence, except in one instance, a fantasy upon Lassen, the Swedish composer's, *Hagen und Kriemhild*.* But, in the way of adaptations for the piano, there are delightful trifles like the *Frühlingsnacht* of Schumann. Many other songs by Schumann were transcribed at this time; and there must be some charming pieces among the twelve songs by that forgotten lieder writer, Robert Franz. Mosonyi's *Grabgeleit*, an elegy to the dead composer, dates from this period. There is, also, an arrangement for piano of Herbeck's *Tanz-Momente*, a delightful piece of Viennese salon music, cleverly reduced from the orchestral score. The *Valse d'Adèle*, arranged from Count Zichy the one-armed pianist's opera, is another amusing relic of this time; and, to conclude the list, we have an adaptation for piano of Saint-Saëns' *Danse Macabre*, which is, at least, a more pleasant work than that 'cemetery farce' in the form it originally took.

All these things are small and of little importance; but, having once resumed his stay in the Villa d'Este, we shall expect to find Liszt more at leisure and in an environment that inspired him to work. The *Cyprès de la Villa d'Este* and the *Jeux d'Eaux* are the early instances of this renewed creativeness. The storms raised by the Cossack Countess had abated, the excitement of Bayreuth was over, he was working again with Princess Wittgenstein upon a revised version of their life of Chopin, and the last seven years of his life open in peaceful, untroubled circumstances.

We must consider it probable that some rumours of Weimar or Budapest had reached the Vatican, for, as soon as it was clear that he had resumed the ascetic life, and when two or three autumns in the Villa d'Este had been safely accomplished, Liszt received the only Church promotion that was ever accorded to him. On 12 October 1879, he was made a Canon of Albano, an honour which he owed to his patron, Cardinal Hohenlohe. This gave him the right, which he never exercised, to wear a purple soutane. The whole Seminary of Albano, to the number of forty persons, came over to Villa d'Este to a banquet in celebration of this event, in curious contrast to those banquets of forty years before in

*Lassen was the conductor at Weimar.

Budapest and in Vienna, when Liszt was presented with the jewelled sabres, and when he gave superb dinners, in return, to the Magnates of Hungary and the Austrian aristocrats.

In further commemoration of his elevation to the rank of Canon, Cardinal Hohenlohe founded a Mass to be said for him in perpetuity in the Cathedral of Albano, every second day of April. And it is only in keeping with the strange personality with whom we are dealing that we should find that Liszt raised the necessary funds to pay the expenses and the attendant fees from his publishers. He, in fact, finished and despatched to them, only two days before the ceremony, two manuscripts for which they had been waiting. These were the Sarabande and Chaconne from Handel's *Almira*, and his own Second *Mephisto-Waltz*.

This is the Abbé Liszt, in character, as it is said of great actors. He was not changed from the Lovelace, or the Leonhardt, of fifteen years before. 'A striking, uncanny figure: his black silk cassock fluttering ironically behind him. Some maintain that he is burnt out and that only the outer walls remain, from which a little ghostlike flame hisses forth.' That was how Gregorovius saw him; and our view of him, fifteen years later, can only confirm that learned opinion. He had not altered, and was incapable of change. Mephistopheles is still disguised as an Abbé, and the close of every chapter is still the end of Lovelace—till the next episode begins.

CHAPTER XLI

Liszt and the modern Russian school of composers—Moussorgsky—Borodin—Balakirev—Liapounov—Tchaikowsky

When last concerned with the details of his life, we took leave of Liszt at a moment when he had acquired the right to exchange his black soutane for a shade of purple. It was a privilege of which he never availed himself; and the new Canon of Albano, we have noted, had paid for his elevation with fees derived from a Sarabande of Handel and a *Mephisto-Waltz* of his own composing. That was in October

1879, and the autumn of the next year finds him back, once more, at Villa d'Este in circumstances no less true to every detail that we know about his character. There had been a concert in Rome of the great Anton Rubinstein, and Liszt writes to the Princess, who was unable or unwilling to be present, that he opened the programme, himself, with his new *Tarantelle Russe*. The evening, in fact, marked an important date in musical history for it signified in public form the interest that Liszt had lately begun to take in Russian music.

The Tarantella in question was his transcription of the *Tarantelle Slave*, for four hands, by Dargomijsky,* but this association extended beyond that rather unknown composer to more important figures in Russian music. As early as 1873 he had come across the music of Moussorgsky. In that year the *Chambre d'Enfants*, a collection of seven children's songs, was published, and Liszt in his enthusiasm expressed his desire to transcribe the whole work for piano solo and to dedicate a composition of his own to Moussorgsky. A letter from that composer to our old friend Stassov (see pp. 104–106) expresses his delight at this unexpected appreciation. Unfortunately Liszt never accomplished his ambition, and these two great names were never honoured together in this way. Whether Liszt ever saw a copy of *Boris Godounov* it is impossible to ascertain, though it is at least probable that he must have been sent this opera on publication.

He was familiar, at any rate, with *Prince Igor*, for Borodin made a special journey to Western Europe with two of his pupils, in 1877, in order to make the acquaintance of Liszt. A delightful account of their friendship is to be found in Borodin's letters to his wife.† He presented himself with some trepidation at the door of the Hofgärtnerei, but Liszt came downstairs to greet him; and, a moment later, they were seated together at the piano while Liszt told him how he had played his Symphony in E Flat, only two days before to the Grand-Duke. And Liszt with his long fingers began to play passages from the scherzo, as he said this. The old magician overwhelmed him with encouragement. He was in the right path, and must continue in it without paying heed to the

---

*An orchestral version, scored by Vittorio Rieti, used to be performed by Diaghilev as an interlude.

†*Borodin and Liszt. Borodin's Letters*, edited by A. Habets, translated by Rosa Newmarch, London, 1895.

counsels of convention. No good music, he assured Borodin, had ever met with anything but neglect and hostility, at first.

Four years later Borodin came back again to Europe and found Liszt at the Magdeburg Festival. He followed the master to Jena, and describes the arrival of Liszt to conduct a rehearsal in the cathedral. He was wearing his soutane, and walked with Baroness Meyendorff on his arm at the head of a cortège of musicians. He heard Liszt conduct without a baton, play the organ and piano, and accompany the cello sonata of Chopin. This time he was made so welcome by Liszt that he returned with him to Weimar.

He spent all his time with Liszt. He attended the lessons of his pupils, took his meals with Liszt and the Baroness, and went in the evenings to the Grand-Duke's receptions, or else to those of the Baroness. Spiridion, the Montenegrin servant of Liszt, took a special fancy to Borodin. Lazarewitch Knejewitch liked the Russian composer because he was Russian and Orthodox, and because of the Russo-Turkish war in which the 'little white father' had taken it upon himself to defend the Orthodox against the Turkish infidel. And Borodin was not the only Russian attached to the court of Liszt, at Weimar. Vera Timanova,★ whose talent as a player when only fifteen years old had been noted by Miss Amy Fay, had now blossomed into an extremely pretty girl and a pianist of at least adequate distinction. She was the favourite of Liszt, the sultana of his school of pupils; and Borodin describes how she played a rhapsody, and how Liszt embraced her, afterwards, while she kissed his hand. The Baroness was used to this; or it may have been as a distraction that she persuaded Borodin to sing them a chorus from *Prince Igor*. He had a fine voice, and after he had sung them one or two songs he played some of the dances, the famous Polovtsian dances. In this way Liszt heard the finest things from an opera that was only produced after his death, was left unfinished by the composer and never heard performed by him, and that only became known to Western Europe in the second decade of this century.

His association with Borodin brought Liszt into contact with all the other Russian musicians, with Rimsky-Korsakov, César Cui and Liadov. He writes to them in congratulation upon the success of their *Variations et Paraphrases*, a set of piano pieces based upon the nursery tune universally known as 'Chopsticks'! He even

★Vera Timanova was born in 1855.

made a contribution himself to the series, but his biographers unite as one man in contempt of his share in this venture.

With Balakirev, perhaps the most interesting of all the Russian composers, he was also upon familiar terms. When Liszt made his sensational first appearance in Russia, in 1842, one of the earliest and most fervent of his converts had been Glinka. Liszt, in fact, owed his Russian fame to the support and admiration of Glinka. In return for this, Liszt's propaganda for Russian music took early and tangible form in his publication of a paraphrase upon Tchernomor's March from *Russlan and Ludmilla*, in 1847. Liszt had already, therefore, at the date we have now arrived at, had some association with Russian music for no less than thirty years. Balakirev was the person in whom Glinka centred his hopes and communicated his ideas for the future of Russian music. This was, in itself, a sufficiently strong link between Balakirev and Liszt; and another bond between them was the fact that Balakirev was, himself, a pianist of quite exceptional powers. He was interested, because of this, in every branch of Liszt's activity as composer, in his virtuoso studies as much as in his symphonic poems. Glinka and Liszt were, indeed, his models.

The fruits of his admiration for Liszt are his two chief works, *Thamar* and *Islamey*, and they show, respectively, his cult for the orchestral and the pianistic side of Liszt's genius. The slowness with which Balakirev's works matured can only be compared to the laborious processes by which Flaubert perfected his books. *Thamar* was so long in appearing that its fires were stolen by Rimsky-Korsakov. *Schéhérazade* was the result of this; and the person who is familiar with it and who hears *Thamar* for the first time will reverse the processes of truth and will accuse Balakirev in his mind of stealing from Rimsky-Korsakov. Yet *Schéhérazade* is but the cheap popular edition of *Thamar*, pirated before publication. *Thamar* foreshadows every trick and device used by the Russians in order to achieve Circassian or Tartar effects in their music, just as the symphonic poem *Russia*, written by the same composer more directly under Glinka's influence, is the epitome of all specifically Russian music. *Thamar* is dedicated to Liszt, and it is a true development of the new principles that Liszt had discovered. It is more authentically the progeny of Liszt than the symphonic poems of Richard Strauss. Balakirev had the sense of beauty: he was artist as well as craftsman. In comparison with him, it is difficult to find a single instance in Strauss where the poet comes out above the outstanding technique, the superb mechanism, of his score.

Islamey, which shows the admiration of Balakirev for Liszt as virtuoso, is no less the direct descendant of our hero. As transcendental piano music, as a vehicle for virtuosity, it will only bear comparison with the most exacting of Liszt's piano works. And it is something more than a mere virtuoso piece. It is the only great piano work of the whole Russian school, written directly under Liszt's inspiration and due almost entirely to his example. Liszt was the fervent partisan of this work, and played through it frequently with his pupils. There is a delightful anecdote connecting Liszt with *Islamey*, told by Strelezki, a pupil of the master.*

The narrator visited Liszt, at Weimar, in 1869. 'The second time that I saw Liszt was three days after I had delivered my letter of introduction to him; I had been to lunch and was walking back home to practise, as I intended, for a couple of hours, when to my surprise and delight I almost ran against him as he came out of a cigar-shop. He was accompanied by one of his pupils only, a certain Karl Heymann, who later on rose to a high position as virtuoso. On seeing me, the dear old Abbé graciously held out his hand and said: "Ah! lazybones; you ought to be at home, studying". I explained that I had already practised four hours that morning, and was on my way home to continue my work. "Ah, then," Liszt exclaimed, 'if you have already done four hours' slavery to-day, come up home with me; only my young friend Heymann is with me, and we can chat and play all the afternoon. Come along!"

'I was only too delighted, so off I went with them. No sooner had we got to the house than Liszt went straight to the piano, without even taking his cloak off, and commenced playing something. After several minutes he called out to Heymann, "Karl, what is that? It has been running in my head all the afternoon, and I can't for the life of me think what it is; it is most beautiful." He kept playing it over again and again, till at last I thought I recognized it. Heymann seemed altogether puzzled; so I begged leave to speak, and I suggested it was the slow middle movement from Balakirev's *Islamey*. "Why, of course it is", said Liszt.

*A. Strelezki, *Conversations with Liszt*. E. Dunajowski & Co., London, 1887.

"Bravo! bravo! I haven't heard it played since Tausig studied it with me, and it has haunted me all the afternoon." ' The reader will agree that no more delightful picture of Liszt could be imagined than an afternoon spent in this way with him. Is it to be wondered at that his pupils loved him? But we must return from anecdote to narrative.

If Balakirev had an intense enthusiasm for Liszt it is only to be expected that there are other instances in which he reveals himself as his disciple. This is certainly the case where the major part of his piano music is concerned, very typically, for example, in his mazurkas and scherzos, which have the echo of *Thamar* and of *Islamey*, the reflection of his strange originality, running through them, tinged by the virtuosity that he loved and admired and emulated. But Balakirev, both as composer and as a personality, is so little known in comparison with the other Russian composers that it is difficult to discover more than the bare outlines of his career. The protracted birth of his compositions, together with his long spells of musical inactivity due to some form of religious mania, have combined together to form a life, which, though it lasted from his early association with Glinka in the 'fifties down to his last spell of activity and the productions of his two symphonies in 1898 and 1908, is almost completely unknown and unchronicled. Balakirev is so interesting to the Liszt student that this has to be mentioned. The movement of which Liszt was instigator cannot be completely studied until Balakirev has received the consideration due to him.

It would be desirable, too, to prolong that investigation in order to include his disciple, Liapounov. This composer, who died as recently as 1924, was the author of some transcendental études that give him as important a place in the Liszt school as that occupied by Tausig; and these études, it may be said, are more original than any of the relics left by that favourite pupil of the master. The *Lesghinka* and the *Terek*, two studies in the form of Caucasian dances, deserve the attention of any pianist who wishes to enlarge his repertory beyond the ordinary, familiar limits.

Finally, in order to conclude Liszt's contact with the Russian school, it is necessary to mention his name in conjunction with that of Tchaikowsky. It is apparent in Liszt's letters to Countess Mercy-Argenteau, the propagandist of Russian music, that his interest was directed towards the entirely nationalist school. This was not calculated to please Tchaikowsky, and his ill humour is reflected in his letters.* He writes in 1877 to his patroness, his invisible benefactor, Nadejda von Meck: 'Last year I met Liszt. He was sickeningly polite'. And he writes to her again, two years later, à propos the 'Chopsticks' Variations which Liszt had admired: 'Only amateurs can suppose that every piquant harmony is worthy to be given to the public. Liszt, the old Jesuit, speaks in terms of exaggerated praise of every work which is submitted to his inspection. He is at heart a good man, one of the very few great artists who have never known envy, but he is too much of a Jesuit to be frank and sincere.'

He does not seem ever to have altered his opinion of Liszt, though he admired some of his music, the *Faust Symphony*, for instance. But he always suspected Liszt's good intentions. The year before he died, when Liszt had been dead for six years and his letters were being collected for publication by La Mara, he writes to his publisher: 'I only possess one short note from Liszt, which is of so little importance that it is not worth your while to send it to La Mara. Liszt was a good fellow, and ready to respond to everyone who paid court to him. But as I never toadied to him, or to any other celebrity, we never got into correspondence. I think he really preferred Messrs. Cui & Co., who went on pilgrimages to Weimar, and he was more in sympathy with their music than with mine. As far as I know, Liszt was not particularly interested in my works.' This opinion is one of the few unfavourable pictures of Liszt that we have to present. But, at the same time, it must be put on record that, despite the charge of lack of interest in his works, Liszt published, in 1880, a most spirited transcription of the Polonaise from *Eugene Onegin*. It is, indeed, about the best of Liszt's later transcriptions.

To this extent, though, Tchaikowsky's opinion of him was true, that he was more interested in César Cui & Co. But not so much in César Cui, as I hope we have proved, as in Borodin, Balakirev, and Moussorgsky. His encouragement of these Russian composers was the most important of his interests in later life. After *The Ring* had been produced, when little more was to be expected of Wagner, his enthusiasm became intensified. It became stronger still when *Parsifal*, obviously the last work that Wagner would

The Life and Letters of Tchaikowsky, by Modeste Tchaikowsky, translated by Rosa Newmarch. John Lane & Co., 1924.

ever write, was produced; and yet more strong when Wagner was dead and when Liszt knew that all that chapter of music was closed. The music of the future was already accomplished. It was necessary to look a little further in front of him.

CHAPTER XLII
Liszt as pianist—Rubinstein—Busoni—Paderewski

The survival of Liszt into the eighteen-eighties of last century brings the memory of his fabulous exploits into the actual experience of a few persons still alive. In the words of the late Mr. Fuller-Maitland, in Grove's *Dictionary of Music*, 'Even to those who only heard him in the last year of his life, his playing was a thing never to be forgotten, or approached by later artists.' This was when he came to London in 1886, only three months before he died. Of Liszt at an earlier period, in the 'seventies, another authority tells us,* 'Words cannot describe him as a pianist; he was incomparable and unapproachable. I have seen whole rows of his audience, men and women alike, affected to tears when he chose to be pathetic; in stormy passages he was able by his art to work them up to the highest pitch of excitement.' And even these words refer to a period when he had already retired for some quarter of a century from the concert platform.

We are now intent, though, upon the Liszt of living memory, not the legendary genius of a hundred years ago. His unique qualities came from many circumstances acting together in combination. As the inventor of piano playing, as it is now understood, his technique was beyond discussion; but this was united to an extraordinary gift of personality, of the sort only to be met with in the case of an actor like Irving. He had the highest dramatic gift, and the physical appearance most suited to its expression. This must have been much assisted by his black soutane, his ecclesiastic's cloak. We feel tempted, indeed, while dealing with this late paragon of the Romantic Age, to assert that his entry

*Fifty Years of Experience in Pianoforte playing, by Oscar Beringer.

into the Church, his adoption of a priest's dress, is comparable in the annals of romance to Byron's decision to go to Greece. The years of Liszt's youth had been signalized, we must remember, by more than one of such romantic gestures. There had been, for instance, the exile of St. Helena as well as the prophet of Hellenic liberty. And the age had been consecrated by many early deaths —Shelley, Keats, Chopin, Petőfi, Pushkin. Liszt's retirement from his rôle of virtuoso, and his eventual entry into the priest-hood, are like successive stages of the most romantic suicide. No lover of the dramatic could fail to congratulate Liszt upon his admirable interpretation of this part he had chosen for himself.

If he was possessed of so much dramatic gift where the greater decisions of his life were concerned, these qualities were intensified to the highest degree possible on occasions when he played. He would, for example, play the same piece over again for an encore, but perform it in such a different manner that it was barely to be recognized. And this power over his audience did not only reside in the wonders of his technique and in his physical appearance; it was, also, the result of his unrivalled experience. To persons who heard him play in the 'eighties Liszt was the child who had been kissed by Beethoven, who had known Schubert. He had been the friend and associate of Chopin. Together, they had created the piano as an instrument of poetry. And, finally, Liszt was the pro-phet of Wagner, the apostle of the music of the future.

His repertory, to those who heard him play in private, was without any limits. It included, in the first place, all those for-gotten composers whose works he had displaced with his own, and by his performances of Chopin and of Schumann. Kalk-brenner, Clementi, Herz, Moscheles, were among these. They were the composers of the 'thirties. In his own words, 'When in London, in '41, I often visited Moscheles. I have played a duet with Cramer; I was the poisoned mushrooms, and I had at my side my antidote of milk.'

Such was his opinion of the music he displaced. He was, in the other direction, the first person who introduced Beethoven to the public. His performance of, for instance, the *Hammerklavier Sonata*, we may well believe to have been unrivalled. He played Weber, he revived Bach, he helped to rediscover Schubert, he announced Scarlatti, he was the protagonist of Berlioz and Wagner, he was the prophet of the later Russian composers. Of the person who was the pupil of Salieri, the rival of Mozart, it is surely remarkable to read, 'He played Borodin's little polka and Liadov's Valse several times, and he gave to Rimsky-Korsakov's peal of bells a never to be forgotten rendering.' If indeed, the life of Liszt had been prolonged by only another five or six years, until he was little more than eighty years of age, we should have to record, we may feel certain, his discovery of Debussy and his enthusiasm for *L'après-midi d'un faune.**

When, indeed, the operas, the symphonies, and the orchestral music, generally, that Liszt produced during his years at Weimar are added to his repertory of piano music it will be agreed that his experience was wider and more comprehensive than that of any musician known to history. Debussy and Albéniz are almost the only composers in the half-century since his death who would have merited his attention; and the second of these, as we shall see, was his pupil for a short time.

But even these subsidiary factors, his physical appearance, his dramatic gift, his place in history, his unrivalled knowledge, do not explain the miracle of his playing. The ingredients, so to speak, are known, but the secrets of their composition are lost. The mystery was heightened, of course, by the rarity of his appearances. Liszt was a legend for more than half of his own lifetime.

It is probably more easy to explain Liszt's pre-eminence as a pianist by comparison with his successors. Of these the first person ever to approach his fame was Anton Rubinstein. Those fortunate enough to hear both Liszt and Rubinstein play are agreed in giving the palm to Liszt; but it appears that Rubinstein was so formidable a competitor that he was not so far behind Liszt in their estimation. Where he lost, by comparison with Liszt, was in all questions of intrinsic, apart from pianistic, qualities. As composer, he was inexhaustible; there being so much of bad to go with what was good in his compositions, that, in the end, all has been forgotten. All the more wonderful, therefore, must his playing have been, if he could approach so near to Liszt without any of Liszt's extraneous aids to fame.†

* *L'après-midi d'un faune* was written in 1893. Had he lived, Liszt would have been eighty-two years of age at that time.

†It is remarkable that there is so little written upon Rubinstein in the English language. Almost the only exception is the little book by his secretary, A.

Rubinstein was the first virtuoso to achieve fame in more than one continent. His American tour was in 1872, when he played in two towns nearly every day, and, altogether, performed at 215 concerts. Liszt calls it a 'Steeplechase de concerts'. No one but a person of his herculean strength could have withstood the fatigues of such a journey sixty years ago when there were no motor cars and no hotels in the middle west, and nothing but the cold discomfort of the train. A proposal was made to Liszt, in 1874, that he should undertake a similar tour of the United States, to last for seven months, and he was offered six hundred thousand francs by one impresario, and five hundred thousand francs by another, but wisely declined any further negotiations upon the subject. Rubinstein had the requisite energies, and perhaps a sort of brutal vitality that such experiences could not injure. He was able, therefore, to make enough money from the enterprise to devote his leisure to his own compositions. These included four or five symphonies; one of them, *The Ocean*, in seven movements, for the Seven Seas; five concertos; several operas; and a project to set the whole of the Bible, or so it would seem, in the form of dramatic oratorios. He wrote too much, of this there can be no doubt, and its result has been that his music is unjustly forgotten.

It is obvious that Rubinstein, as artist, was an entirely different person from Rubinstein the composer, or the individual man. He is described as coming on to the platform with his curious, shambling walk, looking like an old animal. He had something animal about his downcast, shaggy head and the shape of his limbs and back. He was like a bear led along on a chain; so awkward were his legs, with their appearance of being jointed the wrong way, that he was even compared by some witnesses to an elephant. This curious impression that he gave continued until he touched the piano. Then, everything altered. His head was held high in the air, and he assumed a magnificent leonine presence. As soon as his fingers touched the notes, the transition came over his whole personality. His first attack was famous and unforgettable. All descriptions of him tally in this respect. The present writer was told by Diaghilev of a concert at which

Macarthur, where the rout of Liszt and Rubinstein at Rotterdam is described. There is, also, a small book, published in 1900, by Cuthbert L. Cronk. This curiously named individual should be the brother of Luther L. Cronk whose books also appear in the catalogue of the British Museum Library.

Rubinstein played a concerto, not long before he died. His memory had begun to fail and he only played his own compositions. Diaghilev described the extraordinary manner in which his mood changed and his personality returned to him; he struck the opening notes, gave the time to the orchestra, and dominated the scene like a giant. It would appear that with Rubinstein this first moment of his entry into the music was an experience that no listener could ever forget. Perhaps the echoes of it are to be found in the opening bars of Tchaikowsky's Piano Concerto in B flat minor which was written with a view to performance either by Anton Rubinstein, or by his brother, Nicholas, who, with something of the same mannerisms, was not much inferior as a pianist.

We have given some account of Rubinstein in his old age, when his health and memory were ruined by the excess of his exertions, but in his prime he had an unbelievable power over his audience. He could play some simple piece by Mozart or Schubert and reduce them to tears. Nor could he ever be relied upon to play the same piece, twice over, in the same manner. And, on occasion, he was seized with an extraordinary, raging wildness, intoxicating and fiery beyond description, as though he was, himself, drunk with the effects he was producing. At such moments wrong notes appeared again and again, but it did not matter.

If we want to understand this strange personality it is wise to remember his Jewish origin. In its greatest men this race has the faculty of producing the almost perfect counterfeit; that is why so many of the finest actors have been Jews. They are not creators but interpreters. In the case of Rubinstein we have the perfect counterfeit of a Russian; he was as Russian as Peter the Great or Potemkin. He was surrounded by what seemed to be inextricable disorder and confusion. His students in the Conservatoire at St. Petersburg never knew for a moment what Rubinstein would do next. His lectures were unprepared and delivered impromptu, and he was incoherent in about five or six languages at once. This same lack of logic was carried into every detail of his life. He would fast, when he should have been hungry; and would eat enormous, colossal meals when he had made no exertion. He had a passion for gambling, and seemed to be without intellectual interest of any sort, or love of the arts. Rubinstein was more Russian than the Russians; he was Potemkin to the life; but a Potemkin whose hobby was to look like Beethoven, who, in fact, was acting

Beethoven. As we have said, with Rubinstein there was the wildest disorder and confusion in every detail of his life. How, then, could it come about that this unkempt, untidy prodigal was an artist instinct with any and every shade of poetry; and that his memory for music was on a scale that is beyond belief? This was his mystery; but, while the same problem has been concerned with many other great artists, it is seldom so inexplicable as in the case of Rubinstein.

This wonderful player must have been at his best, as a pianist, when he undertook his great farewell tour of Europe, in 1886. This took him to Berlin, Vienna, St. Petersburg, Moscow, Paris and, finally, to London. The year 1886 was, in fact, a year of remarkable experience for the music lovers of London. In April it was the farewell of Liszt; and in May and June that of Rubinstein. It was during these months that he gave his famous historical programmes, designed to show every school of music. So remarkably comprehensive were his programmes that we give the details of two of the series. At his fifth recital he played the following pieces by Liszt:

1. D flat major Étude.
2. Valse Caprice.
3. Two Consolations, E major and D flat major.
4. *Au bord d'une source.*
5. The Sixth and Twelfth Rhapsodies.
6. *Soirées musicales de Rossini.*

> *La Gita in Gondola.*   *La Serenata.*
> *La Regata Veneziana.*   *La Danza* (Tarantella).

7. Schubert–Liszt.

> *Auf dem Wasser zu singen.*
> *Ständchen.*
> *Erl König.*

8. Schubert–Liszt. *Soirée de Vienne.*
9. Meyerbeer–Liszt. *Robert le Diable Fantasia.*

At another concert he played the following:

Domenico Scarlatti:	*Fugue du chat.*
	Sonata.
William Byrd:	*Carman's Whistle.*
John Bull:	*King's hunting jig.*

Couperin:	*La Ténébreuse, La Favorite, La Fleurie, Le Bavolet flottant, La Bandoline, Le Réveil du matin.*
Rameau:	*Le Rappel des Oiseaux, La Poule,* Gavotte et variations.
Philipp Emanuel Bach:	*La Xénophone, Sibylle, Les Langueurs tendres, La complainte;*

while, at the last concert, devoted to Russian music, he played pieces by Glinka and Tchaikowsky, and ended with the *Islamey* of Balakirev. In fact, as with Liszt, nearly all imaginable piano music was in his repertory. It comes as a surprise to find Rubinstein playing Byrd and Bull, Couperin and Rameau. If there are any omissions, at all, in this fantastic series of programmes, they are the names of Debussy and Albéniz. These two composers apart, it can only be said that programmes do not seem to have altered in the slightest degree during the last half-century and that Rubinstein showed a much greater enterprise and search after novelties than is to be met with in the programmes of any of our contemporary pianists.

But we must leave Rubinstein and come to Busoni. This was the most wonderful pianist it has been our good fortune to hear, and even in the short space that we can devote to him some most interesting problems emerge to occupy the critical mind. Rubinstein had, of course, known Liszt well, ever since the year 1840; but Busoni, as we learn from Professor Dent's life of him, only heard Liszt play once, in Vienna, in 1877 or 1878, when Liszt had injured his left hand, and had to play a Beethoven concerto without using his fourth finger at all. Busoni was 'bitterly disappointed. Accustomed to the fiery style of Rubinstein, he found his interpretation cold and uninspiring'. His model as a pianist was Rubinstein. It was from Rubinstein that he derived his monumental style. Only much later in life did he come to appreciate Liszt; who came, eventually, to assume such an importance in his eyes that he placed Bach and Liszt as the two poles, the two centres of gravity of all music.

Those who remember the playing of Busoni will realize its echoes of Rubinstein. But Busoni, who is universally acknowledged as one of the very greatest intellects ever devoted to music, was, in his pianism, paying the compliment of imitation to someone whom he cannot have admired as a composer, and whose genius was, certainly, of the emotional and not the intellectual kind. The characteristics of Busoni's own playing were masculine force and intellect combined in such manner that it was not every kind of music that could stand up against his interpretation. Physically, he outsized Chopin. He did not care to play Chopin, except the twenty-four *Preludes*. In all the lesser Chopin the drawing-room atmosphere, the satin and the flounces, became too apparent when he played. It was when Busoni played Chopin, and not when Pachmann played, that one realized the truth of Legouvé's remark that Chopin was the natural son of Weber and a Duchess. But the same thing in Busoni's performance that belittled Chopin, enlarged Bach, or the last sonatas of Beethoven, beyond all the bounds of ordinary experience. They had the magnificence of the most splendid classical architecture, of Vitruvian masterpieces that never reached creation. Only by such an analogy is it possible to describe a fugue played by Busoni.

He could make Liszt sound equally important and convincing. No other pianist, but the composer himself, can have played Liszt as well as he. Structure and ornament were inherent. Neither the bones nor the flesh of this music held any terrors for Busoni; and by his technique, which made such achievements easy for him, he was enabled to show us Liszt in his true character, an exceptional and magical being living in a world of his own in which the ornaments and the passages of scales were, perhaps, the air itself of his world, as the realms of light were the later world of Turner. Liszt dwelt in his own exceptional atmosphere, maintaining himself in it by means of these sudden flashes, these elaborate descents and landings. He lives in his own element as much as the falcon or the eagle. They sail along the winds, or hover, and whether they move, or are immobile and lazy in the airs, we cannot think of them as living by such simple limbs as a man, or any quadruped. Or, if we carry our imagination to another element, for another rarefied being who lives by such swift and sudden manipulation, we can think of him as a pike seen on a sunny evening in the reeds. He belongs to our age of motor car and speed boat. He is streamlined and tapering, calculated for his own purposes of speed and prey, gone in the flash of a second, then lying in the shallows, fierce and sharklike, trimmed for war, and gone again in a flash with one arpeggio of his fins. He was designed expressly for his own especial purposes; so are the plumes and the airy cells of an eagle's wings; and this element of virtuosity, this virtuoso air with which our book is concerned, cannot expect to be inhabited by a being not specially adapted to its circumstances. He must have been physically built and designed for his peculiar environment, just as dancers are born with particular muscles to develop and are given a physical structure that suits them to these purposes. Such was Liszt; and, in our lifetime, it has never been more clearly postulated than when Busoni played the music of Liszt.

Towards the end of his life this master of the monumental, the architectural, devoted most of his attention to Mozart. So enormous was his repertory that he had exhausted nearly every other possibility of choice. During the last few years of his life some ten or twelve of Mozart's piano concertos were performed by him. Perhaps Mozart was coming to occupy the place formerly held by Bach in his estimation. This was the time of his last and most critical opinions upon his art, and hardly any music passed the censor of his judgement. We know, from Professor Dent's book, that in 1924, the year he died, Busoni was preparing for another concert tour in England when he hoped to appear in an altogether new style of pianoforte playing, a style for which his whole repertory was useless. The music of an Irish composer, whom the English themselves had forgotten—Field's *Nocturnes**—lay on his table, annotated with grace notes and cadenzas. Field's *Nocturnes* had for him a 'chastity' which Chopin had corrupted; Chopin's were too dramatic, too sensual. But this journey to England was never undertaken; Busoni was already a dying man.

If it was the semi-Italian character, the cantilena of Field's melodies, that appealed to Busoni, part of his attraction towards Liszt was to be found in the same quality. As Professor Dent says, 'Busoni was not converted to Liszt until he began to see Liszt as something more than a mere virtuoso, as the only link that there had ever been between the Italy of Bellini and the Italy of his own time'. If his belief in Liszt was shaken for a time, his faith in Bach and Beethoven passed through the same stage of disillusionment, for these three composers had an equal importance in his mind.

*An interesting little book on Field's *Nocturnes* was published by Liszt, in French and in German, in 1859. It is the best, and almost the only book written upon this forgotten Irish composer. *Vide* Appendix IV.

The Italian form of Mozart, his Italian graces and geniality, came more and more to be his predilection. It was an architecture in music, not an outlet for the emotions that Busoni was ever in search of. Architecture, more than poetry, was his concern.

And now we arrive at the only other pianist who can claim to be mentioned with the three that have gone before. Paderewski has, indeed, achieved a fame that never fell to the lot of Busoni. His name was world famous, sixty years ago, in the 'nineties. In distinction to Busoni, whose quality was that architectural importance that we have stressed, Paderewski was a musician whose effects were those of poetry. The extraordinary quality of his touch was a poetical evocation; and, long ago, when he was in the prime of his playing, when his physical appearance was that of Swinburne, only a Swinburne made physically normal, it cannot have been possible to speak of his artistry in terms of the intellect. It was not through the mind that he appealed to his audience, but through those very things that the reason denies. An extremely romantic appearance, of the sort that all poets must envy, was certainly a great aid to his universal success; and this was still further assisted by his possession of patriotic qualities never met with before in a musician that place him upon a level of importance with Kossuth or with Garibaldi as an inspirer or regenerator of national liberties. Nor can it be said that his fame as a musician has been unduly helped by such external qualities, because he was famous long before he undertook those duties, and was, indeed, chiefly able to do so because of the renown he had won as a pianist.

If we consider him then entirely from that standpoint, we have to admit that he must have been the most poetical player that has ever appeared. Of late years it had been his practice to concentrate almost entirely upon Chopin, to the exclusion of all other composers. His Chopin was, indeed, inimitable; but, if a personal opinion may be hazarded, the poetical powers that we associate with the name of Paderewski were even better exemplified when he played little pieces by Schumann, than which no more lovely experience could be imagined. Paderewski never heard Liszt play, and may often have heard Rubinstein; but his own art must be thought of as something entirely different from that of either of his predecessors. When he played more complicated pieces he did so with a perfection which was enhanced by the apparent difficulties of his task, as if it were even more arduous than the reality.

Nothing more different than the method of, for instance, Tausig, could be imagined in this respect.

It is the poetical atmosphere that he evoked, and the poetical wonders of his touch, that made Paderewski a great artist. The physical truth of such a thing as his touch it is impossible to investigate, though it may be imagined that the resonance must have come from his whole body, as it must surely do in the case of such a miraculous player as Menuhin, who, if he was handed the same violin that other artists had just played upon could obviously produce an entirely different resonance and a tone and quality which it would be beyond their powers to draw from the instrument. Paderewski was not a great intellect devoted to music; his playing was not a great architectural conception; but it was a poetical experience of the deepest and most vital sort.

If we collect our impressions of what all four of these great artists must have achieved in their best and most inspired moments, we shall find our thoughts reverting again and again to Liszt. Even if we divest our minds of any appeal made to us by his noble character we have to admit his living contact with the music he played. This cannot be said of any of the other performers mentioned, not even of Rubinstein. With Paderewski and Busoni all the music that they played was dead, dead before it reached their fingers. Chopin, for instance, had been dead for forty years before either of these great pianists was in his prime. But Liszt, himself, belonged to the great epoch of this music. It is my belief that Rubinstein is the person who must have approached most near to him. He had not the intellect of Busoni, or the romantic appearance of Paderewski; his supremacy was only while he played, but it is easy to believe that in his extreme moods, in his tenderness and in the wild raging fury that sometimes seized him, he may have possessed an emotional force of extraordinary quality. The nature of this is, perhaps, visible in the contrast between his features and those of Liszt. His leonine, his essentially animal head, is marked with tremendous impulses; he has not the control of that aquiline face. It is like the contrast between the classical repose of a head of Augustus, and the imaginable features of, say, Jenghis Khan, whose barbarian force created an equal stir in the world, but it was a storm which will die down and leave nothing behind it. And it is precisely this which has happened in the case of Rubinstein.

In any case, the century of the great virtuoso is over and accomplished. Hardly anything written since 1850 has been added to their repertory; their very existence is in the past of three generations ago. How can they expect to survive, when the mystery that must surround them has been dissipated by so many forms of cheap reproduction? Their plight, in the end, must be as difficult as that which might be imagined for the epic bards when the art of printing was invented. We must be prepared, then, for their disappearance; and their place will be taken by universal competence. This is the case, already; there are a hundred good pianists and not a single great virtuoso. All the more interest attaches, therefore, to their epoch of fame. Having heard the two of these artists who were contemporary to ourselves, we are the more curious about their greater predecessors whom we missed. We once saw Paderewski arriving at Victoria Station for his tour of England. This rare being, still majestic and magnificent in appearance, looked like the ghost of himself in the glare of the electric lights. He walked slowly forward, across the platform, into the waiting motor-car, like some spectral survival from the great Romantics, like the incarnation of—whom shall we say? Like a Swinburnian hero, grown old: with the colour and fire of Swinburne, with his separateness from all other human beings. And like a drawing by Beardsley; or like one of the Three Musicians, in his poem. And he was gone, while one still wondered about him. He drove off—to the Carlton Hotel—and left one sighing for Liszt and for Rubinstein. One would sooner, still, for instance, have seen the arrival of Liszt at Weimar, when he returned from Rome and walked up to the Altenburg through the dark night, meeting who knows how many phantoms upon his way.

CHAPTER XLIII

Position of Liszt in art—His position in Romantic Art compared with that of Bernini in Baroque Art—The force of his experiments

A last opportunity now presents itself of trying to assess the true position of Liszt in the history of art. There have been so many attempts to demolish his reputation, so many assurances that we must have a natural antipathy to his music and need not, for that reason, take any trouble to increase our knowledge of him. When the reputation of Liszt is reduced to its smallest shreds and tatters we are allowed his transcriptions of Schubert's songs, and, perhaps, his *Faust Symphony*. More than that his detractors will not permit. It is inconceivable that any curiosity should be so easily satisfied. Possibly the *B minor Sonata* will be admitted into those things of which it is permissible to speak; but any further additions are likely to come into that category where everything else that Liszt wrote is thrown indiscriminately into a heap and classified as 'having too many notes'. This silly sophism is equivalent to accusing Byzantine art of its gilded background, or Rococo art of its curves. Persons who cannot progress beyond that stage of comprehension must own that their tastes are too simplified to be of deep standing.

There are, of course, many prejudices, many false ideas to be removed. When Liszt lived in Paris and was the associate of Chopin he was not a Frenchman, any more than he can be counted as a German composer on the score of his residence in Weimar and his friendship with Wagner. If Liszt is thought of as a German composer he suffers, at once, as being outside their stream of direction. Nor, though he has so many of the national traits of his race, can Liszt be considered as an Hungarian. He was, in truth, a great internationalist, and his entry into the Roman hierarchy, if it was regarded in the sense in which it was intended, should be looked upon as the affirmation of this. He belonged, by virtue of his decision, to the only truly universal body in the civilized world. And before justice can be done to him he must be removed, first and foremost, from the shadow of Wagner. He was content to live in that shade because of his devotion to that great genius, but his importance to posterity may consist in other things than that particular fidelity. Liszt was, also, as we have sought to prove, very much more than a mere virtuoso. There must, surely, be enough incidents in his career that prove how continually he transcended those limits of fame.

Liszt is not the only instance in history of a great man whose personality was certain to keep the attention of the public, and who was then blamed because of his sensational talents. There are enough examples of this sort of genius, from Alcibiades downwards, and when we arrive at the Romantic Period we have not yet reached the age of Fabianism. The historian of an age that produced Byron and Liszt must expect some fustian. But it was this very thing which Liszt was fighting all through his early life, until, eventually, he vanquished it by retiring altogether from the public stage. Even this, and, later on, even his entry into the Church, were construed as attempts to stimulate the interest of the public; though, by continuing his career as virtuoso, he need never have abated their enthusiasm and would have been a rich man, many times over, by the most simple means open to his talent.

Instead, he chose poverty, and devoted himself to furthering the music of others. This is the one side of his character which it is unnecessary to discuss, for it has been universally accepted. But need we, on the other hand, have this national antipathy to his own music? Is it really 'against the grain'? Is there, really, something about it that a self-respecting Englishman cannot swallow? The attitude of the great body of public opinion towards him is still that of old editions of Italian guidebooks, when there is any mention of Bernini. The two men are, in fact, reproached with the same faults. Too much exuberance, restless surface, a striving to catch the attention, a wish to be original at all costs, these are some of the accusations brought against both Bernini and Liszt. Nor was this opinion of Liszt confined to England, for it was equally true of critical circles in France and Germany. But, in England, the feeling has persisted. There used to be a native pianist, Miss Arabella Goddard, whom the critics preferred in the 'sixties and 'seventies to Rubinstein or to von Bülow. Perhaps there are still Miss Arabella Goddards in our midst! Certain it is that the same school of public opinion still denounces those things to which the amateur standard cannot be applied.

But the art of Liszt has so many different facets, and is so immense in its scope that it can hardly fail to appeal, in some form, to every shade of taste, if only it is allowed the chance. There is no one who loves music who will not admire some side of his talent, and who could not, if he would, be continually surprised at the discovery of some new, unsuspected excellence. The very slightest amount of patient exploration will result in a changed opinion of his merits. Little by little, the vast complex of his musical personality will begin to emerge. It becomes an absorbing, and never-ending study. New directions open continually to the eyes, and so many of them are paths which have remained un-explored since his day. We are thinking, at this moment, of his orchestral works, his Symphonic Poems; but, perhaps, more interest still attaches to the experiments of his old age, when he wrote only to amuse himself. *La Lugubre Gondola*, the *Mephisto-Waltzes*, the *Weihnachtsbaum*, are things unique in their way; while it may be said with truth that his basic sin of bringing in 'too many, unnecessary notes', is conspicuously absent. In a piece like *Les Jeux d'Eaux à la Villa d'Este*, a subject which might well have tempted him to be prodigal, he writes with the economy of Ravel. And, when a curiosity for such things has been stimulated, a piece written by Liszt, perhaps forty years before this, will suddenly emerge to light and prove no less astonishing in its qualities. The *Eglogue*, for instance, from the Swiss volume of the *Années de Pèlerinage*, is as fraught with future possibilities as *Les Jeux d'Eaux*.

His works can become a never-ending source of pleasure. Trains of musical thought which he followed up all through his life can be pursued to their ultimate development in some piece written only a year or two before his death; while there are great, isolated instances, like the *Deux Légendes*, which remain un-approached, and to which it is impossible to find a parallel in music. Things which are completely unknown to the public are legion. It would, indeed, be feasible to give whole concerts devoted to first performances of Liszt works; and this is much to be desired. This principle might well be applied, both to a piano recital and to an orchestral concert. There is so much of the highest possible interest lying completely unknown and forgotten in that immense dust-heap into which all his works have been indiscriminately thrown. His last symphonic poem, *Von der Wiege bis zum Grabe*, his *Triomphe Funèbre de Tasso*, his last *Mephisto-Waltzes*, the *Salve Polonia* interlude from the projected oratorio *St. Stanislas*, the *Malédiction Concerto*, could fill an orchestral programme, and would all be first performances so far as the living public is concerned.

The great, the abiding importance of Liszt, even in the neglect to which he has been condemned by ignorance, consists in his unrivalled experience. He is not one of the giant brains of music; he must not be studied for his intellectual content, but his natural gift was of so extraordinary a nature, the circumstances of his life brought him into so many contacts, and, withal, he was of such prodigal energy, and so inventive, that we are dealing with a career which is absolutely without precedent. His culture was not derived from books, from the printed page, as, with all our reverence for Busoni, the nature of that genius might be characterized; but the culture of Liszt came from his living contact with the things he interpreted and created. His perceptions were quickened by experience until they reached that pitch of intensity, through knowledge, which geniuses of a higher order arrive at through instinct and intuition. This it is which gives such peculiar value to the *Faust Symphony*, and makes that work haunting and haunted as no other music.

It is impossible to deny that Liszt was lacking in some of the expected requisites of great composers; but so was Berlioz, and both men, by their different sorts of genius, triumphed over their difficulties and appear in moments of their highest inspiration as more truly flying and hovering in those exalted regions than their brother composers to whom wings were granted and of whom a steady and unremitting flight might be taken for granted. The mechanics of their system of flight, and the problem of how it is sustained without feathers, make Berlioz and Liszt two of the most interesting of all geniuses known to the arts. Of the two, no one would deny that Berlioz had more frequent and complete moments of success; but then, while Liszt is so little inferior to him, and so often his equal and even his superior, we have, behind our appreciation of Liszt, the knowledge that he was the greatest executive musician known to history, and that far from being a born orchestral writer, as was Berlioz, he had little or no experience of this until he was thirty-six years of age, when he abandoned his natural career and gave rein to his new genius in a series of experiments, some of which still astonish after the lapse of over a century. Over and above this, we have sought to prove that one, at least, of his orchestral works is the masterpiece of the Romantic Age.

There is, perhaps, one explanation of the fervency of expression in both men, when fully aroused and working at the highest pressure of inspiration. Both Liszt and Berlioz might be described as Bible readers; but it was not the Bible they read. In the case of Berlioz, it was Shakespeare and Virgil; with Liszt, it was Dante, Tasso, and Goethe's *Faust*. These books were their testament, and their musical utterance was coloured to an extraordinary degree by the phrases and the imagery, which, through constant reading, had become so integral a part of their natures. As much as Bach was founded and derived in his music from Holy Scripture, so much were Liszt and Berlioz the products of their favourite poets. Liszt, who was so used to reading his breviary, went on through his life, so far as we can see, consulting these books to which he was accustomed. In smaller ways he would read political memoirs or historical works, but does not seem to have been interested in the literature of his own time, except when it concerned people whom he knew. He attacks Disraeli, whom he had met in England, in 1840, for putting living characters into his *Lothair;* and, later on, he discovers Flaubert and reads *La Tentation de St. Antoine*. But his inspiration, so far as it had a literary source, was in the past. Dante, Tasso, and Goethe were all he needed.

The Romantic Movement had failed in painting and in architecture. We find Liszt writing enthusiastically to Princess Wittgenstein upon the restoration of the Wartburg, saying that this would be to future ages as much the document of its time as Versailles is the embodiment to us of the age of Louis XIV. It was not only the restored architecture of the Wartburg that Liszt admired, but the frescoes of Moritz von Schwind drew the warmest expressions of admiration from him. A few years later, the designs for *Parsifal* elicit his high praises. Any person who has seen the castle of Hohenschwangau will realize what *Parsifal* must have been like from the visual point of view. The pale mysticism of this opera, its landscape of meres and green reeds, of walled rose gardens, of wistful and virginal chivalry, would have found a fitting equivalent in Burne-Jones, who could have given the music a certain loveliness of setting in the style of his Kelmscott tapestries; but, in the actual production at Bayreuth, the scenes designed by Joukowsky will have been one of the final condemnations of the whole Romantic Age.

The strength of that movement never lay in painting, or in architecture. Even the achievement of a Delacroix cannot alter this. The whole forces of the Romantic Revival were directed into poetry and into music. With Liszt, as with Berlioz, the strength and the weakness of their inspiration were derived from its sources in literature. This is accounted a fault; but the same charge is never brought against Bach for his close attention to the Bible. It is, therefore, unreasonable to blame Liszt for using Dante, Tasso, and Goethe as the spurs to his imagination.

If the Romantic Movement is denied its pictures and its buildings, we find the whole of this enormous and battlemented edifice living only upon paper, existing only upon the printed page. It is there that the winds howl through the waste lands of *Ossian*; that the lovers read romances together by the clandestine flames; that their innocence turns to guilt, because of the fires of poetry, and the shuddering, frightful whirlwinds carry them away for ever and toss their souls to and fro, with never rest nor peace. It is there that the crooked streets and the students' cellars of Hoffmann are to be found; it is there that we read the dreams of Byron, from his Italian exile. The sighings and the wailings of Romanticism are a palimpsest, a chronicle in which one tragedy is written above another on the paper—they never came to life away from the printed page.

Their only contradiction is in music. This tangible, hourlong life, that dies away with the dying echoes, is invested with an extraordinary importance, when, for instance, the *Faust Symphony* is played. This could be compared to a great building, prepared and put up for an hour. It gives as deep an impression of the age of romance as we could get from wandering in the permanence of some castle or palace of the time. And we know that there is none of these worthy of the great poets; that we cannot turn from the poetry to the architecture of the age. Away from poetry, the Romantic Age is only made manifest in the few masterpieces of music that it produced.

It is our endeavour, then, to place Liszt upon the same footing of importance as Byron. That world-famous figure, the greatest of Englishmen after Shakespeare and Dickens, is known more for those things of which he was the implication and the embodiment than, directly, as an artist. We can admire him as a poetical figure, but not as a poet.

It may seem to us that the career of Liszt is not less romantic and remarkable. He raised the whole status of his art; he invented virtuosity, established standards of technique, and carried the possibilities of the instrument that he played to the extreme limits of which it was capable. This same instrument he endowed with a repertory of studies and parade pieces designed to show it off in all the ranges of its expression. He carried his fame as an executant to every corner of Europe, enjoying triumphs of success such as have never fallen to the lot of any poet, or any actor. Pianists who came after him have never rivalled him, for he was first in the field. We, then, see him, at the height of his renown, abandon that career, in order to devote himself to his music and to what he considered to be the best interests of his art. The unselfishness and the true humility of his life for the rest of his days are without parallel. He gave his services free, raising great sums of money for others, and teaching hundreds of pupils without asking payment for his pains. He lived contentedly upon some three or four hundred pounds a year, having no luxuries, drinking the cheapest and coarsest of wines; and even where his one weakness was concerned, in the matter of cigars, he would give away good ones that had been presented to him and smoke, for preference, the cheapest sorts that he could buy. This venerable and kind old man, whose life was spent in travelling in order that he could be at the service of others, was not even able to afford to ride first-class upon the railways. He must have broken the strength of his iron constitution through his exertions; and, but for this, he might well have lived for another ten years.

The romantic incidents of his life must have been sufficiently apparent through the course of these pages. His is a great name; and he is of the sort of greatness that leaves behind it the achievement of good. He must ever be among the foremost names in the history of his art; for he personifies the most dazzling gifts that music can bestow; he was the friend and associate of some of its greatest heroes; his own name is synonymous with nobility and fineness of character; and, in a few instances, he was a great and neglected composer. No one, in the words of another musician who knew him, is such an incarnation of the flourish, the 'panache', of the Romantic Age. He is as important ,in that, as Bernini is to the age of the Baroque. The century of Byron or of Keats is incomplete without Liszt; and, perhaps, it is only the fact that he lived for so long, when those other paragons died young, before they could exhaust their talents, that has worked against the recognition of so many remarkable achievements.

After being, in youth, the Romantic Age in person, Liszt reached out towards other and fresh directions. The force of his experiments is not yet spent; and, even if the Symphonic Poems have accomplished their purpose, have altered the future of music and are, now, forgotten because they have little more to say which has not been developed by other hands, his last and lonely experiments remain unheeded and, as the last fruits of such an unrivalled musical experience, they deserve the closest attention.

It is only when Liszt can be studied in every facet of his music that it will be possible to deliver the final verdict upon him, and that day is still so far distant that judgement must be indefinitely postponed. It looks, indeed, as if the occasion might never arise, so neglected is his music, in all but its more trivial examples. But history is travelling away from him so fast that the era of his revival may be more near than is suspected. If, and when, that epoch arrives, there will be surprising and unexpected discoveries. Meanwhile, he has at least a safe and firm position—even now when his credentials are hardly examined. His place is among the very greatest names in music, and any investigation into his forgotten works only serves to accentuate his fame. He was a great artist, not one of those born to the very highest flights of genius, but one whose perceptions were quickened by experience until they reached that intensity, through knowledge, which geniuses of a higher order arrive at through instinct and intuition. And his will ever be one of the first names that come into the mind when music is spoken of, and the very first when its nobler virtues are meant.

CHAPTER XLIV

The garden of the Villa d'Este—The Academy of Music at Budapest—Lina Schmalhausen—The Palazzo Vendramin—Death of Wagner—La Lugubre Gondola—The Weihnachts-baum—Ungarische Bildnisse—The Mephisto-Waltzes, and Mephisto-Polka—The Ballads, or Melodramas—Other works by Liszt, published and unpublished—Liszt at Weimar—Eugène d'Albert—Albéniz—Jules Zarembski—Moriz Rosenthal—José Vianna da Motta—The Liverpool Festival—His last stay in Rome, and farewell to Princess Wittgenstein

Our penultimate chapter begins at Villa d'Este. The Roman winter of blue sky and sparkling air could own no more lovely dwelling place for a poet or musician than Tivoli, the town of waters. Lovely in the heat of summer, and no less lovely in winter. A hillside of water falling, a ravine, an amphitheatre of water with the temple of Vesta, most graceful of Roman temples, to overlook the tumult and the seething sound. Yet this is but the play before the curtain. For the waters find their voices only through the fountain masks in this garden of the Renaissance. The waters are disciplined: they are trained to music. They are pipes for the fauns to play with, and are reeds which the stone giants blow, lying on their beds of moss. The great cypresses climb above them to the terrace, and the palace is simple and empty in comparison with the play below.

Here dwelt the old magician, the black-gowned Merlin, who began his day at four o'clock in the morning, going, lantern in hand, to early Mass. He lived in utter simplicity, taking his meals on that incomparable terrace, until the early evening drove him indoors to the candlelight. Then, perhaps, he would play and the long, empty corridors would fill with sound; but most evenings, he was weary, and weary, not least, with his own skill. And there were letters to write; last of all, before he went to sleep, his letter to the Princess.

So did he pass the winter days for the last six years of his life, from 1880 onwards. And about the middle of January he would leave Rome on his long journey to Budapest. Here, at last, in January 1881, we find him living in his long-promised apartment in the Royal Academy of Music. Curtains and sofa covers had been embroidered by the ladies of society; and if, as Liszt says, the luxury would have impressed Balzac we may feel more certain than ever of its ugliness.

In spite of his complaints to Princess Wittgenstein there is evidence that he had come to like his life in Budapest. Four times a week, from three in the afternoon till six, he gave lessons to about a dozen of his pupils, of both sexes. This labour apart he was free to lead his own life, and the constant references in his correspondence to all the noble names of Hungary, Esterházy, Festetics, Palffy, Batthyány, Apponyi, show that he could not complain of neglect from the aristocracy of his native land. He was drawn naturally, it must be remembered, to this kind of society, and he liked to alternate between it and the company of his fellow-musicians. His exquisite manners may have been a little wasted in entirely professional circles.

And there were other consolations during the months of exile from Rome. He had a new and charming companion, Lina Schmalhausen,* who often travelled with him and made Budapest the centre of her attentions, safe, as it was, from the prying eyes of his two guardian princesses. The months of spring may have passed quickly enough in this agreeable fashion, the atmosphere of which may be gleaned from the pages of Janka Wohl; and it was varied by excursions into the Hungarian countryside, to Szezgard, the home of the Augusz family, and to Kalocsa, a little cathedral town where he stayed with the Archbishop and was accommodated, as Canon of Albano, with a stall among the other canons in the choir. On another occasion he ventured as far afield as Kolozsvár in Transylvania, where he was the guest of Count Teleky. Whenever he went on these trips into the country he was serenaded and acclaimed with the wildest enthusiasm. The Hungarians, in fact, accorded him the honours of a national hero.

But it is not possible to follow Liszt in all his peregrinations during these last five or six years of his life. He is to be found, at random, in Vienna, Berlin, Stuttgart, Carlsruhe, and Strasbourg, wherever a concert programme included one of his works, or he could do a service to some pupil, or some charity, by his

*The *Mephisto-Polka* is dedicated to Lina Schmalhausen.

presence. And he would travel, occasionally, as far as Brussels and Antwerp, where two of the more enthusiastic of his pupils, Franz Servais and Jules Zarembski, organized no less than a Liszt concert. His own music was, by now, so universally neglected that he could not forgo the opportunity to hear it played. It is probable, too, that his old habits of youth had returned to him and that he had to travel, as if on tour, for the state of his nerves, in the same way that old soldiers who are used to marching have to go for long walks every day to keep their health.

We find him, then, travelling incessantly during these years, never still for more than a couple of months at a time. Up till now the interest of his musical life was still the music of Wagner. In the autumn of 1880 he stayed some days with Wagner and his family at Torre Fiorentina, just outside Siena. His own seventieth birthday came the following October, and in July 1882 he is at Weimar for the production of *Parsifal*. His enthusiasm is boundless, *Parsifal* is the miracle of the century. There has never been anything in the history of the theatre to equal it. At the end of November we find him staying with Wagner and his family at the Palazzo Vendramin, in Venice. Wagner had rented this from the Duca della Grazia, son of the Duchesse de Berri; and they were installed in a suite of eighteen rooms, finely furnished, with their own chief servants brought from the Villa Wahnfried at Bayreuth, and two gondoliers always waiting at the door. There was a parish church where Liszt attended Mass every day only a hundred paces from the door; and, on Sundays, he went by gondola to High Mass in St. Mark's. Life was very peaceful, and Liszt was able to make some progress with his Oratorio on *St. Stanislas*, but suddenly he put this away and started on a new work, one of the strangest experiments of his old age, *La Lugubre Gondola*.

At the end of six weeks he was off again to Budapest, where the news reached him of Wagner's death at Venice, in February 1883. It is said that he was writing at his table when a friend came in and announced the news to him. At first he did not believe it, did not look up from his table, or stop writing, and would say no more than the words 'Pourquoi pas?' He had so often been announced as dead, himself, ever since those days in Paris, sixty years ago, when the printshops published a portrait of him with the date of his death printed below it. But then the telegrams began to arrive, confirming the news. There was no longer any doubt about it,

and in a low voice Liszt was heard to say the words: 'Lui aujour-
d'hui, moi demain!' He had only a little more than three years to
live, himself. *La Lugubre Gondola* was of curiously appropriate
inspiration. He had written it only some three weeks before
Wagner's death, 'as though', in his own words, 'it was a presen-
timent'. It is, in effect, an elegy; a very odd, peculiar piece of music,
of strangely haunting character. And of experimental nature, as
though the composer was reaching out towards some untraversed
world of harmonies. It is not like any other piece of music. In
these last few years of his life he wrote to distract himself and to
experiment. He was not in search of either money or reputation and
cared nothing whether such works were ever performed or not.

His inspiration, which had slackened in him since he finished
Christus and *St. Elizabeth* at the end of the 'sixties, returned to him
in something of its full force about this time. The last things that
he composed are free of both the virtues or the vices, whichever
way they are regarded, of his youth and maturity. And of this
important body of his works, *La Lugubre Gondola* is not the least
surprising achievement.

The *Weihnachtsbaum*, or 'Christmas tree', a collection of twelve
little pieces, is another worthy example of the ageing magician.
These are manifestly little things, but it is not possible to imagine
any works more redolent of a supreme skill attuned to the smaller
perfections and to the poetry of sentiment. And, as pieces, they
are delightfully and supremely varied.

Another work, quite unknown to the public, is the *Ungarische
Bildnisse*. We find Liszt writing from Antwerp to his Hungarian
publisher, Taborszky, on 8 June 1885: 'From Weimar, where I
shall be once more in ten days' time, you will receive at the
beginning of July some short Hungarian pianoforte pieces, which
I shall orchestrate later on. They are entitled

TO THE MEMORY OF

Stephan	Széchenyi
Franz	Deák
Josef	Eötvös

Ladislas	Teleky
Michael	Vörösmarty
Alexander	Petőfi

'To these six portraits you can add, as the seventh, Mosonyi's *Grabgeleit* (an elegy to the memory of Mosonyi), which you have already had by you for fifteen years. These seven numbers will make, altogether, sixty pages of print.' Liszt never survived to orchestrate these curious pieces; and, by some odd chance, when all his later works are so difficult to procure and so fraught with mystery, these *Ungarische Bildnisse* are often confused with the later *Mephisto-Waltzes*.

These latter, which are the greatest of his later works, are three in number; or four, if the waltz from Lenau's *Faust* (the 'Dance in the Village Inn') is included as the First *Mephisto-Waltz*. The Second *Mephisto-Waltz* was written at Villa d'Este, and orchestrated in 1880-1. It is an orchestral piece, of which Liszt, later on, made a reduction for the piano. The Third *Mephisto-Waltz*, for piano, is a still later composition, dating from 1885, and orchestrated by his pupil Reisenauer, as we know from a letter written to him by Liszt, from Weimar, on 1 September 1885.

Finally, there is the *Mephisto-Polka*, written in 1884,[*] and a Fourth *Mephisto-Waltz*, published recently in London by the Liszt Society. Besides that generally known as the *Mephisto-Waltz*, which is, in reality, an episode from Lenau's *Faust*, there are, in fact, three more *Mephisto-Waltzes*; one, orchestrated by Liszt; one, by Reisenauer with Liszt's advice; and one, only for pianoforte, recently published. The *Mephisto-Polka* is for pianoforte alone.

It has been necessary to state these facts in detail because there is such a state of confusion where the *Mephisto-Waltzes* are concerned. Is it too much to hope that, one day, a whole evening could be given to Liszt's Mephisto-music? Some competent hand should orchestrate the last of the waltzes and the polka. The three *Mephisto-Waltzes* and the *Polka* would fill the first half of the programme, with the Two Episodes from Lenau's *Faust*, and the *Faust Symphony*, to end with.

If these are the important, big works of his old age there are, also, many smaller things instinct with the finer shades of his personality. Let us mention, in this context, the three delightful *Valses Oubliées*, more especially the first of them; a *Valse Elégiaque* and a *Romance Oubliée*. All these date from the 'eighties. Among minor curiosities must be some specimens of the Czárdás, including a *Czárdás obstiné* and a *Czárdás macabre*. There are also the

[*]This is printed, and there is a copy of it in the British Museum.

late, and unknown rhapsodies, from the sixteenth, a little rhapsody written in 1879 in honour of the painter Munkácsy, to the still unpublished twentieth,★ and there is a recently discovered Rumanian dance, or rhapsody, *Rhapsodie nach Siebenbürgischen und Walachischen Motiven*, which must have been composed when Liszt paid his visit to Kolozsvár in Transylvania, as the guest of Count Teleky.†

He was working, also, towards the end of his life, upon a series of ballads or melodramas, for declamatory voice and piano accompaniment. There are quite a number of these. There is the wild and grisly *Der traurige Mönch*, to a poem by Moritz Jókai. It might be described as one of the curiosities of music, for, apart from its peculiar mood, it is said to anticipate the whole-tone experiments of Debussy. The two best of the other melodramas are probably a ballad by Petőfi, and a poem by Moritz Jókai upon the death of this same romantic and extraordinary person. These melodramas by Liszt are complete novelties, and when the subject, or the poem chosen, was sufficiently inspiring it is probable that they may be strangely effective and exciting. This is very likely to be the case where Petőfi is concerned; and Liszt, who was obviously deeply stimulated by the life and incredible adventures of this poet, has left another memorial to him in the form of a piano piece, *Dem Andenken Petőfi*, found among Liszt's papers after his death and published posthumously.

Having rid our narrative of this last ballast of fact the gliding of his ultimate years of life becomes more easy and unencumbered in the contemplation. We have resigned ourselves not to follow him on all his round of travels, and we come back to his life after the death of Wagner. For the purposes of this chapter there are still nearly three years to run, until the end of 1885, when Liszt set out upon his last and most triumphant journey.

In the spring of 1883 we find him back again, as usual, at Weimar, where he organizes a concert in memory of Wagner,

---

★The nineteenth and twentieth rhapsodies were edited by Busoni, but the twentieth is still unpublished.

†In the way of religious music Liszt was no less industrious during these years. The *Cantico del Sol of St. Francis of Assisi* for baritone solo, male chorus, and orchestra, was written as late as 1885. He published, also, in this same year, a Choral Mass in A minor for full choir and organ; and, a year or two before this, a collection of twelve Motets for choir.

upon Wagner's birthday, and a string quartet inscribed with his name, the only piece of chamber music by Liszt, is performed. For a whole year he does not seem to have returned to Rome but to have spent his time at Weimar and in Budapest. At the end of May 1884 part of his new Oratorio on *St. Stanislas* was ready for performance, and the interlude, *Salve Polonia*, was given for the first time.

These months at Weimar were almost his last session with his pupils. Only once more did he return there for any length of time, so that we can take this year of 1884 as the culmination of his career as pedagogue. This is the last, the ultimate generation of his pupils, and its interest to us lies in the fact that some few of their names were till recently before the public. But, first of all, to name but the chief of his pupils who are no longer alive, it is necessary to mention Eugène d'Albert, who died in 1932. Until the vagaries of his health affected both his memory and his technique d'Albert must, from all the evidence, have been one of the most astounding pianists that have ever appeared. Unfortunately, owing to the reasons that have been stated, it has been nearly impossible during the last thirty years of his life to form any correct opinion of what his powers may have been during his maturity, and the assurance of them has to be taken for granted.

In contrast with a renown of such evanescent nature as that of d'Albert it is more easy to see the effect of Liszt upon Albéniz. This delightful and engaging personality, not less in his music than in all the accounts that we have of his character, when he was eighteen years old, gave concerts until he had collected sufficient money to set off for Budapest expressly to see his idol Liszt, whom he admired beyond all men living.* They had several interviews, Albéniz played to him with much success, and we are told that in the same year, 1878, he followed Liszt to Weimar and to Rome where he had lessons from Liszt and profited by the counsel that was given to him. It is certainly possible to see Albéniz as compounded, in equal parts, of his native Spanish idiom, of Debussy, and of Liszt. His association with the master was of short duration, but the strength of that influence is easily apparent in the suite *Ibéria* and in all of his more serious, mature works. The easy charm

*Albéniz et Granados, par Henri Collet, p. 30 *et seq*. Paris, Librairie Félix Alcan, 1926.

of his tunes is enhanced by a glittering brilliancy that is due to his study of Liszt. *Ibéria* is essentially full-blooded, there is nothing of French economy in its procedure, and without the lessons of the wonderful technique at which he had worshipped it may be considered doubtful if Albéniz could have given such dazzling expression to his ideas.

Another musician, completely forgotten in our day, who was the pupil of Liszt to a much greater extent than Albéniz, and who is mentioned over and over again in Liszt's letters, was Jules Zarembski, a native of Poland. After studying with Liszt he took up a post as teacher in Brussels, and it was due to his efforts that a regular Liszt revival was set on foot in Brussels and in Antwerp. In his last years Liszt paid frequent visits to these two cities in order to attend the concerts organized by Zarembski, who was assisted by another Liszt pupil, Franz Servais. Liszt had a very high idea, indeed, of his talents. He regarded Zarembski as the chief of the 'jeunes matadors du piano', and it would appear that he was a forceful, romantic player, and, personally, was one of the most extreme offshoots of the Romantic Movement. As composer, Liszt says that his mazurkas, polonaises, cracoviennes, danses galiciennes, are 'worthy of Chopin. That is to say a lot of him, but not too much'.* And, in another place, he uses the same words of praise to describe his new danses galiciennes, mazurkas for four hands, and polonaise. It should be put on record that in 1881 Liszt orchestrated the *Deux Danses Galiciennes* for Zarembski, and, as an example of Liszt's later orchestral writing, these pieces demand performance. But his hopes of Zarembski were doomed to disappointment, for he became consumptive and died in 1885, making a final romantic gesture by putting on his best and most picturesque clothes, seating himself at the piano, and actually dying in the act of playing Chopin's funeral march. This 'jeune matador' perished, in fact, in the arena. He was scarely thirty years old.

And they are all dead, all the pupils that have been mentioned. Reisenauer is dead, a fine pianist, who, in Liszt's words, was 'malheureusement trop sujet à l'embonpoint!' Siloti is dead, 'who possessed the very favourable negative advantage of not being a composer', and who revived the dead and forgotten *Totentanz* of Liszt, much to Liszt's delight, performing it with extraordinary

*Letter to Princess Wittgenstein, from Weimar, 6 September 1883.

and unforgettable effect even forty years later, in the years just after the first World War.

Then there was Emil Sauer, who, in the 1930's, lived in Vienna: a romantic and wonderful artist in his way, a master of delicate nuance and fine shades. Felix Weingartner was familiar enough to London audiences. Moriz Rosenthal, who became a pupil of Liszt in 1877 and who died only in 1946 in New York. His rendering of Liszt's *Don Juan Fantasia* was an amazing pyrotechnical exhibition, never to be forgotten; and then this impassive old gentleman, of imperturbable, heavy-lidded eyes, of head that was once a magnificent mane of hair, looking aloof and dignified with his Polish moustache and masklike features, would play a whirling, incredible fantasia upon Strauss waltzes. This had to be heard to be believed.

To conclude with the pupils of Liszt there is our Mr. Frederic Lamond, from Glasgow, whom we shall meet again in the next chapter, and there is the Portuguese, José Vianna da Motta, who was born in 1868 in a strange place, the Portuguese island of São Thomé off the coast of Guinea, a cocoa island which was almost the last resort of the African slave trade. Da Motta studied with Liszt at Weimar and became a musician precociously occupied with transcendental technique. He worked with Busoni on the monumental edition of Liszt for the Franz-Liszt Stiftung, lived in Germany and in Geneva, and then returned to Lisbon. His proclivity for Liszt led him to compose five *Portuguese Rhapsodies*, and other pieces of that nature; while his interest in transcendental technique led him to study the works of Alkan, and he published what is described as an admirable transcription of Alkan's *Huit prières pour orgue, ou piano à clavier de pédales*, Opus 64, a work of hideous and almost inextricable difficulties. From Liszt to Alkan is a transition that the merest amateur of the latter's music can readily understand, but it is a branch of art in which the last word has been said, and it is a matter for regret that nobody sought out da Motta and persuaded him to give his recollections and opinions.

In his old age the chief pleasure of Liszt was in his pupils, and we have given sufficient details of some few of them to justify his enthusiasm and his interest in their future. When Wagner was dead he put his faith more and more in the Russian composers; he was not content, like most old men, to live in the past. We find

him writing in this very same year, 1884, declining an invitation
to transcribe the *Devin du village*, a little piece by Jean-Jacques
Rousseau, for a French society who were engaged in editing and
publishing the operas of Lully and Rameau. He explains that he is
unable to help them. Without being lacking in respect towards
his ancestors he had devoted all his own energies to their modern
descendants. This was the absolute truth about himself, and almost
the only contradiction to it is the Sarabande arranged by him from
Handel's *Almira*. In music, he liked the living and not the dead.
He did not, for this reason, grudge the time that his pupils
absorbed; his years of vagabondage had made it impossible for
him to keep still for long, which accounted for his 'vie trifurquée';
and, also, he had reached a state of disillusionment about himself
which made him careless of the time he wasted, so long as it was
of benefit to others. We must expect Liszt, from now till the end,
never to stop travelling until he dies.

There is no respite from those incessant journeys. In this same
year, we hear of the poor old man on his way from Weimar to
Budapest having to walk about the platforms in Vienna railway
station for 'only an hour and a half, at five o'clock in the morning', and not informing any friend or relation in Vienna of the
fact, so as not to disturb their rest. This was, we may add, on a
February morning. It is hardly a matter for surprise that his health
began to fail under this incessant strain. In 1881 he had a severe fall
on the stairs of the Hofgärtnerei, from the results of which he
took a long time to recover; and, about the period we are speaking of, he began to age rapidly. By the end of 1884 he was unable
to keep awake after dinner. He writes from Weimar of a dinner
party given on his seventy-third birthday. Friends came in to
greet him, including the Hereditary Prince, but he was asleep and
only woke up to the strains of an admirable harpist, who had come
all the way from Berlin to play to him. He seems to have dozed
away again after this, and was in bed and asleep at ten o'clock, a
very early hour for the Liszt to whom we are accustomed.

Not long after this he is back once more at the Villa d'Este,
where in January we find him writing the fourth and last *Mephisto-
Waltz*, which was only recently published. His spirits had not failed
him altogether, and after a stay of only a few weeks in Rome he
sets off on an even wider scope of travel than usual. He will visit
Florence, Venice, Vienna, Pressburg, Budapest, Weimar, Leipzig,

Munich, Aix-la-Chapelle, Strasbourg, and Antwerp. 'Je perds mon temps plus ou moins volontairement', he writes to the Princess. At Antwerp, where he stays with his friends, the Lynens, they give a 'bal costumé' in his honour, with tableaux vivants. Everywhere, there is a growing excitement about him. The public seem suddenly to have awoken to his fame, just because he had for so long survived it. An immense curiosity, if only for this reason, began to attach to his person and, still more, to his playing.

This became sensationally increased as he approached his seventy-fifth birthday.* His name was a legend to the public, but he still existed, and it was rumoured that his artistry was un-dimmed by age and that he played as well as ever. He had been, we must remember, as sparing with his playing as he was averse to the inclusion of any of his works in concert programmes. It was only to his pupils that he was willing to play, or when the object was to raise money for some charitable enterprise of which he approved. In a letter to Marie Lipsius, written in 1879, Liszt says: 'Since the year 1847 I have only played in public twice in Rome —'63 and '64—at the gracious command of Pio IX; often in Budapest, later on—twice in Vienna—once in Pressburg and in Oedenburg—nowhere else. Since the end of '47 I have not earned a farthing by teaching, playing, or conducting.' And we know, also from his own evidence, that even in Budapest, where he says he played 'often enough', the occasions on which this happened amounted only to nine times in fourteen years.

Yet an extraordinary ignorance prevailed as to his intentions. As late as 1874 a musical festival was held at Liverpool, and the secretary wrote to Liszt, as if to any ordinary pianist, asking him to reply, stating his terms. This drew a dignified response from Liszt. 'Dear Sir, Your kind communication rests upon a harmless mistake. You are presumably not aware that for twenty-six years I have altogether ceased to be regarded as a pianist, hence I have for a long time not given any concerts, and only very occasionally played the piano in public, for some very special reason, to aid some charity or to further some artistic object, and then only in Rome, in Hungary (my native country), and in Vienna—nowhere

* Many small books and pamphlets appeared at this time in celebration of his jubilee. From one of them, by Frederick S. Buffen, we cull the following irresistible sentence—it comes in the preface: 'I confess to an enthusiasm for art, and I recognize in Shakespeare the secretary of the world.'

else. And on these rare and very exceptional occasions no one has ever dreamed of offering me any remuneration in money. Excuse me, therefore, dear sir, that I cannot accept your invitation to the Liverpool Musical Festival, inasmuch as I could not think of wearying the public with my, whilom, piano playing.'

The occasions on which he played at concerts are, therefore, of historic importance, though he seems to have restricted his own contribution down to the very smallest possible limits and never to have played any of his own compositions unless absolutely obliged to do so. Thus at a concert at Vienna, in 1877, to celebrate the fiftieth year after the death of Beethoven, he at first refused, and then only consented to play if no music of his own was included in the programme. He played, eventually, the *Emperor Concerto*, the piano part in the *Choral Fantasia*, and accompanied some of the Scotch songs arranged by Beethoven.*

Liszt had, of course, no kind of misgiving as to his abilities as pianist, he knew well that his powers were unimpaired by age, but he was weary of the easy astonishment he created. He had known enough of that kind of success. It pleased him to live in a halo of mystery, and it amused his cynical humour to deprecate every attempt to drag him to the piano. He writes as follows, in 1876, to the violinist Reményi: 'Rossini used to amuse himself by signing a lot of his photographs "Pianiste du troisième classe". For my part, I am not in the least ambitious to earn myself the title of Ex-pianiste invalide (without either class or déclassement of any sort whatever).' At the same time, as we have shown, his services had only to be asked where it was a question of some worthy object, and he would give all his energies to the enterprise. The last thing he would do, however, was to play any of his own music.

As the months went on, it became obvious that his seventy-fifth year would involve him in the most immense and fatiguing exertions. When he reached Rome, at the end of 1885, he seems to have been almost prostrated with fatigue. 'It would be better for me not to go out this evening,' he writes to the Princess. 'My fatigue in living is extreme and, in spite of my wish to do so, I no longer feel good for anything. Do not send an answer to this sad letter.' It was his last visit to Rome, and his few weeks' rest there must have given him just sufficient energy to undertake the formidable programme that he set before himself for his seventy-

* Busoni, a child of eleven, was present at this concert.

fifth year. He was not, yet, too old to work. At the beginning of 1886 he was able to send his last completed manuscripts to the publishers. They were two additions to his cult of the Russian composers; a transcription of a song, *Autrefois*, by an amateur, Count Wielhorsky, and the transcription of a Tarantella by César Cui. This was of elaborate nature and cost him a good deal of trouble, as is proved by his letters on the subject to Countess Mercy-Argenteau. It was intended as a pendant to the Tarantella by Dargomijski, and is the latest work published during the lifetime of Liszt.

Meanwhile, he was preparing to leave Rome as if for the last time. A concert of his works was given and he was induced to play. A few days later came his farewell to the Princess. She was still surrounded with her manuscripts, for the *Causes intérieures* was, now, nearly completed. They must, both, have known it was for the last time; her timed and punctual senses will have told her how long they had to live by the amount of manuscript she had to finish. A matter of a few months; but she was content to die, and so was her lover. He must, often enough, have assured her of that. So, perhaps, when they parted, it was the sort of farewell where there is not the temptation to turn back and linger for a moment. The parting had, in effect, taken place long ago. This was not the farewell of a pair of lovers.

At the same time, it is a moving, an emotional thought to think of the slow, the laborious tread with which he came downstairs in the Via del Babuino, and said good-bye to the servants, and was helped into the wretched Roman fiacre at the door. This was Liszt, the wreck of his own great Glanz-Periode, bidding farewell to Princess Wittgenstein. His way of parting took him, always, from Italy to his native Hungary, but this was a very different Liszt from the young man who left San Rossore to conquer fame, nearly fifty years before. His eyes were beginning to fail him. He was a living proof of the dignities and the indignities of age; for age is decay, and the most venerable appearance, the most snow-white hair, cannot hide this. He is no longer even the Liszt whom Gregorovius saw: no longer Lovelace, and scarcely Mephisto any more. Nothing but the picture of benignity; and the appearance of this with more true applications of its verity, by deed and by thought, than have fallen to the history of most other persons with the renown of sanctity.

CHAPTER XLV

His last tour—Paris—Account of his stay in London—Plays to Queen Victoria at Windsor Castle—The Grosvenor Gallery— Faust at the Lyceum with Sir Henry Irving—Cardinal Manning—Holy Week at Antwerp—Paris again—Back to Weimar—His last jurney to the Castle of Colpach in Luxembourg—He returns to Bayreuth, and catches cold in the train— Death of Liszt at Bayreuth—Death of Princess Wittgenstein in Rome

It was a journey of sixty hours from Rome to Budapest, broken by nights at Venice and at Gorizia. He enjoyed some two months of comparative repose in Budapest, and then the fatigues of his last tour began. In celebration of his seventy-fifth year, which would be completed in October, he had promised his English pupil Walter Bache to attend a performance of *St. Elizabeth* in London. He had, also, undertaken to visit Paris, for the same purpose, on his way to and from London, for a performance of the *Messe de Gran* in St. Eustache on 25 March, and, again, for *St. Elizabeth* which was to be given at the Trocadéro, at the end of April. He even accepted an offer to visit St. Petersburg at the instance of the Grand-Duke Constantine, but this came to nothing because at the only time Liszt could have made the journey the Russian Court were in the Crimea and his patron would have been away.

London and Paris, in any case, may be considered as being sufficiently tiring, in view of his age, and there were also to be subsidiary concerts at Liège and at Antwerp. He was in Liège for the first of these celebrations at the end of March, and a day or two later arrived in Paris at the Hôtel de Calais, rue des Capucines. He had not been in Paris since 1878, when he came for a few days as member of a jury connected with the exhibition of that year. Now, he was received with every honour; and he may have left with the illusion that his works were coming into a popularity which has actually failed of fulfilment.

He arrived, at last, in London, on the evening of Saturday, 3

April 1886; and drove at once to the house he was to stay at, Westwood House, Sydenham, where he was the guest of Mr. and Mrs. Littleton. Walter Bache had met him at Dover; Mr. Littleton and Sir Alexander Mackenzie went as far as Calais to greet him,* and crossed the Channel in his company. At Westwood House, as soon as dinner was over, three or four hundred persons were admitted to welcome him and he was given a great ovation as he came into the music-room. Walter Bache and other artists gave a programme of music, and although he must have been tired out with the journey, to the delight of everyone present Liszt went to the piano and played a Nocturne of Chopin, Opus 32 (2). It had been expected that if he played at all it would be one of his own compositions. His choice of music by another was typical of his whole character.

The next day, Sunday, was passed in comparative quiet, but in the evening he played the greater part of his E flat concerto before a few friends. Monday was the rehearsal of *St. Elizabeth* at St. James's Hall. More than fifteen hundred persons were present; and in the evening of that day he improvised most beautifully on some of the themes from it. On Wednesday he was entertained by the Royal Academy of Music at Tenterden Street; the Liszt Scholarship, raised by the exertions of Walter Bache, was formally presented, and a programme of music given. To the delight of everyone present Liszt walked to the piano and played the first of his *Glanes de Woronince*. The evening of this day was the concert; *St. Elizabeth* was conducted by Sir Alexander Mackenzie, and the enthusiasm and applause were endless.

On the following day, at the invitation of Queen Victoria, Liszt proceeded to Windsor Castle, where he was received by the Queen and played to her an improvisation; Chopin's Nocturne in B flat minor, No. 1; a Rhapsody; and the Miracle of the Roses from *St. Elizabeth*. On 8 April came the great reception in honour of Liszt at the Grosvenor Gallery. Walter Bache had asked three or four hundred persons representing every branch of art and all ranks of society to meet him. Nearly every celebrity of the time was present, and many people realizing the importance of the occasion brought their children. Burne-Jones was among the former, and the late Duke of Westminster among the

* Sir Alexander Mackenzie denied this to me, but Liszt states it in a letter to the Princess, 6 April 1886.

latter section of the audience. Liszt played the finale of Schubert's *Divertissement à l'Hongroise* and the second *Hungarian Rhapsody.*

This reception at the Grosvenor Gallery, the headquarters and centre of propaganda for Burne-Jones and the later Pre-Raphaelites, was a memorable occasion. Liszt had not been in London since 1841. Perhaps his original liaison with Madame d'Agoult had done as much to keep him from England as anything else; but now, on his return after nearly fifty years' absence, he was the lion of London, accorded nearly that welcome which is, now, the sinecure of every single American film star, male or female. In 1840, Liszt had been the friend of Lady Blessington, of Count d'Orsay; the world had altered much, but lest the reader should think that Liszt was altogether out of place in this paradise of the Pre-Raphaelites he must know that Liszt, in the year 1880, had contributed a charming song, 'Go not, happy day', to the Tennyson album.

The afternoon of Friday, 9 April, by way of a rest, was spent with the Orczys, Hungarian friends of Liszt. In spite of his failing sight Liszt played through his *Tasso* and *Les Préludes* on two pianos, with Madame Boursot, his *Dante Symphony*, and most of Baron Orczy's latest opera from the score. In the evening there was a big concert of his works, followed by a smoking concert at which the Prince of Wales, whom he had met previously at the performance of *St. Elizabeth*, made Liszt sit by his side. The next day, another Liszt concert at the Crystal Palace, and, on the Sunday, a Mass of Palestrina at Brompton Oratory, followed by tea with the old Duchess of Cambridge, whom he had known forty years before. She was eighty years old, and deaf, and he played her one or two little pieces with the help of the pedal while she leaned her head towards him in order to hear. When he had finished they both had tears in their eyes. That night he dined with the Prince of Wales at Marlborough House, where many famous beauties, including the late Lady Ripon, were invited to meet him. He played several little things as 'chasse-café', to while away the time after dinner. Every day was full of appointments; and his visit, which had been intended to last for a week, had to be doubled in length. He sat for his bust to Boehm and was received by Cardinal Manning.

His last week was just as full of interesting occasions. He attended, we may note, the London début of his pupil Mr.

Frederic Lamond at St. James's Hall on 15 April. And there was the gala performance of *Faust* at the Lyceum. In the interval the orchestra played a Hungarian March by Liszt, and the applause was so great that he had to come to the front of the Royal box with Ellen Terry. Afterwards, Irving entertained him to supper underneath the theatre, in the rooms of the Beefsteak Club, of which Sir Martin Harvey gives so fine a description in his *Memoirs*—mysterious, underground vaults leading to rooms hung with stage armour, passages haunted by Kean and still trod by actors who had known and could imitate his walk, while Irving, his host, had no less ghostly a tread. Altogether, this performance of *Faust* was a memorable one, of much poetic implication, to those who can admire either Liszt or Irving; and it is impossible to pass by that most lovely and theatrical of London theatres—now a dance-hall—without thinking of Liszt arriving for *Faust*, in the gaslight, and of his banquet afterwards with Irving in the vaults below.

The last evening of his stay in England a dinner was given at Westwood House for twenty-six people. It may have been of this day that Sir Alexander Mackenzie tells us the following most typical story: 'Again, when at Westwood House, when a talkative pianist had ruffled him, Liszt abruptly left us. I silently followed him to ascertain whether he had gone to his room and saw him gazing out of a window halfway up the staircase. After a few minutes' reflection he slowly descended and joined us as if nothing had happened to upset him.' This anecdote, so true to his benevolence and kindness, may have happened on the afternoon of this last day. In the evening, as we have said, there was the banquet; and Liszt played the Crusaders' March from *St. Elizabeth*, two Chopin études (A flat major and F minor), a nocturne, and, to end with, as an exhibition of his powers, the Fantasia on the Tarantella from Auber's *Masaniello*. The following morning he left London for Antwerp, promising to return the next year.

At Antwerp he was again the guest of the Lynens, and he spent the entire Holy Week in that city, attending all the sacred offices. This was his last peace on earth. It is interesting to think of him at Antwerp, making the round of the churches, fulfilling the sacred programme as he had done so often in Rome, and admiring the pictures of Rubens above the altars. Then, by way of Brussels, he reached Paris on 5 May where he stayed with Munkácsy in his fine but, we may be certain, ugly house, at 53 Avenue de Villiers. The performance of *St. Elizabeth* was an enormous success. His portrait was painted by Munkácsy; he lived in the company of Gounod, Saint-Saëns and Planté; called on Princess Mathilde, and dined with Prince Napoléon. 17 May found Liszt back again at Weimar, returning by way of Antwerp and Sondershausen. At Weimar he had a few weeks of comparative rest, and, on 3 July, went to Bayreuth to attend the wedding of his granddaughter Daniela with von Thode, a young historian. That same day he wrote to his pupil Sofie Menter: 'For a month past I have been quite unable to read and almost unable to write, with much labour, a couple of lines. Two secretaries kindly help me by reading to me and writing letters at my dictation. After the Festspiel at Bayreuth, at the end of July, I must, alas!, put myself under the, to me, very disagreeable cure at Kissingen, and in September an operation to the eyes is impending for me with Gräfe, at Halle.' Liszt was, in fact, threatened with a severe form of cataract, and it was obvious, by now, that his health was failing.

In spite of this, he undertook the last of his long list of excursions with a visit to the Castle of Colpach, in Luxembourg, the luxurious and even uglier property of Munkácsy. He had still the strength to dictate a few letters, and he even wrote a little music, the last of all his compositions, consisting of a few bars from Mackenzie's opera, *The Troubadour*, upon which he intended to write a Fantasia. Among the guests at Colpach was Cardinal Haynald, who was Primate of Hungary and something of a historian. He had been the religious sponsor of Liszt for more than twenty-five years. They passed a delightful evening together, although Liszt had missed his train and only arrived after the grand dinner was over, for which he was expected; avoiding, by this, all the orations which had been prepared for him on his arrival at the station in Luxembourg. The Cardinal had to leave very early the next morning, and begged Liszt not to put himself out to see him off. He did not realize that Liszt habitually got up at four a.m., or even, so we are told, an hour earlier than that. Therefore the Cardinal, as soon as he rose, was greeted with strains of music. Liszt was playing a March by Schubert of which the Cardinal had expressed his admiration the evening before.

The excitable Janka Wohl from whom this anecdote has been culled assures us that this was the last occasion on which Liszt touched the piano, but such is not the case. He stayed a fortnight at Colpach, until 19 July, and on that evening attended a concert of the Luxembourg Musical Society, and was persuaded to play an étude by Chopin. The next day he left Colpach for Bayreuth to attend the festival that was beginning there. It was his intention to stay at Bayreuth for this purpose until 23 August.

We have been unable to inform ourselves of the details of his last voyage from Luxembourg to Bayreuth, but it is reasonable to surmise that this entailed passing a night in the train. The next morning, on the last stage of his journey, the door of his second-class compartment was flung open, at a wayside station, and a young honeymoon couple climbed into the carriage. They sat, we may suppose, side by side, clasped in each other's arms, kissing each other before the open window, while they looked out on the golden cornfields or the dark romantic forests. The cold air from those pine woods came in through the window, it struck a chill into his heart; but Liszt was the last person to foreclose upon an atmosphere of romance by insisting that a window should be drawn up. He left them to enjoy their happiness, and when, at last, Bayreuth was reached he had to retire to bed immediately with a feverish cold. He was not even in the comfort of the Villa Wahnfried, but had rooms in a house near by.

The next day he stayed in bed, and, in the evening, played a little whist. He moved to the Wahnfried upon the following day and on the Sunday, disregarding the doctor's orders, insisted upon attending the performance of *Tristan*. He sat through the opera in the private box of the Wagner family, at the back of the theatre, in darkness, invisible to the audience. After the death of Isolda he could bear no more, and was carried back to the Wahnfried. On the following morning he was very ill; and, when on the Tuesday pneumonia declared itself, it was soon apparent that his case was hopeless. At the same time the doctor made the fatal mistake of forbidding him his brandy, just at the time when he was most in need of a stimulant. His temperature rose very high and he became delirious. He had always been superstitious, and in a lucid moment he asked his servant if the day was a Thursday. It was, in fact, a Friday; and Liszt remembered, then, that the year had begun on a Friday, and that his own birthday had fallen on that day. This was of evil omen, and he knew that he was doomed.

At about two o'clock, the next night, he rose up in delirium from his bed, uttering the most appalling cries, and possessed of such strength that he knocked down his servant who tried to calm him. It is an ugly thought to imagine the dreams, or nightmares, that must drive a dying man to such a supreme effort of his strength. When day came, it was Sunday the first of August, the last sacraments were given to him. He lay dying all that day. At ten o'clock at night, at theatre time, his lips moved; and by those who put their ears close to his mouth, he was heard to say the one word, 'Tristan'. Just at midnight he died.

He was buried at Bayreuth, where he died, although requests were made that he should be interred at Weimar and at Budapest. Eventually, an extremely ugly little chapel was raised above his remains. There was a large attendance at his funeral, but Walter Bache,* who came over from England for the purpose, was shocked beyond measure at the manner in which the musicians present joked together after the ceremony. They had forgotten Liszt already, on the day of his funeral. Bache sat by himself nursing his grief for the great and noble soul who was dead. As for Liszt, it is doubtful whether he would have wished it to be otherwise. He died, we may be certain, without ambitions, unless it was the humble desire just to live until the twenty-second of October, his seventy-fifth birthday. He had always loved an anniversary.

Meanwhile, in Rome, in the Via del Babuino, Princess Wittgenstein will have been praying for the repose of his soul. When news came of his death she closed her doors for ever. She saw no one, and wrote no letters. Her last energies were reserved for the *Causes intérieures*. All through the winter she worked at it, and at the end of February 1887 the twenty-fourth, and final, volume was finished. A fortnight later she was dead herself, having accomplished her readerless task. She is buried, far from her lover, in Rome, where she died.

*Walter Bache did not long survive his hero. He died in July 1888.

APPENDIXES

APPENDIX I
A NOTE UPON ALKAN

Where so much of the piano music of Liszt has been mentioned there is reasonable excuse for a short notice of Alkan. By the side of Liszt, Alkan is the only other comparable composer of transcendental music for the piano. In the words of Busoni, prefacing the great edition of Liszt for the Liszt-Stiftung, 'the greatest of the post-Beethoven composers for the piano, Chopin, Schumann, Alkan, Brahms'. The information, given below, is taken principally from the article on Alkan by Kaikhosru Sorabji in his book, *Around Music* (London: Unicorn Press, 1932).

Alkan was his nom de plume, his real name being Charles Henri Victorin Morhange. He was born at Paris, in 1813, of Jewish origin, and died in Paris, in 1888. By profession he was a music teacher, and he does not seem to have emerged at any time from this semi-obscurity, though such leading musicians as Liszt and Rubinstein expressed their admiration for his works. His early compositions are comparatively simple, until we reach his Opus 35, *Douze Études dans tous les Tons Majeurs*, and Opus 39, *Douze Études dans tous les Tons Mineurs*. Mr. Sorabji draws especial attention to the fifth étude of the first set, an '*allegro barbaro*'; to the seventh, '*l'incendie au village voisin*'; and to the last, which is a bravura piece, in octaves. The other set of twelve études, '*dans tous les Tons Mineurs*', is still more interesting and unique in character. Four of these études are intended to form a symphony for piano, and another four of them form a concerto. The seventh étude is '*En rhythme molossique*', of a most remarkable and odd effect. The twelfth, and last, étude is '*Le Festin d'Esope*', a magnificent set of variations on a theme of eight bars, akin to that of Paganini's sixth capriccio. Mr. Sorabji does not hesitate to place these beside the Diabelli variations of Beethoven and the Paganini variations of Brahms.

Our same authority praises the forty-eight *Esquisses* and the *Trois Grandes Études*, Op. 76. One of these is for left hand alone, and one for right hand alone, while the third is the great '*Etude en mouvement semblable et perpetuel*'.

The other works by Alkan that should be mentioned include the curious Op. 27, *Le Chemin de fer*, a piece the name of which must not be taken as relating it in any way to Honegger, and two études of bravura, military effect, the Op. 50, *Le Tambour bat aux champs*, and the *Capriccio alla Soldatesca*. This pair of études might be described as the most immediately effective of his works.

The titles chosen by Alkan, a typical example is *Le Chapeau plat*, must not mislead anyone into supposing that he possessed any affinities to Erik Satie. He has been, on the contrary, entirely neglected by every shade of musical opinion in France, and the revival of Alkan, if revival there has been, was due entirely to the curiosity of Busoni. An adequate study of Alkan and his works has not yet been published in France. The transcendental character of his music, and its effect, in the words of Mr. Sorabji, as 'an entirely novel and unfamiliar system of decorative design', as, in fact, a new and unknown musical style, makes the works of Alkan particularly difficult to describe in words. The extraordinary, robust vigour of it is the first impression produced; nor can the excess or ornament be called unnecessary, since it is an end in itself, and no more artificial and false—because of this—than, say, the practice of dancing 'sur les pointes', which, once it has been accepted as the convention of ballet-dancing, comes to be expected as inevitable—as indeed the starting-point of dancing. His music lives on a plane of virtuosity where the most difficult feats of pianism are looked upon as a commonplace. That is the approach to Alkan; but, the flourishes of virtuosity apart, his tunes, unadorned, have often the fresh exuberance and vitality of Chabrier.

Alkan must have developed independently from Liszt. The extent to which he avoided all imitation of Liszt is, indeed, not the least remarkable feature in his music. He devised for himself a structure of complex but inherent ornament, and his music may be said to take its place among the most elaborately curious of human inventions. For research in his material, and for its fantastic, exuberant oddity when finished, Alkan must be compared to someone of the character of Bernard Pallissy, to some French artificer of the sixteenth century; while the elaborate processes by which he perfected his transcendental études make him comparable to such slaves to craftsmanship as the Japanese lacquerers whose passion for technique produced the most elaborate and technically finished productions in all the history of the arts. To such as these is Alkan akin, in his music; and, because of this, his music is almost completely unknown.

It is not likely that this situation will ever be altered. Alkan will remain one of the curiosities of music, but a curiosity whose extraordinary qualities place him on a level with the great masters.

That fine Liszt player, Mr. Gordon Watson, a pupil of Egon Petri, and therefore grandpupil of Busoni, informs me of the tradition that Alkan, a Rabbinical scholar, died through falling from a ladder in his library while looking for a lost Rabbinical volume. Alkan was a Danish-Jewish name, and the sporting painter Henry Alken, of all people, was of the same origin.

APPENDIX II

LISZT PLAYS TO ME

An extract from My Musical Life, *by the Rev. H. Haweis.*

This incident must have taken place in 1880. It probably refers, not to La Campanella, *which was written in about 1838, but to the piece entitled* Angelus *in the Third Book of the* Années de Pèlerinage. *This will have been composed at about the year in question.*

We had again reached the upper terrace of the Villa d'Este, where the Abbate's midday repast was being laid out by his valet. It was a charming situation for lunch, commanding that wide and magnificent prospect to which I have alluded; but the autumn was far advanced, there was a fresh breeze, and the table was ordered indoors. Meanwhile, Liszt laying his hand upon my arm, we passed through the library, opening into his bedroom, and thence to a little sitting-room (the same which commanded that view of the Campagna). Here stood his grand Erard piano. 'As we were talking of bells,' he said, 'I should like to show you an "Angelus" I have just written' and, opening the piano, he sat down. This was the moment which I had so often and so vainly longed for.

When I left England, it seemed to me as impossible that I should ever hear Liszt play, as that I should ever see Mendelssohn, who has been in his grave for thirty-three years. How few of the present generation have had this privilege! At Bayreuth, I had hoped, but no opportunity offered itself, and it is well known that Liszt can hardly ever be prevailed upon to open the piano in the presence of strangers. A fortunate pupil, Polig, who was then with him at the Villa d'Este, told me he rarely touched the piano, and that he himself had seldom heard him—'but,' he added with enthusiasm, 'when the master touches the keys, it is always with the same incomparable effect, unlike anyone else, always perfect'.

'You know,' said Liszt, turning to me, 'they ring the "Angelus" in Italy carelessly; the bells swing irregularly, and leave off, and the cadences are often broken up thus': and he began a little swaying passage in the treble—like bells tossing high up in the evening air: it ceased, but so softly that the half-bar of silence made itself felt, and the listening ear still carried the broken rhythm through the pause. The Abbate himself seemed to fall into a dream; his fingers fell again lightly on the keys, and the bells went on, leaving off in the middle of a phrase. Then rose from the bass the ring of the Angelus, or rather, it seemed like the vague emotion of one who, as he passes, hears, in the ruins of some wayside cloister, the ghosts of old monks humming their drowsy melodies, as the sun goes down rapidly, and the purple shadows of Italy steal over the land, out of the orange west!

We sat motionless—the disciple on one side, I on the other. Liszt was almost as motionless: his fingers seemed quite independent, chance ministers of his soul. The dream was broken by a pause; then came back the little swaying passage, of bells, tossing high up in the evening air, the half-bar of silence, the broken rhythm—and the Angelus was rung.

APPENDIX III
NOTE UPON SIVORI, THE ONLY PUPIL OF PAGANINI

The only actual pupil of Paganini was Ernesto Camillo Sivori, though two violinists, Ole Bull, a Norwegian, and Wilhelm Ernst, a German, were strongly influenced by him. Sivori was born at Genoa, Paganini's birthplace, in 1817. The mother of Sivori was with child when she heard Paganini play, and Sivori was born the next day after the concert. When he was six years old Paganini met the child, and was so impressed that he gave him lessons and wrote six sonatas for him, with accompaniment of guitar, alto, and cello—and also, a concertino for the same instruments. Paganini used, himself, to accompany Sivori in these pieces upon the guitar. When a little older, Sivori travelled over Europe as a virtuoso, spending two whole years in the British Isles. In 1846 he went to the United States, and travelled through them to Mexico, and throughout Central and South America. He returned to Genoa in 1850, and resumed his tours of Europe, being heard in England in 1853. The critic Janin, in the *Journal des Débats*, wrote of Sivori at this period as 'youthful, slight, and smiling, reminding us of a statue of dance and song, standing on the yet empty tomb of the mournful and gloomy Paganini'. After living for many years in Paris, Sivori died at Genoa, in 1894.

If he was the pupil of Paganini it can be seen from the above description that he did not possess many points of resemblance to his master. He seems to have been without much personality. His compositions, which are numerous, and forgotten, include Tarantellas beyond count, and pieces with such names as *Fleurs de Naples*, *Carnaval du Chili*, and *Carnaval de Cuba*, being, in fact, no more than the embellishment of popular airs.

It is more probable that a correct counterfeit of Paganini was to be found in a violinist who made the tour of the English music halls especially in that character, with a careful make-up to resemble that ghostly figure, with a special arrangement of shaded lights, blue spectacles, the correct black clothes, and every detail carefully copied from the original. This man, whose name, I believe, was Levy, is described as a good violinist and, in appearance, an extraordinarily good copy of Paganini. I have some recollection, in my childhood, of having seen a music-hall 'turn' of this description, but it must have been by a copy of this copy, for Levy, if that was his name, must have died many years before. It may be added that the famous Charles Peace, an amateur of some powers, used to give concerts in Sheffield and its neighbourhood in which he was announced as the second Paganini, and I have known people who had heard him play. With his well-known power of altogether disguising his appearance by dislocating his jaw, it is possible that Peace may have been most weird and macabre in a rôle so fraught with sinister possibilities as that of Paganini. It is, indeed, even unpleasant to dwell upon the thought of it.

APPENDIX IV
A NOTE UPON JOHN FIELD

John Field, who came of a family of musicians, was born at Dublin, in 1782. He made his début as a pianist in London in 1794. He then became piano salesman in Clementi's London shop, and had the benefit of lessons from Clementi. Spohr met him there and describes him in his autobiography: 'Clementi kept him to his old trade of showing off the pianos in the warehouse, and there he was to be found, a pale melancholy youth, awkward and shy, speaking no language but his own, and in clothes which he had far outgrown; but who had only to place his hands on the keys for all such drawbacks to be at once forgotten.'

Clementi left London in 1804, and Field moved abroad and settled in St. Petersburg as teacher. His lessons were much sought after and extraordinarily well paid. In 1808 he married Mlle Percheron; and in 1823 he went to Moscow and met with even greater success, there, than in St. Petersburg. He was known, by this time, as 'Russian' Field. In 1832 he played a concerto of his own, in London, at a concert of the Royal Philharmonic Society. Thence, he travelled to Paris, and through Belgium and Switzerland to Italy. But at Milan, Venice, and Naples, his playing did not please the aristocratic audiences and his concerts did not pay. He began to be marked for disaster. Habits of intemperance grew upon him, he suffered the agonies of fistula, and his situation at Naples became worse and worse. He lay in a hospital for nine months in the most deplorable condition, from which, at last, a Russian family, named Romanow, rescued him, on condition that he came back with them to Moscow. He was heard again in Vienna, where he elicited transports of admiration by the exquisite playing of his *Nocturnes*. But his health had gone. Hardly had he arrived at Moscow than he succumbed, in the summer of 1837.

His interest lies in the influence he must undoubtedly have had upon Chopin. It was not only by his invention of the title of Nocturne; but the graces and the sentiment of Chopin are to be found in Field. His compositions include seven piano concertos, a *Polonaise en forme de Rondeau*, a *Rondeau Écossaise*, and the twelve *Nocturnes*. Field would seem to have been a pianist of exceptional delicacy and poetic power, unrivalled in his exquisite ornaments. If his name is still familiar to everyone, the same thing cannot be said of his actual music, which is little known so far as the public is concerned. He is of national interest as an Irishman, and it is most curious to see so much of what is typically Chopinesque foreshadowed in this pale, Chatterton-like poet, whose last days were so unhappy and pathetic. Busoni, it may be added, intended to play his Nocturnes on the last English tour that he projected in 1924, but his death intervened. The best account of Field is in the little pamphlet published in French and German by Liszt in 1859. It would appear from this that Liszt was personally acquainted with Field, and had heard him play. Of late, it is true that Field's *Nocturnes*, at least, have made their appearance on the programmes of English pianists. With this accomplished, English music can no longer be reproached with having produced nothing between the time of Handel and that of Elgar. But, perhaps, the melody of Field is more typical of Ireland than of England. Whatever its origin may be, it is extremely beautiful.

It may be added, in final parenthesis, that Glinka was a piano pupil of Field, so that this Irish musician is to some extent connected with the origins of the modern Russian school of composers.

APPENDIX V

A NOTE UPON WALTER BACHE, THE ENGLISH DISCIPLE OF LISZT

The Bache family were natives of Birmingham. The elder brother, Fancis Edward (1833–1858), died too early to become associated with Liszt. The younger brother, Walter, who was born in 1842, went out to Rome when he was about twenty years of age, in 1862, and made the acquaintance of Liszt. At their first meeting Walter Bache was so nervous, and was so untidily dressed, that Liszt thought he must have come to him to borrow money and asked in the kindest manner whether he could be of any assistance. Walter Bache became a fanatical follower of Liszt, and his admiration for the master was of the most touching description. Being possessed of some means, he used to organize annual concerts of Liszt's works in London at a permanent financial loss. He was a considerable pianist, himself, and used to take part in these concerts. It was due, chiefly, to his insistence that Liszt came over to England for his final visit in 1886. Walter Bache was heartbroken at the death of Liszt and writes a pathetic description of his funeral. He gave his last concert of Liszt's music on Liszt's birthday, 22 October 1887, and died soon afterwards, in July 1888. His sister, Miss Constance Bache, born in 1846, was no less enthusiastic a partisan. She published *Brother Musicians*, a book about her two dead brothers, and the part of this work devoted to Walter Bache contains many of his letters, which are full of references to Liszt and most interesting in that respect. She also translated a selection of Liszt's letters, taken from the La Mara edition, in two volumes, in 1894; and the *Early Correspondence of Hans von Bülow*, in one volume, in 1896. Miss Constance Bache died in 1903.

NOTE

One of the main difficulties that befall the biographer of Liszt is the problem of a correct catalogue of his works. It is said that there are, in all, between 1200 and 1300 items, of which seven hundred are original compositions. The catalogue printed below has been drawn up with great care, after consulting all the available printed authorities. Probably the best system of all was that invented and adapted by Mr. Frederick Corder in his book on *Liszt* published by Kegan Paul & Co., in 1925, in their admirable 'Masters of Music' series. His system is infallible, but not quite full enough; and, while I cannot sufficiently express my indebtedness to his example, it may, perhaps, be claimed that this present catalogue carries his principles of arrangement into greater detail. The problem is, of course, made more complicated by the many versions of the same work that Liszt often published, and by the fact that, in many cases, publication only took place some years after the work was written. In such instances, I have tried to give the date of composition, as well as the year of publication; adding, sometimes, where there is a flagrant instance of such ill usage, the date of first performance of a work written many years before. Finally, in order to furnish the amateur of Liszt with some kind of guide through the maze of his works, I have adopted the practice of Baedeker, awarding one star where a work is important, curious, or of historical moment, and two stars where indubitable masterpieces are concerned. This supreme prize has been so sparingly awarded that it is hoped its bestowal will carry conviction.

(i)

Original Works for pianoforte solo

À la Chapelle Sixtine. Tone poem based upon Mozart's   1862
    Ave Verum, and a phrase from the *Miserere* of Allegri.
    (Also for organ.)

Album d'un Voyageur. Three books of pieces.　　　　　1835
　　(i) *Impressions et Poésies* (7 pieces).
　　(ii) *Fleurs Mélodiques des Alpes* (3 pieces).
　　(iii) *Paraphrases: Trois Airs Suisses.* The final version
of (iii) was not published until 1872.

Années de Pèlerinage. Première Année: Suisse. This is an　　1852
improved version of the *Album d'un Voyageur.* Some of
the smaller pieces were omitted, but the Swiss Airs
were published in the end as a separate work.

　　1. *Chapelle de Guillaume Tell.*　　5. *Orage.*
　★2. *Au lac de Wallenstadt.*　　　　★6. *Vallée d'Obermann.*
　　3. *Pastorale.*　　　　　　　　　　★7. *Eglogue.*
　★4. *Au bord d'une source.*　　　　8. *Le Mal du Pays.*
　　　　　　　9. *Les Cloches de Genève.*

Années de Pèlerinage. Seconde Année: Italie. All these had　　1848
been separately published, but were now revised.
　★1. *Sposalizio* (on Raphael's picture in the Vatican).
　★2. *Il Penseroso* (on the tomb of Lorenzo de Medici, by
Michelangelo, in the Cappella Medici at Florence).
　　3. *Canzonetta di Salvator Rosa.*
　★4–6. *Tre Sonetti di Petrarca.* (First written as songs.)
The best of the three is probably the second in E major.
It was orchestrated by Busoni, in 1911.
　★7. *Fantaisie, quasi Sonate: d'après une lecture de Dante.*
(Upon Victor Hugo's poem of that name.)
　　8–10. *Venezia e Napoli.* Gondoliera, Canzone, Tarantella. These three pieces were not added to the collection until the edition of 1861. The Gondoliera is the
gondolier's song heard 'off-stage' in Rossini's opera
Otello.

Années de Pèlerinage. Troisième Année. This third volume,　　1883
all of which had been issued separately, was not published until 1883, but its publication had been intended
and prepared for long before.

　　1. *Angelus.*
　　2. *Cyprès de la Villa d'Este.*
　　3. *Cyprès de la Villa d'Este.*
　★★4. *Les Jeux d'Eaux à la Villa d'Este.*

5. *Sunt lacrymae rerum* (en mode hongrois).
6. *Marche Funèbre* (to the memory of the Emperor Maximilian of Mexico).
7. *Sursum corda.*

Apparitions. Three pieces.   1835

Ave Maria. (Arranged, also, for choir.) Written in 1851.   1863

Ballade No. 1 In A minor.   1854

**Ballade No. 2 In B minor.*   1854

Berceuse.   1854

Bülow March.   1884

Trois Valses-Caprices.   1840

    1. *Valse di Bravura.*
    2. *Valse Mélancholique.*
  **3. *Valse à Capriccio* (re-written in 1852).
On themes taken from *Lucia di Lammermoor* and from *Parisina*, a forgotten opera by Donizetti. The latter theme is nearly identical to the adagietto in *Les Biches*, by Francis Poulenc.

Consolations. Six pieces.   1850

Élégie.   1868

Élégie No. 2.   1870

Élégie No. 3. (*La Lugubre Gondola* is sometimes mentioned   187?
as being one of the *Élégies.*)

Études de Concert. No. 1 in A flat.   1849
            No. 2 in F minor.
            No. 3 in D flat.

Deux Études de Concert.   1849–63
  **1. *Waldesrauschen.*   *2. *Gnomenreigen.*

Epithalamium. (Published, also, with a violin part.)   1872

Études en Forme de Douze Exercices pour Piano. This was   1830
his Opus 1 published at Marseilles. The *Grandes Études Transcendantes* were derived from these.

Les Funérailles.   1850?

La Lugubre Gondola. Written in Venice in the Palazzo   1883
Vendramin, just before the death of Wagner.

Grandes Études. Another reissue of the *Douze Exercices.*   1831

Études d'Exécution Transcendante. The final form of the   1854
Grandes Études.

1. *Preludio.*	7. *Eroica.*
2. A minor.	★ 8. *Wilde Jagd.*
3. *Paysage.*	★ 9. *Ricordanza.*
4. *Mazeppa.*	10. F minor.
★5. *Feux Follets.*	11. *Harmonies du Soir.*
6. *Vision.*	12. *Chasse-Neige.*

★*Ab–Irato: Étude de Perfectionnement.* First published in   1854
1852. A tremendous transcendental study; an epilogue,
as it were, to the Twelve Great Études.

Grand Galop Chromatique. A modern audience can   1838
stand this, but it was the great war-horse of Liszt's
Glanz-Periode, and, as such, deserves attention.

Heroic March in the Hungarian Style. This was the original   1844
form of the Symphonic Poem *Hungaria.*

Hymne du Pape.   1865

Harmonies Poétiques et Religieuses. First published as four   1851
pieces; eventually as ten pieces in four books. A ★★ is
deserved by the third piece in this collection, the
Bénédiction de Dieu dans la Solitude.

Impromptu in F Sharp.   1877

Deux Légendes.   1866
    1. *St. François d'Assise prédicant aux Oiseaux.*
★★2. *St. François de Paule marchant sur les Flots.*

Liebesträume. Three Nocturnes; and, in the first place,   1850
songs.

Mazurka Brillante.   1851

Mephisto-Waltz. ★★No. 2. Written for orchestra. Liszt,   1881
later on, made a piano version of it.
    ★★No. 3. Written for piano. Orchestrated by   1885
    Riesenauer.
    ★No. 4. (Recently published by the Liszt Society   1885
    in London)

Mephisto-Polka.   1884

Mosonyi's Grabgeleit. Elegy written to the memory of 1870
Mosonyi, the Hungarian composer.

Pensée des Morts. Afterwards printed in the *Harmonies* 1835
Poétiques.

Deux Polonaises. No. 1 in E. No. 2 in C minor. 1852

Romance Oubliée. Also arranged for violin and piano. 1881
This is mentioned by Grove as unpublished; there is,
therefore, perhaps another, and unpublished, *Romance
Oubliée* in the Liszt Museum at Weimar.

Scherzo and March. 1854

Grand Solo de Concert. Composed in 1850. Also published 1865
as a Concerto for two pianos.

**Sonata in B minor.* 1854

*Ungarische Bildnisse. Seven pieces, intended as portraits 1883–5
of Hungarian characters. The seventh piece is *Mosonyi's
Grabgeleit.* It was Liszt's intention to orchestrate these
pieces, but his death intervened. In June, 1886, Arthur
Friedheim orchestrated and conducted four of these
pieces at a festival in Sondershausen, but the score of
them is lost. Liszt, who died the next month, was
present at the concert.

Grande Valse de Bravura. 1836

Valse Impromptu. Written in 1843. 1853

*Trois Valses Oubliées. These are among the best pro- 1879–86
ductions of his old age.

Valse Élégiaque. 188?

Via Crucis. 1865

*Weihnachtsbaum. The Christmas Tree, a collection of 1882
twelve enchanting and delightful pieces; one of the
best works of his old age.

(ii)
National Airs

HUNGARIAN

Fifteen Hungarian Rhapsodies. Four more were published 1851–4
later (1879–86?), and another, the Twentieth Rhapsody,
is unpublished. The MS. is in the Liszt Museum at
Weimar. Busoni prepared an edition which was never
published.

The Third Rhapsody is the *Héroïde Funèbre* ; the
Ninth is the *Carnaval de Pesth*; the Fifteenth is the
Rákóczy March.

When the series was resumed the Sixteenth was a
little rhapsody written in honour of the painter Munkácsy, in 1879, and the three last were very late works
written in 1884–6. Out of the whole series, a ★ is
deserved by the Second, Ninth, Tenth, Eleventh,
Twelfth and Thirteenth. The last five of the Rhapsodies
are practically unknown, and most interesting.

Attention should be drawn to the imitation of the
Hungarian cymbalon in the Tenth, and the opening of
the Eleventh Rhapsodies.

Czárdás obstiné. (These pieces have now been published 1883–5
Czárdás macabre.　　and performed)

Five Hungarian Airs.	1872
Hussitenlied.	1841
Rákóczy March. (In various versions.)	1852

FRENCH

La Marseillaise.	1841
Deux Chansons du Béarn. 1. *Faribolo Pastour.*	184?

　　2. *Chanson du Béarn* (dedicated to his first love,
Caroline de Saint-Cricq, who came from Béarn.)

ENGLISH

God Save the Queen.	1841
Rule Britannia.	1841

ITALIAN

Notturno: Canzone.	?
Napolitana.	1839
La Romanesca; mélodie du 16ième siècle.	1860

RUSSIAN

Deux Arabesques. 1. *Le Rossignol.*	1853
2. Chanson Bohémienne.	

SPANISH

Rhapsodie Espagnole. (Based, partly, upon the *Folies* 1845
d'Espagne of Corelli. A version of this for pianoforte
and orchestra was published by Busoni, in 1894.)

El Contrabandista; Rondo sur un thème espagnol. (On a song 1837
by Manuel Garcia, sung by his daughter, Malibran.)

SWISS

Trois Airs Suisses.	1835–1872

(iii)

Operatic Transcriptions

Auber.	Fantasia on the *Tyrolienne* from *La Fiancée.*	1829
	*Tarantella de Bravura from *Masaniello.* (One of the greater virtuoso pieces.)	1847
Bellini.	*Réminiscences de Puritani.*	1837
	Grande Fantaisie sur La Sonnambula. (In two different editions.)	1840–8
	Grande Fantaisie sur Norma.	1841
Donizetti.	*Fantaisie sur des motifs de Dom Sebastian.*	1841
	Réminiscences de Lucia di Lammermoor. (In two parts.)	
	Réminiscences de Lucrezia Borgia. (In two parts.)	1841
Glinka.	Tchernomor's March from *Russlan and Ludmilla.*	1847
Gounod.	Berceuse, from *La Reine de Saba.*	1864

	Les Adieux, from *Roméo et Juliette*.	1868
	**Waltz, from *Faust*. (This may have been written some years before 1868. It is, perhaps, the most successful of all these pieces.)	1868
Halévy.	*Réminiscences de La Juive*.	1836–8
Lassen.	*Hagen und Kriemhild*.	1879
Meyerbeer.	*Réminiscence de Robert le Diable*.	1841
	Réminiscences des Huguenots.	1837–9
	Le Prophète (4 separate parts).	1841
	L'Africaine (2 parts).	1865
Mosonyi.	*Zep Ilonka*.	1868
Mozart.	**Don Juan Fantaisie*. (An altogether exceptional work.)	1841
	Figaro Fantaisie. (Left unfinished, and completed by Busoni in 1912.)	1843
Pacini.	*Fantaisie sur le Niobe*.	1836
Raff.	*King Alfred*.	1853–4
Saxe-Coburg (Duke of).	Hunting Chorus from *Toni*.	1841
Tchaikowsky.	*Polonaise from *Eugène Onegin*. (One of the best of the operatic transcriptions.)	1880
Verdi.	*Ernani Fantaisie*.	1860
	I Lombardi.	1860
	Jerusalem, 'Salve Maria.'	1870
	Rigoletto. (The famous quartet.)	1859
	Trovatore. (At least as good as the foregoing.)	1860
	*Two illustrations from *Don Carlos* : *Coro di Festa* and *Marcia funebre*. (An especially good example of the *Fantaisies Dramatiques*.)	1867
	Réminiscences de Simone Boccanegra. (This is much to be recommended.)	1882–3
	Aïda (two parts).	187?
Wagner.	*Rienzi Fantasia*.	1861
	The Flying Dutchman. Spinning Chorus.	1862
	Senta's Ballad.	1873

Tannhäuser: (The Overture).		1849
'O Star of Eve.'		1849
Entry of the Guests (March).		1853
Chorus of the Younger Pilgrims.		1864
Lohengrin: Elsa's Dream.		1864
Lohengrin's Warning.		1857
Bridal Procession.		1853
Introduction to Act III.		1853
Tristan and Isolda: Isolda's death scene.		1858
Rheingold: Entry of the Gods into Valhalla.		1875
Meistersinger: Walter's introduction.		1871
Parsifal: March to the Castle of the Holy Grail.		1883

Tannhäuser: (The Overture). 1849
'O Star of Eve.' 1849
Entry of the Guests (March). 1853
Chorus of the Younger Pil- 1864
grims.
Lohengrin: Elsa's Dream. 1864
Lohengrin's Warning. 1857
Bridal Procession. 1853
Introduction to Act III. 1853
★*Tristan and Isolda*: Isolda's death scene. 1858
Rheingold: Entry of the Gods into Valhalla. 1875
Meistersinger: Walter's introduction. 1871
Parsifal: March to the Castle of the Holy 1883
Grail.

(iv)

Transcriptions of Songs

Arcadelt. *Allelujah* and *Ave Maria*.   1861

Beethoven. *An die ferne Geliebte*, song cycle. (Six songs.)   1850

Hans von Bülow. *Tanto gentile*, Canzonetta.   1860

Chopin. ★*Six Chants polonais*.   1860

Dessauer. Three songs.   1847

Donizetti. ★*Nuits d'Été à Pausilippe*.   1838

  1. *Barcarola.*   2. *Notturno.*
  3. *Canzone Napoletana.* (See below, Mercadante and
    Rossini.)

Robert Franz. Twelve songs.   1875

A. Goldschmidt. Two songs.   1880

E. Lassen. Two songs.   ?

F. Liszt. Six songs.   1860

  ★1. *Lorelei.*   4. *Es war einmal ein König.*
  2. *Am Rhein.*   5. *Der du von dem Himmel bist.*
  ★3. *Mignon's Song.* ★6. *Angiolin da biondo crin.*
  (The third and sixth of these are most beautiful.)
★★*Tre Sonetti di Petrarca.* (In the second book of the   1839
Années de Pèlerinage.)

Trois Chansons: 1. *Avant la Bataille.*   1850
                 2. *La Consolation.*
                 3. *L'Espérance.*
(Transcriptions of part-songs for male voices.)

Glanes de Woronince: three transcriptions of Polish   1849
melodies. (Part of the first is similar to the *Mädchens
Wunsch* of Chopin's Chants polonais. Liszt, therefore,
treated this melody more than once. The *Glanes de
Woronince* are exceedingly lovely, and occupy an
exceptional place in Liszt's works.)

Mercadante. *Les Soirées Italiennes.*   1838

1. *La Primavera.*   4. *La Serenata del Marinaro.*
2. *Il Galop.*   5. *Il Brindisi.*
3. *Il Pastore Svizzero.*   6. *La Zingarella.*

The three *Nuits d'Été à Pausilippe* of Donizetti were
added to these songs by Mercadante in order to form
the *Soirées Italiennes,* as a pendant to the *Soirées
Musicales de Rossini.*

Meyerbeer. *Le Moine.*   1870

Mozart. *Ave Verum.*   1860

Rossini. *Les Soirées Musicales.*   1838

   1. *La Promessa.*   7. *La Partenza.*
  *2. *La Regata Veneziana.*   8. *La Pesca.*
   3. *L'Invito.*   * 9. *La Danza* (Tarantella).
  *4. *La Gita in Gondola.*   *10. *La Serenata.*
   5. *Il Rimprovero.*   11. *L'Orgia.*
   6. *La Pastorella delle Alpi.* 12. *Li Marinari.*

These songs—apart from the *Stabat Mater,* the *Petite
Messe Solennelle,* and the hundreds of miniature pieces
written in the last decade of his life, from which Diaghilev assembled the music for *La Boutique Fantasque*—
are the only productions of Rossini during the forty
years of his retirement. Liszt had adapted them for the
piano with the same care that he devoted to Schubert's
songs. They may be described as a delightful entertainment. *La Danza,* by the way, is the actual Tarantella in
La Boutique Fantasque. For some half-century it was the
most popular Neapolitan song.

Rubinstein. Two songs.   1881

    1. *O wenn es doch immer.*   2. *Der Asra.*

Schubert. In all, Liszt set between fifty and sixty of 1838–
Schubert's songs, but their exact enumeration is 1856
difficult, because in many cases he published new versions of them amounting in some instances to an
entirely new transcription. Most of the Schubert
transcriptions were published in the 'forties.

Abschied.	*Erstarrung.*
Am Meer.	*Frühlingsglaube.*
★*Auf dem Wasser zu singen.*	*Gretchen am Spinnrade.*
Aufenthalt.	*Frühlings-Sehnsucht.*
Ave Maria.	*Gute Nacht.*
Das Fischermädchen.	*Himmelsfunken.*
Das Wandern.	*Hymne.*
Dad Wirthshaus.	*Ihr Bild.*
Der Atlas.	*Im Dorfe.*
★*Der Doppelgänger.*	*In der Ferne.*
Der Jäger.	*Kriegers Ahnung.*
★*Der Leiermann.*	*Liebesbotschaft.*
Der Lindenbaum.	*Litanei.*
Der Müller am Bach.	*Lob der Thränen.*
Der stürmische Morgen.	*Mädchensklage.*
Der Wanderer.	★*Meeresstille.*
Die böse Farbe.	*Muth.*
Die Forelle.	*Rastlose Liebe.*
Die Gestirne.	*Sei mir gegrüsst.*
Die junge Nonne.	★*Ständchen.*
Die Nebensonnen.	*'Hark, Hark! the lark!'*
Die Post.	*Sterbeglöcklein.*
Die Rose.	*Täuschung.*
Die Stadt.	*Trockne Blumen.*
Die Taubenpost.	*Ungeduld.*
Du bist die Ruh'.	*Wasserfluth.*
★*Erlkönig.*	*Wohin?*

It is certain that more of these Schubert songs, besides those indicated, deserve an asterisk.

Schumann. *An den Sonnenschein.*	1860
Widmung.	1849
★*Frühlingsnacht.*	1872
Provenzalisches Minnelied.	1881
Schumann (Robert and Clara). Thirteen songs.	1875
Spohr. A song.	1876
Weber. A song (from *Preciosa*).	1847
Schlummerlied.	1849
Leier und Schwert.	1848
Lützows wilde Jagd.	1848
Count Wielhorsky. *Autrefois*, Romance.	1885

(v)

Transcriptions of Instrumental Pieces

Johann Sebastian Bach. Fantasia and Fugue for Organ, in G minor.	1839
★Six organ Preludes and Fugues.	1839
★Original variations on the Prelude, *Weinen, Klagen.*	1850
Variations on a theme from the Mass in B minor.	?
Beethoven. Septet.	1840
All the Nine Symphonies. (Though these were not published till this date, they had been written twenty-five years before.)	1865
Berlioz. *Benvenuto Cellini, Bénédiction et Serment.*	1854
Harold en Italie, Marche des pèlerins.	1840
Faust, Danse des Sylphes.	1866
Les Francs-Juges, Overture.	1845
King Lear, Overture. (The publication of this cannot be traced.)	1836
★*Symphonie Fantastique.*	1836–40
Harold en Italie (the whole work).	1880
Bulhakov. *Russischer Galopp.*	1846
Conradi. *Zigeuner Polka.*	1849
César Cui. Tarantella. (The last publication of Liszt in his lifetime.)	1886

Dargomijski. *Tarantella.   1880

Ferdinand David. *Bunte Reihe* (a transcription of 24 violin   1851
pieces.)

Diabelli. Variations on a waltz. (The first music by Liszt   1824
ever published. It is the ninth of the 24 variations by
different hands.)

Donizetti (Giuseppe, brother of Gaetano). *Paraphrase de la*   1847
Marche d'Abdul Medjid Khan.

*Handel. Sarabande and Chaconne from *Almira.*   1880

Hexameron. Introduction, variations, and finale to March   1837
from the *Puritani* of Bellini.

Herbeck. *Tanz-Momente.* (A piece of Viennese salon   1881
music.)

Hummel. Septet.   1841

Lassen. *Symphonic Intermezzo.*   1883
       Music to *Hebbela.*   1879

Louis of Prussia. Elegy on themes by.   1847

*Mendelssohn. Wedding March and Dance of the Elves   1856
from the *Midsummer Night's Dream.*

Meyerbeer. *Schiller March.*   1859

Paganini. *Grande Fantaisie sur La Clochette (La Cam-*   1834
panella). This was withdrawn, and republished, eventually finding its place in:
    Six Grandes Études d'après les Caprices de Paganini.   1851

Rossini. Overture to *William Tell.* (Written in 1838.)   1846

Saint-Saëns. *Danse Macabre. (A great improvement upon   1877
the original.)

Schubert. *Divertissement à l'Hongroise.*   1846
           Hungarian Melodies: Two Books.   1830–40
           Four Marches.   1838–46
      Les Soirées de Vienne (nine delightful Waltzes).   1852

Széchenyi. Introduction and Hungarian March.   ?

Weber. Overture, *Der Freischütz.*   1846
       Overture, *Jubel.*   1854
       Overture, *Oberon.*   1854

G. Zichy. **Valse d'Adèle.*   1877

(vi)

Works for Pianoforte and Orchestra

Beethoven. Fantasia upon themes from *The Ruins of*   1865
Athens (written in 1853).

Bellini. *The Hexameron.* (This was another version, for   1837
piano and orchestra, of the variations on the March
from *Puritani.*)

Liszt. *Concerto No. 1, in E Flat.*   1857
  Concerto No. 2, in A Flat.   1863
  Hungarian Fantasia.   186?
  Malédiction (for pianoforte and strings).   185?
  **Totentanz (Variations on the *Dies Irae*). (Written   1850–5
  1849, not performed until 1881.)

Weber. Polacca in E major.   1852–3

(vii)

Works for Two Pianos

Beethoven. Pianoforte concertos, Nos. 3, 4, and 5.   1860–70?
  Concerto pathétique.   1845–51

Liszt. *Totentanz.*   1849–55

(viii)

Original Orchestral Works

Symphonies.   ***The Faust Symphony.*   1853–61
  1. *Faust.*   2. *Gretchen.*
  3. *Mephistopheles.* Ad libitum choral
      ending.
  Dante's *Divina Commedia.*   1856
  1. *Inferno.*   2. *Purgatorio.*
  3. *Paradiso* (Magnificat, with choral
      ending).

Symphonic Poems 1. *Ce qu'on entend sur la Montagne:*   1857
(*Berg-Symphonie*).

                Composed for pianoforte 1840,
                scored 1849, performed, and
                again revised.

351

　　　　2. Tasso–Lamento e Trionfo.　　　　　1856
　　　　　Epilogue, Triomphe Funèbre de　　1868–78
　　　　　Tasso.
　　　　3. *Les Préludes.*　　　　　　　　　　1856
　　　　4. *Orpheus.*　　　　　　　　　　　1854–6
　　　　5. *Prometheus.* (Choruses added from　1850
　　　　　Herder's poem in 1859.)
　　　　6. *Mazeppa.*　　　　　　　　　　　1858
　　　　7. Festklänge. (Composed 1853, per-　1860
　　　　　formed, and revised.)
　　　　8. *Héroïde Funèbre.*　　　　　　　1857
　　　　　(The *Symphonie Révolutionnaire* of　1857
　　　　　1830, revised and rewritten.)
　　　　9. Hungaria.　　　　　　　　　　　1856
　　　　10. *Hamlet.* (First performed in 1886.)　1859
　　　　11. Hunnenschlacht.　　　　　　　1856
　　　　12. *Die Ideale.*　　　　　　　　　　1859
　　　　13. *Von der Wiege bis zum Grabe.* In　1883
　　　　　three parts. (Written some quar-
　　　　　ter of a century after the other
　　　　　Symphonic Poems.)

Two Episodes from Lenau's *Faust.* **1. The Night Ride.　1862
**2. Dance in the Village Inn. (Generally known as
the *Mephisto-Waltz*, being No. 1 of the four *Mephisto-Waltzes*.)

Les Morts. Oraison pour orchestre.　　　　　　　　1860

Salve Polonia and Two Polonaises. Interludes from the　1882
unfinished Oratorio on *St. Stanislas.*

Goethe Festmarsch.　　　　　　　　　　　　　　1849

Huldigungs Marsch. (For the Duke of Saxe-Weimar.)　1858

Künstler Festzug. (For the Schiller Festival.)　　　1859

Ungarische Sturmmarsch.　　　　　　　　　　　1876

Ungarische Krönungsmarsch. (Hungarian Coronation　1867
March.)

Vom Fels zum Meer.　　　　　　　　　　　　　1865
　　　(All these Orchestral pieces were published, also, for
two or four hands, and many, as well, for two pianos.)

(ix)
Orchestral Arrangements

Hans von Bülow. *Mazurka Fantaisie.*   1867

Liszt. Six of the *Hungarian Rhapsodies* with the assistance   186?
of his pupil, Döppler.

    Three of the later Rhapsodies, written in 1884–6,   1886
Nos. 17, 18, and 19 were, also, orchestrated.

    Szózat and Hymnus (Hungarian National Airs). 1872–5

    Three Songs: 1860

        1. *Mignon's Song.*   3. *Three Gypsies.*

        2. *Lorelei.*

    Marche Funèbre, orchestrated from the Third Book   1861
of the *Années de Pèlerinage.*

Schubert. Four Marches.   1859–71

    Four Songs (for small orchestra).   1860

Zarembski. *Deux Danses Galiciennes.*   1881

(x)
Religious Works
(a) Oratorios

The Legend of Saint Elizabeth.   1862

Christus.   1866

Saint Stanislas (begun in 1874, and left unfinished).   1874

(b) Other Works, Masses, Psalms, Hymns, etc.

Cantantibus Organis. Alto solo, chorus, and organ.   1881

For St. Cecilia's Day. Soprano solo, female choir, and   1875
organ.

Cantico del Sol di S. Francesco Assisi. Baritone solo, male   1885
choir, and orchestra.

Chorale *Nun danket alle Gott.* Chorus, brass and organ.   1884

Hymns. *An den heiligen Franciscus.* Male voice, bass, and   1862
organ.

    Die heilige Cecilia. Mezzo-soprano solo, chorus,   1876
and orchestra. (Also, pianoforte, harp, and
harmonium.)

Natus est Christus.   1886

Hymne de l'enfant à son réveil.   1862

Masses. Mass for four male voices. (First published in   1871
1848.)

       Missa choralis in A minor, for full choir and   1886
organ.

       Graner Mass (the Messe de Gran) for chorus, soli,   1855
and full orchestra.

       *Hungarian Coronation Mass (written partly in   1867
Hungarian rhythms.)

Motets. Twelve Chorales, or Motets.   1883

       Pax Vobiscum, for male voices and organ.   1886

Psalms. *Psalm xiii. Tenor solo, choir, and full orchestra.   1863
(Composed in 1855.)

       Psalm cxvi, for choir and pianoforte.   1871

       Psalm cxxviii, for choir and organ.   1866

       Septem Sacramenta, 7 pieces for chorus, solo,   1878
and organ.

(xi)
Choral Music of a Secular Nature

Choruses from Herder's Prometheus.   1862

Festival Album for Goethe Centenary.   1849

Beethoven Cantata (for unveiling of Beethoven statue   1846
at Bonn).

Chorus of Angels from Goethe's Faust.   1849

*Die Glocken des Strasburgen Münsters (The Golden Legend   1874
of Longfellow).

Mariengarten, Vocal Trio, with organ accompaniment.
(Posthumous.)

An die Künstler, for male chorus and orchestra.   1853

Festlied to Schubert, for male chorus.   1859

Morgenlied, children's chorus.   1859

Die Allmacht (Schubert), arranged for tenor solo, chorus,   1870
and orchestra.

Twelve Part Songs, for male voices.   1861

Several more Part Songs for male voices were published posthumously.

(xii)
Songs by Liszt

Fifty-five collected songs.   1860
  The songs of Liszt were so often republished in new versions that it is extremely difficult to arrive at the correct facts about them. The best of them are probably *Mignon's Song*, and *Angiolin da biondo crin*. It is, also, necessary to remember the *Three Sonnets of Petrarch; Die Lorelei*; the *Liebesträume*; and a song 'Go not, happy day', written for the Tennyson Album in 1880.

Jeanne d'Arc au bûcher, scena for mezzo-soprano and   1845
pianoforte.
    Another edition for orchestra   1876

Le Crucifix, for contralto, with pianoforte, or organ   1884
accompaniment.

Psalm cxxix. *De profundis*, for baritone or alto, with   1883
pianoforte, or organ accompaniment.

Psalm xiii. For tenor, harp, and organ.   1859

Threnodie. Three pieces for voice and organ.   1869

Mention must, also, be made of the *Musical Recitations* 1870–5
by Liszt; poems to be declaimed with pianoforte accompaniment. They were written, chiefly, in the 'seventies. There are several of these, and it is probable that the best are:
>   *Lenore*, ballad, by Bürger.
>   *Der blinde Sänger*, by Lenau.
>   *Der ewige Jude*, by Victor Hugo.
>   **Der traurige Mönch*, by Moritz Jókai.
>   *Des todten Dichters Liebe*, by Moritz Jókai.

(xiii)
Works for Organ

***Bach Fugue, upon the name B.A.C.H.* (Also in a splendid   1857
edition for pianoforte.)

**Ad Nos ad Salutarem Undam, Fantasia and Fugue, upon   185?
the Chorale from Meyerbeer's *Le Prophète*. (An
edition for pianoforte was published by Busoni in
1897.)

Introduction, Fugue, and Magnificat from Liszt's own   185?
Dante Symphony.

Der Gnade Heil, from Wagner's *Tannhäuser*.   1864

Agnus Dei, from Verdi's *Requiem*.   1879

Chopin, the fourth and ninth Preludes.   1869

Rosario, three pieces for organ. (Published posthumously.)   1861

Ora pro nobis, Litany for organ.   1864

The Organ, symphonic poem for organ on lines from
Herder's poem of that name. (Unpublished.)

(xiv)
Miscellaneous Works

Airs from the *Stabat Mater* of Rossini, arranged for   1848
pianoforte.

La Charité of Rossini, arranged for pianoforte.   1848

Epithalamium, for pianoforte and violin.   1872

Romance Oubliée, for pianoforte and violin.   1881

Am Grabe. Elegy for Richard Wagner, for string quartet.   1883
(The only music ever written for this combination
by Liszt).

Twelve books of technical studies.   1870–80

Editions of pianoforte works by Weber, Schubert, and
Chopin.

**Dem Andenken Petőfi*, for pianoforte; an elegy in   1886
memory of Petőfi. (Published posthumously.)

Le Dieu des Magyars, for choir of male voices and piano-   1881
forte, upon a Ballad by Petőfi; also a special pianoforte arrangement for left hand only, written for
Count Géza Zichy.

(xv)
Literary Works by Liszt

Lohengrin et Tannhäuser de Wagner.	1851
De la Fondation Goethe à Weimar.	1861
Robert Franz (an essay on the song writer).	1872
Frédéric Chopin.	1852
Die Zigeuner und ihre Musik in Ungarn (published in German and Hungarian). An English edition, *The Gipsy in Music*, translated by Edwin Evans, Senior, was published in 1926.	1816
Über Fields Nocturnen (published in French and German).	1859

Liszt contributed many articles to numerous musical papers, and his essays on Wagner and on Berlioz did much to establish their fame. Altogether, his literary works fill six volumes.

As this book first went to press, in February 1934, Josef Szigeti had just given the first performance in England of a violin rhapsody written for Reményi by Liszt. It was edited and arranged by Hubay. This composition probably dates from the 'sixties, when it has been noted that Liszt proposed to write a concerto for Reményi. The rhapsody in question was preserved in manuscript by Reményi, and was now printed for the first time. It was enthusiastically received. In all probability this is the rhapsody played by Liszt and Reményi at the open window: cf. p. 227.

An omission in this catalogue of works is the *Galop in A minor* of 1841 (?) which is to be preferred to the *Grand Galop Chromatique* on many counts. It was orchestrated by Gordon Jacob for use in the Sadler's Wells ballet *Apparitions*. This brilliant piano piece, which deserves a **, was never published in Liszt's lifetime, and only appeared in the Collected Edition in 1928.

1811. 22 October. Franz Liszt is born at Raiding, on the Austrian estates of Prince Esterházy.

1820. He gives his first concert at Oedenburg.

1821. He is taken to Vienna by his father. He studies under Salieri and Czerny, is taken to see Beethoven, and meets Schubert.

1823. 11 December. He arrives in Paris.

1824. He visits England, and plays to George IV at Carlton House.

1825. He returns again to England, plays to George IV at Windsor Castle, and gives a concert at Manchester. On 17 October, his opera, *Don Sanche*, is given at the Académie Royale in Paris.

1827. Visits England again. His father dies at Boulogne in August.

1829. He publishes the first of his operatic fantasias, upon the Tyrolienne from Auber's *La Fiancée*.

1830. The Revolution of July. About this period Liszt meets Chopin, Berlioz and Paganini.

1833. He completes his piano-version of the *Symphonie Fantastique* of Berlioz, and meets the Comtesse d'Agoult.

1835. He goes to Geneva with Madame d'Agoult. Their daughter, Blandine, is born on 18 December.

1836. George Sand visits them. The trip to Chamonix. Liszt returns to Paris in December in order to compete with Thalberg.

1837. He returns to Italy with Madame d'Agoult. Cosima is born at Como on 25 December.

1838. He plays in Vienna, on behalf of the victims of the Danube flood.

1839. He spends some months in Rome, where his son, Daniel, is born. In November he separates, temporarily, from

Madame d'Agoult and returns to Vienna and to his
native Hungary. This is the start of his career as virtuoso.

1840. He gives concerts in Vienna, and elsewhere, to raise money
for the Beethoven Memorial at Bonn. He visits London
again. He plays to Queen Victoria at Buckingham Palace.

1841. He visits England once more, playing at the Royal Philharmonic Society's Concert, on 14 June. This is his last
visit to England till 1886.

1842. His Russian tour.

1843–4. Tours Russia, Turkey, Moldavia, Poland, Denmark, etc.
His break with Madame d'Agoult dates from April of
this year.

1845. Visits Spain and Portugal.

1846. Germany, Russia, etc.

1847. He meets Princess Carolyne Sayn-Wittgenstein, at Kiev.
He gives his last public concert at Elizabetgrad in
Southern Russia. Henceforward he does not earn a
single farthing by playing, teaching, or conducting.

1848. Start of the Weimar period. He lives at the Villa Altenburg
with the Princess. This period of his life, which lasts
until 1861, is his time of greatest activity. He publishes
the definitive editions of his *Transcendental Études*, *Paganini Études*, *Hungarian Rhapsodies*, and writes the Twelve
Symphonic Poems, the *Faust* and *Dante Symphonies*, and a
host of minor works. He also produces operas and
orchestral works beyond number in the course of his
official duties at Weimar, and champions Wagner, whom
he first met in 1842.

1859. He resigns from Weimar. The Princess leaves Weimar for
Rome, but Liszt stays for two more seasons.

1861. His marriage to the Princess, arranged to take place in
Rome on his fiftieth birthday, is suddenly postponed.
This is the start of his Roman period. He lives chiefly in
retirement, and composes numerous religious works,
Legend of St. Elizabeth, *Christus*, etc., hoping to be given
an official position as musical director to the Vatican.

1865. 25 April. Liszt receives minor orders in the Roman Church, and becomes an Abbé.

1867. Hungarian Coronation Mass given in Budapest for the crowning of Franz-Josef.

1869. He emerges from retirement and returns for a part of each year to Weimar, living in the Hofgärtnerei and giving lessons to numerous pupils. The 'vie trifurquée' begins, between Rome (the Villa d'Este), Weimar, and Budapest. Owing to the troubles over the Olga Janina episode, Liszt avoids Rome for a time and only returns regularly to the Villa d'Este after 1873–4.

1876. Death of Comtesse d'Agoult and of George Sand.

1879. He is made a Canon of Albano.

1880–5. The last period. The number of his pupils steadily increases, and included among them are Felix Weingartner, Moriz Rosenthal, Frederick Lamond, and Emil Sauer. Liszt travels on an ever-increasing scale of activity, giving his services wherever they can help any useful purpose. He also enters on a final and interesting period of composition, the fruits of which are three *Mephisto-Waltzes*, the *Jeux d'Eaux à la Villa d'Este*, the *Weihnachtsbaum*, *La Lugubre Gondola*, and other pieces.

1886. His last tour, in celebration of his forthcoming seventy-fifth birthday. He returns to Paris, and visits London, once again, after a lapse of forty-five years. He spends a triumphant two weeks in England in April; his orchestral works are played under Sir Alexander Mackenzie, and he is heard, himself, on more than one occasion. He stays at Westwood House, Sydenham, with Mr. and Mrs. Littleton; plays to Queen Victoria at Windsor Castle; attends a reception in his honour at the Grosvenor Gallery; and goes to a gala performance of *Faust* at the Lyceum with Irving.

He leaves London and spends Holy Week at Antwerp, returning to Paris on 5 May. *St. Elizabeth* is performed with enormous success. 17 May, he returns to Weimar, then to Bayreuth for wedding of his granddaughter, Daniela. In July, he stays with the painter Munkácsy at his Castle of Colpach in Luxembourg, returns to Weimar,

20 July, catches a chill, attends festival performance of *Tristan*, develops pneumonia, and dies on 31 July.

1887. In February, Princess Wittgenstein finishes the twenty-fourth, and last, volume of the *Causes Intérieures*; and dies a fortnight later.

BIBLIOGRAPHY

The biographer of Liszt is faced with an enormous mass of literary authority. Certain works are, of course, indispensable, beginning with the admirable essays upon Liszt in the *Encyclopædia Britannica*, and in Grove. And there is the well-known *Vie de Franz Liszt*, by Guy de Pourtalès, charmingly written, and conveying most of the necessary information with a subtlety that the reader does not realize until he has finished the book. The author had the benefit of oral tradition from members of Liszt's family, so that the details of his life are both interesting and reliable. My indebtedness to this delightful book will be obvious in many places. I should like, also, to express my thanks for the book on Liszt by Sir Frederick Corder, published by Kegan Paul & Co., in 1926; and to the *Life of Ferruccio Busoni*, by Professor E. J. Dent, Oxford University Press, 1933. The Catalogue of Liszt's works, in the former of these volumes, is invaluable; the latter book is the absolute model of its kind, and has been an encouragement in attempting this far from easy task.

It may be asserted without fear of contradiction that this is the first full-length study of Liszt to appear in our language. English literature on this subject is, in fact, very small in quantity, and confined almost entirely to the Bache family. *Brother Musicians*, the account written by Miss Constance Bache of her two brothers, contains more mention of Liszt than any other publication of the kind. A two-volume collection of Liszt's Letters was edited and translated by this lady, in 1894, from the edition of his Letters collected by La Mara. On the whole, these were admirably done, although, as Sir Frederick Corder points out, it is puzzling, at first, to find the German title of *The Taming of the Shrew* translated into *The Subduing of the Refractory Ones*. Nevertheless, this translation of Liszt's Letters is the leading authority on the subject, and more of his life is to be gleaned from reading it than is to be found in any other publication in English. A translation, by Miss Cowdery, of Mme Lina Ramann's immense work, *Franz Liszt als Künstler und Mensch*, never progressed beyond the first volume, which goes no further than the year 1840.

Compared with this paucity of authorities in English, the

362

sources of information are legion, in German, in French, and in Italian. The Bibliography, printed below, is an attempt to name at least the chief and most valuable of these. An immense quantity of Liszt's own correspondence remains unpublished; and, at its best, it may be remarked that such sources of information are deprived of half their value if the letters are not published at the same time as the answers to them.

With regard to the unpublished correspondence of Liszt, a tantalizing beginning was made in the *Correspondance de Liszt et de Madame d'Agoult,* edited by their grandson, M. Daniel Ollivier (Éditions Bernard Grasset: Paris, 1933). But the letters stop in 1840, just as they reach the highest stage of interest. It is to be hoped that the rest of the correspondence, from 1840 to 1844, will see the light as soon as possible. Also the *Memoirs of Count Albert Apponyi* have been published in this country. These contain many mentions of Liszt. In conclusion, it can indeed be truly said that the sources of information for the final study of our hero, Liszt, are as yet in great measure unpublished and un- available. It is my hope that this present book may at least lay claim to a conscientious study of the extant authorities. Perhaps it is only by attempting to stimulate an interest in Liszt that we may hope for the complete publication of all sources of informa- tion about him.

Franz Liszt's Briefe—in 8 volumes. Leipzig: Breitkopf und Härtel, 1893–1905.

These letters, collected by La Mara (Marie Lipsius), are for the most part in French. Four of the volumes contain his letters to the Princess Sayn-Wittgenstein; one volume consists of his letters to Agnes Street Klindworth; and the other three are miscellaneous correspondence. Three volumes were also published of letters written to Liszt; and one volume of his letters to his mother.

An edition of Liszt's letters, in two volumes, was translated and edited by Miss Constance Bache in 1894.

Where the letters of Liszt are quoted in this book, I have, more often than not, made use of my own translation from the French into English.

Letters of Liszt and von Bülow: published by La Mara, in one volume. An English edition was translated and edited by Miss Constance Bache in 1896.

Letters of Liszt and Wagner: published in 1919. Edited by Kloss. 1 volume.

Letters of Liszt and Karl Alexander of Saxe-Weimar. 1 volume.

Lettres de Berlioz et de la Princesse Carolyne de Sayn-Wittgenstein. The complete publications of *Liszt*—all his literary works, that is to say—were published in six volumes. Leipzig, 1894–1905.

Mme de Moukhanoff-Kalergis: Lettres à sa fille. Leipzig, 1907. A life of *Marie Kalergis* was published by Constantin Photiades. Paris, Plon-Nourrit, 1924.

The letters of *Adelheid von Schorn and Princess Sayn-Wittgenstein* were published in 1904. Paris, Dujarric.

The Memoirs of Daniel Stern: (The Comtesse d'Agoult) published by Daniel Ollivier. Paris, Calman-Lévy, 1927.

Blackwood's Magazine for September 1901 has 'Recollections of Liszt' by Charles Salaman.

Robert Bory: Une retraite romantique en Suisse. Geneva, 1923. This work is concerned with the stay of Liszt in Geneva, and the trip to Chamonix.

Adolphe Pictet: Un Voyage à Chamonix.

George Sand: Lettres d'un voyageur.

Lina Ramann: Franz Liszt als Künstler und Mensch: an English translation of vol. i of this work was published by Miss Cowdery, but the translation was proceeded with no further, and the fortunes of Liszt are only followed till the year 1840.

K. d'Isoz: Lettres de Liszt et de Berlioz conservées au musée de Weimar. S.I.M., 1911. No. 11. Also, in the same publication, an interesting article, by Vincent d'Indy, on Liszt at Weimar in 1873.

Revue Musicale. 1928. A special number devoted to Liszt.

James Huneker: Liszt, 1911. This book, a piece of enthusiastic propaganda, and a veritable mine of information, however ill-arranged and over-expressed, was published in 1911, for the centenary of Liszt's birth.

M. Calvocoressi: Franz Liszt, 1906. A standard biography of Liszt.

Guy de Pourtalès: La vie de Franz Liszt. Paris, Librairie Gallimard, 1932. I hope I have sufficiently expressed my indebtedness to this delightful book.

J. G. Prod'homme: Franz Liszt, 1910. Excellent, but too brief.

J. Chantavoine: Franz Liszt, 1911.

A. Habets: Letters of Liszt and Borodin. English translation by Rosa Newmarch. London, 1895. This is an invaluable account, in Borodin's own words, of his visits to Liszt at Weimar, in 1877–81.

Amy Fay: Music Study in Germany. London, Macmillan & Co., 1886. (Dover Reprint, 1965.) A delightful, if naïf, account of Liszt at Weimar in 1869–70.

The Fortnightly Review, September, 1886, has a good article on Liszt by F. Hueffer.

Janka Wohl: Franz Liszt, Souvenirs d'une compatriote. Paris, 1887. An English translation, by B. P. Ward, was published in the same year.

Camille Saint-Saëns: Souvenirs et portraits. 1900.

Robert Franz: 'Souvenirs d'une Cosaque.' 'Souvenirs d'une Pianiste.' These are the two novels published in 1874–5, by Olga Janina, the Cossack Countess, under the pseudonym of Robert Franz. Two more works of fiction came out at the same time: 'Les amours d'une Cosaque—par un ami de l'Abbé X.', and 'Le Roman du pianiste et de la Cosaque', by someone writing under the name of *Sylvia Zorelli.*

Baron Ernest von Wolzogen: Der Kraftmayr. Stuttgart, 1897. A novel dealing with Liszt and his circle at Weimar.

Adolphe Boschot: Le Crépuscule d'un Romantique. Hector Berlioz, 1913. (The author of several other works upon Berlioz.)

Anton Strelezki: Personal recollections of chats with Liszt. London: E. Dunajowski & Co., 1893.

Gregorovius: Roman journal. English translation by Mrs. Gustavus. W. Hamilton. London, 1911.

Léon Escudier: several volumes of memoirs and collected articles.

G. S. B. E. W. Legouvé: Dernières pages, 1904: and other books.

Heinrich Heine: The Florentine Nights, translated by S. A. Stern. New York, 1873.

Lillian Day: Paganini of Genoa. New York, 1929. This book contains an extraordinary amount of interesting information upon the subject, and is warmly to be recommended for the anecdotal, if not the musical, side of Paganini's life.

Julius Kapp: Paganini, 1923.

Leopold Auer: My Long Life in Music. London, 1924.

Sir Alexander Mackenzie: A Musician's Narrative. London, 1918.
He was also the author of two short books upon Liszt.

William Wallace: Liszt, Wagner, and the Princess. London,
Kegan Paul & Co., 1927.

Alexander Macarthur: Anton Rubinstein. London, 1889.

Cuthbert L. Cronk: Anton Rubinstein. London, 1900.

Peter Raabe: Franz Liszt. 1931.

Bruno Schrader: Franz Liszt. Berlin, 1927.

Julius Kapp: Franz Liszt. 1931. New edition.

Julius Kapp: Hector Berlioz. 1917.

J. G. Prod'homme: Souvenirs et voyages de Hector Berlioz. Paris,
1932.

Adolphe Jullien: Hector Berlioz, sa vie et ses œuvres. 1888

Life and Letters of Sir Charles Hallé: edited by his son. London,
1896.

Gustave Bertrand: Nationalités musicales étudiées dans le drame
lyrique. Dijon, 1872.

G. Radiciotti: Gioacchino Rossini, 3 vols. 1927–1929. The
definitive biography of Rossini, written in the greatest
detail, and well illustrated and indexed.

Letters of Liszt to Princess Sayn-Wittgenstein, edited by Howard
E. Hugo. Harvard, 1953.

Postscript

POSTSCRIPT TO THE REVISED EDITION

Although only fifteen months have elapsed since the Introduction to this new edition of Liszt was written, one or two new points of view have arisen, some few facts have come to light, and it is in general an opportunity for the writer to gather together and put into shape his final views. During this short space of time a most informative and detailed study has appeared by Mr. Humphrey Searle.* This could be described as the first adequate study of Liszt as a composer to be written in our language, and it is fascinating reading even to those not technically interested in his compositions. But Mr. Searle is not concerned with the biographical details of Liszt's career, which must be our own excuse and apology for once again testing this life of Liszt upon the public. Those few persons who are even more deeply interested in his music should refer to the tremendous catalogue of Liszt's compositions drawn up by Mr. Searle and printed in the new edition of Grove. It is not likely to be improved upon.

It has been my endeavour to write of Liszt as one might write of Rubens or of Byron. That is to say, to treat of him as an artist *and* a man of action. I think Liszt is in every way not less interesting than either the paragon of the High Renaissance, or the hero of the whole Romantic Movement. He was, after all is said and done, the greatest virtuoso in human history. And it was not only the music of other gods that this Orpheus performed upon his lyre. For that is often the case with great executants. But Liszt was the supreme composer for his own instrument, and to recount his other and manifold achievements would be but to repeat what is already set down in the body of this book.

This is, in any case, a postscript or appendix and not a preface or an introduction. Twenty years ago, when this book first appeared, there were pupils of Liszt still appearing on the concert platform. At about that time, or earlier, I heard Moriz Rosenthal, Siloti, and Frederic Lamond. In 1930, or thereabouts, in Egypt, at the hotel in Assuan, I heard wonderful playing of Liszt and Chopin from the floor beneath and discovered after a morning or two that

* *The Music of Liszt*, by Humphrey Searle. London, Williams & Norgate Ltd., 1954. (Dover Reprint, 1966.)

it was the veteran Emil Sauer. Such experiences are now impossible, for it is doubtful if there is a pupil of Liszt still surviving. I attended, I think, every concert given in London by Ferruccio Busoni during the years after the conclusion of the First World War. And Busoni, if he was not a pupil of Liszt, had at least seen and heard the master play. I was taken to see Sir Alexander Mackenzie who first remembered Liszt in 1861, and had most interesting conversations with him on the subject of both Liszt and Anton Rubinstein. I talked, also, to Madame Misia Sert who, as a child, remembered him and heard him play; and to Baron Meyendorff, son of the third and ultimate of Liszt's nine, or more, Muses. There was the additional interest that Baron Meyendorff, first president of the Russian Duma, politician and expert on international law, had no ear for music. He could speak, therefore, of Liszt as a man, not as a musician, but he was, none the less, victim of that mesmeric spell.

Friends and pupils of Liszt have disappeared, all, or nearly all, of them. And the situation has altered in many other ways. This was borne in upon me as I read these proofs. The radio has changed many things. The details of Chopin's stay in Scotland, to which I refer as something worthy of investigation, are now familiar from 'feature' programmes. In another place I write of Liszt's *Fantaisie, quasi Sonate: d'après une lecture de Dante* as though entirely unknown to the audience, but it has since been heard by thousands of ballet enthusiasts at Covent Garden. The same thing is true of the *Galop in A Minor*, orchestrated by Gordon Jacob for the Sadler's Wells Ballet *Apparitions*, in which, as well, the Second and Third *Mephisto-Waltzes* are performed. This is in token of Constant Lambert's admiration and love of Liszt. But, as well, the *Galop Chromatique* has been heard more often on programmes lately than during the previous three-quarters of a century since it was written. But the greatest change of all in matters concerning this present book since it was first published is the increasing popularity of Liszt's *B Minor Sonata*, now an almost inevitable feature of the recital programme. At the time when Busoni gave an extraordinary and electrifying performance of it at the Wigmore Hall it was seldom, if ever, played. I have to admit, too, for what it is worth, that I have altered my own view of the Sonata and would now put it among the supreme masterpieces, next to the '*Appassionata*' and the '*Waldstein*'.

There has been yet another and more recent development than broadcasting, and this is the long-playing gramophone record. In only a year or two a fantastic quantity of unfamiliar music has been made available, thanks to which it has been possible to hear Berlioz's *Lélio*, a work which, I believe, had only been given one performance, at Cologne, during the years 1918–1952 that the present writer waited, and waited in vain, to hear it played. *Lélio* is most interesting and curious, but after becoming familiar with its romantic asides and outpourings I would no longer say, as in the Introduction, that Liszt's arrangement of parts of it as a piano concerto is of all Liszt's unperformed and unpublished music that piece which I would most like to hear. It is also true of the last two decades that the ever multiplying opportunities of hearing Berlioz may have somewhat diminished the ardour of other enthusiasts and partisans, beside myself. I can no longer admire his *Te Deum*, too reminiscent of the ugly architecture of Saint Augustin and other mid-nineteenth-century churches in Paris; his *Symphonie Funèbre et Triomphale* I now find jejune and childish, and can only admire the few moments of true genius in his *Grande Messe des Morts*. The same slightly ridiculous youthfulness inhabits his *Harold in Italy*, and makes the *Marche Troyenne* in *Les Troyens* like the *idée fixe* of a small boy of eight or ten years old. This, one may suspect, was the whole germ and origin of those two nights of opera. But the *Chasse Royale et Orage* from that opera, the *Queen Mab Scherzo*, and the *Corsair* overture remain imperishable masterpieces and supreme marvels of orchestration, Meanwhile, the *Symphonie Fantastique* is performed as frequently as the Fifth Symphony, and if it were given less often one might recapture more of its originality and fire of creation.

Another and no less strong and eccentric personality from the youth of Liszt has perhaps increased in interest. Paganini, I think, is more and not less extraordinary than he seemed to be. He has become one of the eternal concepts, and is of the company of Dr. Faustus and the Wandering Jew. His strange physical appearance is for ever immortalized in the statuette by Dantan; but he is no less interesting in the photograph of a splendid portrait of him that I was sent lately from the U.S.A. Unfortunately it has been impossible to get permission to reproduce this. The portrait in question was painted in London by George Patten in 1834, and

must be the best 'straight' likeness of Paganini in existence.* The
features are at once recognizable as those of the great violinist,
who is to be known, too, by his length of hair. It is the portrait of
an extremely striking and handsome man, being in no way a
caricature. The most remarkable point in it is his huge dark eyes,
of which there is, of course, no sign in Dantan's statuette. Perhaps
we have only to glance at the other woodcut portraits in the
Musée Dantan to realize that they are all parodies and exaggera-
tions and that Paganini in the flesh was neither as bony nor as
grotesque as contemporary accounts would have him be. The
music of this extraordinary being is now receiving more attention,
though the moment may not yet have come to express any
considered opinion of it.

Before we return finally to Liszt, himself, a word should be
said in extension of what is already written in this book concerning Balakirev and Liapounov. The *Mazurkas* of Balakirev are a
thing unique in piano literature, being compound of Chopin and
of that Orient to which *Thamar* and *Islamey* belong. A particularly
beautiful example is the Mazurka which forms one movement in

* George Patten (b. 1801) practised miniature painting up to 1830, when he
devoted himself to portraiture in oil. He went to Italy in 1837, and in the same
year was elected an A.A. He painted the Prince Consort in Germany in 1840,
and was appointed as his portrait painter. In the latter part of his life he lived
at Ross, in Herefordshire, dying in London in 1865. Amateurs of Paganini
interested in any and every portrait of him should have their attention drawn to
an exceedingly rare lithograph of Paganini playing at the Leeds Music Hall on
17 January 1832, of which there is a reproduction in Vol. XXXIII, Part III, of
the *Transactons of The Thoresby Society*, 16 Queen Square, Leeds, 1932, p. 446.
One of the only two or three copies of this lithograph in existence was known
to that fine pianist, the late Frederick Dawson, a native of Leeds, who after
many years' search discovered another copy in a curiosity shop at Wolverhamp-
ton, and presented it to the Thoresby Society. I would conclude this long footnote with an identification of the *famulus* of Paganini, Mr. George Harrys or
Harris of Hanover, communicated to me in a curious letter from Lachine, P.Q.,
Canada, written to me in 1934 by a correspondent whose name I was unable to
decipher. He quotes from a book published in 1913 by the late Chief-Rabbi of
Hanover on the old Jewish families of that town. From this it appears that
soon after 1805 the youngest son of Salomon David, named Herz, became
converted at the age of twenty-five years, and that he adopted the name of
Carl Georg Harrys. He seems to have died at some date before 1844. Hermann
Harrys, a son of Georg Harrys, published a translation of Tasso's *Madrigals* in
1895. His father, Georg Harrys, was connected with the circles in which the
poet Heine moved. It is some satisfaction to have discovered even this much
of so curious and elusive a personality.

Balakirev's pianoforte sonata. The *Transcendental Études* of his pupil Liapounov are now available for study in the records made of them by Mr. Louis Kentner for the Maharajah of Mysore's Musical Foundation. There, in addition to the pair of Caucasian dances that I mentioned, we can hear *Carillon*, but this is a piece based not on the carillons from the belfries of Flemish town halls but on the deep booming bells of Russian steeples; and there is, also, a fine and lengthy étude in memory of Liszt.

More should have been written in the body of this book on Smetana, who is another over-neglected writer for the piano, himself, like Balakirev, a performer and virtuoso of the first rank. The influence of Liszt is visible in the texture and ornament of his *Polkas* and his *Bohemian Dances*, as well as in other more extended pieces. But progress in these directions, which are not byeways, is slow and gradual, and the piano music of Alkan, for an example, is hardly more familiar than it was twenty years ago when I wrote the footnote which is printed in this book as Appendix I. And this paragraph might be made complete by further mention of probably the most eminent of all Liszt's pupils, the Portuguese Viana da Motta. His life of Liszt, which is in Portuguese, has not been translated, and his musical correspondence with Liszt, von Bülow, Busoni, d'Albert, Albéniz, and other musicians has not even been printed.

The influence of Liszt on Debussy and on Ravel is another topic on which enough has not been said. The influence of Liszt on Ravel's *Jeux d'Eau*, deriving from the former's *Jeux d'Eaux à la Villa d'Este*, is at once apparent. It is no less strong in *Le Gibet* and *Scarbo* from his *Gaspard de la Nuit*. Debussy, born in 1862 and thirteen years older than Ravel, was equally an admirer of Liszt and during his years in Rome at the Villa Medici had the opportunity of hearing him play, a fact of which I was not aware at the time I wrote this book.*

Liszt, for we now come back to him, does certainly make more frequent appearance in recital programmes than before. Mr. Louis

---

*Debussy met Liszt at the house of Sgambati in 1884, and heard the master and his pupil play Saint-Saëns' *Variations* for two pianos on a theme of Beethoven (Op. 35). Liszt left Rome the next day, never to return. On another occasion Debussy and Vidal played to Liszt the *Valses romantiques* of Chabrier : cf. *Debussy*, by Edward Lockspeiser. J. M. Dent & Sons, 1951, pp. 29, 30.

Kentner, and a younger generation of pianists including Mr. Gordon Watson, a pupil of Egon Petri, have to this extent deepened public knowledge. The latter player has broadcast more than one performance of the delightful *Nuits d'Été à Pausilippe*, which are paraphrases by Liszt upon songs by Donizetti. In Liszt's vast output fantastic ingenuities are often hidden in unsuspected places. Such a case in point is No. 2 of his *Illustrations du Prophète*, which is in fact the skating waltz *Les Patineurs* from Meyerbeer's opera. This piece is now in the repertory of both the pianists mentioned in this paragraph, a fantastic display of fireworks on a frozen lake. But during all the years I have been interested in Liszt I never remember a performance of either the *Valse Infernale* from *Robert le Diable* (a favourite with Anton Rubinstein), or of the *Marche Indienne* from the *Illustrations de l'Africaine*. The conjunction of Liszt with Meyerbeer, once the wonder of his age, is worth stressing because of the extraordinary qualities of the *Organ Fantasia and Fugue* on the chorale *Ad Nos ad Salutarem Undam* from *Le Prophète*. This is a work of the same alloy as the *Faust Symphony* and the *Sonata in B Minor*, and it is in many ways typical of Liszt that he should have been roused to so astonishing a feat of the arts of metamorphosis or transformation by a 'faked' chorale in a grand opera by Meyerbeer. This is one of the greatest of Liszt's works, a compound of all his fascinating qualities of good and bad, and a glass into which to look long and often in order to watch the reflections of that uncanny mind and soul.

If the reader will turn for a moment to the photograph of Anton Rubinstein (facing page 243), for as long as physiognomy has any meaning there will be visible the difference between Liszt and Rubinstein as performers upon their instrument. I have known persons who heard both and preferred the latter. How interesting that Professor Walter Starkie in his recent book *In Sarah's Tents* should mention that occasion when Anton Rubinstein was taken to the Café de Chinitas in Málaga and initiated into the golden age of Cante Hondo and Flamenco music! What a meeting of East and West! It is now time to hear fewer of Liszt's *Hungarian Rhapsodies* and more of the *Magyar Dallok* and the *Magyar Rhapsodiák*, which is the form in which they originally appeared. The childhood background of both Liszt and Rubinstein, the one in the Hungarian plain and the other in Moldavia, must be a racial explanation of their genius as players. To say that such things count for nothing, and that childhood in Manchester or Liverpool could achieve the same results is no argument, for all is possible, but both virtuosos were born and spent their early years on the borders of the Orient, while their equivalent has not yet appeared from out our cities of soot and fog.

When the original draft of this book had been completed and was in proof I had the benefit of Constant Lambert's corrections and advice. He was an ardent admirer of Liszt in all, or nearly all, his manifestations, and helped me with his criticisms and with a few points of detail. I, also, had conversations with, and received one or two letters from, Bernard van Dieren; and benefited from the writings of my friend Kaikhosru Sorabji. These friends apart, I had for stimulus my admiration for Liszt as the greatest virtuoso and executant in history, and for drawback my technical ignorance in music; enthusiasms and deficiencies which it was not easy to combine into a book that could be read with pleasure. This new and revised edition now appears with another set of illustrations which have been carefully chosen alike for their interest and their unfamiliarity. Thus, some may read the book for the first time, while other and older readers open it anew and turn the page.

March 1955.

As this book goes to press (April 1955) Mr. Humphrey Searle informs me that the MS. of a *Fourth Valse Oubliée* (see page 342) has now turned up in the U.S.A., and has been published there (Theodore Presser Co., Bryn Mawr, Pennsylvania). Liszt gave the MS. in 1885 to his pupil, May Holtzke, who went to live in America, and her son gave it to the Library of Congress.

INDEX

INDEX

Index

Index

Index

Index

Index

Index

A CATALOGUE OF SELECTED DOVER BOOKS
IN ALL FIELDS OF INTEREST

A CATALOGUE OF SELECTED DOVER BOOKS
IN ALL FIELDS OF INTEREST

THE NOTEBOOKS OF LEONARDO DA VINCI, edited by J.P. Richter. Extracts from manuscripts reveal great genius; on painting, sculpture, anatomy, sciences, geography, etc. Both Italian and English. 186 ms. pages reproduced, plus 500 additional drawings, including studies for Last Supper, Sforza monument, etc. 860pp. 7⅞ x 10¾. USO 22572-0, 22573-9 Pa., Two vol. set $15.90

ART NOUVEAU DESIGNS IN COLOR, Alphonse Mucha, Maurice Verneuil, Georges Auriol. Full-color reproduction of Combinaisons ornamentales (c. 1900) by Art Nouveau masters. Floral, animal, geometric, interlacings, swashes — borders, frames, spots — all incredibly beautiful. 60 plates, hundreds of designs. 9⅜ x 8¹/₁₆. 22885-1 Pa. $4.00

GRAPHIC WORKS OF ODILON REDON. All great fantastic lithographs, etchings, engravings, drawings, 209 in all. Monsters, Huysmans, still life work, etc. Introduction by Alfred Werner. 209pp. 9⅛ x 12¼. 21996-8 Pa. $6.00

EXOTIC FLORAL PATTERNS IN COLOR, E.-A. Seguy. Incredibly beautiful full-color pochoir work by great French designer of 20's. Complete Bouquets et frondaisons, Suggestions pour étoffes. Richness must be seen to be believed. 40 plates containing 120 patterns. 80pp. 9⅜ x 12¼. 23041-4 Pa. $6.00

SELECTED ETCHINGS OF JAMES A. McN. WHISTLER, James A. McN. Whistler. 149 outstanding etchings by the great American artist, including selections from the Thames set and two Venice sets, the complete French set, and many individual prints. Introduction and explanatory note on each print by Maria Naylor. 157pp. 9⅜ x 12¼. 23194-1 Pa. $5.00

VISUAL ILLUSIONS: THEIR CAUSES, CHARACTERISTICS, AND APPLICATIONS, Matthew Luckiesh. Thorough description, discussion; shape and size, color, motion; natural illusion. Uses in art and industry. 100 illustrations. 252pp. 21530-X Pa. $3.00

TEN BOOKS ON ARCHITECTURE, Vitruvius. The most important book ever written on architecture. Early Roman aesthetics, technology, classical orders, site selection, all other aspects. Stands behind everything since. Morgan translation. 331pp. 20645-9 Pa. $3.75

THE CODEX NUTTALL. A PICTURE MANUSCRIPT FROM ANCIENT MEXICO, as first edited by Zelia Nuttall. Only inexpensive edition, in full color, of a pre-Columbian Mexican (Mixtec) book. 88 color plates show kings, gods, heroes, temples, sacrifices. New explanatory, historical introduction by Arthur G. Miller. 96pp. 11⅜ x 8½. 23168-2 Pa. $7.50

CREATIVE LITHOGRAPHY AND HOW TO DO IT, Grant Arnold. Lithography as art form: working directly on stone, transfer of drawings, lithotint, mezzotint, color printing; also metal plates. Detailed, thorough. 27 illustrations. 214pp.
21208-4 Pa. $3.50

DESIGN MOTIFS OF ANCIENT MEXICO, Jorge Enciso. Vigorous, powerful ceramic stamp impressions — Maya, Aztec, Toltec, Olmec. Serpents, gods, priests, dancers, etc. 153pp. 6⅛ x 9¼.
20084-1 Pa. $2.50

AMERICAN INDIAN DESIGN AND DECORATION, Leroy Appleton. Full text, plus more than 700 precise drawings of Inca, Maya, Aztec, Pueblo, Plains, NW Coast basketry, sculpture, painting, pottery, sand paintings, metal, etc. 4 plates in color. 279pp. 8⅜ x 11¼.
22704-9 Pa. $5.00

CHINESE LATTICE DESIGNS, Daniel S. Dye. Incredibly beautiful geometric designs: circles, voluted, simple dissections, etc. Inexhaustible source of ideas, motifs. 1239 illustrations. 469pp. 6⅛ x 9¼.
23096-1 Pa. $5.00

JAPANESE DESIGN MOTIFS, Matsuya Co. Mon, or heraldic designs. Over 4000 typical, beautiful designs: birds, animals, flowers, swords, fans, geometric; all beautifully stylized. 213pp. 11⅜ x 8¼.
22874-6 Pa. $5.00

PERSPECTIVE, Jan Vredeman de Vries. 73 perspective plates from 1604 edition; buildings, townscapes, stairways, fantastic scenes. Remarkable for beauty, surrealistic atmosphere; real eye-catchers. Introduction by Adolf Placzek. 74pp. 11⅜ x 8¼.
20186-4 Pa. $3.00

EARLY AMERICAN DESIGN MOTIFS. Suzanne E. Chapman. 497 motifs, designs, from painting on wood, ceramics, appliqué, glassware, samplers, metal work, etc. Florals, landscapes, birds and animals, geometrics, letters, etc. Inexhaustible. Enlarged edition. 138pp. 8⅜ x 11¼.
22985-8 Pa. $3.50
23084-8 Clothbd. $7.95

VICTORIAN STENCILS FOR DESIGN AND DECORATION, edited by E.V. Gillon, Jr. 113 wonderful ornate Victorian pieces from German sources; florals, geometrics; borders, corner pieces; bird motifs, etc. 64pp. 9⅜ x 12¼.
21995-X Pa.' $3.00

ART NOUVEAU: AN ANTHOLOGY OF DESIGN AND ILLUSTRATION FROM THE STUDIO, edited by E.V. Gillon, Jr. Graphic arts: book jackets, posters, engravings, illustrations, decorations; Crane, Beardsley, Bradley and many others. Inexhaustible. 92pp. 8⅛ x 11.
22388-4 Pa. $2.50

ORIGINAL ART DECO DESIGNS, William Rowe. First-rate, highly imaginative modern Art Deco frames, borders, compositions, alphabets, florals, insectals, Wurlitzer-types, etc. Much finest modern Art Deco. 80 plates, 8 in color. 8⅜ x 11¼.
22567-4 Pa. $3.50

HANDBOOK OF DESIGNS AND DEVICES, Clarence P. Hornung. Over 1800 basic geometric designs based on circle, triangle, square, scroll, cross, etc. Largest such collection in existence. 261pp.
20125-2 Pa. $2.75

150 MASTERPIECES OF DRAWING, edited by Anthony Toney. 150 plates, early 15th century to end of 18th century; Rembrandt, Michelangelo, Dürer, Fragonard, Watteau, Wouwerman, many others. 150pp. 8⅜ x 11¼.   21032-4 Pa. $4.00

THE GOLDEN AGE OF THE POSTER, Hayward and Blanche Cirker. 70 extraordinary posters in full colors, from Maîtres de l'Affiche, Mucha, Lautrec, Bradley, Cheret, Beardsley, many others. 9⅜ x 12¼.   22753-7 Pa. $5.95

SIMPLICISSIMUS, selection, translations and text by Stanley Appelbaum. 180 satirical drawings, 16 in full color, from the famous German weekly magazine in the years 1896 to 1926. 24 artists included: Grosz, Kley, Pascin, Kubin, Kollwitz, plus Heine, Thöny, Bruno Paul, others. 172pp. 8½ x 12¼.   23098-8 Pa. $5.00
23099-6 Clothbd. $10.00

THE EARLY WORK OF AUBREY BEARDSLEY, Aubrey Beardsley. 157 plates, 2 in color: Manon Lescaut, Madame Bovary, Morte d'Arthur, Salome, other. Introduction by H. Marillier. 175pp. 8½ x 11.   21816-3 Pa. $4.00

THE LATER WORK OF AUBREY BEARDSLEY, Aubrey Beardsley. Exotic masterpieces of full maturity: Venus and Tannhäuser, Lysistrata, Rape of the Lock, Volpone, Savoy material, etc. 174 plates, 2 in color. 176pp. 8½ x 11.   21817-1 Pa. $4.50

DRAWINGS OF WILLIAM BLAKE, William Blake. 92 plates from Book of Job, Divine Comedy, Paradise Lost, visionary heads, mythological figures, Laocoön, etc. Selection, introduction, commentary by Sir Geoffrey Keynes. 178pp. 8½ x 11.
22303-5 Pa. $4.00

LONDON: A PILGRIMAGE, Gustave Doré, Blanchard Jerrold. Squalor, riches, misery, beauty of mid-Victorian metropolis; 55 wonderful plates, 125 other illustrations, full social, cultural text by Jerrold. 191pp. of text. 8⅛ x 11.
22306-X Pa. $6.00

THE COMPLETE WOODCUTS OF ALBRECHT DÜRER, edited by Dr. W. Kurth. 346 in all: Old Testament, St. Jerome, Passion, Life of Virgin, Apocalypse, many others. Introduction by Campbell Dodgson. 285pp. 8½ x 12¼.   21097-9 Pa. $6.00

THE DISASTERS OF WAR, Francisco Goya. 83 etchings record horrors of Napoleonic wars in Spain and war in general. Reprint of 1st edition, plus 3 additional plates. Introduction by Philip Hofer. 97pp. 9⅜ x 8¼.   21872-4 Pa. $3.50

ENGRAVINGS OF HOGARTH, William Hogarth. 101 of Hogarth's greatest works: Rake's Progress, Harlot's Progress, Illustrations for Hudibras, Midnight Modern Conversation, Before and After, Beer Street and Gin Lane, many more. Full commentary. 256pp. 11 x 14.   22479-1 Pa. $7.95

PRIMITIVE ART, Franz Boas. Great anthropologist on ceramics, textiles, wood, stone, metal, etc.; patterns, technology, symbols, styles. All areas, but fullest on Northwest Coast Indians. 350 illustrations. 378pp.   20025-6 Pa. $3.75

MOTHER GOOSE'S MELODIES. Facsimile of fabulously rare Munroe and Francis "copyright 1833" Boston edition. Familiar and unusual rhymes, wonderful old woodcut illustrations. Edited by E.F. Bleiler. 128pp. 4½ x 6⅜. 22577-1 Pa. $1.50

MOTHER GOOSE IN HIEROGLYPHICS. Favorite nursery rhymes presented in rebus form for children. Fascinating 1849 edition reproduced in toto, with key. Introduction by E.F. Bleiler. About 400 woodcuts. 64pp. 6⅞ x 5¼. 20745-5 Pa. $1.50

PETER PIPER'S PRACTICAL PRINCIPLES OF PLAIN & PERFECT PRONUNCIATION. Alliterative jingles and tongue-twisters. Reproduction in full of 1830 first American edition. 25 spirited woodcuts. 32pp. 4½ x 6⅜. 22560-7 Pa. $1.25

MARMADUKE MULTIPLY'S MERRY METHOD OF MAKING MINOR MATHEMATICIANS. Fellow to Peter Piper, it teaches multiplication table by catchy rhymes and woodcuts. 1841 Munroe & Francis edition. Edited by E.F. Bleiler. 103pp. 4⅝ x 6. 22773-1 Pa. $1.25

THE NIGHT BEFORE CHRISTMAS, Clement Moore. Full text, and woodcuts from original 1848 book. Also critical, historical material. 19 illustrations. 40pp. 4⅝ x 6. 22797-9 Pa. $1.35

THE KING OF THE GOLDEN RIVER, John Ruskin. Victorian children's classic of three brothers, their attempts to reach the Golden River, what becomes of them. Facsimile of original 1889 edition. 22 illustrations. 56pp. 4⅝ x 6⅜. 20066-3 Pa. $1.50

DREAMS OF THE RAREBIT FIEND, Winsor McCay. Pioneer cartoon strip, unexcelled for beauty, imagination, in 60 full sequences. Incredible technical virtuosity, wonderful visual wit. Historical introduction. 62pp. 8⅜ x 11¼. 21347-1 Pa. $2.50

THE KATZENJAMMER KIDS, Rudolf Dirks. In full color, 14 strips from 1906-7; full of imagination, characteristic humor. Classic of great historical importance. Introduction by August Derleth. 32pp. 9¼ x 12¼. 23005-8 Pa. $2.00

LITTLE ORPHAN ANNIE AND LITTLE ORPHAN ANNIE IN COSMIC CITY, Harold Gray. Two great sequences from the early strips: our curly-haired heroine defends the Warbucks' financial empire and, then, takes on meanie Phineas P. Pinchpenny. Leapin' lizards! 178pp. 6⅛ x 8⅜. 23107-0 Pa. $2.00

ABSOLUTELY MAD INVENTIONS, A.E. Brown, H.A. Jeffcott. Hilarious, useless, or merely absurd inventions all granted patents by the U.S. Patent Office. Edible tie pin, mechanical hat tipper, etc. 57 illustrations. 125pp. 22596-8 Pa. $1.50

THE DEVIL'S DICTIONARY, Ambrose Bierce. Barbed, bitter, brilliant witticisms in the form of a dictionary. Best, most ferocious satire America has produced. 145pp. 20487-1 Pa. $1.75

THE BEST DR. THORNDYKE DETECTIVE STORIES, R. Austin Freeman. The Case of Oscar Brodski, The Moabite Cipher, and 5 other favorites featuring the great scientific detective, plus his long-believed-lost first adventure — 31 New Inn — reprinted here for the first time. Edited by E.F. Bleiler. USO 20388-3 Pa. $3.00

BEST "THINKING MACHINE" DETECTIVE STORIES, Jacques Futrelle. The Problem of Cell 13 and 11 other stories about Prof. Augustus S.F.X. Van Dusen, including two "lost" stories. First reprinting of several. Edited by E.F. Bleiler. 241pp. 20537-1 Pa. $3.00

UNCLE SILAS, J. Sheridan LeFanu. Victorian Gothic mystery novel, considered by many best of period, even better than Collins or Dickens. Wonderful psychological terror. Introduction by Frederick Shroyer. 436pp. 21715-9 Pa. $4.50

BEST DR. POGGIOLI DETECTIVE STORIES, T.S. Stribling. 15 best stories from EQMM and The Saint offer new adventures in Mexico, Florida, Tennessee hills as Poggioli unravels mysteries and combats Count Jalacki. 217pp. 23227-1 Pa. $3.00

EIGHT DIME NOVELS, selected with an introduction by E.F. Bleiler. Adventures of Old King Brady, Frank James, Nick Carter, Deadwood Dick, Buffalo Bill, The Steam Man, Frank Merriwell, and Horatio Alger — 1877 to 1905. Important, entertaining popular literature in facsimile reprint, with original covers. 190pp. 9 x 12. 22975-0 Pa. $3.50

ALICE'S ADVENTURES UNDER GROUND, Lewis Carroll. Facsimile of ms. Carroll gave Alice Liddell in 1864. Different in many ways from final Alice. Handlettered, illustrated by Carroll. Introduction by Martin Gardner. 128pp. 21482-6 Pa. $2.00

ALICE IN WONDERLAND COLORING BOOK, Lewis Carroll. Pictures by John Tenniel. Large-size versions of the famous illustrations of Alice, Cheshire Cat, Mad Hatter and all the others, waiting for your crayons. Abridged text. 36 illustrations. 64pp. 8¼ x 11. 22853-3 Pa. $1.50

AVENTURES D'ALICE AU PAYS DES MERVEILLES, Lewis Carroll. Bué's translation of "Alice" into French, supervised by Carroll himself. Novel way to learn language. (No English text.) 42 Tenniel illustrations. 196pp. 22836-3 Pa. $3.00

MYTHS AND FOLK TALES OF IRELAND, Jeremiah Curtin. 11 stories that are Irish versions of European fairy tales and 9 stories from the Fenian cycle — 20 tales of legend and magic that comprise an essential work in the history of folklore. 256pp. 22430-9 Pa. $3.00

EAST O' THE SUN AND WEST O' THE MOON, George W. Dasent. Only full edition of favorite, wonderful Norwegian fairytales — Why the Sea is Salt, Boots and the Troll, etc. — with 77 illustrations by Kittelsen & Werenskiöld. 418pp. 22521-6 Pa. $4.50

PERRAULT'S FAIRY TALES, Charles Perrault and Gustave Doré. Original versions of Cinderella, Sleeping Beauty, Little Red Riding Hood, etc. in best translation, with 34 wonderful illustrations by Gustave Doré. 117pp. 8⅛ x 11. 22311-6 Pa. $2.50

EARLY NEW ENGLAND GRAVESTONE RUBBINGS, Edmund V. Gillon, Jr. 43 photographs, 226 rubbings show heavily symbolic, macabre, sometimes humorous primitive American art. Up to early 19th century. 207pp. 8⅜ x 11¼.
21380-3 Pa. $4.00

L.J.M. DAGUERRE: THE HISTORY OF THE DIORAMA AND THE DAGUERREOTYPE, Helmut and Alison Gernsheim. Definitive account. Early history, life and work of Daguerre; discovery of daguerreotype process; diffusion abroad; other early photography. 124 illustrations. 226pp. 6⅙ x 9¼.
22290-X Pa. $4.00

PHOTOGRAPHY AND THE AMERICAN SCENE, Robert Taft. The basic book on American photography as art, recording form, 1839-1889. Development, influence on society, great photographers, types (portraits, war, frontier, etc.), whatever else needed. Inexhaustible. Illustrated with 322 early photos, daguerreotypes, tintypes, stereo slides, etc. 546pp. 6⅛ x 9¼.
21201-7 Pa. $6.00

PHOTOGRAPHIC SKETCHBOOK OF THE CIVIL WAR, Alexander Gardner. Reproduction of 1866 volume with 100 on-the-field photographs: Manassas, Lincoln on battlefield, slave pens, etc. Introduction by E.F. Bleiler. 224pp. 10¾ x 9.
22731-6 Pa. $6.00

THE MOVIES: A PICTURE QUIZ BOOK, Stanley Appelbaum & Hayward Cirker. Match stars with their movies, name actors and actresses, test your movie skill with 241 stills from 236 great movies, 1902-1959. Indexes of performers and films. 128pp. 8⅜ x 9¼.
20222-4 Pa. $3.00

THE TALKIES, Richard Griffith. Anthology of features, articles from Photoplay, 1928-1940, reproduced complete. Stars, famous movies, technical features, fabulous ads, etc.; Garbo, Chaplin, King Kong, Lubitsch, etc. 4 color plates, scores of illustrations. 327pp. 8⅜ x 11¼.
22762-6 Pa. $6.95

THE MOVIE MUSICAL FROM VITAPHONE TO "42ND STREET," edited by Miles Kreuger. Relive the rise of the movie musical as reported in the pages of Photoplay magazine (1926-1933): every movie review, cast list, ad, and record review; every significant feature article, production still, biography, forecast, and gossip story. Profusely illustrated. 367pp. 8⅜ x 11¼.
23154-2 Pa. $7.95

JOHANN SEBASTIAN BACH, Philipp Spitta. Great classic of biography, musical commentary, with hundreds of pieces analyzed. Also good for Bach's contemporaries. 450 musical examples. Total of 1799pp.
EUK 22278-0, 22279-9 Clothbd., Two vol. set $25.00

BEETHOVEN AND HIS NINE SYMPHONIES, Sir George Grove. Thorough history, analysis, commentary on symphonies and some related pieces. For either beginner or advanced student. 436 musical passages. 407pp.
20334-4 Pa. $4.00

MOZART AND HIS PIANO CONCERTOS, Cuthbert Girdlestone. The only full-length study. Detailed analyses of all 21 concertos, sources; 417 musical examples. 509pp.
21271-8 Pa. $6.00

THE FITZWILLIAM VIRGINAL BOOK, edited by J. Fuller Maitland, W.B. Squire. Famous early 17th century collection of keyboard music, 300 works by Morley, Byrd, Bull, Gibbons, etc. Modern notation. Total of 938pp. 8⅜ x 11.
ECE 21068-5, 21069-3 Pa., Two vol. set $15.00

COMPLETE STRING QUARTETS, Wolfgang A. Mozart. Breitkopf and Härtel edition. All 23 string quartets plus alternate slow movement to K156. Study score. 277pp. 9⅜ x 12¼.
22372-8 Pa. $6.00

COMPLETE SONG CYCLES, Franz Schubert. Complete piano, vocal music of Die Schöne Müllerin, Die Winterreise, Schwanengesang. Also Drinker English singing translations. Breitkopf and Härtel edition. 217pp. 9⅜ x 12¼.
22649-2 Pa. $5.00

THE COMPLETE PRELUDES AND ETUDES FOR PIANOFORTE SOLO, Alexander Scriabin. All the preludes and etudes including many perfectly spun miniatures. Edited by K.N. Igumnov and Y.I. Mil'shteyn. 250pp. 9 x 12.
22919-X Pa. $6.00

TRISTAN UND ISOLDE, Richard Wagner. Full orchestral score with complete instrumentation. Do not confuse with piano reduction. Commentary by Felix Mottl, great Wagnerian conductor and scholar. Study score. 655pp. 8⅛ x 11.
22915-7 Pa. $11.95

FAVORITE SONGS OF THE NINETIES, ed. Robert Fremont. Full reproduction, including covers, of 88 favorites: Ta-Ra-Ra-Boom-De-Aye, The Band Played On, Bird in a Gilded Cage, Under the Bamboo Tree, After the Ball, etc. 401pp. 9 x 12.
EBE 21536-9 Pa. $6.95

SOUSA'S GREAT MARCHES IN PIANO TRANSCRIPTION: ORIGINAL SHEET MUSIC OF 23 WORKS, John Philip Sousa. Selected by Lester S. Levy. Playing edition includes: The Stars and Stripes Forever, The Thunderer, The Gladiator, King Cotton, Washington Post, much more. 24 illustrations. 111pp. 9 x 12.
USO 23132-1 Pa. $3.50

CLASSIC PIANO RAGS, selected with an introduction by Rudi Blesh. Best ragtime music (1897-1922) by Scott Joplin, James Scott, Joseph F. Lamb, Tom Turpin, 9 others. Printed from best original sheet music, plus covers. 364pp. 9 x 12.
EBE 20469-3 Pa. $7.50

ANALYSIS OF CHINESE CHARACTERS, C.D. Wilder, J.H. Ingram. 1000 most important characters analyzed according to primitives, phonetics, historical development. Traditional method offers mnemonic aid to beginner, intermediate student of Chinese, Japanese. 365pp.
23045-7 Pa. $4.00

MODERN CHINESE: A BASIC COURSE, Faculty of Peking University. Self study, classroom course in modern Mandarin. Records contain phonetics, vocabulary, sentences, lessons. 249 page book contains all recorded text, translations, grammar, vocabulary, exercises. Best course on market. 3 12" 33⅓ monaural records, book, album.
98832-5 Set $12.50

MANUAL OF THE TREES OF NORTH AMERICA, Charles S. Sargent. The basic survey of every native tree and tree-like shrub, 717 species in all. Extremely full descriptions, information on habitat, growth, locales, economics, etc. Necessary to every serious tree lover. Over 100 finding keys. 783 illustrations. Total of 986pp.
20277-1, 20278-X Pa., Two vol. set $9.00

BIRDS OF THE NEW YORK AREA, John Bull. Indispensable guide to more than 400 species within a hundred-mile radius of Manhattan. Information on range, status, breeding, migration, distribution trends, etc. Foreword by Roger Tory Peterson. 17 drawings; maps. 540pp.
23222-0 Pa. $6.00

THE SEA-BEACH AT EBB-TIDE, Augusta Foote Arnold. Identify hundreds of marine plants and animals: algae, seaweeds, squids, crabs, corals, etc. Descriptions cover food, life cycle, size, shape, habitat. Over 600 drawings. 490pp.
21949-6 Pa. $5.00

THE MOTH BOOK, William J. Holland. Identify more than 2,000 moths of North America. General information, precise species descriptions. 623 illustrations plus 48 color plates show almost all species, full size. 1968 edition. Still the basic book. Total of 551pp. 6½ x 9¼.
21948-8 Pa. $6.00

HOW INDIANS USE WILD PLANTS FOR FOOD, MEDICINE & CRAFTS, Frances Densmore. Smithsonian, Bureau of American Ethnology report presents wealth of material on nearly 200 plants used by Chippewas of Minnesota and Wisconsin. 33 plates plus 122pp. of text. 6⅛ x 9¼.
23019-8 Pa. $2.50

OLD NEW YORK IN EARLY PHOTOGRAPHS, edited by Mary Black. Your only chance to see New York City as it was 1853-1906, through 196 wonderful photographs from N.Y. Historical Society. Great Blizzard, Lincoln's funeral procession, great buildings. 228pp. 9 x 12.
22907-6 Pa. $6.95

THE AMERICAN REVOLUTION, A PICTURE SOURCEBOOK, John Grafton. Wonderful Bicentennial picture source, with 411 illustrations (contemporary and 19th century) showing battles, personalities, maps, events, flags, posters, soldier's life, ships, etc. all captioned and explained. A wonderful browsing book, supplement to other historical reading. 160pp. 9 x 12.
23226-3 Pa. $4.00

PERSONAL NARRATIVE OF A PILGRIMAGE TO AL-MADINAH AND MECCAH, Richard Burton. Great travel classic by remarkably colorful personality. Burton, disguised as a Moroccan, visited sacred shrines of Islam, narrowly escaping death. Wonderful observations of Islamic life, customs, personalities. 47 illustrations. Total of 959pp.
21217-3, 21218-1 Pa., Two vol. set $10.00

INCIDENTS OF TRAVEL IN CENTRAL AMERICA, CHIAPAS, AND YUCATAN, John L. Stephens. Almost single-handed discovery of Maya culture; exploration of ruined cities, monuments, temples; customs of Indians. 115 drawings. 892pp.
22404-X, 22405-8 Pa., Two vol. set $9.00

CONSTRUCTION OF AMERICAN FURNITURE TREASURES, Lester Margon. 344 detail drawings, complete text on constructing exact reproductions of 38 early American masterpieces: Hepplewhite sideboard, Duncan Phyfe drop-leaf table, mantel clock, gate-leg dining table, Pa. German cupboard, more. 38 plates. 54 photographs. 168pp. 8⅜ x 11¼. 23056-2 Pa. $4.00

JEWELRY MAKING AND DESIGN, Augustus F. Rose, Antonio Cirino. Professional secrets revealed in thorough, practical guide: tools, materials, processes; rings, brooches, chains, cast pieces, enamelling, setting stones, etc. Do not confuse with skimpy introductions: beginner can use, professional can learn from it. Over 200 illustrations. 306pp. 21750-7 Pa. $3.00

METALWORK AND ENAMELLING, Herbert Maryon. Generally conceded best all-around book. Countless trade secrets: materials, tools, soldering, filigree, setting, inlay, niello, repoussé, casting, polishing, etc. For beginner or expert. Author was foremost British expert. 330 illustrations. 335pp. 22702-2 Pa. $4.00

WEAVING WITH FOOT-POWER LOOMS, Edward F. Worst. Setting up a loom, beginning to weave, constructing equipment, using dyes, more, plus over 285 drafts of traditional patterns including Colonial and Swedish weaves. More than 200 other figures. For beginning and advanced. 275pp. 8¾ x 6⅜. 23064-3 Pa. $4.50

WEAVING A NAVAJO BLANKET, Gladys A. Reichard. Foremost anthropologist studied under Navajo women, reveals every step in process from wool, dyeing, spinning, setting up loom, designing, weaving. Much history, symbolism. With this book you could make one yourself. 97 illustrations. 222pp. 22992-0 Pa. $3.00

NATURAL DYES AND HOME DYEING, Rita J. Adrosko. Use natural ingredients: bark, flowers, leaves, lichens, insects etc. Over 135 specific recipes from historical sources for cotton, wool, other fabrics. Genuine premodern handicrafts. 12 illustrations. 160pp. 22688-3 Pa. $2.00

DRIED FLOWERS, Sarah Whitlock and Martha Rankin. Concise, clear, practical guide to dehydration, glycerinizing, pressing plant material, and more. Covers use of silica gel. 12 drawings. Originally titled "New Techniques with Dried Flowers." 32pp. 21802-3 Pa. $1.00

THOMAS NAST: CARTOONS AND ILLUSTRATIONS, with text by Thomas Nast St. Hill. Father of American political cartooning. Cartoons that destroyed Tweed Ring; inflation, free love, church and state; original Republican elephant and Democratic donkey; Santa Claus; more. 117 illustrations. 146pp. 9 x 12. 22983-1 Pa. $4.00
23067-8 Clothbd. $8.50

FREDERIC REMINGTON: 173 DRAWINGS AND ILLUSTRATIONS. Most famous of the Western artists, most responsible for our myths about the American West in its untamed days. Complete reprinting of *Drawings of Frederic Remington* (1897), plus other selections. 4 additional drawings in color on covers. 140pp. 9 x 12. 20714-5 Pa. $5.00'

How to Solve Chess Problems, Kenneth S. Howard. Practical suggestions on problem solving for very beginners. 58 two-move problems, 46 3-movers, 8 4-movers for practice, plus hints. 171pp. 20748-X Pa. $3.00

A Guide to Fairy Chess, Anthony Dickins. 3-D chess, 4-D chess, chess on a cylindrical board, reflecting pieces that bounce off edges, cooperative chess, retrograde chess, maximummers, much more. Most based on work of great Dawson. Full handbook, 100 problems. 66pp. 7⅞ x 10¾. 22687-5 Pa. $2.00

Win at Backgammon, Millard Hopper. Best opening moves, running game, blocking game, back game, tables of odds, etc. Hopper makes the game clear enough for anyone to play, and win. 43 diagrams. 111pp. 22894-0 Pa. $1.50

Bidding a Bridge Hand, Terence Reese. Master player "thinks out loud" the binding of 75 hands that defy point count systems. Organized by bidding problem—no-fit situations, overbidding, underbidding, cueing your defense, etc. 254pp. EBE 22830-4 Pa. $3.00

The Precision Bidding System in Bridge, C.C. Wei, edited by Alan Truscott. Inventor of precision bidding presents average hands and hands from actual play, including games from 1969 Bermuda Bowl where system emerged. 114 exercises. 116pp. 21171-1 Pa. $2.25

Learn Magic, Henry Hay. 20 simple, easy-to-follow lessons on magic for the new magician: illusions, card tricks, silks, sleights of hand, coin manipulations, escapes, and more —all with a minimum amount of equipment. Final chapter explains the great stage illusions. 92 illustrations. 285pp. 21238-6 Pa. $2.95

The New Magician's Manual, Walter B. Gibson. Step-by-step instructions and clear illustrations guide the novice in mastering 36 tricks; much equipment supplied on 16 pages of cut-out materials. 36 additional tricks. 64 illustrations. 159pp. 6⅝ x 10. 23113-5 Pa. $3.00

Professional Magic for Amateurs, Walter B. Gibson. 50 easy, effective tricks used by professionals —cards, string, tumblers, handkerchiefs, mental magic, etc. 63 illustrations. 223pp. 23012-0 Pa. $2.50

Card Manipulations, Jean Hugard. Very rich collection of manipulations; has taught thousands of fine magicians tricks that are really workable, eye-catching. Easily followed, serious work. Over 200 illustrations. 163pp. 20539-8 Pa. $2.00

Abbott's Encyclopedia of Rope Tricks for Magicians, Stewart James. Complete reference book for amateur and professional magicians containing more than 150 tricks involving knots, penetrations, cut and restored rope, etc. 510 illustrations. Reprint of 3rd edition. 400pp. 23206-9 Pa. $3.50

The Secrets of Houdini, J.C. Cannell. Classic study of Houdini's incredible magic, exposing closely-kept professional secrets and revealing, in general terms, the whole art of stage magic. 67 illustrations. 279pp. 22913-0 Pa. $3.00

THE MAGIC MOVING PICTURE BOOK, Bliss, Sands & Co. The pictures in this book move! Volcanoes erupt, a house burns, a serpentine dancer wiggles her way through a number. By using a specially ruled acetate screen provided, you can obtain these and 15 other startling effects. Originally "The Motograph Moving Picture Book." 32pp. 8¼ x 11. 23224-7 Pa. $1.75

STRING FIGURES AND HOW TO MAKE THEM, Caroline F. Jayne. Fullest, clearest instructions on string figures from around world: Eskimo, Navajo, Lapp, Europe, more. Cats cradle, moving spear, lightning, stars. Introduction by A.C. Haddon. 950 illustrations. 407pp. 20152-X Pa. $3.50

PAPER FOLDING FOR BEGINNERS, William D. Murray and Francis J. Rigney. Clearest book on market for making origami sail boats, roosters, frogs that move legs, cups, bonbon boxes. 40 projects. More than 275 illustrations. Photographs. 94pp. 20713-7 Pa $1.50

INDIAN SIGN LANGUAGE, William Tomkins. Over 525 signs developed by Sioux, Blackfoot, Cheyenne, Arapahoe and other tribes. Written instructions and diagrams: how to make words, construct sentences. Also 290 pictographs of Sioux and Ojibway tribes. 111pp. 6⅛ x 9¼. 22029-X Pa. $1.75

BOOMERANGS: HOW TO MAKE AND THROW THEM, Bernard S. Mason. Easy to make and throw, dozens of designs: cross-stick, pinwheel, boomabird, tumblestick, Australian curved stick boomerang. Complete throwing instructions. All safe. 99pp. 23028-7 Pa. $1.75

25 KITES THAT FLY, Leslie Hunt. Full, easy to follow instructions for kites made from inexpensive materials. Many novelties. Reeling, raising, designing your own. 70 illustrations. 110pp. 22550-X Pa. $1.50

TRICKS AND GAMES ON THE POOL TABLE, Fred Herrmann. 79 tricks and games, some solitaires, some for 2 or more players, some competitive; mystifying shots and throws, unusual carom, tricks involving cork, coins, a hat, more. 77 figures. 95pp. 21814-7 Pa. $1.50

WOODCRAFT AND CAMPING, Bernard S. Mason. How to make a quick emergency shelter, select woods that will burn immediately, make do with limited supplies, etc. Also making many things out of wood, rawhide, bark, at camp. Formerly titled Woodcraft. 295 illustrations. 580pp. 21951-8 Pa. $4.00

AN INTRODUCTION TO CHESS MOVES AND TACTICS SIMPLY EXPLAINED, Leonard Barden. Informal intermediate introduction: reasons for moves, tactics, openings, traps, positional play, endgame. Isolates patterns. 102pp. USO 21210-6 Pa. $1.35

LASKER'S MANUAL OF CHESS, Dr. Emanuel Lasker. Great world champion offers very thorough coverage of all aspects of chess. Combinations, position play, openings, endgame, aesthetics of chess, philosophy of struggle, much more. Filled with analyzed games. 390pp. 20640-8 Pa. $4.00

SLEEPING BEAUTY, illustrated by Arthur Rackham. Perhaps the fullest, most delightful version ever, told by C.S. Evans. Rackham's best work. 49 illustrations. 110pp. 7⅞ x 10¾.   22756-1 Pa. $2.00

THE WONDERFUL WIZARD OF OZ, L. Frank Baum. Facsimile in full color of America's finest children's classic. Introduction by Martin Gardner. 143 illustrations by W.W. Denslow. 267pp.   20691-2 Pa. $3.50

GOOPS AND HOW TO BE THEM, Gelett Burgess. Classic tongue-in-cheek masquerading as etiquette book. 87 verses, 170 cartoons as Goops demonstrate virtues of table manners, neatness, courtesy, more. 88pp. 6½ x 9¼.
                                                                                22233-0 Pa. $2.00

THE BROWNIES, THEIR BOOK, Palmer Cox. Small as mice, cunning as foxes, exuberant, mischievous, Brownies go to zoo, toy shop, seashore, circus, more. 24 verse adventures. 266 illustrations. 144pp. 6⅝ x 9¼.   21265-3 Pa. $2.50

BILLY WHISKERS: THE AUTOBIOGRAPHY OF A GOAT, Frances Trego Montgomery. Escapades of that rambunctious goat. Favorite from turn of the century America. 24 illustrations. 259pp.   22345-0 Pa. $2.75

THE ROCKET BOOK, Peter Newell. Fritz, janitor's kid, sets off rocket in basement of apartment house; an ingenious hole punched through every page traces course of rocket. 22 duotone drawings, verses. 48pp. 6⅞ x 8⅜.   22044-3 Pa. $1.50

CUT AND COLOR PAPER MASKS, Michael Grater. Clowns, animals, funny faces . . . simply color them in, cut them out, and put them together, and you have 9 paper masks to play with and enjoy. Complete instructions. Assembled masks shown in full color on the covers. 32pp. 8¼ x 11.   23171-2 Pa. $1.50

THE TALE OF PETER RABBIT, Beatrix Potter. The inimitable Peter's terrifying adventure in Mr. McGregor's garden, with all 27 wonderful, full color Potter illustrations. 55pp. 4¼ x 5½.   USO 22827-4 Pa. $1.00

THE TALE OF MRS. TIGGY-WINKLE, Beatrix Potter. Your child will love this story about a very special hedgehog and all 27 wonderful, full-color Potter illustrations. 57pp. 4¼ x 5½.   USO 20546-0 Pa. $1.00

THE TALE OF BENJAMIN BUNNY, Beatrix Potter. Peter Rabbit's cousin coaxes him back into Mr. McGregor's garden for a whole new set of adventures. A favorite with children. All 27 full-color illustrations. 59pp. 4¼ x 5½.
                                                                            USO 21102-9 Pa. $1.00

THE MERRY ADVENTURES OF ROBIN HOOD, Howard Pyle. Facsimile of original (1883) edition, finest modern version of English outlaw's adventures. 23 illustrations by Pyle. 296pp. 6½ x 9¼.   22043-5 Pa. $4.00

TWO LITTLE SAVAGES, Ernest Thompson Seton. Adventures of two boys who lived as Indians; explaining Indian ways, woodlore, pioneer methods. 293 illustrations. 286pp.   20985-7 Pa. $3.50

HOUDINI ON MAGIC, Harold Houdini. Edited by Walter Gibson, Morris N. Young. How he escaped; exposés of fake spiritualists; instructions for eye-catching tricks; other fascinating material by and about greatest magician. 155 illustrations. 280pp. 20384-0 Pa. $2.75

HANDBOOK OF THE NUTRITIONAL CONTENTS OF FOOD, U.S. Dept. of Agriculture. Largest, most detailed source of food nutrition information ever prepared. Two mammoth tables: one measuring nutrients in 100 grams of edible portion; the other, in edible portion of 1 pound as purchased. Originally titled Composition of Foods. 190pp. 9 x 12. 21342-0 Pa. $4.00

COMPLETE GUIDE TO HOME CANNING, PRESERVING AND FREEZING, U.S. Dept. of Agriculture. Seven basic manuals with full instructions for jams and jellies; pickles and relishes; canning fruits, vegetables, meat; freezing anything. Really good recipes, exact instructions for optimal results. Save a fortune in food. 156 illustrations. 214pp. 6⅛ x 9¼. 22911-4 Pa. $2.50

THE BREAD TRAY, Louis P. De Gouy. Nearly every bread the cook could buy or make: bread sticks of Italy, fruit breads of Greece, glazed rolls of Vienna, everything from corn pone to croissants. Over 500 recipes altogether. including buns, rolls, muffins, scones, and more. 463pp. 23000-7 Pa. $4.00

CREATIVE HAMBURGER COOKERY, Louis P. De Gouy. 182 unusual recipes for casseroles, meat loaves and hamburgers that turn inexpensive ground meat into memorable main dishes: Arizona chili burgers, burger tamale pie, burger stew, burger corn loaf, burger wine loaf, and more. 120pp. 23001-5 Pa. $1.75

LONG ISLAND SEAFOOD COOKBOOK, J. George Frederick and Jean Joyce. Probably the best American seafood cookbook. Hundreds of recipes. 40 gourmet sauces, 123 recipes using oysters alone! All varieties of fish and seafood amply represented. 324pp. 22677-8 Pa. $3.50

THE EPICUREAN: A COMPLETE TREATISE OF ANALYTICAL AND PRACTICAL STUDIES IN THE CULINARY ART, Charles Ranhofer. Great modern classic. 3,500 recipes from master chef of Delmonico's, turn-of-the-century America's best restaurant. Also explained, many techniques known only to professional chefs. 775 illustrations. 1183pp. 6⅝ x 10. 22680-8 Clothbd. $22.50

THE AMERICAN WINE COOK BOOK, Ted Hatch. Over 700 recipes: old favorites livened up with wine plus many more: Czech fish soup, quince soup, sauce Perigueux, shrimp shortcake, filets Stroganoff, cordon bleu goulash, jambonneau, wine fruit cake, more. 314pp. 22796-0 Pa. $2.50

DELICIOUS VEGETARIAN COOKING, Ivan Baker. Close to 500 delicious and varied recipes: soups, main course dishes (pea, bean, lentil, cheese, vegetable, pasta, and egg dishes), savories, stews, whole-wheat breads and cakes, more. 168pp. USO 22834-7 Pa. $2.00

COOKIES FROM MANY LANDS, Josephine Perry. Crullers, oatmeal cookies, chaux au chocolate, English tea cakes, mandel kuchen, Sacher torte, Danish puff pastry, Swedish cookies — a mouth-watering collection of 223 recipes. 157pp.
22832-0 Pa. $2.25

ROSE RECIPES, Eleanour S. Rohde. How to make sauces, jellies, tarts, salads, pot-pourris, sweet bags, pomanders, perfumes from garden roses; all exact recipes. Century old favorites. 95pp.
22957-2 Pa. $1.75

"OSCAR" OF THE WALDORF'S COOKBOOK, Oscar Tschirky. Famous American chef reveals 3455 recipes that made Waldorf great; cream of French, German, American cooking, in all categories. Full instructions, easy home use. 1896 edition. 907pp. 6⅝ x 9⅜.
20790-0 Clothbd. $15.00

JAMS AND JELLIES, May Byron. Over 500 old-time recipes for delicious jams, jellies, marmalades, preserves, and many other items. Probably the largest jam and jelly book in print. Originally titled May Byron's Jam Book. 276pp.
USO 23130-5 Pa. $3.50

MUSHROOM RECIPES, André L. Simon. 110 recipes for everyday and special cooking. Champignons à la grecque, sole bonne femme, chicken liver croustades, more; 9 basic sauces, 13 ways of cooking mushrooms. 54pp.
USO 20913-X Pa. $1.25

THE BUCKEYE COOKBOOK, Buckeye Publishing Company. Over 1,000 easy-to-follow, traditional recipes from the American Midwest: bread (100 recipes alone), meat, game, jam, candy, cake, ice cream, and many other categories of cooking. 64 illustrations. From 1883 enlarged edition. 416pp.
23218-2 Pa. $4.00

TWENTY-TWO AUTHENTIC BANQUETS FROM INDIA, Robert H. Christie. Complete, easy-to-do recipes for almost 200 authentic Indian dishes assembled in 22 banquets. Arranged by region. Selected from Banquets of the Nations. 192pp.
23200-X Pa. $2.50